ELEANOR ORMEROD, LL.D.

ECONOMIC ENTOMOLOGIST

AUTOBIOGRAPHY

AND

CORRESPONDENCE

EDITED BY ROBERT WALLACE

Elibron Classics
www.elibron.com

Elibron Classics series.

ISBN 1-4021-6707-5 (paperback)
ISBN 1-4021-0271-2 (hardcover)

This Elibron Classics Replica Edition is an unabridged facsimile of the edition published in 1904 by John Murray, London.

ELEANOR ORMEROD, LL.D.

The Printed Works of Miss Ormerod.

The Cobham Journals. Abstracts and Summaries of Meteorological and Phenological Observations made by Miss Caroline Molesworth, at Cobham, Surrey, in the years 1825 to 1850. *Stanford* (out of print).

A Manual of Remedies and Means of Prevention for the Attacks of Insects on Food Crops, Forest Trees, and Fruit. One vol., fully illustrated, with portrait (second edition 1890). Demy 8vo, pp. xiv, 410. 5s.

A Text-Book of Agricultural Entomology, being a Plain Introduction to the Classification of Insects and Methods of Insect Life, with Means of Prevention of Insect Ravage ; suited for the use of agriculturists and agricultural teachers and students. One vol., pp. 238 ; 164 figures. Crown 8vo, 3s. 6d.

Handbook of Insects Injurious to Orchard and Bush Fruits. With Means of Prevention and Remedy. Demy 8vo, 300 pp., 3s. 6d. Profusely Illustrated.

Notes and Descriptions of a few Injurious Farm and Fruit Insects of South Africa. This work contains observations on Australian Bug (*Icerya purchasi*). Crown 8vo (out of print).

Observations on Warble Fly or Ox Bot Fly. An Abstract of Information, contributed mainly by British observers during the years 1884-1894, on the History and Habits of the Warble Fly ; and Means of Prevention and Remedy. Fully Illustrated. Royal 8vo, 64 pp. 6d.

Flies Injurious to Stock, being Life-histories and Means of Prevention of a few kinds commonly Injurious, with Special Observations on Ox Warble or Bot Fly. Demy 8vo, 64 pp. Fully Illustrated. 6d.

Ox Warble Fly, or Bot Fly, with Methods of Prevention and Remedy. Demy 8vo, 40 pp. Fully Illustrated. 3d.

Annual Reports on Injurious Insects for the Twenty-four years, 1877-1900 (with **General Index,** 1877-1898. Compiled by ROBERT NEWSTEAD, F.E.S., Curator of the Grosvenor Museum, Chester. With Preface by E. A. ORMEROD). Royal 8vo. Fully Illustrated. Price 1s. 6d. each.

LONDON : SIMPKIN MARSHALL & CO., LTD.

Elliott & Fry, Photo — Walker & Cockerell Ph. Sc.

Eleanor A. Ormerod

ELEANOR ORMEROD, LL.D.
ECONOMIC ENTOMOLOGIST. AUTO-BIOGRAPHY AND CORRESPONDENCE

EDITED BY ROBERT WALLACE

PROFESSOR OF AGRICULTURE AND RURAL ECONOMY
IN THE UNIVERSITY OF EDINBURGH

WITH PORTRAIT AND ILLUSTRATIONS

LONDON
JOHN MURRAY, ALBEMARLE STREET
1904

DEDICATED

TO ALL

MISS ORMEROD'S CORRESPONDENTS

IN

ECONOMIC ENTOMOLOGY.

PREFACE

THE idea that Miss Ormerod should write her biography originated with the present writer during one of many visits paid to her at St. Albans. Miss Ormerod had unfolded in charming language and with admirable lucidity and fluency some interesting chapters of her personal experiences and reminiscences. The first working plan of the project involved the concealment of a shorthand writer behind a screen in the dining-room while dinner was proceeding, and while the examination of ethnological specimens or other attractive objects gave place for a time to general conversation on subjects grown interesting by age. Although the shorthand writer was selected and is several times referred to in letters written about this period (pp. 304–7), Miss Ormerod, on due reflection, felt that the presence, though unseen, of a stranger at these meetings *in camera* would make the position unnatural, and dislocate the association of ideas to the detriment of the narrative.

She then bethought herself of the method of writing down at leisure moments, from time to time as a suitable subject occurred to her, rough notes (p. 122) to be elaborated later, and when after a time a subject had been exhausted, the rough notes were re-written and welded into a narrative (pp. 304–21). Some four or five of the early chapters were thus treated and then typewritten, but the remainder of the Autobiography was left in crude form, requiring much piecing together and editorial trimming. Had the book been produced on the original plan, it was proposed to name it "Recollections of Changing Times."[1] It would have dealt with a number of subjects of general interest, such as the history of the Post Office, early records of floods and

[1] See letter to the Editor dated June 14, 1900, p. 304.

earthquakes, as well as newspapers of early date. The introduction of Miss Ormerod's letters to a few of her leading correspondents was made necessary by the lack of other suitable material. The present volume is still mainly the product of Miss Ormerod's pen, but with few exceptions general subjects have been eliminated; and it forms much more a record of her works and ways than it would have done had she been spared to complete it. From the inception of the idea the present writer was appointed editor, but had Miss Ormerod lived to see the book in the hands of the public his share of work would have been light indeed. Armed with absolute authority from her (p. 318) to use his discretion in the work, he has exercised his editorial license in making minor alterations without brackets or other evidences of the editorial pen, while at the same time the integrity of the substance has been jealously guarded.

As in Miss Ormerod's correspondence with experts only scientific names for insects and other scientific objects were employed, it was found expedient to introduce the common names within ordinary or round brackets. Much thought and care have been given to the arrangement of the letters, and a sort of compromise was adopted of three different methods that came up for consideration, viz., (1) according to chronological order, (2) according to the subjects discussed, and (3) grouping under the names of the individuals to whom they were addressed. While the third is the predominant feature of the scheme the chronological order has been maintained within the personal groups, and precedence in the book was generally given to the letters of the oldest date. At the same time, to complete a subject in one group written mainly to one correspondent, letters dealing with the subject under discussion have been borrowed from their natural places under the heading of "Letters to Dr. ——" or "Letters to Mr. ——." While Miss Ormerod's practice of referring to matters of minor importance and of purely personal interest in correspondence dealing mainly with definite lines of scientific research, has not been interfered with in a few instances, in most of the other groups of letters on technical subjects editorial pruning was freely practised to prevent confusion and to concentrate the subject matter. The chief exceptions occur in the voluminous and interesting correspondence with Dr. Fletcher, in her specially confidential letters to Dr. Bethune, and in the very general correspondence with the editor. It was felt that to remove more of the friendly references and passing general remarks to her correspondents would have been to invalidate the letters and show the writer of them in a character alien to her own.

The figures of insects which have been introduced into the correspondence, to lighten it and increase its interest to the reader, have been chiefly borrowed from Miss Ormerod's published works; and among them will be found a number of illustrations from Curtis's "Farm Insects," for the use of which her acknowledgments were fully given to Messrs. Blackie, the publishers.[1] The contents of this volume will afford ample evidence of Miss Ormerod's intense interest in her subject, of the infinite pains she took to investigate the causes of injury, and of the untiring and unceasing efforts she employed to accomplish her object; also that her determinations relative to the causes and nature of parasitic attacks upon crops, give proof of soundness of judgment, and her advice, chiefly connected with remedial and preventive treatment, was eminently sensible and practical. Mainly by correspondence of the most friendly kind she formed a unique connecting link between economic entomologists in all parts of the world; and she quoted their various opinions to one another very often in support of her own preconceived ideas.

The three biographical chapters, III., XI., and XII., were added to the autobiographical statements which she had left, with the object merely of supplying some missing personal incidents in an interesting life. Other deficiencies in the Autobiography are made up by Miss Ormerod's correspondence, and the history of her work is permitted to evolve from her own letters.

A strong vein of humour runs through many parts of her writings, notably in the chapter on "Church and Parish." The reader will not fail to notice the splendid courtesy and deference to scientific authority, as well as the fullest appreciation of and unselfish sympathy with the genuine scientific work of others, which pervades all she wrote. Prominent among these characteristics of Miss Ormerod should be placed her scrupulous honesty of purpose in acknowledging to the fullest extent the work of others.

The work of collecting material, sifting, and editing has been going on for nearly two years, and could never have been accomplished but for the kindly help rendered by so many of Miss Ormerod's correspondents, all of whom I

[1] Figs. C. and D. (pp. 160 and 162) are borrowed from Yarrell's *British Birds* by permission of Messrs. Gurney & Jackson.

now cordially thank for invaluable sympathetic assistance. Special acknowledgments are due to Sir Wm. Henry Marling, Bart., the present owner of Sedbury Park, and to Miss Ormerod's nephews and nieces, who have been delighted to render such assistance as could not have been found outside the family circle. Besides Mr. Grimshaw, Mr. Janson, Dr. Stewart MacDougall, Professor Hudson Beare, and Mr. T. P. Newman who read the proofs critically, last, but not least, do I thank Mr. John Murray, whose friendly reception of the first overtures made to him as the prospective publisher of this volume brightened some of the dark moments near the close of Miss Ormerod's life. I have had as editor the much appreciated privilege of drawing, in all cases of difficulty, upon Mr. Murray's great literary experience.

In making these pleasing acknowledgments I in no way wish to shift the responsibility as Editor from my own shoulders for defects which may be discovered or for the general scheme of the work, which was, with slight modifications, my own. If it be said in criticism that the Editor is too little in evidence, I shall be all the more satisfied, as that has been throughout one of his leading aims.

ROBERT WALLACE.

UNIVERSITY OF EDINBURGH,
1904.

LIST OF ERRATA.

Page 70, line 31, for "*Tenebroides*" read "*Tenebrioides.*"
" 130, " 11, for "*Ceutorhyncus*" read "*Ceuthorhyncus.*"
" " in description of Fig. 14, for "CEUTORHYNCUS" read "CEUTHORHYNCUS."
" 144, line 7, for "importad" read "imported."
" 185, " 1, for "*Lucania*" read "*Leucania.*"

CONTENTS

LIST OF ILLUSTRATIONS IN THE TEXT

LIST OF FULL-PAGE PLATES

CHAPTER I

BIRTH, CHILDHOOD AND EDUCATION

I WAS born at Sedbury Park, in West Gloucestershire, on a sunny Sunday morning (the 11th of May, 1828), being the youngest of the ten children of George and Sarah Ormerod, of Sedbury Park, Gloucestershire, and Tyldesley, Lancashire. As a long time had elapsed since the birth of the last of the other children (my two sisters and seven brothers), my arrival could hardly have been a family comfort. Nursery arrangements, which had been broken up, had to be re-established. I have been told that I started on what was to be my long life journey, with a face pale as a sheet, a quantity of black hair, and a constitution that refused anything tendered excepting a concoction of a kind of rusk made only at Monmouth. The very earliest event of which I have a clear remembrance was being knocked down on the nursery stairs when I was three years old by a cousin of my own age. The damage was small, but the indignity great, and, moreover, the young man stole the lump of sugar which was meant to console me, so the grievance made an impression. A year later a real shock happened to my small mind. Whilst my sister, Georgiana, five years my senior, was warming herself in the nursery, her frock caught fire. She flew down the room, threw herself on the sheepskin rug at the door, and rolled till the fire was put out. But she was so badly burnt that the injuries required dressing, and this event also made a great impression on me. Other reminiscences of pleasure and of pain come back, in thinking over those long past days, but none of such special and wonderful interest as that of being held up to see King William IV. Little as I was, I had been taken to one of the theatres, and my father carried me along one of the galleries, and raised me in his arms that I might look through the glass window at the back of one of the boxes and see His Majesty. I do not in the least believe that I saw the right man. However, it is something to remember that about the year 1835, if I had not been so frightened, I might have seen the King.

In regard to any special likings of my earliest years it seems to me, from what I can remember or have been told, that there were signs even then of the chief tastes which have accompanied me through life—an intense love of flowers; a fondness for insect investigation; and a fondness also for writing. In my babyhood, even before I could speak, the sight of a bunch of flowers was the signal for both arms being held out to beg for the coveted treasure, and the taste was utilised when I was a little older, in checking a somewhat incomprehensible failure of health during the spring visit of the family to London. Some one suggested trying the effect of a supply of flower roots and seeds for me to exercise my love of gardening on, and the experiment was successful. I can remember my delight at the sight of the boxes of common garden plants—pansies, daisies, and the like; and I suppose some feeling of the restored comfort has remained through all these years to give a charm (not peculiarly exciting in itself) to the smell of bast mats and other appurtenances of the outside of Covent Garden market.

My first insect observation I remember perfectly. It was typical of many others since. I was quite right, absolutely and demonstrably right, but I was above my audience and fared accordingly. One day while the family were engaged watching the letting out of a pond, or some similar matter, I was perched on a chair, and given to watch, to keep me quiet at home, a tumbler of water with about half-a-dozen great water grubs in it. One of them had been much injured and his companions proceeded quite to demolish him. I was exceedingly interested, and when the family came home gave them the results of my observations, which were entirely disbelieved. Arguing was not permitted, so I said nothing (as far as I remember); but I had made my first step in Entomology.

Writing was a great pleasure. A treat was to go into the library and to sit near, without disturbing, my father, and "write a letter" on a bit of paper granted for epistolary purposes. The letter was presently sealed with one of the great armorial seals which my father wore—as gentlemen did then—in a bunch at what was called the "fob." The whole affair must have been of a very elementary sort, but it was no bad application of the schoolroom lessons, for thus, quite at my own free will, I was practising the spelling of easy words, and their combination into little sentences, and also how to bring pen, ink, and paper into connection without necessitating an inky deluge. In those days children were not "amused" as is the fashion now. We neither went to parties, nor were there children's parties at home, but I fancy we were just as happy. As soon as possible a certain amount of lessons, given by my mother, formed the backbone of the day's employment. In the higher branches requisite for preparation for Public School work, my mother was so successful as to have the pleasure of receiving a special message of appreciation of her work sent to my father by Dr. Arnold, Head-master of Rugby. All my brothers were educated under Dr. Arnold, two as his private pupils, and the five younger as Rugby schoolboys, and he spoke with great appreciation of the sound foundation which had been laid by my mother for the school work, especially as regarded religious instruction. From the fact of my brothers being so much older than I, the latter point is the only one which remains in my memory; but I have a clear recollection of my mother's mustering her family class on Sunday afternoons, *i.e.*, all whose age afforded her any excuse to lay hands on them. Whether in the earlier foundation or more advanced work, my mother's own great store of solid information, and her gift for imparting it, enabled her to keep us steadily progressing. Everything was thoroughly learned, and once learned never permitted to be forgotten. Nothing was attempted that could not be well understood, and this was expected to be mastered. In playtime we were allowed great liberty to follow our own pursuits, in which the elders of the family generally participated, and as we grew older we made collections (in which my sister Georgiana's love of shells laid the foundation of what was afterwards a collection of 3,000 species), and carried on "experiments," everlasting re-arrangement of our small libraries, and amateur book-binding. All imaginable ways of using our hands kept us very happily employed indoors. Out of doors there was great enjoyment in the pursuits which a country property gives room for, and I think I was a very happy child, although I fancy what is called a "very old-fashioned" one, from not having companions of my own age.

On looking back over the years of my early childhood,

the period when instruction—commonly known as education—is imparted, it seems to me that this followed the distinction between education and the mere acquirement of knowledge (well brought out by one of the Coleridges), and embraced the former much more fully than is the case at the present day. There was no undue pressure on bodily or mental powers, but the work was steady and constant. The instruction, except in music, was given by my mother, who had, in an eminent degree, the gift of teaching. Although at the present time home education is frequently held up to contempt, still some recollections of my own home teaching may be of interest. The subjects studied were those included in what is called a "solid English education." First in order was biblical knowledge and moral precepts, practical as well as expository, which seem to have glided into my head without my being aware how, excepting in the case of the enormity of any deviation from truth. In each of the six week-days' work came a chapter of Scripture, read aloud, half in English, and half in French, by my sister and me. The "lessons," *i.e.*, recitation, inspection of exercises, &c., followed. The subjects at first were few—but they were thoroughly explained. Geography, for example, was taken at first in its broad bearings, viz., countries, provinces, chief towns, mountains, rivers, and so on (what comes back to my mind as corresponding to "large print"), and gradually the "small print" was added, with as minute information as was considered necessary. Use of the map was strictly enforced, and repetition to impress it on the memory. I seem to hear my mother inculcating briskness in giving names of county towns—"Northumberland? Now then! quick as lightning, answer." "Newcastle, Morpeth and Alnwick, in Northumberland"; and to enforce attention a tap of my mother's thimble on the table, or possibly, if stupidity required great rousing, with more gentle application on the top of my head. If things were bad beyond endurance, the book was sent with a skim across the room, which had an enlivening effect; but this rarely happened. My mother gave the morning hours to the work (unless there was some higher claim upon them, such as my father requiring her for some purpose or other) but she always declared that she would have nothing to do with the preparation of lessons in the afternoon. If all went fairly well, as usual, the passage for next day's lesson was carefully read over at my mother's side, and difficulties explained, and then I was expected to learn it by myself. What we knew as "doing lessons"—which now I believe passes under the more advanced name of "preparation"—was left to my own care, and if this proved next morning not to have been duly given I had reason to amend my ways. The preparation hour was from four to five o'clock, but if the lessons had not been learned by that time they were expected to be done somehow, though I think my mother was very lenient if any tolerably presentable reason were given for short measure. If the work were completed in less than the allotted time, I was allowed to amuse myself by reading poetry, of which I was excessively fond, from the great volume of "Extracts" from which my lesson had been learned. This plan seems to me to have had many advantages. For one thing, I carried the morning's explanations in my head till called upon, and for another, I think it gave some degree of self-reliance, as well as a habit of useful, quiet self-employment for a definite time. This was, in all reason, expected to be carefully adhered to, and I can well remember when I had hurried home from a summer's walk how the muscles in my legs would twitch whilst I endeavoured to learn a French verb.

One educational detail which, as far as my experience goes, appears to have been much better conducted in my young days than at present, was that reading aloud to the little people had not then come into vogue. I have no recollection of being allowed to lie about on the carpet, heels in the air, whilst some one read a book to me. There was also the peculiarity to which, if I remember rightly, Sir Benjamin Brodie attributes in his autobiography some of his success in life, viz., work was almost continuous. There was never an interval of some weeks' holidays. A holiday was granted on some great occasion, such as the anniversary of my father and mother's wedding-day and birthdays, and on the birthdays of other members of the family, but (if occurring on consecutive days) somewhat under protest; and half-holidays were not uncommon in summer. These consisted of my being excused the afternoon preparation of lessons, and as the pretext for asking was generally the weather's being "so very fine," I conjecture it was thought that an extra run in the fresh air was perhaps a healthy variety of occupation. Any way, the learning lost must have been small, for excepting the written part of the work the lessons were expected to appear next morning in perfect form, however miscellaneously acquired. One way or other there were occasional breaks by pleasant episodes such as picnics, on fine summer days, to one of the many old ruined castles, or disused little Monmouthshire churches, or Roman remains in the neighbourhood, where my father worked up the material for some forthcoming archæological essay and my mother executed some of her beautiful sketches (plate VI.). The carriage-load of young ones enjoyed themselves exceedingly, and prevented the work from becoming monotonous or burdensome. And there were joyful days before and after going from home, and now and then, when it was impossible for my mother to give her morning up to the work, if she had not appointed one of the elder of the young fry her deputy for the occasion. I remember, too, that I took my book in play hours, when and where I wished; sometimes on a fine summer afternoon the "where" might be sitting on a horizontal bough of a large old Portugal laurel in the garden. And I fancy that the perch in the fresh air, with the green light shimmering round me, was as good for my bodily health (by no means robust) as my entertaining little book for my progress in reading.

It was remarkable the small quantity of food which it was at one time thought the right thing for ladies to take in public. I suppose from early habit, my mother, who was active both in body and mind, used to eat very little. At lunch she would divide a slice of meat with me. Although now the death, in her confinement, of the Princess Charlotte, "the people's darling," which plunged the nation in sorrow, is a thing only of history, yet it is on record how she almost implored for more food, the special desire being mutton chops. Though not in any way connected with the Royal Family, my mother held in memory the unhappy event from its consequences. Sir Richard Croft, whose medical attentions had been so inefficient to the Princess, was shortly after called to attend in a similar capacity on Mrs. Thackeray, wife of Dr. Thackeray, then or after Provost of King's College, Cambridge. For some reason or other he left his patient for a while, and the story went that, finding pistols in the room where he was resting, he shot himself. Miss Cotton—Mrs. Thackeray's sister—was a friend of my mother. Miss Thackeray, the infant who was ushered into the world by the death of both her mother and the doctor, survived, and in her young-lady days was particularly fond of dancing; and I have the remembrance of my first London ball being at her aunt's house.

PLATE I.

Sedbury Park House and Grounds, distant view.

Mansion House, Sedbury Park; Miss Georgiana Ormerod on the left, Miss Eleanor Ormerod on the right.
(*pp. 14, 48.*)

To face p. 6.

CHAPTER II

PARENTAGE

THE situation of Sedbury (plate I.), rising to an elevation of about 170 feet between the Severn and the Wye, opposite Chepstow, was very beautiful, and the vegetation rich and luxuriant. My father purchased the house and policy grounds from Sir Henry Cosby about 1826, and it was our home till his death in 1873. He retained Tyldesley, his other property in Lancashire, with its coal mines, but we did not reside there, as the climate was too cold for the health of my mother and for the young family.

[The original purchase was called Barnesville, and earlier still Kingston Park, and it consisted of a moderate-sized villa with the immediately adjoining grounds. The property was added to by purchases from the Duke of Beaufort, and it was renamed Sedbury Park after the nearest village. To the house the new owner added a handsome colonnade about 10 feet wide, and a spacious library. Sir Robert Smirke, the architect of all the improvements, was the man who designed the British Museum, the General Post Office, &c.[1] Barnes Cottage on the property, at one time 'Barons Cottage,' was kept in habitable repair because it secured to the estate the privilege of a seat in church.]

About sixteen miles from Sedbury Park are still to be seen the interesting ruins of the Great Roman station of this part of the country, Caerwent or the white tower, the Venta Silurum of Antonine's "Itinerary."[2] Its trade and military

[1] About that period it was the practice for men who became leading architects to undergo a thorough classical training, including a lengthened course of practical study on the continent of Europe—the results of which are in evidence in so many public buildings then erected in London.

[2] See George Ormerod's *Strigulensia, Archæological Memoirs relating to the district adjacent to the confluence of the Severn and Wye* (1861).

importance were transferred to Strigul, now known as Chepstow, after the Norman Conquest. Sedbury Park is believed to have been an outlying post of this chief military centre, and it was occupied by soldiers "guarding the beacon and the look-out over the passages" of the Severn. Considerable finds of Roman pottery (plate XI.) were discovered about 1860, while drains about 4 feet deep were being cut near to the Severn cliffs. They consisted chiefly of fragments of rough earthenware—cooking dishes and cinerary urns, &c. There was also a small quantity of glazed, red Samian cups and one piece of Durobrivian ware and great quantities of animals' teeth and bones, but no coins (p. 174). After the death of my father it was found that much of the best ware had been stolen.

My father (pl. II.) is well known for the high place he takes amongst our English County historians, as the author of "The History of the County Palatine, and City of Chester," published in 1818. He came of the old Lancashire family of Ormerod of Ormerod, a demesne in the township of Cliviger, a wild and mountainous district, situated along the boundaries of Lancashire and Yorkshire. The varied watershed (transmitting the streams to the eastern and western seas); the beauties of the rocks and waterfalls; the shaded glens, and the antique farmhouses (where fairy superstition still lingered till the beginning of the past century), have been written about by Whitaker in his "History of Whalley."[1] There, in the year 1810, in an elevated position, amongst aged pine and elm trees, and surrounded by high garden walls of dark stone, the mansion, (pl. XXVIII.)—since greatly enlarged by the family of the present proprietor—stood in a dingle at the side of a mountain stream, which rushed behind it at a considerable depth. Beyond the stream, the rise of the ground to the more elevated moors includes a view of the summit of Pendle Hill, of exceedingly evil repute for meetings of witches and warlocks, and congenerous unpleasantnesses, in the olden time.

The family of Ormerod was settled in the locality from which they took their name, as far back as the year 1311, the estates continuing in their possession until, in 1793 (by the marriage of Charlotte Ann Ormerod, sole daughter and heiress of Laurence Ormerod, the last of the generation of the parent stem in direct male descent), they passed to Colonel John Hargreaves; and by the marriage of his eldest

[1] See pp. 345, 355, 3rd edition.

PLATE II.

GEORGE ORMEROD, ESQ., D.C.L., LL.D., F.R.S., F.S.A.,
OF SEDBURY PARK, GLOUCESTERSHIRE, AND TYLDESLEY, LANCASHIRE,
FATHER OF MISS ORMEROD.

From a painting after Jackson, date circa 1820.
(pp. 11, 14.)

To face p. 8.

daughter and co-heiress, Eleanor Mary, with the Rev. William Thursby, they became vested in the Thursby family,[1] represented until recently by Sir John Hardy Thursby, Bart., of Ormerod House, Burnley, Lancashire, and Holmhurst, Christchurch, Hants. Sir John showed thoughtful, philanthropic feeling to his Lancashire district, by presenting the land for a public park to Burnley, and, in connection with his family, he also gave the site for the neighbouring "Victoria Hospital." In 1887, he served as High Sheriff of Lancashire, and was created Baronet. Dying on March 16, 1901, he was succeeded by his eldest son, John Ormerod Scarlett Thursby, of Bankhall, Burnley, who, in his surname and baptismal names, keeps alive the connection with the old family stock and the families with which the last two co-heiresses of Ormerod were connected by marriage. With these matters of possessions, however, the collateral branch of Ormerod, of Bury in Lancashire (from the special founder of which my father was descended in direct male line), had nothing to do. From Oliver Ormerod, who became permanently resident at Bury shortly after the close of the seventeenth century, descended his only son, George Ormerod of Bury, merchant. From him descended George Ormerod (an only child), who died on October 7, 1785, a few days before the birth of his only child—my father—yet another George Ormerod. In a mere statement of the names of the representatives of successive generations, of whom no specially distinguishing points appear to have been recorded, there is, perhaps, little of general interest. But possibly some amount of interest attaches to the proofs of representatives of one family having lived quietly on from generation to generation in one locality since the early part of the fourteenth century. The connections and intermarrying of the Ormerods with many of the Lancashire families of former days give the subject a county interest to those who care to search out the genealogical, historical and heraldic details given at great length in my father's volume of "Parentalia." Here and there some member of the family appears to have come before the world, as in the case of Oliver Ormerod, M.A., noted as a profound scholar, theologian, and Puritan

[1] See *Parentalia, Genealogical Memoirs*, by Geo. Ormerod, D.C.L., F.R.S., pp. 3–8, for records and evidences regarding successive generations of the family from 1311 onwards, as existing in Inquisitions; Pedigrees in College of Arms; Duchy Records; Clithero Records, and other official sources quoted in the work.—(E.A.O.)

controversialist, and author of two polemical works—one entitled "The Picture of a Puritan," published in 1605, and the other "The Picture of a Papist," published in 1606. Oliver Ormerod was presented to the Rectory of Norton Fitzwarren, Co. Somerset, by William Bourchier, third Earl of Bath, and afterwards to the Rectory of Huntspill in the same county, where he died in the year 1625.

Something, however, occurred in 1784 of much interest to our own branch of the family, leading subsequently to great increase of property, and likewise in some degree, connecting us with the Jacobite troubles of 1745. This was the marriage of my grandfather with Elizabeth, second daughter of Thomas Johnson, of Tyldesley. Thomas Johnson (my great grandfather) having married, secondly, Susannah, daughter and co-heiress of Samuel Wareing, of Bury and Walmersley, got with her considerable estates, inherited from the Wareings, the Cromptons of Hacking, and Nuthalls of Golynrode. On the occasion of the march of Charles Stewart to Manchester in 1745, "Tyldesley"—to use the form of appellation often given from property in those days—suffered many hardships. As one of the five treasurers who had undertaken to receive Lancashire subscriptions in aid of the reigning monarch, King George the Second, and as an influential local friend of the cause, he was one of those who suffered the infliction of domiciliary military visitation, and also threat of torture by burning his hands to induce him to give up government papers and money in his possession. I have still in my house (1901) the large hanging lamp of what is now called "Old Manchester" glass, which lighted the dining-room when my great grandfather stood so steadily to his trust that although the straw had been brought for the purpose of torture (or to terrify him into submission) extremities were not proceeded to. He was ultimately left a prisoner on parole, in his house, until released in December, 1745, in consequence of the retreat of the rebel army. But disagreeable as this state of things must have been at the best, it was to some degree lightened by kindness (or at least absence of unnecessary annoyance) on the part of the Jacobite officers, of whom stories remained in the family to my own time. One especial point was their kindness to my eldest great aunt,[1] then a little child, whom they used to take on their knees to show her what she described as their "little guns." The drinking of the healths of the rival

[1] Anne, born 1739, by a first marriage, married Charles Ford.

FAMILY GROUP—GEORGE ORMEROD AS A CHILD; HIS MOTHER SEATED BEHIND HIM; HER BROTHER, THOMAS JOHNSON, ESQ., OF TYLDESLEY, LANCASHIRE, STANDING; AND THEIR MOTHER SEATED ON THE RIGHT.

Composition from miniature, circa 1780.

To face p. 10.

princes, which probably often led to a less peaceful ending, was mentioned by my father in his History of Cheshire, as a notable instance of consideration.

"On one occasion when the Scotch officers who caroused in their prisoner's house, had given their usual toast KING JAMES, and the host on request had followed with his, and undauntedly proposed KING GEORGE, some rose, and touched their swords; but a senior officer exclaimed, 'He has drunk our Prince, why should we not drink his? Here's to the Elector of Hanover."[1]

During the disturbed time, when any one bearing the appearance of a messenger would assuredly have been seized with the papers which he carried, the difficulty of transmitting information was met by the employment at night of two greyhounds trained for the service. The documents were fastened to the animals and thus carried safely to the adherent's house, from which as opportunity offered they could be passed on. The greyhounds, having been well fed as a reward and encouragement to future good behaviour, were started off on their return journey. In the present day this plan of transmission would very soon be discovered, but in those times the nature of the country, the nocturnal hours chosen, and also the deeply-rooted superstitions of the district, all helped to make the four-footed messengers very trusty carriers.

In 1755 Thomas Johnson served as Sheriff of Lancashire. He died in 1763, leaving a widow (who survived him until 1798), one son, and three daughters—the only survivors of a family of eleven children, of whom seven died in infancy, three on the day of their birth. Of the four children who reached maturity, Elizabeth, the second daughter (plate III.) married my grandfather, George Ormerod of Bury, at the Collegiate Church, Manchester, on the 18th of October, 1784. He died in 1785, a fortnight before the birth of my father, who was the sole issue of this marriage.

My father, George Ormerod (plate II.), heir to his grandfather, was born October 20, 1785. He was co-heir of, and successor to the estates of his maternal uncle in 1823, and sole heir to his surviving maternal aunt in 1839. He was D.C.L., LL.D., F.R.S., F.S.A., and a magistrate for the counties of Cheshire, Gloucester, and Monmouth. On August 2, 1808, he married my mother, Sarah, eldest daughter of John Latham, Bradwall Hall, Cheshire, Fellow

[1] *Hist. Ches.*, vol. i. p. 43.

and sometime President of the Royal College of Physicians, Harley Street, London.[1]

My grandfather in the female line, John Latham, M.D., F.R.S. (plate IV.), the eldest son of the Rev. John Latham, came of an old family stock, and was born in 1761 in the rectory house at Gawsworth, Cheshire. He was educated first at Manchester Grammar School, and thence proceeded (with the view of studying for orders) to Brasenose College, Oxford, but the strong bent of his own wishes towards the medical profession induced him to alter his plans, and he took his degree of M.D. on October 10, 1788. "His first professional years were passed at Manchester and Oxford, where he was physician to the respective infirmaries. In 1788 he removed to London, was admitted Fellow of the College of Physicians, and elected successively physician to the Middlesex, the Magdalen, and St. Bartholomew Hospitals. In 1795 he was appointed Physician Extraordinary to the Prince of Wales, and reappointed to the same office on the Prince's accession to the throne as George IV. In 1813 Dr. Latham was elected President of the College of Physicians; in 1816, founded the Medical Benevolent Society; and in 1829 finally left London, retiring to his estate at Bradwall Hall, where he died on April 20, 1843, in the eighty-second year of his age."

He indulged in the practical pleasures of country life, and maintained a home farm, on which he kept a dairy of sixty cows. He was a man of great force of character and of decisive action. On one occasion a man who had been told that if he returned he would be summarily ejected, came back to crave an audience. On being reminded of the fact he pleaded, "Oh! doctor, you do not really mean it." "Yes, I do," was the prompt reply as an order was given to the butler to turn the intruder out.

Dr. Latham married, in 1784, Mary, eldest daughter and co-heiress of the Rev. Peter Mayer, Vicar of Prestbury, Cheshire, by whom he had numerous children, of whom three sons and two daughters lived to maturity. My

[1] For details and genealogical tables of descent (accompanied by armorial bearings) regarding the above-named families, and many others of the old families of the Counties Palatine of Lancashire and Cheshire, now more or less passed away, see *Parentalia*, by George Ormerod, cited *ante* in note, p. 9, with an absolutely enormous amount of reference to documentary evidence, often in itself of much antiquarian interest (E.A.O.).

PLATE IV.

JOHN LATHAM, ESQ., M.D., F.R.S., PHYSICIAN EXTRAORDINARY TO GEORGE IV., MATERNAL GRANDFATHER OF MISS ORMEROD, IN HIS ROBES AS PRESIDENT OF THE ROYAL COLLEGE OF PHYSICIANS, 1813 TO 1819.

To face p. 12.

mother, his eldest daughter, survived him, as did also her brothers. Of these the second son, Peter Mere Latham, M.D., of Grosvenor-street, Westminster, one of Her Majesty's Physicians Extraordinary, was long well known as an eminent consulting physician regarding diseases of the chest, until his own severe sufferings from asthma obliged him to retire to Torquay, where he died on July 20, 1875.

From our being related to John Latham and his wife, Mary Mayer (although in point of rank the difference was so enormous between the head from whom we could trace and ourselves), it is permissible to allude to our connection with the family of Arderne of Alvanley, and consequent descent from King Edward the First and his wife, Eleanor of Castile. This gave us our claim of "founder's kin" in the election to the "Port Fellowship" of Brasenose College, to which distinction in my time my brother—Rev. John Arderne Ormerod—was elected. He was the last Port Fellow on the above foundation. The record of each generation will be found in the genealogical table of "Arderne" in my father's "Parentalia," and also on reference to the pedigrees of the many families of which members are named in the "History of Cheshire."

CHAPTER III

REMINISCENCES OF SEDBURY BY MISS DIANA LATHAM [1]

MY cousin Eleanor Anne Ormerod was the youngest of a family of ten—seven brothers and three sisters—all clever, energetic creatures, and gifted with a strong sense of humour. A large family always creates a peculiar atmosphere for itself; it also breaks up into detachments of elder and younger growth, and the elder members are beginning to take places in the world before the younger are out of the schoolroom. Eleanor's eldest brother was a Church dignitary while she was still a child, teased and petted by her young medical student brothers, and the darling of her elder sister Georgiana. The father and mother of this numerous flock were both remarkable people. Mr. Ormerod, historian and antiquary, always occupied with literary or topographical research, was an autocrat in his own family and intolerant of any shortcomings or failings that came under his notice. He could, however, on occasion, relax and tell humorous stories to children. The family discipline was strict; the younger members were expected to yield obedience to the elders, and it was said that the spaniel Guy (he came from Warwick), who ranked as one of the children, always obeyed the eldest of the family present. My aunt had a large share of the milk of human kindness added to much practical common sense and a touch of artistic genius in her composition; it was from her that her daughters inherited their eye for colour and dexterity of touch. Mr. Ormerod was a neat draughtsman of architectural subjects, but my aunt had taste and skill and a delight in her own branch of art—flower painting—that lasted all her life.

Sedbury Park (plate I.) was a beautiful home; the house, a handsome family mansion with comfortable old-fashioned

[1] The daughter of Mr. Henry Latham, resident in Italy.

furniture, good and interesting pictures, old china, and a splendid library, afforded also ample space for its inmates to follow their various hobbies, and many were the arts and crafts practised there at various times. The carpenter's bench, the lathe, wood-carving, electro-typing, modelling and casting for models each had their turn, and in all this strenuous play Eleanor had her full share. Society played a very secondary part in life at Sedbury; calls were exchanged with county neighbours at due intervals, and there was some intimacy with Copleston, Bishop of Llandaff, the Bathursts of Lydney Park, and the Horts of Hardwicke. But though Mr. Ormerod attended to his duties as magistrate, and went duly to meetings of the bench at Chepstow, he was quite without sympathy for field sports and the pursuits of his brother magistrates. He was absorbed in his own studies, and something of a recluse by nature.

[Miss Ormerod has herself written of the elaborateness of the arrangements and the great formality which were associated with the regular county dinner party, the chief method of entertainment at Sedbury sixty years ago. She referred to the anxieties experienced lest the coach should not arrive in time with the indispensables including fish—"the distance of Sedbury from London involving twenty-four hours or more of transmission in weather favourable or otherwise." Miss Ormerod continues:—

"One very important matter in the far gone past times in the arrangement of the dinner table, was the removal of the great cloth and of two cloths laid, one at each side, just wide enough to occupy the uncovered space before the guests, and long enough to reach from one end of the table to the other. The removal required a deal of care and dexterity, and I do not think it was practised at many other houses in our neighbourhood. When the table was to be cleared for dessert of course everything was removed, including the great tablecloth itself—one of the handsomest of the family possessions, and of considerable length when there were the usual number of about eighteen or twenty guests. The operation was performed as follows:—The butler placed himself at the end of each strip successively, and a few of the house servants or of those who came with guests along each side. The butler drew the slips in turn and the servants took care there should be no hitch in the passage of the cloths, and so each was nicely gathered up.

"But the removal of the great tablecloth which was the

next operation was a more difficult matter. The great heavy central epergne of rosewood had to be lifted a little way up by a strong man-servant or two, whilst the tablecloth was slipped from beneath it and the cloth was started on its travels down the table till it came into the hands of the butler, who gathered it up. The beautifully polished table then appeared in full lustre. The shining surface sparkled excellently and presently reflected the bright silver and glass and the fruit and flowers with a brilliance which to my thinking was much more beautiful than the arrangement of later days."]

The annual visit to London was a great delight to my aunt, who enjoyed meetings with her own family and friends, and visits to exhibitions, &c. Her husband had always occupation in the British Museum, and her daughters took painting and other lessons. Mary, the eldest, was a pupil of Copley Fielding; Georgiana (pl. XXVII.), and Eleanor later, had lessons from Hunt and learnt from him how to combine birds' nests and objects of still life with fruits and flowers into very lovely pictures. Both were excellent artists with a slight difference in style: Georgiana's pictures had great harmony of colour and composition; Eleanor's had more *chic*. Hunt was a very touchy little man—almost a dwarf—and if by any chance my aunt did not see him and bow as she drove past he cherished resentment for days after. At Sedbury driving tours or picnic excursions to the ruined castles and other objects of interest (pls. V., XVI., XXV.), in the neighbourhood were frequent, and the sketches that resulted were often reproduced as zincographs. Now and then a tour abroad was achieved, but such tours were few and far between. The beautiful copy of Correggio's "Marriage of St. Catherine" which ultimately became Eleanor's property, was acquired on a visit to Paris and the Louvre.

This self-contained family life did not lead to the marriage of the daughters, and three only of the seven sons married —one very late in life. Mary, the Princess Royal of the family, was the centre of the first group—herself and four brothers; Georgiana that of the second, consisting of two brothers older than herself, one younger, and Eleanor. Georgiana was a most lovable person; she always believed in her younger sister's capacity and in her projects, which were not approved of nor taken seriously by some of her elders, and could not have been carried out until after the break up of the home on the death of Mr. Ormerod. Meantime,

PLATE V.

Ruins of Tintern Abbey, Monmouthshire.

Frith photo.

To face p. 16.

the naturalist element in Eleanor was free to lay up knowledge for future use, and her country life gave leisure and opportunity for observation of bird, plant, and insect life, to say nothing of reptiles. Any snake killed on the estate was brought to Eleanor, and if it was remarkable for size or beauty she took a cast of it to be afterwards electrotyped, or had it buried in an ant-hill in order to set up its skeleton when the ants had cleaned the bones. The casts, which resembled bronze, were sometimes attached to slabs of green Devonshire marble, and made handsome paper weights. Wasps were at one time a subject of special study and interest to her brother Dr. Edward Ormerod, and she and Georgiana once conveyed a wasp's nest to him at Brighton. I believe he did not allow the wasps to exceed a certain number, out of consideration for the neighbouring fruiterers.

The premature deaths of Edward and William, physician and surgeon, were heartfelt sorrows to the two sisters nearest in age. If Eleanor's lot had been cast in later days she might have become a lady doctor of renown; she had many qualifications for the medical profession and a liking for domestic surgery; she had strong nerves and inspired confidence and used to say that she never went a journey without some fellow-passenger going into a detailed account of all her ailments. Besides strong nerves she had strong eye-sight and a delicate but firm touch. Her brothers did not encourage anatomical studies, but she could prepare sections of teeth and other objects for the microscope as beautifully as any professional microscopist. Some of my cousins were strong sighted and very short-sighted, and much inclined to be sceptical as to my long-sighted vision.

My last visit to Sedbury was in the autumn of 1853 in company with my step-sister Margaret Roberts, then just beginning to try her powers as an authoress. Eleanor must then have been twenty-five or twenty-six, but was considered to be quite young by her family, and in some respects was really so. She no longer played such pranks as embarking in a tub to navigate the horse pond, but her fine dark eyes would shine with mischief, and she was the licensed jester to the family circle.

The routine of life at Sedbury usually began, on the part of the younger members of the family, with a walk after breakfast prefaced by a visit to the poultry yard and greenhouses. Georgiana was chief hen-wife, and kept an account of the eggs and chickens. The park, lying on high ground between the Severn and the Wye, had beautiful points of view and fine timber, and there were lovely views beyond its precincts. "Offa's Dyke" ran through a corner of the estate, and the discovery of some Roman pottery in its neighbourhood had given my cousins much occupation in sticking broken fragments together and re-building them into vases (plate XI.). Our most beautiful walk, rather too long for the morning strolls, was to the "double view," a projecting promontory above the Wye where the river curves and from whence a lovely view is visible both up and down the stream. From the morning walk we always brought back something from hedge or field for my aunt to draw as she lay on her sofa with her drawing table across it. She was then in failing health, but still able to draw, and she used to make studies of flowers in pencil on grey paper, touching in the high light with Chinese white. Each drawing when finished was shut up in a large book, and there kept until some gathering of the family took place, when the drawings were produced and a lottery ensued, each person choosing a drawing in turn according to the number on the ticket they had drawn. I have a book of these beautiful drawings (plate VI.) which I greatly prize. In her youthful days she had painted in oils, and there were some fine copies of Dutch flower pictures in the drawing-room made by her. In later life the care of her large family left scant time for Art, but she cherished it in her daughters, and it was again a resource in her advanced age. The great sculptor Flaxman was a friend of her father and had encouraged her youthful efforts in Art. She had amazing industry and had copied many of his designs on wood as furniture decorations.

Georgiana and Eleanor usually had some painting or other industry on hand, or copying to do for their father. In the afternoon we often took a drive and were taken to see Tintern or the Wynd Cliff or some other point of interest. After dinner we sat in the library, a fine room with a splendid collection of books shut up in wire bookcases. Each member of the family had a key to the imprisoned books, but a visitor felt that to get one extracted for personal use was rather a ceremony. The beautiful illustrated books were brought out for the evening's entertainment and then safely housed again. On Sundays we walked or drove to Tidenham Church, a "little grey church on a windy hill" (plate VII.). We took a walk in the afternoon, and in the evening Mr. Ormerod read a sermon in the library to us and the servants. Such was the routine of life that autumn at Sedbury. At the time of our visit, the Gloucester Musical

PLATE VI.

Portion of Norman Work from Chepstow Parish Church.

From a drawing by Mrs. Ormerod, 1844.

(p. 6.)

To face p. 18.

Festival was going on, but there was no thought of going to hear it. In later years Eleanor possessed a good piano and studied the theory of music, but I think that was prompted by her general cleverness and activity of intellect rather than by any special gift for music. She was teaching herself Latin during our visit, and as time went on she acquired other languages. She made beautiful models of fruits by a process of her own invention. A collection of these was sent to an International Exhibition at St. Petersburg and she acquired sufficient knowledge of Russian to correspond with the department of the Exhibition receiving them.

After the break-up of the Sedbury home, consequent on the death of Mr. Ormerod, who survived his wife [1] for many years, Mary bought the lease of a house in Exeter and settled there for the rest of her life; the two younger sisters took a house for three years in Torquay, where we were then living as well as their, and our, old and beloved uncle, Dr. Mere Latham. Wishing to be nearer London, they removed to Isleworth and some years later to Torrington House, St. Alban's, where they spent the remaining years of their lives.

DIANA LATHAM.

[1] Sarah Ormerod died in 1860 aged 75 years.

CHAPTER IV

CHURCH AND PARISH

OUR Parish Church (plate VII.), that is to say, the Church of St. Mary the Virgin, Tidenham, Gloucestershire, in which parish my father's Sedbury property was situated, was of considerable antiquarian interest, as, although the hamlet of Churchend in which it stands is not mentioned in the Saxon survey of 956, the original church was in existence in the year 1071. The fabric of the church when I knew it was of later date, and, as shown by the accompanying sketch, chiefly in the architecture of the fourteenth century, excepting the south doorways of the nave and chancel and the tall narrow trefoil-headed windows in the north aisle. The chief point of archæological interest, however, lies in its possession of a leaden font (plate VII.) in perfect repair, referable from its style to the transition period of Saxon and Anglo-Norman architecture, and considered not likely to be more recent in date than the eleventh century. The subject derives additional interest from the circumstance of the precise correspondence of this font in Tidenham Church with the leaden font in the church of the adjoining small parish of Llancaut, making it demonstrably certain that both the fonts were cast from the same mould.[1] The decorations

[1] Alfred C. Fryer, Ph.D., M.A., begins an admirable, fully illustrated paper on "Leaden Fonts" in the *Archæological Journal*, March, 1900, with the following statements: There are 27 leaden fonts situated in 12 counties in the south, east and west of England—8 in Gloucester, 3 in Berks, 3 in Kent, 3 in Sussex, 2 in Oxford, 2 in Hereford, 1 in Derby, 1 in Dorset, 1 in Hants, 1 in Lincoln, 1 in Norfolk and 1 in Surrey. Several of these date from the latter part of the 11th and the 12th centuries. A few belonged to the 13th, 14th and 15th centuries, and the latest has the date 1689 impressed upon it. They are all tub-shaped, with the exception of two, namely, a hexagon and a cylindrical bowl. The older fonts all possessed covers, and several retain the markings to which the locks were attached. The deepest bowl (outside measurement) is 16 inches. The most shallow bowl is at Parham in Sussex, and it is only 8¼ inches in depth. The diameters also vary considerably from 32 inches to 18½ inches.—(Ed.).

PLATE VII.

LEADEN FONT IN TIDENHAM CHURCH.

CHURCH OF ST. MARY THE VIRGIN, TIDENHAM, GLOUCESTERSHIRE. THE VAULT ON S.E. SIDE OF THE CHURCH, ABOUT 15 FT. SQUARE, IS THE GRAVE OF MISS ORMEROD'S FATHER AND MOTHER.

From a sketch by Miss Georgiana E. Ormerod.

To face p. 20.

on the fonts are in *mezzo relievo*. These consist of figures and foliage ranged alternately, in twelve compartments, under ornamental, semi-circular arches resting on pillars; the design—two arches containing figures alternating with two arches containing foliage—being thrice repeated. The details will be better understood from the accompanying plate than from verbal description, but may be stated as representing respectively under each of the two thrice-repeated arches a venerable figure seated on a throne, the first of the two holding a sealed book, the second raising his hand as in the act of benediction, after removal of the seal from a similar book which is grasped in his hand. Each of these figures was considered to represent the Second Person of the Trinity.[1] On this point I am not qualified to offer an opinion, but whatever may be the case as to ecclesiastical adaptation in the representation in the second of the two figures, the first of the throned figures appears to coincide with the description of the vision of the Deity, given in the "Revelation" of St. John, chap. v. verse 1,[2] rather than with any representation of "The Lamb" that "stood," as it had been slain, and "came and took the book out of the right hand of him that sat upon the throne" (verses 6 and 7 of the chapter quoted).

The illustration is taken from very careful "rubbings" of the Tidenham Font. The Llancaut font has suffered considerable damage, and likewise the loss of two of the original twelve compartments. These had presumably been removed to make the font more suitable to the exceedingly small size of the little Norman chapel (pl. VIII.). This church, which in my time was almost disused, measured only about 40 feet in length by 12 in breadth, and possessed nothing of an architectural character, excepting one small round-headed window at the east end, with plain cylindrical side shafts without capitals, and a small cinquefoil piscina. The situation, on one of the crooks of the Wye, and just above the river, is romantic in the extreme. The ground rapidly slopes down to it from above, clothed with woodland from the level of the top of the precipitous cliffs which rise almost immediately beside it to a great height above the

[1] *Strigulensia Archæological Memoirs relating to the District adjacent to the confluence of the Severn and the Wye*, by Geo. Ormerod, D.C.L., F.R.S., of Tyldesley and Sedbury Park, MDCCCLXI., pp. 84–88. Re-arranged from a Memoir in *Archæologia* (by above author), XXIX., p. 17.

[2] "And I saw in the right hand of Him that sat on the throne, a book written within, and on the backside sealed with seven seals."

river. Access on that side is thus only possible by boat, or by a rough way, known as the Fisherman's Path, along the front of the cliffs. Nevertheless, because of the exceeding picturesqueness of the spot, it was a favourite resort on the twelve Sundays in the year on which (I believe under some legal necessity) service was there, in my time, performed. The scene, on the only occasion I was ever present (when our parish church was closed), might have furnished an excellent subject for a painting, as the congregation (far too many for the little church to hold), in their bright Sunday dress, emerged from the sloping glades or woodland, to the open space close by the church. Comfort was a matter of minor importance. Those who disposed themselves on the grass, where they had full enjoyment of the fresh summer air, and heard, through the open door, as much of the service as they chose to listen to, doubtless enjoyed themselves, but within it was not so agreeable. The squire's family were of course installed in *the* pew, and there we were packed as tightly as could be managed, so that we all had to get up and sit down together. We had a "strange clergyman," reported to be of vast learning; and my juvenile terror, along with my physical condition from squeezing, has imprinted the morning's performance on my recollection as something truly wretched.

There being no resident population the chapel has since fallen into ruin, and the font and bell have been removed to the mother parish of Woolastone, the bell now doing duty at the day-school there. In 1890 Sir William H. Marling, Bart. (patron of the living) carefully restored the font and placed within it a brass plate bearing the following inscription :—

"Perantiquum hunc fontem baptismalem e ruinis sacelli scī Jacobi Lancaut in comū Gloucē servatum refecit Gulš Heñs Marling Barš A.D. 1890."

The venerable relic stands in the hall at Sedbury Park.

The history of the "Church" in our parish of Tidenham, whether interpreted as the body of believers or the building in which they worshipped, might be well taken, during about the fifty middle years of the past century, as an illustration of "changing times." In the year 1826—or thereabouts—when my father purchased the property, Tidenham Church was no exception to many other

NORMAN CHAPEL, LLANCAUT, WYE CLIFFS.

To face p. 22.

churches in rural districts. The interior comes back to my remembrance as dark, dingy, and very decidedly damp, as shown by the green mould on pillars and walls. One of the first improvements was the placing of two good stoves in the church,—one presented by my father, and the other (rather, I believe, against local wishes) by the Parish. I well remember the presence of the stoves, as it was considered by the churchwardens, or whoever arranged these matters, that the time which was most decorous for stirring the fires was during the singing as "it drowned the noise." What our local choir consisted of I do not remember, but I rather think it was simply vocal, and started by a "pitchpipe." But at least there was nothing ridiculous about it. We did not, as in a church at no great distance, have the violinist and his instrument carried in on a man's shoulders because the unfortunate musician was without legs!

The sittings for the congregation were (I suppose as a matter of course in those days) all in closed pews with doors—the pews of a size, form, and respectability of appearance, likewise of comfort and fittings, according to the social position of their holders. It could not, however, be said that the chief parishioners had the best places, for our two large, roomy, square seats were mounted up, side by side, a few steps above the others at the end of the north aisle, with a good wall between us and the chancel, effectually preventing our seeing what was going on in that direction. Within our special pew, which had curtains more or less drawn, we sat round with our feet at proper times on good high hassocks. When we knelt we all turned round and faced the sides of the pew, and my juvenile sorrows were sometimes great towards the end of the Litany. The fatigue from kneeling on the top of my unsteady perch produced faintness, and I well remember my anxieties increasing with the "odd" feeling till I mustered courage to announce to my eldest sister, whom I held in considerable awe, that I did not feel very well; and measures were taken accordingly. The pew was said to be just over where the soldiers were buried who were killed during the Parliamentarian war at the Battle of Buttington, a locality in the same parish; but on an occasion of some repairs being made, the flooring was discovered to be laid on, or close above the live rock, which rendered this view inaccurate. The surface of the ground was immediately below the floor, and as the family pew had on its east side one of the great east windows of the church, and on the north side a smaller one, both with small panes ill-leaded, and one with a very insufficiently fastened small window, our Sunday devotions in winter were anything but comfortable.

I believe the rural congregation behaved with great propriety, though certainly on one occasion it struck me that a reverence during the creed at the name of Pontius Pilate on the part of the wife of my father's farm-bailiff, was somewhat out of place. But we were free from such lapses in decency of arrangement as occurred elsewhere. The pigeons did not roost in the tower, neither did a turkey sit on her eggs in the pulpit, which, considering that the time of incubation for the turkey hen is four weeks, must have interfered considerably with the due performance of service. Neither were we, so far as I remember, scandalised by attendance of dogs in church, whether avowedly accompanying their masters or making a voyage of discovery as to where their clerical owner might have vanished. And certainly we did not have the disgraceful circumstance which occurred in another church with which I was acquainted, of two ladies of good social position in the parish walking up to the rails of the communion table to receive the sacrament, followed by their great Newfoundland dog!

One practice—certainly objectionable, but perhaps not unusual in country parishes where the church was also used as the week-day schoolroom—was putting the bags holding the provisions which the children brought with them for their dinners on the communion table. I do not think that this was so very shocking, for no irreverence was intended. A table was a table in those days, and not an "Altar," and looking back on the matter it does not appear clear where else the food could have been safely placed. I fancy there was no regular vestry and, excepting the floor, or the seats of the pews, there does not seem to me to have been any other place of moderately safe deposit. However, by and by a room was hired as a schoolroom, and the church was freed from the presence of the children and their dinners. I well remember our going over in form to hold some sort of an examination, which was wound up by my father (who was certainly better fitted to examine witnesses from the magistrate's bench than to probe for what information our little uncivilised urchins possessed) electrifying the audience by desiring to know whether his examinee knew the use of a pocket-handkerchief. My mother was a more efficient aid by paying the schooling of all our own cottagers' children, and also in allaying strife. On one occasion, when a woman wished to remove her children from the parish school because they were better taught at a recently established Unitarian school, she dexterously overcame the difficulty by stating she meddled with nobody's conscience, but if the children went to the parish school she paid, and if they did not go *she didn't.* We heard no more on the subject.

Some of our customs were very pretty. On Palm Sunday, that is the Sunday before Easter Sunday, sometimes known in our part and the district as "Flowering Sunday," it was the custom to dress the graves with flowers. Friends of the family came from a long distance. A son of our head-gardener would come down from Scotland for the occasion, and the wealth of yellow daffodils and white narcissus, which grew by the Wye, close to the little church of Llancaut, helped greatly towards the decoration. Two Crown Imperials were a greatly admired addition which, season permitting, appeared to ornament one special grave. The "flowering" was a touching and pleasing remembrance of the friends whose bodies rested below, until in after years the custom gradually arose of placing artificial flowers along with the fresh blossoms, and then followed the much to be deprecated practice of putting little cases of flowers of tinsel, or anything that was approved of, which might remain on the grave. At Christmas time we had the real old-fashioned church decorations of good large boughs of holly, with plenty of red berries, mistletoe, laurel, and anything evergreen of a solid sort. The squire (*i.e.*, my father) contributed a cartload of evergreen branches, and as a matter of course, they were applied largely to ornamenting our corner pew with more regard to appearance than comfort.

The service was performed simply, as was customary in those days, without any music excepting the singing of the hymns, but as nothing was omitted, and there was, I believe, no curate, it must have been rather fatiguing to the vicar, and it certainly was a terribly long business especially for those not always in good health, if they stayed for the Communion Service on the rare occasions on which it was administered. The drive from the Park to the bottom of the hill on which the Church stood, was upwards of two miles. Then came a wearying walk up the hill until this became so steep that in the Churchyard there were successive little arrangements of steps to help us up the ascent. Within, it seems to me, that the clergyman neither excused himself, nor us, anything that might have lightened the strain, bodily and mental, to the younger attendants. The creed of St. Athanasius was duly gone through as well as the Litany, and addresses, which nowadays are cut very short, came at full length. When, after the return drive, we got safely home, I will not say but that our spiritual state might have been better had our bodily condition been less open to the unsettling influence of a desire for a much-needed meal.

One pleasure of the high days was having the fine old hymns for Easter or Christmas, which no bad singing can spoil, as a variety on Sternhold and Hopkins, but I still bear in mind the absolute depression caused by that doleful production, the hymn called "The Lamentation of a Sinner." To this day it seems to me that it would be better for such a composition to be omitted from our service.

Although it appears to be the correct thing for those who have been before the public in later life to have reminiscences (or for their biographer to invent them), of their precocious piety, I cannot remember that I was ever much given that way. I think that I was as a child kept in steady paths of proper behaviour, and amongst the items taught was certainly scrupulous observance of the fifth commandment in all its branches. Any deviation from truth was another point, the wickedness of which was most sedulously inculcated; and I should say that from my earliest days I was thoroughly well grounded in as much simple and necessary religious information as my small head could carry.

But I did not indulge in fine sentiments, felt or expressed, and I think that my first absolute feeling on religious matters was roused when in one of our spring visits to London, I went regularly on Sunday morning with the family to attend the service at the Vere Street Chapel, where Mr. Scobell was then vicar, and some clergyman of high standing occasionally preached. One thing that was very charming to a girl who had not heard anything of the kind before, was the hymn singing. The splendid hymn "Thou art the way," imprinted itself on my mind, as likewise a part of a sermon by Mr. Scobell, on the basis of our trust in God. He enumerated various of the high characteristics of the Deity; His boundless power, His holiness and other characteristics of His majesty. With the mention of each characteristic he put the question, "Does this give you a claim for acceptance?" until he came to the climax, "His love," with the words "*but His love, that* you may trust." Perhaps if the good man had known how these words would abide to old age as a comfort to one who was then amongst the youngest of his congregation, it would have given him pleasure.

The Archbishop of Dublin, the celebrated Dr. Whately, also preached at this Chapel, and I heard him deliver his grand sermon on "the doubts leading to the assured belief of St. Thomas." I suppose this time was what in some circles would have been called my "awakening," but we in our family neither thought nor spoke of these things; and any allusion to such matters would have brought on me (possibly very rightly) an awakening of another kind, which would have entirely disinclined me to favour the family with any religious views, beyond what might be shown in behaving with propriety and above all doing as I was bid to the best of my ability.

Reverting to early recollections of ecclesiastical matters, or things in which the clergy might have been expected, *ex officio*, to interfere, there certainly was room for improvement, but this was not peculiar to the olden time. Some of the curious circumstances of which accounts reached my young ears are better forgotten. One thing that I remember was the very different position relating to sporting, and also to the divergence in dress from the great precision now in vogue. A clergyman of somewhat high position, being, I suppose, pressed for time on one occasion, performed the funeral service in his "pink" visible beneath his surplice. Another, subsequently a favourite with all his poorer parishioners for his kindness, when a candidate for orders, was encouraged by his father to the necessary mental labour by the promise that if he passed his examination he should have a double-barrelled gun! In a locality not far from the edge of Monmouthshire, I myself saw the incumbent of one of the small livings with his coat off loading a manure cart! He comes back to my memory as doing the work quietly and gravely, and with no more appearance of derogation than if he had been budding the roses in his garden; still the work must have taken a considerable amount of time from the purposes of his ordination.

The "Oxford" or "Tractarian Movement" of 1833-45 [1] made an enormous commotion, and perhaps for a retired locality nowhere more than in our own parish.

After the death of the old vicar, amongst a succession of clergy the most noted was Dr. Armstrong (presented 1846).[2] With him came the full tide of the Oxford Movement, and as he was a highly accomplished man, eloquent in the pulpit, of charming society manner in the drawing-room, and with his heart fixed on driving his own views of reform and restoration forward, the holders of differing ecclesiastical views in the parish were soon very thoroughly by the ears. My father as "squire" and chief resident landowner had always tried (much to his own discomfort at times) to uphold the cause of decency and order. But with the new arrangements came all sorts of trouble from an excess of ceremonial, and peace seemed to have vanished. The attempted setting up of confession caused much trouble, and difference of lay and clerical opinion in the restoration of the Church was a fertile cause of ill-feeling. One special point was the right claimed by the vicar to prevent any of the general congregation entering the church by the chancel door. We had always gone in that way, and it was not convenient to reach the family pew by going round two sides of the church, so my father stuck to his legal rights, and the door was not visibly fastened. But one unlucky day when we, the ladies of the family, arrived as usual and tried to go in, to our consternation it appeared impossible to turn the latch. It was a remarkably pretty handle—I suppose an imitation of mediæval ironwork—but it required more than common woman's strength to make this unlucky invention act in admitting us to the church. However, we were not to be kept out by this ingenious device. Muscularly I was remarkably strong from working in wood and stone,

[1] "The Oxford Movement" or "Catholic Revival" was initiated as a result of statutory changes in the position of the Church of Ireland, which it was feared might ultimately be extended to England. The position and possible danger of the Church were fully discussed in the *Tracts for the Times*, ninety in number, issued from Oxford during the nine years, 1833-41, and chiefly written by Newman, Keble, Pusey, Williams, and Froude. The object of the movement was to rouse the members of the whole Anglican Community to promote corporate reforms in the Anglican Church as a National Institution—changes which the Evangelical Revival of the end of the eighteenth century had failed to introduce. The line adopted in the movement has been described as "a *via media* between Roman Catholicism and Reformation doctrines." (ED.).

[2] Afterwards Bishop of Grahamstown, Cape Colony.

and I was perfectly happy to forward my father's wishes, so thenceforward for many a week I went to church with a round ruler in my pocket, and slipping this into the hanging bit of ironwork, I easily raised the latch and gave my mother and sisters entrance to church. I did not object to my part of the ceremony in the least—rather liked it, in fact—but looking back from graver age it seems to me that it would have been better if the vicar had not driven the squire to defend the rights of the congregation by such forcible measures. After a while the latch (or the vicar's view on the subject) was loosened, and we obtained entrance without, like the violent, being obliged to take it by force.

The real troubles of the times were endless. It was even possible for a sincerely religious man to absent himself from the reception of communion on the ground that he was not able to participate with Christian comfort and in a charitable frame of mind. Within the church building itself the condition of things was not satisfactory. The openings beneath the very "open" seats, whereby was secured free circulation for dogs and draughts, were unpleasant in various ways.

The appointment of our skilled and accomplished vicar, Dr. Armstrong, to the Bishopric of Grahamstown in South Africa, for which he was eminently fitted, was hailed by many of us with heartfelt gratitude. In later years, under the kindly care of the Rev. Percy Burd (successor in 1862 of the Rev. Alan Cowburn) who, without thinking it necessary to push everything to extremities, attended with the utmost care to proprieties of detail of worship in church, to social friendliness, and to care of the poor, we passed along in paths of comfort and peace, for which some of us were deeply grateful.

Amongst various parish or local matters, of which the bodily presence has, to a great degree, passed away, and the remembrance that at one time such things were has probably faded from most of the minds in which they ever held a place, are turnpike gates, with their adjoining toll-houses; also the parish stocks and the parish pound.

In parochial arrangements in my day two great improvements arose, one of which has now long been a regular part of parish work, but was new at least to us. This was a women's clothing club. The other was the commencement of the plan of lending books to those who otherwise would rarely have seen them. It was introduced by my sister,

Georgiana E. Ormerod, when little more than a girl, quite at her own expense. It was continued by her without any pecuniary assistance (unless may-be sometimes some small co-operation from myself) to the end of her long life.

The clothing club was set on foot under some difficulties by the wife of one of the clergy resident in our parish, for the goods procurable at Chepstow, the nearest town, were by no means remarkable for their quality, and Mrs. Morgan thought herself bound to do the best in her power for her poor subscribers. So the matter was accommodated (not without a good deal of grumbling from Chepstow shopkeepers about money being taken out of their pockets) by part of the goods brought from Bristol (where excellent material was to be had) for the women to choose from, being sent previous to "club day" to Mr. Morgan's large and commodious house. In those days, so far as I know, the plan of sending the women with tickets to the shops had not been adopted, and our method, though exceedingly laborious to the lady manager of the club, was good for the women, for it ensured that their choice was confined to the very best materials, all of a useful kind, and at the lowest possible prices.

When a growing up girl, perhaps about sixteen, my sister Georgiana thought it would be a pleasure to the children of our own cottagers to have some entertaining books, and she began by lending them from the small store which had gradually come down from the elders of our generation. She chose carefully what she thought would be of interest, and very soon the elder children took to reading, or sometimes the fathers would read aloud to their families. My sister always either read the books herself or knew the nature of the contents before lending them, and when done with they were brought back and exchanged. The borrowing rapidly spread beyond our own cottagers till it included our farmers and their friends at Gloucester and Bristol. The books were almost invariably treated with all reasonable care, and scarcely ever was one a-missing. Besides the entertainment, they acted as an antidote to the attractions of the public-house. It was a great delight to my sister when she had a request for a book, because Jack or Dick was home from his ship or on a holiday, and they wanted a book that would keep him from the "public." I attribute much of my sister's success to the care with which, even after her book-lending had extended to far-distant localities, she chose the books. On one occasion when she had made a donation of books of her own choosing to the Lending Library, Bethnal Green, London, she was greatly pleased to hear that the boys and girls had passed the word round amongst the factories of the entertaining books that had arrived. Those we found suited best (for I was in some degree her assistant) were accounts of real incidents made into narratives. Ballantyne's earlier books with accounts of the fire brigade, post office, lighthouse and the like were great favourites, perhaps none the less for the conversations being at times a trifle vulgar; but when a writer took up some special view, as of teetotalism, high-churchism, or any other specialism, we dropped him. Stories of olden times, such as the Plague in London, or the Great Fire; risings in Henry the Eighth's time; wars of the time of Charles the First and Cromwell; forest troubles of the time of William Rufus, and the like—told as stories, with the facts correct although the thread on which they were strung was imaginary—were always favourites. We seldom lent absolutely religious books unless they were asked for, and then we took care that they should be of a solid and interesting sort; but whether sacred or secular the number of books lent or given for lending in the course of the year was very great.

My sister was a highly accomplished woman, a good linguist and historian, and a careful scriptural student. As a scientific entomologist and a Fellow of the Entomological Society of London, she was a co-operator with me in my work. She devoted her artistic talent for many years to the execution of excellent diagrams, serviceable for agricultural purposes, of insects injurious to farm and orchard produce, some of which she made over to the Royal Agricultural Society, but the greater number she presented to friends interested in lessening the amount of loss through insect injury, and to Agricultural Colleges. From girlhood to old age she unceasingly carried on her chosen work of distribution of useful healthy literature. She asked no aid, nor made the considerable sums she expended, and the careful cordial thought she gave to this work, matter of public notoriety, but in her last moments it brought a smile to her face when I told her that I purposed to continue her work.

My father when living near Chester had the first news on a Sunday morning before church time, of the Duke of Wellington's success, and that the battle of Waterloo had been fought and won. After service he mounted on a tombstone and announced the glorious news to the assembled congregation. In my early days in Gloucestershire, a neighbour, Captain Fenton, was at times thought to be tedious in his recurrence to the charge of the Scots Greys in which he had served, but it was a grand memory all the same.

In a much humbler sphere and at a different stage of the same great struggle an interesting part was played by a very decent woman—afterwards a servant in our family—at the burial of Sir John Moore at Corunna. She was proud to remember that she was one of those who held a lanthorn at the ceremony alluded to in Wolfe's poem :—

> "We buried him darkly at dead of night
>
> . . . . .
>
> By the struggling moonbeams' misty light
> And the lanthorn dimly burning."

PLATE IX.

MAP OF THE BANKS OF THE WYE.

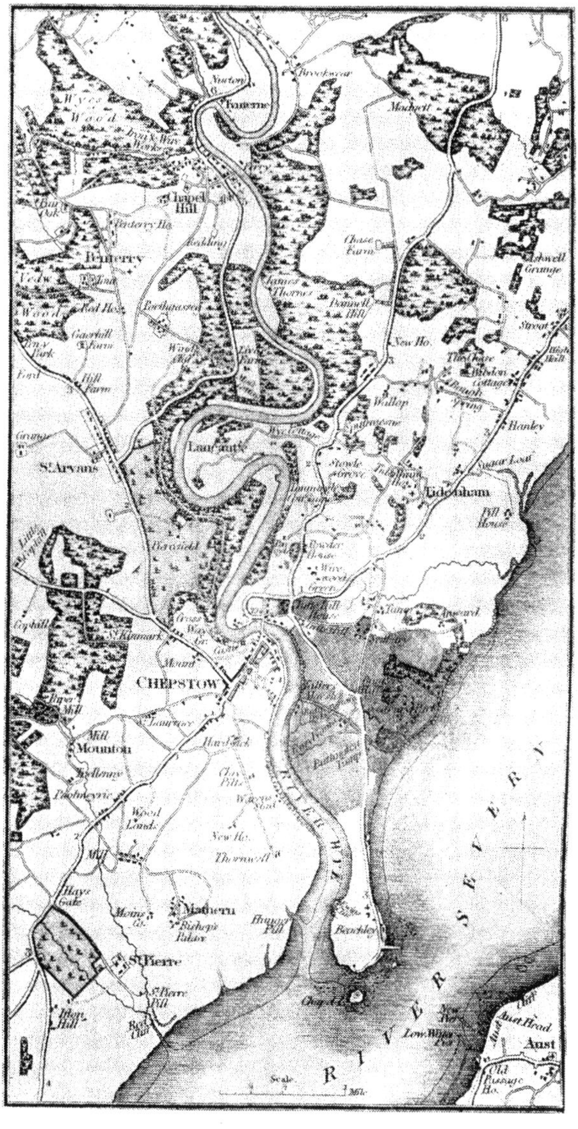

Sedbury Park Property, the darkly shaded area between Severn and Wye.

(pp. 33 and 38.)

To face p. 32.

CHAPTER V

SEVERN AND WYE

THE locality round which most of the recollections of nearly half my life centre is in the district of Gloucestershire, between the Severn and the Wye (opposite Chepstow in Monmouthshire, plate IX.), almost at the extremity of the peninsula, sometimes not inaptly called the "Forest Peninsula," as some of the "Hundreds" comprised in the more widely extended area stretching on to the Forest of Dean near Newnham, are technically called the "Forest Hundreds," although what is commonly thought of (at the present day) as the Forest of Dean, has long since ceased to be connected, popularly speaking, with the lower extremity of the peninsula. This is bounded on the two sides by the Severn and the Wye respectively; and at intervals it presents to the Wye considerable frontage of high cliffs of mountain limestone, and to the Severn red marl, capped more or less with lias. It terminates at the junction of the two rivers in a small area, which is an island at high water, but accessibly connected with the mainland at low water. Here, that is on the rocky ground at the point of confluence of the Wye with the Severn, were still existing in my time (that is up to 1873) the few but massive remains of the Hermitage and Chapels, popularly known collectively as the Chapel of St. Tecla or Treacle Island (plate X.). The name as given by William of Worcester in full form is "*Capella Sancti Teriaci Anachoretæ.*" He describes the locality likewise as "The Rok Seynt Tryacle," but not having now the opportunity of consulting his observations, I am not able to say whether the ancient chronicler gives any reason for the building of this little but massive knot of buildings, or for its overthrow, which must have been a somewhat laborious task, and from the thickness and the solidly built nature of the walls, one that required co-operation. In the short account given by my father in "Strigulensia" from which I borrow some part of these notes, he says, "It would be vain to attempt identification of the Hermit whose name is associated with the ruins, and who does not appear in the calendar of saints, but he occurs as follows in the "Valor Ecclesiasticus" of Hen. VIII., vol. ii. p. 501, "Capella Sancti Triaci valet nihil, quâ stat in mare et nulla proficua inde proveniunt." Whether modern skilled archæologists may have thrown light on the early history of the anchorite and his Severn and seaweed-girt chapel I do not know, but few places could be found less attractive for the archæological picnic-excursions which have become fashionable of late years. Even to my brothers and myself, accustomed as we were to Severn mud, and to picking our way fairly safely over and amongst the coarse brown slippery seaweed fronds (chiefly, if I remember rightly, the *Fucus serratus*), the passage over such parts as were not then submerged was an exceedingly muddy progress, needing a deal of care lest we should take a sudden slide into one of the little rock basins concealed by the "kelp" or other coarse brown seaweed. But once arrived, it was very pleasant to sit in the sunshine and enjoy the glorious view down the Estuary of the Severn, the fresh salt air blowing round us, or otherwise employ ourselves to our fancy. From careful measurements we found the length of the chapel to have been 31 feet 6 inches, the width 14 feet 6 inches, and the thickness of the walls, wherever sufficient remained for observation, approximately 3 feet.[1] We had to be quick in our operations and our return had to be kept in mind, or we should have had to be fetched off in a boat, and under all circumstances it was probably best for the sake of appearances that our walk home should be as far as possible by the fields or under the cliffs where minutiæ as to condition of boots, &c., were unimportant.

The characteristics of the scenery of each of the rivers are wholly different. The Severn above Beachley and Aust (in former days the land-points of the much-used "Old Passage") spreads into a wide area of water, perhaps about a mile wide at the narrowest, and at high tide forming a noble lake-like expanse. The Wye, on the contrary, as shown in the map (plate IX.), takes its sinuous and narrow course between successive promontories, projecting alternately from the Gloucestershire and Monmouthshire banks.

[1] My notes are taken from the copy of a plan (now before me) by my brother Henry Mere Ormerod, solicitor, Manchester: see page 58.

PLATE X.

Ruined Anchorite's Chapel of St. Tecla, on the Chapel Rock where Severn and Wye meet.

From a sketch by Miss E. A. Ormerod.

(p. 33.)

Severn Cliffs, Sedbury Park.

(p. 40.)

To face p. 34.

Across some considerable portion of the river a quarter of a mile or so above Beachley, on the Gloucestershire side, a rocky ledge of limestone called "The Lyde" projects at low tide, causing a backwater of which the steady roar can be heard at a long distance.[1] Cormorants on the rock, and conger-eels below it, were regular inhabitants or visitors—the former presumably attracted by the latter, which served to some degree also as food to the fishermen, although pronounced to be "slobbery-like."

The muddy colour of the Severn was not in itself picturesque—at least I have never heard the point mentioned with admiration; but to me, born as I was by this noblest of our rivers, it seemed to convey a comfortable idea of homeliness and strength. Sometimes, however, in the early morning or in certain conditions of light, the deep rosy colouring was almost as if the whole width of water had been changed to blood; then the effect was very splendid, and as wonderful still as it must have been in days long gone by to Queen Boadicea:—

> "Still rolls thy crimson flood in glory on
> As when of old its deep ensanguined dye
> Told to the warrior Queen her falling throne,
> Her people's death, the foemen's victory."

But, independently of other considerations, a bend in the river was of great local service. It formed a bay of about perhaps three-quarters of a mile across, bounded to the west by our own and the Beachley cliffs, and further protected, or endangered, on the southern side by a low range of rocks running out into the river. With the rising tide the import shipping to Gloucester, which in those days was extensive, put in here to be searched by the Custom House officials. At that time (excepting tugs) it was entirely composed of sailing vessels mostly laden with corn, wine, and timber, and the mixed fleet moving about in the bay with colours flying was a very lively sight. In due time they passed on—the three-masters, ships, and barques, or the graceful chasse-marées, taking the lead; brigs and

[1] The *Sailing Directions for the West Coast of England*, published by the Hydrographic Department of the Admiralty, says:—"Depths: There is a depth of about 46 feet in the river to Chepstow at high water springs, and 36 feet at high water neaps." "Tides: It is high water, full and change, at Chepstow at 7 h. 30 m. local or 7 h. 41 m. Greenwich time; mean springs rise 38 feet and neaps 28½ feet. The tide has, however, been known to rise as high as 56 feet." (E.A.O.)

schooners following, and sloops and—if weather permitted—Severn trows bringing up the rear. These, however, as they differed very little in formation from canal barges, required tolerably fair or at least quiet weather to allow them to proceed in safety. The procession of shipping came along almost beneath our cliffs, the deep channel being on that side, and perhaps it was as well that they were no nearer, or the nautical remarks might have been more often audible to the young people than was desirable!

A special convenience to ourselves was a little creek under the cliffs, called in those parts a "pill" (presumably from the Welsh pwll or pool), which allowed of coals being run in a sloop across from Bristol and carted up to the house by a shorter road than that from Chepstow.

Salmon fishing was carried on partly by nets from fishing boats, partly by rows of baskets known as "putts" or "putchers." The boats during the boat fishing lay above

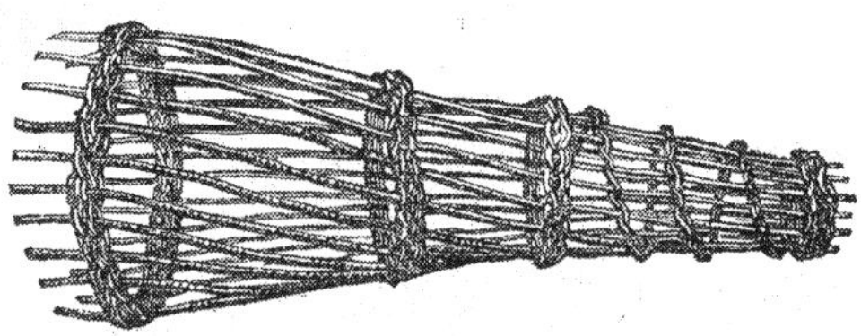

FIG. (A).—PUTCHER FOR CATCHING SALMON.

the edge of the water on the sloping and slippery frontage of the shore. When the tide served for fishing, the men went down from the village above the cliffs to their boats across the flat and precipitously-edged grass, between the base of the low cliffs and the sloping shore. Each man wriggled with might and main at his boat till he loosened its adhesion to the tenacious mud and started it on its slide with its bows foremost towards the water. Once off, of course the pace accelerated; its owner, running behind, held on and clambered in as best he could, and the two arrived safely and with a great jolt on the water. The boats then formed in line, secured by being tied stern to stern at about a boat's length from each other, and presumably anchored also, but this I do not remember. The net of each boat was lowered, and nothing further occurred till a fish was captured; then the net was lifted, the fish, shining in all the beauty of its silvery scales, taken out, and the net lowered again. These were the best fish;

those that were caught in the putts were "drowned" fish, and unless the fishermen were fairly on the alert to secure them before the falling tide had left the baskets long uncovered, there was a very good chance of the eyes being pecked out or the fish otherwise disfigured by birds.

The putcher or basket fishing was carried on by means of very open extinguisher-shaped baskets each long enough to hold, it can hardly be said accommodate, a good-sized salmon. The frame or stand on which these baskets were fixed was formed of two rows of strong poles or upright pieces of wood, running down the shore, across the narrow of the river, for many yards, firmly fixed between high and low tide level, at such a distance as would allow the baskets to reach from one side to the other. Horizontal poles or pieces of wood connected the upright poles, and to these horizontal supports the baskets were attached, so as to form rows with the open ends of the extinguishers facing up stream and all ranged one storey above the other. The fish were drifted into the basket trap, and of course, though they might injure themselves in their struggles, and to some degree their market value, they were powerless to effect their escape and withdraw backward against the set of the tide.[1]

The much larger form of basket described by Mr. Buckland as "putts," and as being used for catching flat fish, was of a slightly different make—formed only of two instead of three pieces; one large piece, so wide at the opening that I, as a girl, had no difficulty in standing within it, and a very much smaller piece, forming a kind of nose. This little adjunct was, I believe, taken off and searched by the fishermen for what it contained. To my sister Georgiana and myself it was a great pleasure to go down to where the two great eel-putts stood on clean shore at very low tide below the longest row of salmon-putchers, and search for anything that was to be found. My sister was a good conchologist. We searched for seaweed, &c., &c., and thereby got a deal of pleasant amusement. The fishermen, who knew us well, made no objection to our investigations, though, as one of the men remarked on one occasion, "It was not everybody they liked to see near the putts."

In our immediate neighbourhood the fishermen were quiet—at least I never heard of their getting into very objectionable difficulties—but about eight miles higher up the river, near Lydney, things in this respect were by no

[1] See Appendix A.

means all that could be wished. On one occasion they captured the Fishery Inspector himself—whose duty it was to ascertain that the meshes were not below a certain measurement—and secured him in the nets. Another time somebody (who, unluckily for him, bore some resemblance to the obnoxious inspector) got nearly sloughed up in one of the great marsh ditches, and would have been left to live or die as might chance—probably the latter—but for the arrival of timely help. My father being one of the acting magistrates of the district, we used to hear from time to time of these and other "mauvaises plaisanteries" in the neighbourhood of the Forest of Dean.

On reference to the portion of the Ordnance Map (plate IX.) it will be seen that there is a broad band marked "mud," of about a sixth of a mile in width at the widest part and extending for about a mile and a half by the side of the deep channel of the Severn, between it and the cliffs of the Beachley and Sedbury Bay.

The most remarkable capture of which I have any recollection as taking place in the waters, or rather in the mud of the Severn, was said to be a "Bottle-nosed whale," or Dolphin, *Delphinus tursio*, Fabr., but it was so many decades of years ago, that I have no means now of turning to any record for verification of the species. The capture itself excited a deal of local interest. It was on a summer morning that one of my brothers, enlivening his vacation studies, as was his custom, by watching through his telescope anything of interest that might be going on amongst the shipping or elsewhere, saw something like an enormous fish struggling and "flopping" on the Beachley pier of the old Passage Ferry. As a matter of course, we young folks set off after luncheon to have our share of the sight, and found the creature had been captured when lying helpless, or half dead, in the mud at the Aust side of the Ferry, and had been towed across behind a boat. At this distance of time I only remember the whale- or dolphin-like shape of the animal, its great size, and that it was apparently of a greyish colour; but this item might very likely be from its being coated with Severn mud. In Bell's "British Quadrupeds" the greatest length recorded of various specimens found in England is 12 feet. The colour of the back is black, with a purplish tinge, becoming dusky on the sides, and dirty white on the belly. This species is considered rare in England and it is of some interest, in referring to the locality of what may be called our own capture, that "The first account which we have of its appearance on our own shores is that of John Hunter," and it was taken with its young one "on the sea coast near Berkeley"; that is about two or three miles higher up the left bank of the Severn than the Aust Cliffs. Another specimen was found in the river Dart in Devonshire, and, it was stated, "was killed with difficulty, the poor animal having suffered for four hours the attacks of eight men armed with spears and two guns, and assisted by dogs. When wounded it made a noise like the bellowing of a bull."[1] In the case of the Old Passage specimen the poor creature was also most barbarously treated, chiefly by being attacked by the running of hay forks, pitch forks, and the like, into its body, and I remember a good deal of chopping with hatchets or axes, but it was quite quiet and, it was to be hoped, was past feeling pain. Immense popular interest, of course, was excited as to the precise nature of the unusual "take," as to whether it was a Leviathan, or possibly the kind of fish that swallowed Jonah—but the affair ended by the creature being shipped off to Bristol to be turned into a little money for the boatmen who secured it, and no other cetacean was taken during the remainder of the years in which Sedbury was my home.

The most observable of the seaweeds, which grew on the rocks or large stones, more or less in the muddy salt water between tide levels at the mouth of the Severn, were of the genus *Fucus*, which at one time was much used in the making of kelp. The ornamental kinds always appeared to me to be unaccountably absent. They were not to be expected to make this place their habitat, but, still, their almost total absence in the masses of drift matter left by the retiring tide struck me as curious. In my most successful searches I do not remember ever being fortunate enough to secure even a fragment of the lovely Oak-leaf, *Delesseria*, with its bright, rosy-veined leaves from as much as 4 inches to 8 inches in length placed along their cylindrical stem, or the Peacock seaweed, *Padina pavonea*, with its concentric markings. Of Iceland Moss there might be a battered morsel. The general composition of the driftage was composed of little except what might be grown in the neighbourhood, mixed with sugar cane or packing material

[1] See quotations in *Hist. of British Quadrupeds, including the Cetacea*, by Thomas Bell, F.R.S., &c. pp. 469–472.

thrown from the vessels. This, however, seemed to me of some interest in connection with the set of the currents. Here, however, I am out of my element, but as my brother Dr. Ormerod employed me as a collector, I am not personally responsible.

The distinct varieties of soil, and also the geographical and the geological surroundings of Sedbury, were unusually favourable to natural history investigations, whether of fauna and flora of the present day, or of fossil remains of saurians and shells. These were easily accessible as they fell from the frontage of lias, or the narrow horizontal strip in the cliffs (plate x.) facing the Severn, well known to the geologists as the "bone bed." At the highest part the cliffs were about 140 feet, calculating from medium tide level. There the face had been quarried back for a supply of lias limestone, used in enlarging the offices of the house, and in so doing had laid bare a fine bed of so-called "Venus" shells. We used to find beautiful specimens of those shells, irrespective of this extra fine deposit, and also of "patens," oysters of some kind, which we sought for unweariedly, hammer in hand. The greatest matters of interest, however, were the saurian, or the fish remains, of which we sometimes found a plentiful supply of specimens of little value, and now and then some of considerable interest.

The Sedbury cliffs lie nearly north of the Aust cliff, and contain the Aust bone-bed, from which the Severn, about a mile wide, or somewhat more, there divides them. Geologically, in all important characteristics, I believe the two cliffs correspond. Of this bone-bed it is noted by Sir Charles Lyell[1]: "In England the Lias is succeeded by conformable strata of red and green marl or clay. There intervenes, however, both in the neighbourhood of Exmouth, in Devonshire, and in the cliffs of Westbury and Aust, in Gloucestershire, on the banks of the Severn, a dark-coloured stratum, well known by the name of the 'bone-bed.' It abounds in the remains of saurians and fish, and was formerly classed as the lowest bed of Lias; but Sir P. Egerton has shown that it should be referred to as the Upper New Red Sandstone." The reasons given are not of interest to the general reader. From the fallen *débris* of this we collected vertebræ, single, or sometimes a few in connection, also bones of the paddles, and any

[1] *Manual of Elementary Geology*, by Sir Charles Lyell, F.R.S., fifth edition, 1855, pp. 337, 338.

Roman Pottery, found in Sedbury Park.
From a drawing by Miss E. A. Ormerod.
(*p. 18.*)

Saurian from the Lias, Sedbury Cliffs.
(*p. 41.*)

To face p. 40.

amount of teeth, also coprolites, the excrementitious matter of the living owners of the bones. These were in great quantity, but I never remember that they were other than irregular lumps, and though some of us were much given to grinding and polishing stones that afforded hope of an ornamental result, it never occurred to us to exercise our talents on these lumps, which might have indicated in their undigested contents some evidence of the diet of their consumers.

The only valuable or interesting specimen of Saurian remains (that is of an animal in moderate degree of entirety) fell from the cliffs after I had ceased to reside there. This was a slab of Lias about 3 feet long by 2 feet broad, and about 7 to 9 inches thick (plate XI.) The history of its fall, as given to me in a letter from Dr. John Yeats, F.R.G.S., then residing at Chepstow, dated September, 1882, was, that "From one of the ledges, or from the top of a slip or subsidence, a fir tree was blown down during the autumn of 1882 . . . The fossil was found beneath the roots," and "the fossil remains were laid bare by a conchoidal fracture." A few detached vertebræ were collected, but unfortunately no part of the head was secured. Of this specimen Professor Richard Owen was good enough to report to Dr. Yeats on the 24th of May, 1883, as follows: "From the concavity of the articular surfaces of the vertebræ, I infer it to be part of an ichthyosaurus, and the number and character of the ribs agree with that deduction. If any part of the jaws or teeth should be found near the locality it would decide the matter."

This fossil is now in the possession of Sir William H. Marling, at Sedbury.

The surface of the cliffs was of a very mixed nature, with ledges of stone projecting slightly in places, and from the effect of weathering, landslips, leading at times to inconvenience, were not infrequent. As we knew the nature of the ground we were careful about going near the edge of the top of the cliff, where a precipice or a crack showed danger, but it happened more than once that a bullock or calf, attracted by food to be found amongst the trees or bushes which in some places clothed the slanting upper part, was tempted beyond safe footing, and toppled down to the bottom to its own destruction. On one occasion, on returning from a walk, my sister Georgiana and I, not having noticed a fall from the cliffs, were cut off by one of these slips from any comfortable advance. It was not a case of danger, but a choice between much wet and dirt from Severn mud, or very considerable discomfort of another sort, as the slip had brought down with it brambles, &c., &c., most unpleasant to brave for the sake of dryness. We preferred the wet passage, feeling our way with our feet through the muddy water from one good-sized stone to another, and presently arrived safely above the high-tide level, but to those who did not know that beneath the muddy surface there was a sound footing if sought for, the little episode might have been unpleasant.

PLATE XII.

ROYAL MAIL STARTING FROM OLD GENERAL POST OFFICE, LONDON.

Original lent by Arthur Ackermann & Son, 191, Regent Street, W.

To face p. 42.

CHAPTER VI

TRAVELLING BY COACH, FERRY, AND RAILWAY

IN my early days much of the passenger transit of South Wales and the south-westerly part of England passed over the old Passage Ferry across the Severn from Beachley to Aust, and consequently the coaches all passed our park gates. It was said there were fourteen coaches a day. On this I am unable to offer an opinion, but there were a great number, and amongst them were two mails. The road to the head of the old Passage Pier, from Chepstow, was about three and a half miles in length, and very hilly (going up one ascent, long or short as the case might be, to go down another), with the exception of two lengths of flat "galloping ground." These well deserved their name, and I can still remember the swing of violent speed at which the high, piled-up vehicle tore past us, causing children and accompanying dogs to allow it a very free passage. The journey was not without risk of disaster, for on one occasion in turning a sharp angle, on the incline of a steep shore-hill, without due care, the coach lurched to the outward side of the curve and made a distribution of its outside passengers on the greensward by our park gates. It certainly would have been a great help in those days if the wish (though not exactly as he expressed it) of the driver of one of the more old-fashioned of the coaches could have been carried out, and "a little akyduct" made to convey the road from the top of one hill to the next, thus avoiding the dangerous descent.

The view from the tops of the coaches as they galloped along the flat road at the summit of the Severn cliffs down to the Ferry pier was very beautiful. On one side was the Severn, a mile wide at the narrowest, with the red Aust cliffs opposite, the Sedbury cliffs above; and, in the distance, about thirty miles away up the river, the hills, near or beyond Gloucester, could be faintly seen. On the other side, about a field or two from the road, was the lowest part of the Wye at its point of juncture with the Severn, and the noble estuary itself opening out from about four miles width till it was lost to view in the distance of the Severn Sea.

The Old Passage, though probably as well managed as was reasonably possible, was, in many respects, a most

TIME TABLE ILLUSTRATING THE METHOD OF TRAVELLING 200 YEARS AGO.

YORK Four Days Stage-Coach.

Begins on Friday *the* 12th. *of* April. 1706.

ALL that are desirous to pass from *London* to *York*, or from *York* to *London*, or any other Place on that Road; Let them Repair to the *Black Swan* in *Holbourn* in *London*, and to the *Black Swan* in *Coney street* in *York*.

At both which Places, they may be received in a Stage Coach every *Monday*, *Wednesday* and *Friday*, which performs the whole Journey in Four Days, (*if God permits*) And sets forth at Five in the Morning.

And returns from *York* to *Stamford* in two days, and from *Stamford* by *Huntington* to *London* in two days more. And the like Stages on their return.

Allowing each Passenger 14l. weight, and all above 3d. a Pound.

Performed By { *Benjamin Kingman.* *Henry Harrison,* *Walter Baynes,*

Also this gives Notice that Newcastle Stage Coach, sets out from York, every Monday, and Friday, and from Newcastle every Monday, and Friday.

Recd. in pt. 05-00-0 of Mr. Bodingfeld for 5 places for Monday the 3 of June 1706.

inconvenient necessity. On one occasion, while fourteen passengers were crossing in a sailing boat, every living thing, except one dog, perished in mid-transit. It was on a stormy Sunday in September, 1838, and the boat was heavily laden with horses as well as the passengers. How the accident happened was never known. One of my brothers had been watching the boat from our cliffs, and on looking again, after a minute or so, she was gone. The conjectural

PLATE XIII.

OLD CHEPSTOW BRIDGE, REBUILT IN 1816, WITH POST-CHAISE CROSSING IT.
From an old picture signed W. Williams, 1783.

To face p. 44.

cause of the disaster was that one of the horses had become unruly. The assignment of the disaster to a judgment for travelling on Sunday, may be looked on as a state of feeling very desirable to be removed by changing times, which have brought a larger charitableness and greater common sense.

A novel custom was associated with the Old Passage. A man suspected of possible infection of hydrophobia, was put into the salt water, and towed about in the Severn at the stern of a boat. In the event of a man having been bitten by a stray dog, this operation made his village acquaintances much easier in their minds about him. They had also the fun, and in any case the patient would not be the worse for a thorough good washing!

The appliances of the ferry were a steam boat and various sailing boats, including one known as the Mail-boat, as well as on the Beachley side, an apparatus acting as a telegraph. This consisted of an arrangement of board which, when at rest, resembled a wooden window shutter about a couple of yards square, fastened to one of the buildings; and, by some code of signals of an exceedingly simple sort, requisite directions were conveyed across the river as to the boat service.

On our side there was one solidly built pier, serviceable for shipment of passengers or goods at all states of the tide, and accessible for all kinds of carriage use from the good road which terminated at the top in front of a small kind of hotel; it likewise had the desirable security, for the greater part of its length, of strong posts with chains between them. On the Aust side there was a high- and also a low-water pier, not far apart, a little way below the inn, and if the tide served for boats to reach these all went fairly well after disembarking, but it was a different matter at half-tide. The half-tide pier was a considerable distance from the others—a quarter or half a mile away beneath the cliffs, and mud and stones and the roughest imaginable affairs in the guise of road had to be got through or over on the way to the inn. The effect of this on the springs, paint, &c., of a good Long Acre-built barouche, when by some unhappy necessity it had to be committed to such a method of transit, may be easily imagined. The passage for a carriage was, at the best, not well arranged. A muster of fishermen or boatmen was made, and the carriage was turned on the pier and dragged more or less rapidly on board, and there, I presume, secured from movement, but, certainly, by no means from danger, for part of the freight might consist of half a dozen or a dozen bullocks, which shifted to one side or the other as the vessel lurched. On the whole the transit by the Old Passage Ferry, so well known in former days, was one link in a chain of necessities which left much room for changing times to improve.

The great change in the method of travelling may be said to have been publicly inaugurated in the spring of 1830[1] by the opening of the Canterbury and Whitstable line of railway.

In the same year the Bill for the Warrington railway was passed by both Houses of Parliament, and permission was also granted to construct a line from Leicester to Swannington, Robert Stephenson being appointed chief engineer to both lines. But the great railway event of that year was the opening, with an imposing ceremonial, on September 15th, of the Liverpool and Manchester Railway. This left nothing to be desired in showing high appreciation of the importance of advance in methods of locomotion. Although a complete success, from the point of view of capabilities of safe and also of rapid travelling, the day was one of great trouble and anxiety. As the train neared Manchester the mob crowded on the lines, and while to have gone forward at any moderate pace would have been death to hundreds, on the other hand, the slow movement allowed the populace to swarm on the carriages and display their political aversion to "the Duke" (Wellington) by throwing brickbats, and by other objectional irregularities. The riot was not so much remembered as the accident which resulted in the death of Huskisson. I can recollect the unsophisticated story of something being seen going along the line at such a speed that it was hardly discernible; and also that a horn was used for train signalling in place of the steam whistle. Carelessness of life through ignorance of the danger was everywhere conspicuous; discipline was much needed. My father while waiting at a station took pleasure in walking along the line to while away the time. Tying horse-carriages on open trucks was not an unusual practice with carriage-people who could afford to pay for the luxury. My father long travelled in his own carriage thus attached, and stepped from the truck on which it stood to the next, but of course at considerable danger to his person.

[1] For some years previously the possibility of transmission, at a low rate of speed, of goods or mineral products had been established by George and Robert Stephenson, against great opposition in some cases.

PLATE XIV.

A West of England Royal Mail *en route.*

Original lent by Arthur Ackermann & Son, 191, Regent Street, W.

To face p. 46.

CHAPTER VII

CHARTIST RISING IN MONMOUTHSHIRE IN 1839

THE remembrance of the Chartist[1] rising in Monmouthshire of November, 1839, must have long faded away, except from the minds of the few survivors who were concerned in its suppression, and those of the younger generation who remember it from the anxiety it caused throughout the district. I came among the latter number. My father was an acting magistrate, and at the time alterations were going on in his house at Sedbury Park. I can well remember the surly, disobedient, and generally insubordinate behaviour of the local workmen in the week preceding Sunday, the 3rd of November. With the return of the workmen, in the course of the following week, the face of affairs had however changed. The rising had taken place, and had been thoroughly crushed. Receiving a reverse, they were there and then seized with panic, and fled. Their chief leaders—by name John Frost, Zephaniah Williams, and William Jones, and others not so deeply implicated—were captured, and to us the result was exceedingly satisfactory. The men when they returned were patterns of obedience and as meek as mice. They did not in the least desire the distinction

[1] Chartism was an excited, and, in some instances, violent political movement which occurred in Great Britain consequent upon the dire distress and poverty of the labouring classes in the thirties of the nineteenth century, and their disappointment with the results of the Reform Bill of 1832. In June, 1839, a monster petition was presented to the House of Commons with 1,280,000 names attached. Its unsympathetic reception fanned the rebellious spirit abroad among the working classes and led to an increase of unruly disturbances, and to the outbreak at Newport, here described. The movement collapsed in 1848, and with the development of the industrial prosperity of the country, largely due to the use of steam power in manufacturing centres, and the vast improvement of the economic and social condition of the people, together with greater political freedom, any return of the perfectly natural, if not even justifiable, spirit of discontent became impossible. (ED.).

of being known, in a magistrate's house, to have taken part in an outbreak which had totally failed. They had thought that by Monday or Tuesday the house would be in their hands and our relative positions reversed, and, indeed, it would have been hard to find a house more indefensible against a disciplined mob than ours. Along two sides of the house (plate I.), ran a broad colonnade of Bath stone, supported by pillars so wide and so placed that in many cases men ascending by ladders put against them, would have been greatly or entirely protected from the discharge of fire-arms from the windows; and the broad flat surface of the top of the colonnade, 10 feet in width, by about 120 feet in length, would have made an admirable mustering ground for scores of men, from which to carry on their unpleasant attacks in conjunction with their allies below. This however we were spared.

The trial of Frost and the other leaders followed speedily by special Commission at Monmouth. It began in the following December and ended in January (1840), with a verdict of guilty of High Treason; and sentence of death according to the treason penalties of the time was pronounced by Lord Chief Justice Tindal as follows:—"That you, John Frost, and you, Zephaniah Williams, and you, William Jones, be taken hence to the place from which you came, and be thence drawn on a hurdle to the place of execution, and that each of you be there hanged by the neck until you be dead, and that afterwards the head of each of you shall be severed from his body, and the body of each, divided into four quarters, shall be disposed of as Her Majesty shall think fit, and may Almighty God have mercy on your souls." A recommendation to mercy, which was mercifully attended to, was added on behalf of the five least guilty men. The possibility of the horrors of the details of the treason penalties (though much mitigated from those of former days on account of their being carried out on the dead body of the offender) created consternation through the district, and the remembrance has remained with me to this day. However, the capital sentence on Frost and his two special associates was commuted to transportation for life, an act of grace coincident with those extended on the marriage of our late Queen of glorious memory.

Only the above disjointed reminiscences of trouble have remained in my mind through the sixty years which have since elapsed, but the rising was so planned that, if it had succeeded, it would have proved a match to light the smouldering Chartism of the Midlands and the North of England, and even under the circumstances the case was described in the Attorney-General's address to the Jury at the commencement of the Monmouth trial as follows:

"There has recently been in this County an armed insurrection, the law has been set at defiance; there has been an attempt to take forcible possession of the town of Newport, there has been a conflict between the insurgents and the Queen's troops; there has been bloodshed, and the loss of many lives. The intelligence of these outrages has caused alarm and dismay throughout the kingdom." [1]

When divested of the repetitions and technicalities of the reports of the sworn witnesses, and also of the addresses of the Lord Chief Justice and legal authorities, the story of the rising possesses much interest as an account in many of its details of what could not happen in the present day. The mountainous nature of the insurgent locality, the extraordinarily stormy weather which threw the undisciplined thousands out in their calculations, and the short, but (for the time occupied) bloody climax would have formed under such a pen as Sir Walter Scott's, a narrative of interest almost equal to some of those of the Covenanting troubles.

The part of the County in which the disturbances took place—was what is called the "hill district" of Monmouthshire (plate XV.), which has been described as an area of triangular form, having for its apex to the south, Risca, a town five miles W.N.W of Newport. The base of the triangle was at a distance of from fifteen to twenty miles in a northerly direction, with the great Beaufort and Nant-y-glo iron works to the west, on the edge of Brecknockshire, and to the east Blaenavon on the Usk in its hilly, or it might be said mountainous, neighbourhood. The area of this hill district is varied with hill and dale, intersected in parts by deep glens, and also by mountain streams, of no inconsiderable force after heavy rains. Picturesquely considered the country is of great beauty, but beneath the surface are rich supplies of coal and iron. For some years before 1839, the mines had been much worked,

[1] *The Trial of John Frost for High Treason* under a Special Commission held at Monmouth, in December 1839, and January, 1840, (p. 58). London, Saunders and Benning, Law Booksellers, 43, Fleet Street, 1840. (E.A.O.)

and the country, instead of being merely inhabited by a small and scattered population, was at the time of the outbreak estimated to contain above 40,000 inhabitants, often, as it was stated, displaying "an extent of ignorance very much to be deplored" and consequently easily led away by the agents of seditious societies and formed into affiliated bodies ready for outbreak when called on.

The matured plan of the rising was arranged on the 1st of November at a meeting at a place called Blackwood, where there was a Lodge or Society of Chartists. At this meeting deputies attended, and orders were formulated, that the men should assemble armed on the evening of the 3rd, the following Sunday. There were to be three principal divisions, one under the command of Frost (then living at Blackwood), the other two to be respectively formed of men from the up-country, and men more from the east and north. These divisions were to meet at Risca at a convenient distance from Newport, their destination, which they purposed to reach about two in the morning. They hoped to find the inhabitants asleep, and to carry out their plans at their own convenience; attack the "intended-to-be-surprised" troops at Newport, break down the bridge over the Usk, and stop the mail. The Newport mails in those days were forwarded over the Old Passage of the Severn to Bristol, from which place at a given time they were sent North. The non-arrival of the mails at Birmingham was to have been a sign of success of the Monmouthshire outbreak, and of a general rising in Lancashire, and other parts of the kingdom. Affairs, however, turned out very differently to what they expected. The night between the Sunday and Monday was the darkest and most tempestuous that had been known for years, and consequently though Frost arrived near Risca early in the night, the other divisions were long behind time. Meanwhile Mr. Phillips, the Mayor of Newport, afterwards Sir Thomas Phillips, a firm and intelligent man, well informed of what was going on, had been quietly making preparations, in view of the intelligence received during Sunday. He had given orders to the Superintendent of Police to have a number of Special Constables ready on that evening. A detachment was stationed at the Westgate Hotel, where the Mayor and another magistrate also located themselves about 9 p.m., and remained watching throughout the night. When day dawned on Monday, November 4th, intelligence was received that the insurgents

PLATE XV.

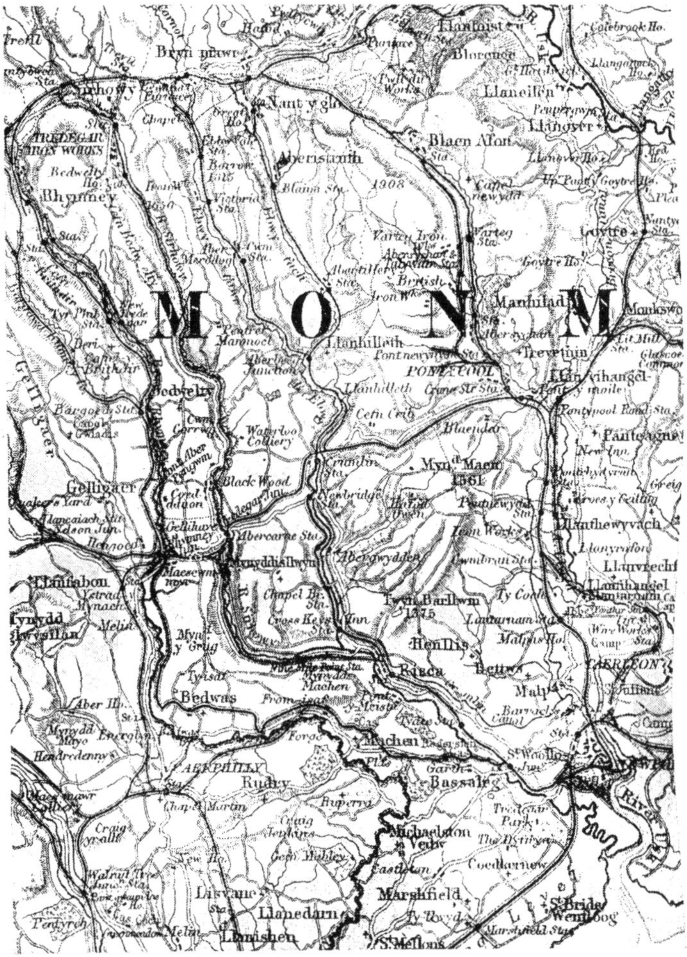

Map showing the District of the Chartist Rising in Monmouth. Newport near the low right-hand corner above the bend of the River Usk.

To face p. 50.

were approaching, and the Mayor sent a request to the barracks for military assistance. There was only one company of soldiers (of Her Majesty's 45th Regiment of foot) stationed at Newport at the time. Of these thirty men, under command of Lieut. Basil Gray, were sent to the assistance of the Mayor. They arrived at the Westgate Hotel about 8 a.m. The soldiers were placed in a room on the ground floor of the hotel with three windows (a bow window with three divisions) coming down within a few inches of the ground, and it should be observed that they did *not* load their muskets until, after being fired upon, they were ordered to do so. Shortly after the rioters were seen advancing, the numbers being technically stated in the indictment for High Treason as "a great multitude . . . . to the number of two thousand and more," probably more accurately computed at 5,000, armed with guns, pistols, pikes, swords, daggers, clubs, bludgeons, and other weapons. Amongst the miscellaneous "weapons of offence" were scythes fixed on poles, and an instrument (of which a specimen was produced in court) called a "mandrel," used for working out coal in the mines, and somewhat resembling a pick-axe in shape. A portion of the rioters formed in front of the hotel, and at once began the attack by firing a volley of small arms at the windows of the room where the soldiers were placed, of which the lower shutters were closed. They gained entrance to a passage, or corridor, communicating with it by a door. The word was immediately given to load with ball cartridge, but whilst the lower window shutters remained closed, the men could not reply. Therefore, with the certainty that they would be fired on, the Mayor and Lieutenant Gray threw back the shutters, and stood unmasked facing the insurgents, who immediately discharged a volley of small arms, whereby the Mayor was wounded in the groin, and seriously in one arm near the shoulder, and Sergeant Daily was badly hit in the head. The order to fire was at once given, and several of the insurgents were wounded, and fell. For the short time that the conflict lasted the rioters in the house continued to try to force the position by rushing up to the doorway; but when they encountered their own dead and received the return fire of the soldiers they faltered, and in less than ten minutes the affray was over. The passage was cleared of all excepting the dead and wounded, and the vast mob of rioters was dispersing with all speed. In the words of one witness, they "ran to all quarters." Another deposed that he met numbers of them near Newport "running back in all directions," and though here and there some men remained, they were without arms, and from the quantity of weapons of offence collected afterwards, it was demonstrable that in many cases the men must have flung them away as they fled. But though short, the affair had been bloody. The rioters lost seven men killed besides a number of wounded, and the casualties to their opponents were in some cases serious, although not fatal. Hundreds hurried from the scene of their repulse with such speed that by ten o'clock a.m. they were passing the Lodge Gate of Tredegar Park, about two miles from Newport. Amongst this crowd was John Frost, ex-draper of Newport and would-be conductor of the outbreak, a man who had proved himself as deficient in courage as he had been inefficient in leadership. He was endeavouring to conceal his identity by holding a handkerchief to his face as if he were crying. But on being spoken to and recognised, he left the road and going through an archway leading to a coppice wood, was lost sight of. A warrant was granted in the afternoon of the same day, and in the evening, on the door being forced open of the house of a man named Partridge (about a quarter of a mile from the Westgate Hotel in Newport), Frost was found and was immediately taken into custody. On being searched, three pistols all loaded, a powder flask, and some balls were found in his pocket.

PLATE XVI.

Chepstow Castle, Monmouthshire.

(*p. 16.*)

To face p. 52.

CHAPTER VIII

BEGINNING THE STUDY OF ENTOMOLOGY, COLLECTIONS OF ECONOMIC ENTOMOLOGICAL SPECIMENS, AND FAMILY DISPERSAL.

So far as a date can be given to what has been the absorbing interest of the work of my life, the 12th of March, 1852, would be about the beginning of my real study of Entomology. I fancy I attended to it more than I knew myself, for little things come back to memory connected with specimens being brought to me to name or look at, one in particular regarding a rare locust. The date was some time before coaches were discontinued, and the usual gathering of people in those days had collected at the door of the George Hotel in Chepstow to see the coach change horses, when, to the astonishment of all, a fine rose-underwinged locust appeared amongst them. Chepstow is on a steep hill, and the "George" about half a mile from the bridge (pl. XVII.). Down the hill set off the locust, pursued by a party from the George, until it was captured at the bridge, and our family doctor conveyed it alive and uninjured to me. On my father sending it up to Oxford to Professor Daubeney as a probable curiosity, he identified it as being the first of the kind which had been taken so far west. If he gave us the name, I have forgotten it. In March I began my studies by buying my first entomological book, and I chose beetles for the subject, and Stephens's "Manual of British Beetles" [1] for my teacher. Those who know the book will understand my difficulties. It has no illustrations, glossary, nor convenient abstracts to help beginners, and, if such things existed in those days, they were not accessible to me. But I made up my mind that I was going to learn, and as *palpi*, *maxillæ*, and names of all the smaller parts of

[1] *Manual of British Coleoptera, or Beetles,* published by Longmans, Green & Co., 1839. In Miss Ormerod's copy is a pencil note: "J. F. S., died 1853."

the insects were wholly unknown to me, I struck out a plan of my own. From time to time I got one of the very largest beetles that I could find, something that I was quite sure of, and turned it into my teacher. I carefully dissected it and matched the parts to the details of the description given by Stephens. The process was very tedious and required great care, but I got a sound foundation, and by making a kind of synopsis of the chief points of classification I got a start. To this day (1891) I have my old Stephens's Manual with my own pencil markings, that started me on my unaided course. Identification was very difficult for a long time, but I "looked out" my beetles laboriously till I thought I was sure of the name, and then, to make quite certain, I took the subject the other way forward—worked back systematically from the species till I found that there was no other kind that it could be. Killing my specimens was another difficulty. I had been told that if beetles were dropped into hot water death was instantaneous. I was not aware that it should be boiling. So into the kitchen I went with a water-beetle, which in after years I found must have been *Dytiscus marginalis*—a large water-beetle which has great powers of rapid swimming—got a tumbler of hot water, and dropped my specimen in. But to my perfect horror, instead of being killed instantaneously, it skimmed round and round on the water for perhaps a minute as if in the greatest agony. This was my second lesson; thenceforward I supplied myself with chloroform.

My first experience in the use of the microscope was gained by helping my brother William to prepare botanical specimens for examination under his microscope. I thus had useful practice early in life, 1849 (?), in the management of a good instrument. I bought my own about 1864, after my brother John's death—one of Pillischer's—a good working instrument with excellent 1-inch and ¼-inch lenses on a nose-piece. I first studied with it the hairs of different animals. I also worked preparations of teeth, showing the fluid contents when in a fresh state.

In the number of the "Gardeners' Chronicle and Agricultural Gazette" for August 1, 1868, the announcement was made that "Throughout the month of August there will be open in the Palace of Industry, in the Champs Elysées, Paris, an Exhibition which we conceive cannot fail to be of great service in extending a knowledge of the destructive

Chepstow with the Road Bridge over the Wye (opened in 1816), Chepstow Castle on the River-bank, and rising ground behind.

Frith photo.

To face p. 54.

or beneficial habits of various species of insects. . . . The Exhibition is organised by the 'Société d'Insectologie Agricole' under the Presidency of Dr. Boisduval, one of the Vice-Presidents of the Horticultural Society of Paris, and under the auspices of the Minister of Agriculture, Commerce, and Public Works. The object of this Society (and consequently of the Exhibition itself) is twofold: firstly, to investigate the economy and to extend the benefits resulting from insects serviceable to mankind; and secondly, to study the habits of those species which affect our gardens, orchards, farms or forests, in order to arrest their ravages or destroy them individually."

Details were given at some length of the classes of subjects to be represented, in the hope that it might attract the attention of the Council of our own Horticultural Society to the desirability of arranging some similar exhibition, and, on the 22nd of August following, the public were informed (again in the "Gardeners' Chronicle," p. 893) that "the desideratum lately pointed out as falling within the province of the Royal Horticultural Society to supply, viz., a Collection of Insects (and their products), is now in a fair way to be made good." A short sketch was given of the plan on which it was proposed to deal with the subject, in which the "insect friends" of the horticulturist were the division to be placed first. Following these were to be "gardeners' enemies," and the plants on which they feed; next to these again, "insects beneficial or injurious to man." Negotiations on the part of the Council of the Royal Horticultural Society with the Science and Art Department resulted in the agreement that, if the Society would form the Collection, the Department would house, care for, and display it. The eminently qualified Fellows of the Society, Mr. Wilson Saunders, Mr. Andrew Murray (pp. 75 and 87), and Mr. M. J. Berkeley, agreed to lend their best assistance in the matter, and Mr. Murray, at the request of the Council, undertook the most laborious part of the task—that of receiving, arranging, and putting in order the various specimens that might be sent from time to time. All collectors and observers who might be willing to help were requested to communicate with Mr. Murray, and without delay I availed myself of the opportunity, in pleasant anticipation of the entomological co-operation giving a use to what had been previously somewhat desultory observation.

I was singularly well situated for the collection of ordinary kinds of injurious insects, and for the observation of their workings, as I then resided on my father's Gloucestershire property. The extent was not very great, only about 800 acres, but the nature of both the land and the cultivation afforded wonderful variety of material for commencing a collection. The wood- and park-land included old timber trees in some instances dating back to the time of the Edwards, and also plenty of ordinary deciduous woodland and coppice. The fir plantations supplied conifer-loving forest pests; the ordinary insects of crop and garden were of course plentiful; the woodland and field pools added their quota; and the diversity in exposure from the salt pasturage by the Severn to the various growths up the face of the cliffs to about 140 feet probably had something to do also with the great variety of insect life. I had willing helpers in the agricultural labourers—when they had made up their minds whether they would assist or not. They had always helped, for we were on very friendly terms, and some of them or their children, like myself, had been born on the estate. But, though I did not know it at the time, I heard afterwards that when I asked for such special help they held a sort of informal meeting to consult whether it should be granted. Happily they settled that I was to be helped because the rural counsel stated I made use of what I got. The verdict was satisfactory in practical results, but I had my own private opinion that what were sometimes called "Miss Eleanor's shillings" helped the cause of collection. From the commencement of work until my father's death, when I ceased to have command of the large area of ground, I collected and sent the results to the charge of Mr. Murray. Communication was entirely carried on by letter.

[N.B.—Miss Ormerod's work was gracefully acknowledged by the Royal Horticultural Society awarding her the Floral Medal (plate XXII.).]

Family Dispersal.

My father's last days were happy and painless, and were passed in comfort under the attendance of my sisters and myself, whom, in the failing condition of his powers of exertion he preferred to all other society. We deeply felt the happiness of ministering to his welfare, for he would not hear of our leaving him for even twenty-four hours, and he objected to visits from my brothers excepting occasionally for a short time. They, not being used to the gentle ways necessary for an aged invalid, worried him.

His last illness, however, was short. On the Monday preceding his decease he was able to come downstairs to his nine o'clock breakfast as usual, and the Thursday following —the 9th of October, 1873—he passed gently away, at the mature age of eighty-seven years.

He was succeeded in the property by his eldest son, the Venerable Thos. Johnson Ormerod, Archdeacon of Suffolk, and Rector of Redenhall-cum-Harleston, Norfolk, who had held the post of Examining Chaplain to two bishops of Norwich, Dr. Stanley and Dr. Hinds, and had been requested to hold it once again by their successor, Dr. Pelham. This however, he declined, not feeling disposed in his own advancing age to continue in the laborious though honourable office. On my father's death, my brother resigned his living,[1] and moved with his two unmarried daughters to Sedbury. From his standing as a clergyman of high position, who had long mixed in literary society, and also as a country gentleman, it had been hoped that he would make Sedbury a literary and county centre, as it had been in my father's time. But his life was unexpectedly closed at the age of sixty-five by a sudden illness. He died on 2nd December, 1874, and the property passed to his eldest son, the Rev. G. T. B. Ormerod, then, or shortly before, curate of Stroud.

[A short account of Miss Ormerod's brothers other than the eldest above referred to—all men of ability and diligent workers—will complete this chapter of family history.

"Two entered the Church; the third brother, John, was the holder of the Port Fellowship of Brasenose and bursar of that college; and the youngest, Arthur, spent his life in parish work as Vicar of Halvergate, in Norfolk.

"The fifth brother, William, and the sixth, Edward, became students at St. Bartholomew's Hospital, to which institution their uncle, Dr. Peter Mere Latham and his father, Dr. John Latham, had been physicians. William's health failing, he left London, and after a few years' practice at Oxford, where he was surgeon to the Radcliffe Infirmary, he retired to Canterbury, and there died at a comparatively early age. Edward distinguished himself as a physician and as a naturalist. He too was debarred by bad health from practising in London, but in Brighton he became physician to the Sussex County Hospital, and was for many years the leading consultant of the town. He wrote several excel-

[1] He had resigned the Archdeaconry in 1868.

lent papers on medical subjects, and his monograph on "British Social Wasps" brought him the fellowship of the Royal Society.

"The second brother, Wareing, and the fourth, Henry, started as solicitors in Manchester. Wareing left Manchester for Devonshire, living first at Chagford, on the borders of Dartmoor, and afterwards at Teignmouth. Geology was his favourite study. He compiled the Index for the publications of the Geological Society, of which he was a fellow, and he made many contributions to its journal.

"Henry Mere Ormerod continued to practise as a solicitor in Manchester till his death in 1898. He also managed his father's Lancashire estates, and to him the other members of his family turned for legal and for practical advice. He was a churchwarden of the Collegiate Church, now the Cathedral, trustee of various important charities, active in all good movements, proud to be of Lancashire origin and a Manchester man. He possessed extensive knowledge and most varied interests. His collections of books, china, and prints were remarkable; and in such subjects as archæology, genealogy, architecture, geology, and certain branches of natural history he was an expert. It was he who presented to the Bodleian Library, Oxford, in accordance with the wishes of his father, the author's copy of the 'History of Cheshire.'"]

* * * * *

EXTRACT FROM ORMEROD'S "HISTORY OF CHESHIRE," VOL. III. PAGE 450 (1ST EDITION), RELATIVE TO THE ORIGINAL OF PL. XVIII. OPPOSITE.

"*P.* 238, *Nantwich Hospital.* The author has in his possession a singularly curious oak chest which he purchased at Erdswick Hall. It had been bought by the tenant at a sale at Hulgreve Hall (an estate of the Astons, who participated in the division of the religious spoil at the Reformation), and it was traditionally said to have come from this hospital. It appears to have been one of the chests used to keep vestments and chalices, &c., in, and is about two feet broad, by five in length, and two feet nine inches in height; at each end are two compartments, and in front five, all of which except the central one are sumptuously carved in imitation of rich Gothic windows with canopies, crockets, finials, buttresses, and shrine work. The centre represents the coronation of Henry VI., and the *single* rose occurs over the *fleur-de-lis* in the ornaments. The chest is figured in Plate 44 of 'Specimens of Gothic Architecture in England,' by Augustus Pugin, 1822; and a description is given at page 27.

"A chest, of a description precisely corresponding with it, was recently offered for sale at Liverpool, with the Brereton painted glass, and described as having been formerly the church chest at Ashton-under-Lyne."

PLATE XVIII.

ANTIQUE CARVED CHEST, AN HEIRLOOM OF THE ORMEROD FAMILY.

To face p. 58.

CHAPTER IX

COMMENCEMENT AND PROGRESS OF ANNUAL REPORTS OF OBSERVATIONS OF INJURIOUS INSECTS

In the spring of 1877 I issued a short pamphlet of seven pages, entitled "Notes for Observations of Injurious Insects,"[1] in which I suggested how much a series of observations in relation to insect ravages on food crops was to be desired; this not merely for scientific purposes, but with a view to finding means of lessening the amount of yearly loss which tells so heavily on individual growers, and also on the country at large. I pointed out shortly that many insect attacks could be remedied, if attention were directed to the subject; and also that many would probably be found, if reliable information could be procured, to be coincident with multiplication or diminution of insect life. On the way in which this increase and decrease were affected by surroundings, such as plants, &c., suitable for food or shelter; by agricultural conditions, such as drainage, nature of the soil and of manures; and also by the state of the weather — I gave some guiding notes, and requested information from agriculturists and entomologists, who were both practically and scientifically qualified to aid in the matter. I also added some short remarks as to the nature of the entomological observations desired; as of date, and amount of appearance of larvæ (grubs); amount of injury caused; and any other points of use and interest that might occur to the observer. And further (as some sort of assistance in the commencement of the plan of campaign) I gave a list of about eighteen of our commonest crop, fruit, and forest insects, with short descriptions in the very plainest words I could use, in most cases accompanied by illustrations.

As my name was then little before the public, although I had worked on entomology for a good many years,

[1] Miss Ormerod had been a contributor to scientific literature for some years before this date. Writing in 1900 she says:—"My first regular paper was printed in the Journal of Linn. Soc., vol. xi., No. 56, Zoology, July 18, 1873, on *The Cutaneous Exudation of the 'Triton cristatus.'* I think it is sound and unusual!"

I requested permission of two of my scientific friends, the Rev. T. A. Preston, one of the masters of Marlborough College, and much interested in phenology (*i.e.*, observation of natural phenomena); and Mr. E. A. Fitch, Secretary of the Entomological Society, to allow me to add their names as referees. To this they kindly consented, but with the stipulation from Mr. Preston that he did not wish to co-operate further. I believe I may say with regard to Mr. Fitch such a very small amount of communication took place that it would not have been worth while to mention the matter, excepting *pro forma*, on account of the names being recorded. These were soon removed from succeeding reports as unnecessary. The pamphlet was widely circulated and the request for observations was responded to far more cordially than could have been expected. Notes regarding insect appearances, together with observations of their habits, and of practicable methods of prevention, were forwarded by observers—who were qualified both as technically scientific and practical workers—from localities scattered over the country as far north as Aberdeenshire in Scotland and south to Hants and Devonshire in England. In fact the communications were quite sufficient to show that the plan was approved of from an agricultural point of view, and might be continued hopefully. In after years I was told that it was very well received by the press. I have been greatly indebted since both to the agricultural and general press, but at the time it did not seem to me to be peculiarly warmly welcomed, nor I think was it likely to be, until it had more to say for itself. The pamphlet was not of many pages; the knowledge of the great mischief caused by insect pests, and the need of prevention of their ravages, was not spread abroad as at the present day, and I was not able at first to utilise to the best advantage the information sent as I had no working reports of my own to help me as to examples of the best methods of arrangement.[1]

[1] To such of my readers as possess some portion only of the early series, it may be of interest to point out that the observations, up to those for 1880 inclusive, were arranged, not as afterwards, as detached papers, placed alphabetically under the heading of the names of the crops to which they referred, but under the numbers given in the successive preceding guide lists issued for the use of observers—as for instance, "6, *Anthomyia ceparum*, Onion fly;" or "25, *Abraxas grossulariata*, Magpie moth" (fig. 9).

These were arranged numerically, from "1" onwards, all the observations on one kind of insect attack being arranged successively in a long unbroken paragraph under the selected number, together with the name of the pest. For want of better knowledge of the requisites

From the first I had excellent contributions. Various members of our Entomological Societies were good enough to send me notes on insects to which they devoted special study, and so also were members of the Meteorological Society, regarding points of natural history, bird life, weather, &c., connected with entomological considerations, and regarding which they were special observers. Agriculturally I had good help also from other quarters, and amongst many who assisted me, I will take leave to especially give the name of the late Mr. Malcolm Dunn, the Duke of Buccleuch's superintendent at the Palace Gardens, Dalkeith, N.B. We never met, but whenever I applied to him he was unfailing in prompt and serviceable reply. As a commencement, the introductions with which he favoured me to the leading foresters and horticulturists of North Britain, were of such invaluable aid that I should be ungrateful not to mention his name as of one to whom I owe a deep debt of gratitude.

In the report for the year 1881 I altered the plan of arrangement to one which so far as I can judge met all that was needed for practical as well as scientific service so conveniently that I have since adhered to it. The information was classed under headings of (*a*) farm crops, (*b*) orchard and bush fruits, and (*c*) forest trees, regarding which observations of insect attack were forwarded. These headings were arranged alphabetically, for instance: Apple, Bean, Corn and Grass, Hop, Oak, Peas, Pine, Turnip, &c., &c. Any information as to live-stock or animal insect pests was similarly placed (that is, alphabetically) amongst the other attacks, under the headings of Deer, Grouse, Horses, &c., &c., as the case might be; but beyond what was absolutely necessary, as in the case of Ox warble, I endeavoured to avoid entering on stock infestations as leading to investigations very unpleasant to myself either to make or to discuss, and very much better left in the hands of veterinary

for a readable as well as useful report, I condensed the information into as few words as possible, with few, if any, breaks in the long paragraphs, and so, until 1880, the results (excepting to technical readers) could not be considered "taking." If any of my entomological readers will turn to a very useful work, the *Forst Zoologie*, of Dr. Bernard Altum, they will see in the second division of the "Insecten" at pp. 36, 37, and again at pp. 162, 163, the difficulties that are thrown in the way of comfortably grasping the subject, by the matter being printed continuously without breaks. This, however, as well as many other things, I had then still to learn. (E.A.O.)

surgeons. Following each heading, the observations were placed which had been contributed during the season, and which appeared to be of sufficient interest to be recorded, regarding the special crop, or fruit, &c., referred to, these being given with locality and date, as far as possible in the contributor's words, and over his own name, unless by request, or for some special reason. This plan of giving the very fullest recognition possible of the source of the information, I, for three very special reasons, most strongly recommend to the consideration of all my readers not fully accustomed to practical reporting:

1. That thus the information may very often carry conviction with it by the name of some well-known agriculturist or cattle-breeder being appended.

2. That to do otherwise is a robbery of the credit of the contributor, and a false appropriation of it by the reporter, wholly unbecoming an honest worker.

3. That the full recognition is a great protection to the reporter or compiler of the reports from plagiarism of his own work. There are people who think nothing of appropriating the credit of true workers, and who absorb also rewards in the shape of salaries and official position based on their own questionable conduct.

In the year 1881 it seemed desirable to change the running heading at the top of the pages. The name of the crop, fruit, or other subject to which the paper referred was henceforward placed at the top of the left-hand page, and the name of each successive attack to it at the top of the right-hand page; as, for instance, Cabbage at the left side, and the different kinds of infestations recorded during the year which might occur to Cabbage, as Cabbage butterfly (large white), Cabbage-root fly, Cabbage moth, on the right-hand heading. At the beginning of each paper, the name of the crop, or fruit, was given in large capitals, and beneath and at the heading of each successive paper, the name of the injurious insect to be referred to, also in English, with the scientific name, and authority for the same following. The observations of contributors were inserted unbroken, so that the methods of prevention and remedy noted as successful by each observer were thus recorded in connection with the accompanying peculiarities of cultivation, soil, manure, weather, &c. The whole life-history of the insect, so far as known or accessible, was given, and sometimes, as in great attacks or in special circumstances, a "summary" of the preceding recorded information; this being, wherever possible, followed by some paragraphs or pages of "Methods of Prevention and Remedy."

In matters of phraseology, selection of the very plainest and shortest words that I could choose was part of my plan, and after the first few years I exchanged the short table of contents for a plain working index.

Illustration always appeared to me a very important part of the work, so that readers might start with the knowledge of the appearance of the insects under consideration, gained by a glance at the accompanying figure, without having the trouble of trying to form a kind of "mind picture" from the descriptions given, often very unlike the true object.[1] At first—in the small beginning—the numbers needed were also small, and I think the little stock of figure blocks with which I started, and for which I was indebted to the kind courtesy of a friend, amounted to *one dozen!* This matter, however, I set right as soon as possible by the purchase from Messrs. Blackie & Sons, of Glasgow, of electros of most of the beautiful wood engravings given in Curtis's "Farm Insects," under an agreement that the accommodation was granted on condition of my using the figures only in my own publications. Some of the illustrations I drew myself on the blocks, and as time went on, and infestations, little or not at all entered on before, required illustration, I engaged the valuable assistance of two brothers,[2] which was continued thenceforward throughout the work. It appears to me that it is hardly possible to exceed the beauty of their work, whether in characteristic representation or in precise and accurate details. I have had great pleasure in the entomological approval which has been bestowed upon it. Illustrations from other sources have of course been used, always, so far as I am aware, most carefully acknowledged; and so far as has been in my power, I have endeavoured that the illustration of each infestation should show the insect (where it was possible to do so) in each of its successive stages of life, as of the caterpillar or maggot (scientifically the *larva*); the chrysalis (*pupa*); and the perfect insect, butterfly, beetle, sawfly, &c., as the case might be. This matter is of great importance agriculturally, for how else (it may be asked) in common circumstances, excepting by a good, plain illustration, is a farmer

[1] This consideration induced the Editor to introduce many figures of insects into the chapters of correspondence in the present volume.

[2] Messrs. Horace Knight and E. C. Knight, of the staff of Messrs West, Newman & Co., 54, Hatton Garden, London.

or fruit-grower to know what the connection is between the grubs and maggots which he finds underground or on his trees and the moths or beetles which he may notice in his fields or orchards. To give a single instance, how seldom the grey, cylindrical, legless grubs of the Daddy Longlegs are known to have anything to do with the large, gnat-like, two-winged flies which are to be seen floating over our grass-fields in legions where the larvæ have been destroying underground. And so the work went on, and I believe that I may say that—from the great amount of useful information contributed, together with my own co-operation in entomological verification, adding requisite details, publishing the year's communications, and distributing them to my contributors—it answered fairly the purpose for which it was set on foot. And year by year we gained knowledge till we possessed serviceable information on the main points, both of habits and means of prevention of the greater number of our really seriously injurious farm, orchard, and forest pests of Britain.

Those who wish to investigate in detail the various kinds of infestation noticed during the first twenty-two years of my observations will find them in "The General Index to my Annual Reports on Injurious Insects, 1877–1898," compiled at my request by Mr. Robert Newstead.[1] In this index the insects are arranged alphabetically under their popular and also under their scientific names, with references to the various Annual Reports in which notices of their observation are recorded, or papers given on them, and also of the pages in each paper containing information on their habits and history and means of prevention. Lists are also given of crops and plants, stock, &c., affected. The index thus affords a fair summary of the advance of our knowledge of crop infestation during the years referred to.[2]

In the year 1881 I published a digest of the information

[1] Curator of the Grosvenor Museum, Chester.

[2] On November 26, 1899, Miss Ormerod wrote to Mr. Newstead:—
"I am delighted with our index—the more I examine it the better I like it. Some acknowledgments have come in already, and they are most pleasantly cordial. All are delighted to have such a good reference work . . . One recipient suggests the index would be more serviceable to him if he had a complete set of my reports! He absolutely enclosed a list of deficiencies, but I thought he had best buy, and only sent him that for 1896."

Other letters she wrote about the index "were on much the same lines, and one refers to the cordial letter received from the Board of Agriculture" (ED.).

sent in up to date in an octavo volume of 323 pages, very fully illustrated, entitled "Manual of Injurious Insects, with Methods of Prevention and Remedy"; and in 1890 I followed this by a much enlarged demy-octavo second edition of 450 pages, bearing the same title. In 1898, under the title of "Handbook of Insects Injurious to Orchard and Bush Fruits, with Means of Prevention and Remedy," pp. 280, I included the special observations on fruit infestations which had been sent me. In 1900 I published a pamphlet (also illustrated) entitled "Flies Injurious to Stock" (pp. 80), [p. 304] giving reports of observations of life history and habits, and also of means of prevention of a few kinds of infestation. These were given as shortly as they could serviceably be dealt with, excepting in the case of the Warble fly, *Hypoderma bovis*. Into this it appeared desirable to enter more fully, it having been under my observation since the year 1884, and having been carefully written on in every detail of habits and means of prevention, as observed by my contributors and myself in this country.

Besides the above publications, I arranged, for gratuitous circulation, various four-page leaflets on our commonest farm pests. Each contained an illustration and as much information as I could manage to condense into the limited space. Among the subjects discussed were the widely destructive Wireworm and equally destructive grubs of the Daddy Longlegs or Cranefly, the Mangold-leaf maggot, the Mustard beetle, the minute Stem eel-worm (which causes the malformed growth of cereal plants known as "tulip root" and does much harm in clover shoots), the Warble fly and the troublesome Forest fly. Our recent investigations have proved this last to be present in two other districts at least, besides the New Forest and its vicinity in Hampshire, to which previously it had been supposed to be almost limited (p. 138). For the leaflet on the Warble fly, its history, and easily practicable methods of prevention and remedy, there has been such a large demand that various issues have been successively printed amounting to 170,000 copies, including 15,000 copies which the Messrs. Murray, of Aberdeen, requested permission to print at their own cost.

The original plan (or rather that which gradually formed in the first few years) of arrangement of the Annual Reports appeared to meet all requirements, so long as the requirements of the case remain unaltered. Year after year such information as had been asked for was sent, gradually

6

completing most of the histories of our seriously injurious crop and orchard insects, but in the report for 1899 it was requisite to make some arrangement for insertion of disconnected additional observations of appearance, habits, &c., of insects, previously referred to. These I gave accordingly in an appendix under the heading of "Short Notices," not to encumber the report with repetitions that could be avoided.

In 1901, when about to publish my report of observa tions of the preceding year, it appeared to me that a large proportion of the new information contributed bore on points of scientific entomological interest, or of occasional appearance of little observed attacks of very little interest or use to the majority of our agriculturists and orchard growers, and quite foreign to the broad scale consideration of pests, which was the object of these reports. It seemed something more than *un*necessary to continue this work, and I, therefore, inserted the following notice in the preface of my Annual Report for 1900, thus closing the series with the closing century :—

"*But now, although with much regret, I am obliged to say that I feel the time has come for discontinuing this series of Annual Reports.* When I commenced the work in 1877, comparatively little was known of the habits and means of prevention of insects seriously injurious to our crops, and of this little a very small amount was accessible for public service, and I undertook the series of reports in the hope (so far as in my power lay) of doing something to meet both these difficulties. Firstly, by endeavouring to gain reliable information of the kind needed; and secondly, by publishing this, with all requisite additions, and especially with illustrations, at a price far below the publication expenses, so that it might be accessible to all who wished to purchase, but especially by sending a copy of each Annual Report to each contributor who had favoured me with useful information. It seemed to be but right and fair that those who kindly helped in the work should have their courtesy acknowledged to the best of my power, and I have continued the reciprocation throughout. But the work was hard; for many years for about five or six months all the time I could give to the subject was devoted to arranging the contributions of the season for the Annual Report of the year, with the addition of the best information I could procure from other sources (in every case, whether of contributors or otherwise, *fully acknowledged*).

As the consultation enquiries were kept up during winter as well as summer, I found the work, carried on single-handed, at times very fatiguing. But so long as there appeared to be a call for it, I have tried to do what I could. Now, however, the necessities of the case have (as a matter of course) been gradually changing. Year after year information has been sent, gradually completing the histories of most of our worst insect pests, and now additional information is rare (as is to be expected after twenty-four years' observations) on points of great agricultural importance.

"I claim no credit to myself in the work; but those who will look over the names of the contributors, given with their information, will see how deeply indebted I am to them, and to other good friends, who have placed their experience and great knowledge at the public service. To them, and to all who have assisted me, and to some who have allowed what began as agricultural communications to ripen into valuable friendship, I offer my grateful thanks and my deep appreciation of their goodness, and I trust they will believe that if, as I well know, much of my work has not been so well done as it would have been in better qualified hands, at least I have earnestly tried to do my very best."[1]

On the publication of the above-mentioned report, I received many kind letters from friends, and I was much gratified by the press allusions on the matter. These, obviously, it would not be desirable for me to do more here than just allude to generally, with my thanks.[2]

[1] Preface to "Twenty-fourth Report of Observations of Injurious Insects." By E. A. Ormerod, LL.D., p. vii.

[2] See Appendix B.

CHAPTER X

SAMPLES OF LEGAL EXPERIENCES

It was a good many years after my name had been before the public as an official Consulting Entomologist that I began occasionally to receive applications to furnish what is called "expert" evidence regarding insect infestation of live crops, or of cargoes of flour. To work this properly, and without risk of being confused under examination by the host of questions, relevant or irrelevant, and, of course, made purposely perplexing by the legal representatives of the opposing side of the case, involved a most inconvenient amount of research and also of mental strain. It was necessary to keep all points in any way likely to be referred to, classed in order in the mind, and available instantaneously without hurry or confusion; and sometimes also necessary in helping non-entomological cross-examiners so to formulate their questions as to admit of any answer being given.

My first experience of anything of this kind was in July, 1889, when I received a copy of a letter written by myself on September 20th of the previous year relative to a certain insect attack, of which specimens, together with samples of the infested plants, had then been sent me. This letter was accompanied by an enquiry whether I could swear to the accuracy of my statements. This, of course, I had no doubts about. It was a perfectly simple case, and I replied accordingly. The result was that one morning before luncheon my sister came into my room in perplexity, and announced that there was a "young man" in my study who wanted to speak to me, but who he was, or where he came from, or anything except that it was just for a minute that he wished to see me, nobody had been able to make out. I believe I guessed pretty well the nature of the mysterious business; but, as for explanation, the young man was perfectly impenetrable, excepting on two points. One that he was to give me a paper which I accepted, and next that he was to give me some small amount of money, which I also accepted, not knowing whether any other course was open to me. As this was the first (and also last) case of a subpœna being served on me, I do not know whether the immense reticence is part of the business, or whether the server is possibly in danger of bad language or unpleasant treatment, but certainly the visitor appeared very uneasy, and took himself off as soon as possible. On examining the paper I found it called me to give evidence on the side of the defendants, which was a little awkward, as after due investigation of details I found that the entomological circumstances would give the case for the plaintiffs. It ran as follows :—

"In the High Court of Justice between Thomas Wilkinson, Plaintiff, and The Houghton Main Colliery Company, Limited, Defendants. Victoria, by the Grace of God, of the United Kingdom of Great Britain and Ireland, Queen, Defender of the Faith, to Miss Eleanor A. Ormerod, of Torrington House, St. Albans, in the County of Herts. Greeting.—We command you to attend before our Justices assigned to take the assizes in and for the West Riding Division of the County of York to be holden at Leeds on Wednesday the 24th day of July, 1889, at the hour of ten in the forenoon and so from day to day during the said assizes until the above cause is tried to give evidence on behalf of the Defenders, &c."

On the back of the document was inscribed (name and address given) that the writ was issued by the London Agents of J. Parker Rhodes, of Rotherham, Yorkshire, defendants' solicitor. I felt myself very unpleasantly situated, more particularly as one of my legal brothers assured me that I should make myself (or be made) quite ridiculous in Court, but I did not see the matter quite in this light, for I was sure of my facts. I explained to the solicitor for the defendants that if put in the witness box I must support the cause of the plaintiff. The case was then withdrawn and costs allowed to the plaintiff.

Ten years afterwards I was employed by Messrs. Ross T. Smyth and Co., 33, Mark Lane, London, E.C. The case was entered on March 9, 1899, and the matter in question was alleged infestation of a cargo of flour, transmitted from New York, U.S.A., to Durban, S. Africa. I gave evidence on oath here, Torrington House, St. Albans, on October 20, 1899, before Mr. E. K. Blyth (of Messrs. Blyth, Dutton,

Hartley and Blyth), appointed a Commissioner of the High Court of Natal, to take my evidence in the cause of Smyth *v.* Findlay. On Tuesday the 24th following, Mr. E. K. Blyth attended with depositions which I read and signed in his presence. Subjoined is a copy of my "Report on Insect Presence," and also an extract from a confirmatory report made by Mr. Oliver Janson doubly confirmed by the report of a representative of the Department of Agriculture, Division of Entomology, Washington :—

"I have examined the contents of the box and bottle this day submitted to me from yourselves, the bottle being under seal of Messrs. Randle Brothers and Hudson, Durban, Natal, &c., &c. I made my examination both with hand magnifiers and microscope and found that in the very small amount of insect presence in the wheat flour and in the spirit or preservative fluid, there were two kinds of beetles represented. One of these was the *Tribolium ferrugineum,* popularly known as the Rusty-red flour beetle (fig. 70). This is a small red-brown, or yellowish-red-brown, beetle, about a sixth of an inch long, somewhat parallel-sided and narrow in proportion to its length; the wing-cases striated longitudinally, and the antennæ (or horns) with a three-jointed club at the extremity. I found this beetle present in all its stages of development; that is, as a comparatively long and narrow larva (grub or maggot) ; in the chrysalis (pupa) state, in which it resembles the beetle with its limbs folded beneath it until development is complete ; and the perfect beetles.

"I also found one specimen of what is called the *Cadelle* in larval (grub or maggot) state. This is a pitchy-coloured beetle, *Trogosita mauritanica* or *Tenebroides mauritanicus,* rather larger than the kind above named, being about four times longer. I examined the whole amount of insect infestation sifted in my presence from the wheat flour under consideration or taken out of the bottle of preservative fluid, and in the very small amount of insect presence observable, I found nothing else to which the slightest degree of importance could be attached. In reply to the inquiry submitted to me, as to the possibility of the bags of wheat flour under consideration having been infested when they were shipped from New York, on or about July the 5th, 1898 ; I can state that I fully believe the flour could not then have been infested, as in such case—consequent on the well-known exceedingly favourable conditions for multiplication of insect presence, through which the bags of flour would pass during the voyage—there would certainly by the date of arrival at Durban, on or about September 14th, have been so great an amount of infestation in all stages, that it could not have been overlooked. And by the further dates named, in the following October and November, it would have been overwhelming. The exceedingly high temperatures through which the shipment would pass are known to be very favourable to rapid propagation of successive generations of *Tribolium*. It is to be borne in mind that the infestation does not lie in a torpid state, but after hatching from the egg (sometimes inaccurately called the "germ"), which soon occurs in high temperatures, it passes through the changes from larva (or grub) to chrysalis, and beetle condition more or less quickly according to warmth of locality; and then the male and female beetles pair, and in the ordinary course die, in the case of the female after egg-laying. Examination of the condition of the flour, had infestation been present, would have shown not only the living infestation, but also the dead bodies of the previous generations of beetles, which being of a hard and horny nature externally, would not have decayed in the flour.

"Further, not only is great warmth favourable to increase of *Tribolium*, but also the conditions, when flour is placed in bags and left unopened for any length of time, are especially suited to their propagation. I can also state that the effect of *Tribolium* infestation on flour is such that its presence even to a small amount could not be unobserved, and these characteristics were wholly absent in the flour submitted to me. To the best of my knowledge and belief I consider it to be absolutely and demonstrably impossible that the infestation regarding which the inquiry is now before me could have been shipped from New York, and after the most careful examination and investigation which I am able to make, I consider that the infestation took place after the arrival of the flour at Durban.

"May I, in addition to the above opinion, be permitted to suggest to you that as this investigation is one of great importance, it might be satisfactory to yourselves if you were also to submit the samples, which I have re-secured under my own seal, to Mr. Oliver E. Janson, F.E.S., as being a skilled entomologist, and so well qualified by personal observation and scientific knowledge of the *Coleoptera* (beetles), to give a correct opinion in the present matter, that I should consider him to be the most thoroughly trustworthy English referee."

Mr. Janson's report was as follows :—

"Having carefully examined the specimens of insects submitted to me under seal of Miss E. A. Ormerod, and stated to have been found in the accompanying sample of flour, named 'Radiant,' 'Strathness,' also the specimens of insects, &c. &c., I identify them as the coleopterous insect, known scientifically as *Tribolium ferrugineum*, in its various stages of larva (grub), pupa (chrysalis), and imago (beetle). I also find a single specimen of *Trogosita mauritanica*. . . In considering the important question as to origin of the infestation, I am of opinion that the evidence afforded clearly indicates the origin of the infestation to have been subsequent to the arrival of the flour at Durban."

[The case never came to trial, but the unanimity of the expert opinion enabled Messrs. Ross T. Smith & Co. to effect a compromise on terms they were willing to accept.]

The following letter addressed to us by Mr. Wm. Simpson of Messrs. R. & H. Hall, Limited, of Cork, Dublin, Belfast and Waterford, shows a similar satisfactory termination to a case in which granary weevils had done serious damage to a cargo of flour from San Francisco.

"WESTPORT, *Feb.* 6, 1900. DEAR MADAM,—Perhaps you have not quite forgotten my visit to you in early summer of last year when I submitted for your inspection a sample of flour with weevil infestation from a cargo landed here. It will I am sure interest you to know that we have just settled the case out of Court by the owners of the vessel paying us £900 and our costs. We are pleased that the matter is thus ended, but I cannot forbear from again thanking you for all the attention and help you gave us in the case and which was to us of the greatest value. Yours very truly, (Sgd) WM. SIMPSON."

CHAPTER XI

BIOGRAPHICAL SKETCH BY THE EDITOR

THE removal of Miss Ormerod and her sister, Georgiana, from Torquay to Spring Grove, Isleworth, was primarily because Torquay did not suit their health and secondarily because at Isleworth they were near Kew Gardens, where they were on intimate terms with Sir Joseph and Lady Hooker. They left again for Torrington House, St. Albans, in September, 1887, partly because Sir Joseph resigned the Directorship of Kew Gardens in 1885 and partly because of the increase of population, and the defective and unwholesome drainage of the house. In a letter (p. 74) to Dr. Bethune, one of her esteemed Canadian correspondents, she refers to her impending change of residence.

DUNSTER LODGE, SPRING GROVE, ISLEWORTH.
August 7, 1887.

"MY DEAR MR. BETHUNE,—I have very often lately been hoping to hear of your safe arrival, and I am very glad to hear of it; but I am so sorry that I cannot have the great pleasure of seeing you to-morrow, for I have to be at St. Albans to meet a number of people on business from noon till 4 p.m. This is a great disappointment to me, for I (we) had much looked forward to a chat with you. I am longing to hear of my kind friends in Canada and especially of Mr. Fletcher and Professor Saunders, and I want much to ask you how to transmit so much of a set of my entomological publications as I can get together for acceptance by the Entomological Society of Ontario.[1] I cannot tell you

[1] The Entomological Society of Ontario was originated by Dr. Saunders and Dr. Bethune nearly forty years ago. Its headquarters are in London, Ontario, and it has branches in Toronto, Montreal and Quebec. Its publications are the monthly *Canadian Entomologist*, now in its thirty-fifth volume, and thirty-three annual reports to the Legislature of Ontario on *Noxious and Beneficial Insects*. Miss Ormerod was an Honorary Member.

how much I respect and admire the working of that noble Society, and I feel myself greatly honoured by being elected one of its members. Hessian fly (fig. 15) is indeed becoming a scourge—and the work is enormous—it is a different story now to when I was so roundly sneered at last year for thinking it had come. If we had our grand Entomological Society of Ontario here things might have been very different. I trust you may be able to spare, if only one hour to give us just time to confer a little on your return. I would put aside any ordinary engagement for the pleasure and also the benefit of an entomological conversation. But now about my sister and myself. This place is fast becoming very unsuitable for us—you will know all that is involved in the rapid increase of the outskirts of London—and we have a notice of most of our garden going to be offered for sale next year for small building plots. Therefore we are making arrangements to move about the end of next month to St. Albans. We have many good friends and fellow-workers there or near, and the place is very healthy, and very accessible both for London and the country, and I can, I trust, do my work much more fully there."

Of Miss Ormerod Lady Hooker has written: "When she was our neighbour during our residence at Kew, she was a frequent visitor at our house and often came in the morning before public hours to the Gardens, to pursue her researches and look for the insects to be found on the trees, shrubs and plants; on these occasions she generally lunched with us and we delighted in her bright and intellectual conversation. She was extremely fond of animals and birds, and could imitate the calls of the animals and the notes of many birds so perfectly that she could collect the creatures around her; it was curious to see the squirrels peep out from the trees when she called to them and venture to her feet for the nuts she scattered for them. Her observation was always on the alert and she saw many minute things in nature that others would have passed by. She was a fine artist—and so was her sister, Miss G. Ormerod. At one time my husband was needing some drawings made for the *Botanical Magazine* and she offered her services and drew three or four very beautifully."

Lady Hooker made a practice of inviting Miss Ormerod and her sister to come over and help to entertain distinguished visitors at great functions and on the occasion of visits of official scientific parties. On one

PLATE XIX.

Torrington House, St. Albans, Herts, Miss Ormerod's last Residence.
(p. 115.)

To face p. 74.

occasion the whole Chinese Embassy, excepting the Ambassador himself, came in Chinese costume. Miss Ormerod asked permission of Lady Hooker to speak to the Naturalist, who talked English very well. The information elicited however was but trifling, amounting to the fact that in China a yellow powder (probably flowers of sulphur) was used to dress plants to ward off disease. She suggested tea as an escape from a disappointing position and then adjourned to the tea-room followed by the whole Embassy. The Entomologist took tea, but another minor member of the group, being reputed at times to indulge in potations to which the hosts were not accustomed, gave great cause for anxiety by taking possession of a wine bottle. Miss Ormerod was successful in spiriting the bottle away and in substituting a cup of tea, but great was her relief when Sir Joseph and Lady Hooker arrived on the scene.

At Kew she also met Andrew Murray, Secretary of the Royal Horticultural Society, who did excellent work in Economic Entomology for the Bethnal Green and South Kensington Museums. Miss Ormerod described him as a "profoundly scientific and intellectual man."

An interesting instance of the widespread benefit of Miss Ormerod's work and the affection with which her name and personality were revered by her distant correspondents was supplied by Dr. Lipscomb, her trusted medical attendant. He says:—

"My sister was talking to a small market gardener in a flower garden she was painting near Penzance, and Miss Ormerod's name happened to be mentioned. The old gardener was beside himself with delight to meet some one who knew Miss Ormerod. He said she had saved him from utter ruin. His flowers had become infected with some injurious insect which bade fair to devastate the whole garden. In despair, hearing of Miss Ormerod, he wrote to her and not only received a kind letter of advice, but also a copy of her work on 'Injurious Insects' with the page turned down and the paragraphs specially applicable to the case marked. No wonder the poor old chap with tears in his eyes said he loved his unknown benefactress."

Miss Ormerod was appointed Consulting Entomologist to the Royal Agricultural Society of England in 1882, and for ten years retained that honourable position to the advantage of the Members and the British public generally.

The need of a Consulting Entomologist was forcibly brought home to the Society, then under the presidency of Mr. J. Dent-Dent, by the disastrous attack in 1881 of the Turnip fly, or more correctly flea beetle, which resulted in an estimated loss of over half a million sterling to farmers in England and Scotland. Leading agriculturists all over the country, but more from the East than the West, supplied information for a report, and special assistance was given by some members of the Royal Agricultural Society, including Mr. J. H. Arkwright of Hampton Court, Herefordshire. The results were embodied in the Annual Report for 1881, published in 1882.

A short time after this event a request was made to Miss Ormerod to indicate whether she would accept the post of Consulting Entomologist to the Royal Agricultural Society. Urged by Mr. Charles Whitehead, Chairman of the "Seeds and Plant Diseases Committee," and by her intimate personal friend Professor Herbert Little, another member of the Council, she accepted, but with hesitation and with considerable reluctance, engendered by the opposition of her sister Georgiana, who believed her strength was not equal to the strain of additional work. The meeting with members of the Council at the Society's offices, 12, Hanover Square, London, at which details were discussed, was unusually trying, in spite of the kindly courtesy of the Secretary (Mr. H. M. Jenkins) for whom Miss Ormerod entertained the deepest regard. She says, writing in 1900, "I was nearly frightened out of my wits in going through the requested ordeal, and the recollections of the experiences remain as uniquely unpleasant. On arriving, I gave my card to the attendant, who led me upstairs, where I expected to meet but two or three people, and I was ushered into a room full of gentlemen standing waiting my arrival, not one of whom except Professor Little was known to me even by sight. I advanced about two feet, my sole thought being of the awkward fix in which I had so suddenly been landed, and how I should get out of it. Scarcely a word was spoken when I was led down again to the Secretary's room, where a discussion took place with Professor Little, Mr. Whitehead, the Secretary, and the President of the Society,—the others remained absent. In the discussion the President attempted a slight examination of my qualifications, but it amounted to little more than eliciting the length of time during which attention had been devoted to

Entomology. My reply was "about thirty years," to which he had nothing further to say. There was a slight departure from the serious nature of the interview when a parcel of Daddy longlegs grubs which had been placed on the table, gave way, and the creatures crawled all over the place. The final result was, that I agreed to take the post of Consulting Entomologist, but I returned home very uneasy in mind and wrote the same evening that I did not wish to accept office. I was, however, pressed into acceptance at the first business meeting and the first work I undertook was the making of drawings to form originals for six diagrams illustrating some common injurious insects with life histories and methods of prevention.[1] This would be the first Tuesday of June, 1882, and I inaugurated my position on the way home by meeting with a severe accident at Waterloo Station, from the results of which I have never recovered. While doubtless rather preoccupied, crossing the road, a rapid incline from Waterloo Road to the station, I did not notice a carriage coming down the slope till the horses' heads were over mine. With no time to run or turn, I sprang and landed on the pavement, but a sharp pain set in, in the muscle above one knee. Whether it originated from a strain or a blow I never knew, but a little flask I carried on the injured side was beaten in as if by a horse's foot or the point of a carriage pole. The injury was not properly attended to and the affected part gradually increasing and spreading gave rise to the lameness accompanied with severe and frequently intermittent pain which necessitated exceeding quiet and bodily inactivity—a state of matters which was in marked contrast to the extremely active life I had led in my early years rambling in the country, and latterly by indulging in the mechanical in addition to the usual æsthetical pleasures of gardening."

She explains in a letter to Dr. Fletcher, dated August 22, 1892 (p. 212) that she was driven by failing health to resign her honorary official work and to concentrate her energies upon her private work, which steadily increased in volume, and especially on the work of her Annual Report.

A conception of the interesting methods adopted by Miss Ormerod in carrying out her work may be gleaned from her

[1] Details were given in a letter to Colonel Coussmaker of August 1, 1885, p. 99.

own words addressed to us in the course of a long and intimate correspondence.

"I will now try and think of something you may care to insert about languages. So far as I can avoid it, I try not to write in any language but my own, but I can read serviceably French, Italian, and Spanish, and also Latin for what I need; likewise, of course, German; Russian I could read once but not so readily now; and with the dictionary I can make something of Dutch and Norwegian."

"Of my very special colleagues who are now gone from us, were Professor Westwood, Life President of the Entomological Society, and Dr. C. V. Riley, Entomologist of the Board of Agriculture of the U.S.A.; and Professor Huxley, in days when I sat on the Council of Education Committee of Economic Entomology, was a valued friend. It was marvellous to see how Huxley with his towering personality led a committee. On one occasion he asked if any one present would express an opinion on the subject under consideration, and he rather suddenly directed his attention to a certain member of committee, who was so startled he nearly got frightened out of his life."[1]

"The regular course of my work brings me into such constantly recurring communication with the Entomological Departments of our own Colonies, also of many of the U.S.A. States, and various Continental Societies or specialists, that I may venture to say that as occasion occurs we interchange—I mean the heads of the Departments and myself—friendly observations, very beneficial and pleasant to me. The plan of my work has long been to reply, if I could do so soundly, to every enquiry on the day of receipt. Often investigation is needed for scientific purposes, but a large proportion of the enquiries may be answered at once so far as the practical needs of the enquirers are concerned. For further purposes my custom is to work up anything new or involved that occurs, for use in the following Annual Report. I do not devolve on my specialist referees the researches (so far as I can ascertain the state of the case), but they tell me if my identification is correct, or correct it for me, and I quite invariably, if the matter be for publication, publish also my acknowledgment. The correspondence continues steadily all the year round, more of course in the warm seasons of the year than at other times, but even in winter it never ceases. My plan has generally been to store up all the observations of the growing (and conse-

[1] See "Letters from Huxley," pp. 85–87.

quently insect-attacking) times of the year till autumn, and then sort them and prepare them for the Annual Report of that year. If some favourite subject be under discussion the letters may be very numerous. I once had a run of 60, 80, to 100 a day for a short time, including on one day a total of 149—but of course on such an occasion I was obliged to get help to keep reply at all in hand. The steady letter work of the year I estimate at about 1,500."

Referring on December 27, 1889, to a proposal which had been made to procure an assistant to relieve her of the enormous pressure of work, she says :—

"I need not point out that, however agreeable the post might be to my so-called 'assistant,' to me the addition would be a trouble—loss of time and other inconveniences beyond telling. It would be more trouble to write to him than to attend myself, and as a referee he would be almost useless. My reference work is to the leading men of the world—those who are known, literally, as the authorities above all others on the special points ; thus I am in no way derogating from the respect I bear to Professor Harker's [1] knowledge, but who that knew anything would have cared for his opinion on *Icerya purchasi* (scale insect of orange trees)? Dr. Signoret's opinion carried all before it. Again, no one's opinion stands like that of Mr. G. B. Buckton on Aphides, and he communicates with me whenever I ask.

"On that most important agricultural matter, *Tylenchus devastatrix*, there is no one in England fit to form an opinion worth comparison with Drs. de Man and J. Ritzema Bos, by whom I am favoured, through being allowed any amount of communication. These, and men like these, pre-eminent each in his own line, are the referees that I personally am honoured by being allowed to ask aid from ; and in my own humble way sometimes I can reciprocate, but 'an assistant' would do me no good in any of these matters. And with regard to agricultural and applied bearings I do not want a *dictum*, but year by year by my own correspondence with agriculturists to work out on the fields the parts of the cases as they occur, and to give the points to the public in my reports. I am responsible for the entomological work of the R.A.S.E., and unless it goes through my hands I do not know what may be going on, and no one would know to whom to write, or, in fact,

[1] The late Allen Harker, Professor of Biology at the Royal Agricultural College, Cirencester.

anything definite about the matter, if there were an assistant. I have my own circle of helpers, my own paid special referee, by whom I reach specialists out of my circle, and my lady amanuensis in the house, besides my good sister's invaluable aid—always promptly and ably given. So long as I can I hope to keep my work in my own hands, and if it were not for the great masses sometimes sent me, which come because I have been (up to the present time) the only Official Entomologist here, the work would not have been so distressing. Professor Harker is, I believe, excellently qualified to hold a good and high entomological post, but not even Professor Riley or Professor Westwood would work a post without referees. Some day, I hope, he may be high in office; then he will, as I do now, have his organised corresponding staff."

"As a meteorological observer, while living at Isleworth my work consisted in taking notes on about eighteen different subjects once a day, beginning at 9 a.m., Greenwich time precisely. These included taking the readings of the maximum and minimum temperatures, and also those other thermometrical conditions, as of dry and wet bulb, solar, earth, and ground thermometers, &c.; likewise of rainfall in the past four-and-twenty hours, of the state of weather at the time; the nature of the clouds, with the amount and direction of them, and likewise the direction and estimated speed of wind. The time occupied out-of-doors in the observations was about twenty minutes, to which had to be added the barometrical reading with that of the attached thermometers, with corrections according to tables furnished for altitude of the barometer, and such minute errors in record of the thermometers as were shown by tables of error furnished by comparison with the instruments at the Royal Observatory, Kew. Altogether the work required some considerable amount of time, and also most scrupulous attention to accuracy, not to say some amount of personal self-denial, as whatever the weather might be at 9 a.m. the work had to be done. Perhaps there would be a thunderstorm, or at other times cold so great that my fingers almost froze to the instruments, as on one occasion, when the thermometer registered nearly down to zero."

Professor Westwood belonged to the good old academic type of scholar who made the responses in church in Latin. He was, till his death, Miss Ormerod's mentor from her

PLATE XX.

Miss Ormerod at her Meteorological Observation Station, near Isleworth.

To face p. 80.

initiation into Entomology, and she regarded him as the greatest living scientific authority in the broad lines of their common subject during the whole period of her advisory work. They "got on famously," and as she said, he "took the privilege," which she highly appreciated, "of knocking her work about," as the subjoined letter, written at an early stage of her career as an authoress, charmingly shows.

UNIVERSITY MUSEUM, OXFORD,
January 10, 1884.

MY DEAR MISS ORMEROD,—I congratulate you on the publication of your "Guide to Methods of Insect Life"—the nicest little Introduction to Entomology with which I am acquainted. You have been very fortunate in obtaining such a good series of woodcuts, many of which were new to me. Allow me to suggest one or two improvements after a hurried glance over the contents. It would have been well to have indicated more precisely the size of some of the objects figured; for instance, the locust, p. 28, is twice the size of the figure—whilst the earwig, on the same page, is about one-half the length of the figure. In p. 98, the Death's-head moth, which is twice the size of the Eyed-hawk moth, is represented smaller than it is in next page. In p. 118 the fly is the *Sirex juvencus*, not the commoner one *S. gigas*. In p. 125 the Bee parasite has not the front portion of the wings black, but as milky as the other part. In p. 73, line 8, for "glassy" read "glossy." I know you will thank me for these hurried suggestions, or I would not have troubled you with them.

Thanks for your kind enquiries. I am thankful to say that after two months' attack of bronchitis I am nearly all right again, but have been much confined to the house, although I have been wanting to go to London. My kind remembrance to your sister. We should be very glad if you could come and give us a visit for a short time.—Yours very truly, J. O. WESTWOOD.

The high terms of approval and appreciation of her work by Miss Ormerod's numerous foreign correspondents are shown in no halting manner in the subjoined letter :—

From Dr. J. A. Lintner, New York State Entomologist.[1]

ALBANY, N.Y.
May 29, 1889.

MY DEAR MISS ORMEROD,—I must congratulate you upon your last Report. It is excellent, and reflects

[1] Who died in Rome while on a visit to Europe.

great credit upon you. I am very glad that your letters have been so appreciated that it has been necessary to summon a lady private secretary to your aid. It will be a satisfaction to you that you will now be able to accomplish much more than before. I am led to think whether I should not ask our next Legislature to provide for an assistant for me.

Your kind letter of the 10th inst. was also duly received. How strange, and how very interesting to me, that you should discover *Cecidomyia leguminicola* (Gnat midge), red maggot, with you, as you have done, working at the root—only "infesting the root," and not, so far as known, attacking the head. If it occurs on the blossoms, you should have been able to find it there by the time that this reaches you, for, as I have somewhere mentioned, the nearly-mature larva shows a disposition to leave the clover heads very soon after they are picked. You ask if I have observed this form in other cecids of the clover. We have, so far as known, but one other clover cecid, and that is your introduced *C. trifolii* (Clover leaf midge). The thought suggests itself to examine some of my dried *leguminicola* larvæ. I am glad to have found in my collection examples preserved in alcohol of the larvæ which I had forgotten. As I put up quite a little quantity of them, I can spare you these, which I am sure will be acceptable to you.

Your investigation of the "warble" presence (p. 110) effect upon the beef-eater will, I am sure, be of much importance. One of our Western agricultural papers has commenced an investigation. Probably your studies and publications have incited them to it.

March 12, 1894.

In going carefully over several pages of your seventeenth report, which came to me last week, I asked myself, "Is not this the best report that Miss Ormerod has written?" You are pleased to bestow praise on my reports, which from you is agreeable to receive, but I think that I can judge of their true value, and very glad indeed would I be if I could feel that they were up to the standard of yours. These are far from words of flattery, but are said because I believe that you need encouragement. Your reports have high merit and value, beyond similar writings of any of your English contemporaries—yes, far beyond.—As ever, sincerely yours,

J. A. LINTNER.

CHAPTER XII

BIOGRAPHICAL SKETCH BY THE EDITOR (*continued*)

As a public lecturer Miss Ormerod achieved a high measure of success. The first effort in this capacity was made at the Royal Agricultural College, Cirencester, where as "Special Lecturer on Economic Entomology," she delivered six interesting and valuable addresses to audiences of about 120 students and professors on: (1) Injurious Insects; (2) Turnip Fly; (3) Effects of Weather on Insects; (4) Wire-worm; (5) Insect Prevention; (6) Œstridæ—Warble or Bot Flies. The first was given in October, 1881, and the last in June, 1884. On the first occasion Lord Bathurst, one of the Governors of the College, was present, and Miss Ormerod was placed between Principal McClellan on the one hand and Professor Harker (biology) on the other, as her sister Georgiana humorously remarked afterwards, "for fear her courage should fail and she run away." Her anxieties in the new capacity knew no bounds.

Although extremely nervous and anxious she succeeded in concealing this from an attentive and appreciative audience, and made an excellent appearance.[1] She declared that while walking from the drawing-room to the large lecture theatre at the opposite corner of the college quadrangle she could not utter a word, and on this, as on other somewhat similar exciting occasions, she experienced a drumming in her head which she failed to moderate by any attempted remedial measures. After about three years' experience as a supernumerary member of the college staff, it was found that the preliminary preparation of the lectures was robbing her steadily increasing general work of time which was inconveniently spared, and, although it was considered an honour to be invited to give special lectures, she felt it to be a duty to her main work to retire.

[1] The Editor, having been present, is able to give this statement on his own authority.

During this period one lecture was delivered before the "Institute of Agriculture," at South Kensington, in April, 1883, in the Lords of Council lecture hall, where as usual she was in a state of trepidation as to what might happen. The audience numbered about five hundred—two hundred and fifty of whom were Government students. The subject was "Insect Injuries to Farm Crops, and their Prevention." A number of minor incidents were nevertheless disturbing. To begin with, the driver who had been engaged to take the lecturer first to South Kensington and again in the evening to Isleworth, started on the wrong journey first, but the mistake was discovered before he had gone very far astray. Then a chairman had failed to appear and another had to be anxiously watched for at the door. A most suitable person was at last found in the President of the Entomological Society. All went well for a time until Miss Ormerod's sight on the left side wholly failed. Being subject to attacks of migraine from overwork, she thought one of these had come on, but on moving a little to the right she discovered that a brilliant light had been arranged to fall on the diagrams, and that to her great discomfort she had got into the line of it.

A rather amusing incident occurred as the last distraction. The object was to place the elements of Entomology before the students in the simplest form possible, but a few definitions were first necessary. They were told to realise in the words of Professor Westwood that insects were "Annulose animals, breathing by tracheæ, having the head distinct and provided in the adult stage with six articulated legs, and antennæ, subject also to a series of moultings previously to attaining perfection, whereby wings are ordinarily developed!"

The audience burst out cheering, thinking, as Professor Tanner[1] explained afterwards, that the scientific terms were being used as a joke.

Apropos of this experience she wrote on October 14, 1890, to Mr. Robert Newstead, "If I could find time I would like to form an instructive book, on the plan of which I enclose a few lines—so as to proceed gradually from a foundation well known to the pupils—thus:—

"*Q.* What is an insect? *A.* A fly is an insect, so is a moth or a butterfly, or a wasp, or a grasshopper, or a cricket.

"*Q.* Is a spider an insect? *A.* No.

[1] The organiser of and first Senior Examiner in the Agriculture Department, South Kensington.

"*Q*. Why not? *A*. Because it has eight legs, and never has any wings. Insects in their perfect state have six legs, and usually either one or two pairs of wings.

"*Q*. Why do you say in their perfect state? And so on.

"I believe that it is an absolute mistake to begin with a definition of an insect such as is usually given—half the words of which are utterly without meaning to the student."

Under strong pressure at a later date, Miss Ormerod delivered in the same hall a course of ten lectures in five consecutive days, on the "Orders of Insects," and these were reproduced in full in her "Guide to the Methods of Insect Life."

The organisation was defective, and very small audiences assembled. Professor Axe and others who gave special lectures in the same course had the same experience. Only £10 was paid to Miss Ormerod for her share of the work, a sum which did not cover outlays, and apart from the annoyance of the bungling the fatigue was great.

About this course, Professor Huxley wrote on November 11, 1883:—"Dear Miss Ormerod,—I am very glad to welcome you as a colleague—and I wish I could come and hear your lectures, being particularly ignorant of the branch of Entomology you have made your own. I shall be very glad if any of my students can find time to profit by your teaching—but I suspect that their hands are pretty full. We shall be very glad to have your sister's work and thank her for the trouble she has taken.—Ever yours very truly," &c.

When a copy of the book reached him in the following January he again wrote:—"Many thanks for your 'Guide to Insect Life.' I know enough of your portion of work to be sure that it will be clear, accurate, and useful, and I hope that the public will show a due appreciation of it. With best wishes, &c.

"T. H. HUXLEY."

Sir Joseph Hooker also wrote as follows:—

ROYAL GARDENS, KEW,
January 11, 1884.

DEAR MISS ORMEROD,—Pray accept my best thanks for the copy of your "Guide to Methods of Insect Life." I have read the first 50 pages at intervals of my work with great pleasure and interest. I was an Entomologist before I took to Botany, as was my father before me, and I do enjoy in my old age the account you give of the forgotten habits of the friends of my early youth. I think it is capitally well done and suited to its purpose, and I shall hope to interest my children with it in the holidays. With united sincere regards to you both, most truly yours,

JOS. D. HOOKER.

In March, 1882, a paper on "Injurious Insects" was read at a meeting of the Richmond Athenæum. The hall was so crammed that the Council were crushed up on the platform. "At the close of the lecture" (Lady Hooker writes) "Miss Lydia Becker, at that time a vigorous upholder of 'Woman's Rights,' rose to speak, and while praising Miss Ormerod's able lecture, instanced her work as 'being a proof of how much a woman could do without the help of man.' Miss Ormerod, in her reply, thanked Miss Becker, but begged to say that she had no right to the praise accorded to her on the ground of her work being so entirely that of a lone woman, for, she said, 'No one owes more to the help of man than myself. I have always met with the greatest kindness and most generous aid from my friends of the other sex, and without their constant encouragement my poor efforts would have had no practical result in being of benefit to my fellow men.'"

In the discussion which followed the lecture Sir Joseph Hooker "referred to the great benefit they had derived at Kew Gardens from Miss Ormerod's researches, remarking that to her and her sister (Georgiana) they owed some of the best illustrations they had of insect ravages upon plants. He could not but allude also to the elegance and clearness of the language employed by Miss Ormerod in her paper as an illustration that scientific matters might be put in a clear and simple form, so that all might understand them. . . . In conclusion he thanked Miss Ormerod and her sister for their services to science."

About 1888 an entomological "At Home" was given at Torrington House, St. Albans, when some sixty people assembled in the drawing-room and listened to a most interesting dissertation on the "Hessian Fly," given by the hostess in a friendly and informal conversational manner.

The Farmers' Club lecture in 1889 was felt by Miss Ormerod to be the most important and most gratifying of all similar public appearances. She prepared it with infinite care and, as the time fixed for its delivery approached, the state of nervous tension was great. Leading agriculturists were present, and a number of ladies came to make inquiries about all sorts of things, but probably the lecturer would have been equally well pleased had none of her own sex put in an appearance.

In 1882 Miss Ormerod was invited by the Lords of the Committee of Council on Education to become a member of a committee to advise in the improvement of the collections relating to Economic Entomology in the South Kensington and Bethnal Green Museums. The other members of committee were Professor Huxley, Mr. W. Thisleton Dyer, Professor J. O. Westwood, Mr. F. Orpen Bower, Professor Wrightson, and Mr. Moore—Colonel Donnelly and Sir Philip Cunliffe Owen being present officially. After serious consideration and a good deal of pressure from influential quarters, Miss Ormerod accepted the invitation and was a most useful member of committee till her withdrawal from it in April, 1886. She continued, however, to assist the supervision of the work, which went on for some time after. At the first meeting she was asked to prepare a scheme for a series of illustrations of Economic Entomology, and her suggestion of classifying injurious insects by the name of leading plant affected, and not by the Natural Orders of the creatures, was accepted. A collection of cases containing natural specimens in all stages of development, as well as accurate drawings of them, though never completed, was made, at first mainly under Professor Westwood's direction, but later on, under Miss Ormerod's supervision. Many of the specimens were taken from Mr. Andrew Murray's earlier contributions.

The collection was in 1885 removed from Bethnal Green to the Western Exhibition Galleries, South Kensington Museum. The value of Miss Ormerod's services and the esteem in which she was personally held by her associates in connection with the work of the committee, may be gathered from the subjoined letter sent to her by Professor Huxley.

March 12, 1883.

DEAR MISS ORMEROD,—Many thanks for the trouble you have taken. Your suggestion about utilising the figures which are not specially wanted for our purpose, for schools, seems to me excellent, and I hope you will bring it forward at our next meeting.

I hope our first discussion has convinced you that we want nothing but to achieve something useful. And as I have at any rate learned how to recognise practical knowledge and common sense, when I meet with them (they are not so common as people imagine) you will find me always ready to do my best to aid in carrying out your views. You really know more about the business than all the rest of us put together. Yours very truly,

T. H. HUXLEY.

While Miss Ormerod was associated with the Bethnal Green Museum she was asked to look at the proofs of a series of insect diagrams illustrating "Gardeners' Friends and Foes" being prepared for publication by the Science and Art Department. She found that an official of the Museum had been guilty of wholesale plagiarism, both in the coloured figures and the descriptive letterpress, and moreover that a number of figures of a popular kind had been introduced which were not drawn with scientific accuracy, that she felt conscientiously impelled to report the irregularities and deficiencies to the authorities. The results were that the diagrams were withdrawn (only a few sets having been presented for private use to certain fortunate individuals); and the removal of the official from the position of trust became a wholesome lesson to those who lightly make use without acknowledgment of the work of others.

At a later date she arranged the descriptive matter of a series of beautiful insect diagrams, the originals of which were drawn and coloured by her sister, Georgiana, for the Royal Agricultural Society, and referred to in the appended facsimile page of a letter addressed to the present writer, and again at p. 210 of her correspondence.

To Miss Anne Hartwell, Miss Ormerod's private secretary and confidential companion, I am indebted for many of the following incidents in the home life. The two sisters, though they were never robust, enjoyed comparatively good health, when Miss Hartwell, in May, 1888, went to reside with them, and were at all times very busy. Miss Ormerod (Georgiana) usually sat in the dining-room working at her diagrams and Miss Eleanor in the study. They generally worked all the morning, and in the afternoon they would

* * * * * *

AN EXCELLENT SPECIMEN OF MISS ORMEROD'S CLEAR AND CHARACTERISTIC WRITING IN WHICH SHE CONDUCTED HER VOLUMINOUS CORRESPONDENCE, PAGE 89 OPPOSITE.

May 12th 1891.

Torrington House
St. Albans.

Dear Prof Wallace.

Your letter was a great pleasure to us, and my sister was delighted to hope that her diagrams may be of such general use

I have now written to Mr Newman begging *him* to write *to you* replying to your enquiries, — and also to send (to your kind acceptance from my sister) by Parcel post samples of the diagrams so far as they are printed completely. That is with the exception of Ichn fly which you have.

You ought I am sure to *see* for yourself just what it is that we are about walk out together, take a drive, or pay calls. They frequently had visitors for a few days, and nephews and nieces would come and go—which was always a pleasure to them. They were devoted to each other and spent much time together. Miss Georgiana's death, on August 19, 1896, was a sad blow to Miss Eleanor, who missed her sister's companionship and sympathy dreadfully. To a casual observer time seemed to heal her wounded feelings and she appeared cheerful and bright, but in reality she was never again quite the same person—they had been such lifelong friends and companions.

In a letter to the Rev. C. J. Bethune she wrote on October 12, 1896:—

"I thank you gratefully for your kind comforting letter; believe me such words as yours are a great consolation and support to me, for I do miss my dear sister exceedingly.

"For her I fully hope that she is safe, and happy, and I love to think of her as without fears or doubts serving the Lord she so humbly trusted—but we were so completely one that I scarcely feel the same person without her. It was not only our sisterly affection and colleagueship, but she had such a good judgment that I am constantly longing for her sound sense to help me. There is no use in idle grief, and I am fairly well again. I have not at all put aside work through all my sorrow, for I felt this would answer no good purpose, and now I am working on my next Annual Report and am arranging to have a good portrait of her as a frontispiece (plate XXVII.). I think she would like it, and I am sure she would have been deeply grateful for the kind respect paid by the good friends whose friendship she so exceedingly valued. I scarcely know how to write about it—there is so much I should like to say. Perhaps I had better not write more, but indeed I value your beautiful words of comfort which I have repeatedly read."

A touchingly sympathetic notice of the death appeared in Miss Ormerod's Annual Report for 1896.

Miss Ormerod rose early, breakfasted at eight o'clock, and then read the "Times." On getting to work she made a special point of replying to inquiries first, saying it served no good purpose to keep people waiting for an answer; and, as a matter of fact, delay or hesitation found no place in any of her actions. Frequently there were specimens to examine and report upon, and probably to put aside in a place of safety to permit of maturation or further development and to undergo subsequent examination.

After the entomological work was finished—work which was a real pleasure, but proved a severe strain as the Annual Report was taking form—her personal correspondence was attended to. She wrote with great facility and with extraordinary rapidity and accuracy. She had many colonial and continental correspondents who held standing invitations to pay her visits, when in this country. Many came, and graciously she received them, and courteously and royally she entertained them with much pleasure to herself. None so honoured can ever forget the cordiality of the breezy welcome which, accompanied by her hearty and genuinely natural and friendly laugh, were merely harbingers of the intellectual treat and the other good things that were in store for them.

Among her most intimate immediate friends were Lord[1] and Lady Grimthorpe, the Bishop of St. Albans (Dr. Festing) and his sister, the Dean (Walter John Lawrence, M.A.), General and Mrs. Bigge, Colonel and Miss Cartwright, Dr. and Mrs. Norman, and Dr. Lipscomb and Miss Lipscomb. She was always pleased to see friends who called, and she was very witty and cheerful with them. It was not at all necessary that they should be scientific. One of the little group mentioned, simply and perhaps too modestly explains, "I always think that when Miss Ormerod sent for me, she descended to my level, and our conversation was generally on the most homely subjects. She would be most interested in the little events of our everyday life and thoroughly enter into our pleasures and enjoyments."

The lively sense of humour which has already been mentioned as a family characteristic remained with her throughout life. The following little anecdote told by Mrs. Evans of Rowancroft, Dorking, is also illustrative of the personal coolness and power of action in times of difficulty which were conspicuous among Miss Ormerod's attributes, and it shows also "the quietly determined manner in which she did some things."

"My poor little story was told to me a good many years ago. My aunt was lunching with some friends, and the peace of the entertainment was suddenly disturbed by the

[1] Edmund Beckett, K.C., LL.D., J.P., 1st Baron (1886), Chancellor and Vicar-General of York, 1877–1900. The work of the restoration of St. Albans Abbey was carried out under his direction. (See p. 296.)

arrival of a large and lively hornet. No one else ventured to interfere with the enemy, but Miss Ormerod waited quietly till the insect came close to her, caught it in her hand, and forthwith deposited it in one of the little chip boxes which she generally carried in her pockets. I leave you to imagine the astonishment and admiration of the other guests, and the quiet chuckle with which my aunt wound up her story with the remark, 'Of course I knew it was a "drone," by the length of the antennæ.'"

Miss Ormerod was not the least nervous in the sense of being afraid. When just a girl living at Sedbury she became the centre of admiration of the workmen on her father's estate by fearlessly seizing a farmyard dog by the back of the neck and hauling him off her own dog, who had been rudely assaulted. Great was the applause of "Miss Eleanor's sperrit."

Another incident with a dog of a much more dangerous character is best given in her own words: "I only remember one instance of rabies. The animal attacked was one of two beautiful Clumber spaniels which had been left one day at our house with a message that the sender, a friend of my brother, desired him to select one of them, and accept it as a gift. The two pretty creatures, named Cæsar and Pompey, were introduced into our establishment, and one of them—Cæsar—became a great favourite with my father. How long it was after their arrival I do not remember, but one day Cæsar vanished, and in the course of the afternoon, although he was not one of the house dogs, he came to me as I was standing in the front hall. To my astonishment when I noticed him as usual, he gave a kind of scream, or extraordinary howl, such as I had never heard before, and I saw that the expression of his eyes was wild and distressed to an entirely unnatural degree. The strange scream made me suspect what might be wrong, and I called one of the head men. We took the dog, who was perfectly gentle, into the butler's pantry and shut the door so that he might not escape, whilst we tried to find out what was amiss. I did not much like the business, but it happened I was the only one at home, excepting a lady relation, who, thinking "discretion the better part of valour," mounted herself *pro tem.* out of harm's way, on the top of a very large stone table, and awaited results in safety. I knew that offering water was a very partial test, but I had some poured out. The effect was instantaneous. The moment the poor dog heard the sound he almost flew to me, as if for protection, and tried to

PLATE XXI.

AP ADAM OAK, SEDBURY PARK.

HEDGEHOG OAK, SEDBURY PARK.

To face p. 92.

wrap his head in my dress so as to exclude the sound, calling out as if in great trouble. I had no right to have my father's favourite dog destroyed on a suspicion in his temporary absence, and the dog so far was not violent; it appeared to me that the only reasonable course to adopt was to have him chained securely and led away to an empty stable, where he was fastened to a pole and the door shut. By this course no harm could happen, except in prolonging the poor creature's sufferings. These, however, though increasingly violent, were not endured for very long. By the time my father returned, in about an hour, the dog was tearing the woodwork all around him to pieces. He was at once destroyed, the attack being pronounced, by those better versed in the matter than myself, undoubtedly a case of rabies."

Miss Ormerod's brother, Dr. E. L. Ormerod, of Brighton, author of "British Social Wasps," testified to the courage and skill with which she assisted him in taking the hanging wasps' nests from trees. The "Ap Adam" oak shown in plate XXI. which she climbed after a hornet's nest by means of the library folding ladder, was one of the very ancient hollow oaks in Sedbury Park, about one-third of a mile from the house. She had a sick headache next day about which her brother John made the sympathetic (?) remark, "If young ladies will play at lamplighters they must take the consequences!" The Hedgehog oak, at the root of which in plate XXI. Miss Ormerod is seen sitting in rather an uncomfortable position, was another hollow remnant of the primeval forest. She had remarked that she thought she was sitting on a wasps' nest when Waring, her second brother, promptly admonished her in the interests of the safety of the party to "sit tight"! The two hollow shells of what must have been at one time splendid timber trees, were historically interesting, having been boundary marks of the country referred to in the time of Edward III. Both trees have been cleared away and the ancient oak now known as that of "Ap Adam" stands only a few hundred yards from the original tree, within the moat which formerly surrounded old Badam's Court. There are several other very ancient oaks in the park. Two on the left of the carriage drive, going in the direction of the mansion house, were christened "Darby and Joan" by Miss Ormerod.

On one occasion the eldest sister, Mary, had the misfortune to run a crochet hook through her hand. The mother fainted away. Miss G. S. Ormerod, who supplied this information, concludes, "My Aunt Eleanor fetched her forceps, nipped off the hook and drew out the stem without waiting for the doctor's arrival, showing not only her courage but her presence of mind." The same authority goes on to say:—

"She was very fond of children and young people. When staying at Sedbury, we always enjoyed our walks with her. She made everything interesting. She taught me a great deal about insects, helped me to begin a collection of butterflies, &c., showing me how to destroy them mercifully and how to set them out properly. I remember stuffing a splendid dragon-fly under her superintendence.

"Fully occupied as her life was up to the time of her last illness, yet she was always full of sympathy and interest for her poorer neighbours, always ready to assist in any good work that came before her.

"You may like to hear how my aunt was beloved by the servants for her practical kindness and for the keen interest she took in all outdoor surroundings. Any curiosity discovered by them, whether animal or vegetable, was always carefully brought in for her inspection. Many were the snakes, birds, nests, insects, fungi, &c., handed to her, especially at the time when she did so much modelling."

She maintained throughout a practical interest in the survivors of her mother's old servants, and she extended her kindness and thoughtfulness to those of her own household. Her strong loyalty was curiously instanced on one of these occasions, on the King's accession to the throne, when she summoned all her household, including outdoor servants, and produced some rare old white port in which they drank the King's health. She subscribed liberally to St. Albans' charities and other public objects in the Abbey parish in which she lived, as well as in St. Michael's, where she attended church. Dr. Lipscomb gives, in a few words, "An instance of her great generosity, so well known to all who were intimate with her, though she ever did such deeds by stealth and blushed to find them fame." He goes on: "I may mention a day she asked me to see her. Being rather late I apologised, telling her that the annual meeting of the governors of our local hospital detained me. She said she hoped we had had a successful meeting, and on my saying 'Yes, with the exception that the accounts showed a deficit of some thirty odd pounds,' she immediately produced her cheque book and gave me a cheque for the amount." She also extended personal sympathy and practical help to many of her poor neighbours by whom she was loved and esteemed.

She never lost taste for the pastime of modelling in plaster of Paris, and at leisure moments, when unable to go out of doors, she would occupy spare time in this way. She modelled some beautiful specimens of common fruits and made the cast of her own hand. In the evening, when tired of writing, she would read or crochet. Her great skill in what is generally regarded as exclusively woman's work is independently testified to by Miss Emma Swan, niece of Professor Westwood, who is so well able to speak with authority, in the following words: "What particularly struck me as a young girl at the time I visited her was the very beautiful needlework she found time to do, and pleasure in doing. Whatever she did, she seemed to do well!" From the same source we learn that "she sang and played the piano very well indeed." She also composed music with facility and might have developed musical tastes, but for the overpowering love of science which was the absorbing interest of her life.[1]

We have it on excellent authority that the very greatest pleasure of all her public recognitions was experienced on April 14, 1900, in the McEwan Hall, Edinburgh, when the LL.D. of the University was conferred upon her in company with a group of distinguished recipients of that honour[2] before an assemblage of about 3,000 people. The

[1] In addition to the individual appreciation of her correspondents and fellow-workers, Miss Ormerod's position in the world of science was recognised by scientific and educational bodies in a manner which was most gratifying to her. She was Honorary Doctor of Laws of the University of Edinburgh; Fellow of the Royal Meteorological Society, London; (for ten years) Consulting Entomologist to the Royal Agricultural Society of England; (for three years) Examiner in Agricultural Entomology in the University of Edinburgh (1896–8); Fellow of the Entomological Society, London; Hon. Fellow of the Entomological Society, Stockholm; Member of the Entomological Society, Washington, U.S.A.; Member of the Association of official Economic Entomologists, Washington, U.S.A.; Hon. Member of the London Farmers' Club; Honorary and Corresponding Member of the Royal Agricultural and Horticultural Society of South Australia; Hon. Member of the Entomological Society of Ontario, and Corresponding Member of the Field Naturalists' Club of Ontario, Canada; and Member of the Eastern Province Naturalists' Society, Cape Colony.

[2] List of the Hon. Graduates of 1900, given in the alphabetical order in which they graduated:—(1) Horatio Robert Forbes Brown, J.P.,

trials of the occasion, which are described in her letters, were greatly lessened by the courtesy and kindness and whispered words of encouragement of his Excellency, the American Ambassador, who was placed beside her during the ceremonial, and preceded her in undergoing the ordeal of capping. In presenting her to the Vice-Chancellor (Principal Sir Wm. Muir) the Dean of the Faculty of Law (Sir Ludovic Grant) said, with his usual eloquence :—

"A duty now devolves upon you, sir, which has devolved upon none of your predecessors, and of which the performance will render the present occasion memorable in the annals of the University. Our roll of Hon. Graduates in Law contains the names of many illustrious men, but you will search it in vain for the name of a woman. To-day, however, a new roll is to be opened—a roll of illustrious women ; and it is matter for congratulation that this roll should begin with a name so honoured as that of Miss Ormerod.

"The pre-eminent position which Miss Ormerod holds in the world of science is the reward of patient study and unwearying observation. Her investigations have been chiefly directed towards the discovery of methods for the prevention of the ravages of those insects which are injurious to orchard, field, and forest. Her labours have been crowned with such success, that she is entitled to be hailed as the protectress of agriculture and the fruits of the earth—a beneficent Demeter of the nineteenth century. It would take long to enumerate her contributions to Entomological and Phenological literature, but I may select for mention the valuable series of reports extending over twenty years, the preparation of which involved correspondence with all parts of the world. Remarkable, too, is the list of the honours which she has received. She was the first lady to be admitted a Fellow of the Royal Meteorological Society, and she has been awarded the Silver Medal of the 'Société Nationale d'Acclimatation' of France. To these distinctions

Editor of the Calendars of State Papers (Venetian) for the Public Record Office. (2) His Excellency the Hon. Joseph Hodges Choate, Ambassador for the United States of America, London. (3) Miss Eleanor A. Ormerod, F.R.Met.Soc., F.E.S. (4) C. D. F. Phillips, M.D., LL.D. (5) The Rev. Thomas Smith, M.A., D.D., lately Professor of Evangelistic Theology in the Free Church College, Edinburgh. (6) William Ritchie Sorley, M.A., Regius Professor of Moral Philosophy, University of Aberdeen. (7) Anderson Stuart, M.D., Professor of Physiology in the University of Sydney.

the University of Edinburgh, sensible of her conspicuous services, and not unmindful of her generous benefactions, now adds its Doctorate in Laws."

The honour referred to, conferred by our cultured neighbours across the channel, was publicly announced in the press in the following words :—

"At the Annual Meeting on the 25th of June, 1891, of the Société Nationale d'Acclimatation de France, M. Le Myre de Vilers, president, in the chair, the large silver medal of the Society, bearing the portrait of Geoffrey Saint-Hilaire, was decreed to Miss Eleanor A. Ormerod, of St. Albans, England, for her work in Economic or Applied Entomology."

To a confidential correspondent she wrote, "You will believe that this pleases me very much."

Plate XXII. shows this medal with three other silver and two gold medals that were presented to Miss Ormerod between the years 1870 and 1900 by home and foreign institutions.

Miss Ormerod preserved very few letters except those necessary for scientific or business purposes, and these she classified and fastened into books for convenience of reference. Nothing else, and especially nothing which if returned to the writer, would hereafter lead to unpleasantness, escaped ordeal of fire. After keeping letters on general subjects for a few days, she would tear them up. The result is that, of the mass of interesting contributions on many subjects, which poured in to the oracle, first of Isleworth and latterly of St. Albans, from all sorts and conditions of men and women, the few sample letters written by prominent public men and reproduced in these pages, are almost all that remain. To some of her relatives she wrote very amusing letters, but—no doubt inspired by the desire to avoid all possible danger of hurting the feelings of people referred to—she exacted the promise that they should not be preserved.

KEY TO MEDALS PRESENTED TO MISS ORMEROD AND SHOWN ON PLATE XXII., OPPOSITE.

Royal Horticultural Society,
Victoria Medal of Honour,
1900.
(Gold Medal.)

Royal Horticultural Society.
For Collection of Economic
Entomology.
1870.
(Silver Medal.)

Société Nationale d'Acclimatation
de France.
Entomologie Appliquée.
1899.
(Silver Medal.)

University of Moscow, 1872
Emperor Peter I., 30th May,
1672.
Emperor Alexander II., 30th May,
1872.
(Gold Medal.)

International Health Exhibition,
London, 1884.
(Silver Medal.)

Moscow Polytechnic Exhibition,
1872.
(Silver Medal.)

PLATE XXII.

MISS ORMEROD'S MEDALS, RECEIVED BETWEEN 1870 AND 1900, AS RECOGNITION BY SCIENTIFIC BODIES OF HER SCIENTIFIC WORK.

(pp. 96, 304.)

To face p. 98.

CHAPTER XIII

LETTERS TO COLONEL COUSSMAKER AND MR. ROBERT SERVICE

Surface Caterpillars—Leopard and Puss Moths—"Hill-Grubs" of the Antler Moth.

THE letters in this the first chapter of correspondence (dealing with a number of moths, the caterpillars of which are destructive to vegetation), were written while Miss Ormerod was resident at Isleworth, and after she had issued seven of her Annual Reports. Apart from the Entomology discussed, the letters show how ready she was to recognise and to commend the meritorious scientific work of others.

To Colonel Coussmaker, Westwood, near Guildford.

DUNSTER LODGE, SPRING GROVE, ISLEWORTH,
August 1, 1885.

DEAR SIR,—Perhaps the best way I can reply to your inquiry about the coloured sheets is to enclose the short description, on the wrapper of one of my reports.[1]

I should mention, though, that they are the property of the Royal Agricultural Society; I only drew them. The insects

[1] "ROYAL AGRICULTURAL SOCIETY OF ENGLAND.

"Coloured Diagrams of Insects Injurious to Farm Crops, suitable for Elementary Schools. Prepared by Miss E. A. Ormerod, F.R.Met.Soc., Hon. Consulting Entomologist to the Society. A series of Six Diagrams, viz.: Large White Cabbage Butterfly; Turnip Fly or Flea Beetle; Beet Fly; Wireworm and Click Beetle; Hop Aphis or Green Fly, with Ladybird; Daddy Longlegs or Crane Fly. In various stages, with methods of prevention. On paper, 5s.; for each Diagram, 1s. Mounted on linen and varnished, 8s.; for each Diagram, 1s. 6d. Procurable from the Secretary."

are drawn greatly magnified, with a view to hanging the sheets on walls of schools. The history, and the simplest means of prevention are given in the very plainest words I could find.

Have you my current report? It contains a good deal on that great pest the Ox warble fly (fig. 5)—contributed by practical men—cattle owners, veterinary observers and the like. I would, with the greatest pleasure, ask your acceptance of a copy if you would permit me to do so. If you have studied its habits in India, I should greatly like to be in communication with you on the subject. The Colonial Company procured me a few estimates of damage to hides—which were of much service as showing comparative amount of injury in different parts of the globe, but I much want to find whether in India the larva is found to penetrate below the subcutaneous tissue into the flesh. I am aware from one of my contributors connected with inspecting army supplies in India, that at one time meat for the troops was apt to be so damaged from what he considered to be this attack, that it was to some extent useless. The locality was not far from Kurrachee. If you, as a student of insect life, could give me any information on this point, I should be thankful for the addition to the notes I am still collecting.

August 4, 1885.

Many thanks to you for so kindly taking the trouble to write about the injury to flesh possibly caused by the Warble maggot; it would be of great service to know about it. Doubtless your care of your cattle had a great deal to do with their being free from injury—if we could but get even the moderate amount of care applied which is needed to put on a dressing when attack is seen it would make an enormous difference.

The Dart or Turnip moth caterpillar is doing damage now—and I do not believe there is a better remedy than scraping out the grubs, but this is very troublesome till they are larger. I see in a report on the "Cutworms," as they call these creatures in the U.S.A., that there is very much less injury from them on ground which has been well salted. It is thought that the salt drawn up into the plant makes it distasteful to the caterpillars. I do not know how this may be, but in a district of the Eastern Counties reported from last year—where previously they had been quite set against anything "artificial"—they were finding the turnips on salted lands answered very much the best. I should much like to try the effect of watering with salt and water, at a safe strength, but from my own garden being so perpetually used for trial ground it is getting free of regular pests. I have found watering with soft soap and a little mineral oil (pp. 66–67, eighth report, 1884), act well on these caterpillars. The application appeared to paralyse the creature so that it could not get away from the poisonous effects of the mixture, which is a very important point.

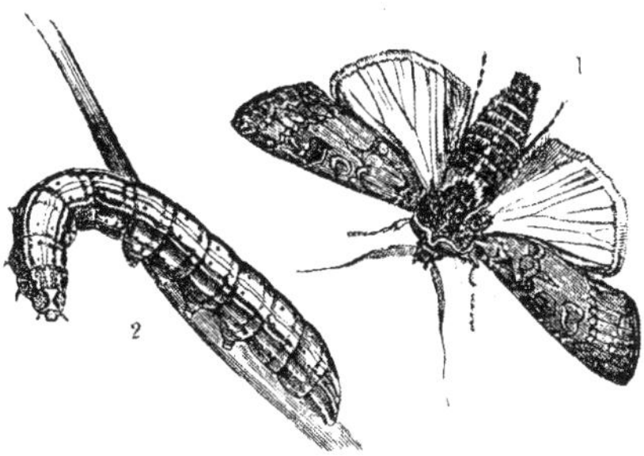

(*a*) 1, Turnip moth ; 2, caterpillar.

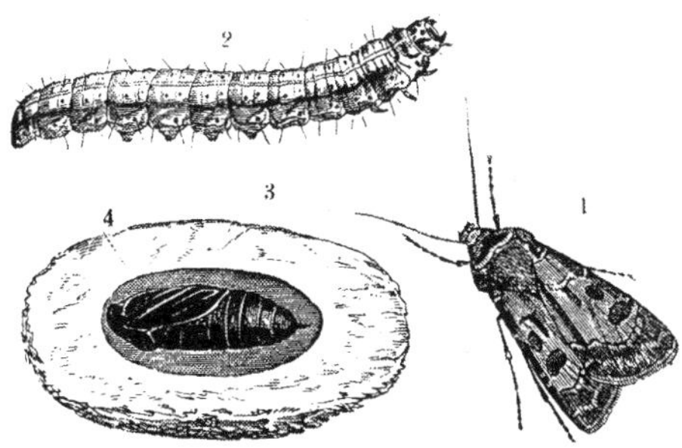

(*b*) 1, Heart-and-dart moth ; 2, caterpillar ; 3, chrysalis in earth-cell.

FIG. I.—SURFACE CATERPILLARS : OF THE TURNIP OR DART MOTH, *AGROTIS SEGETUM*, OCHSENHEIMER, AND OF THE HEART-AND-DART MOTH, *AGROTIS EXCLAMATIONIS*, LINN.

I found this mixture act well on Cabbage green fly, and if you should try it I shall be very much obliged for any observation. The great point is to mix the ingredients at boiling heat. I would try whether the strength noted was safe for any special plant. I rather think it is for cabbage, but certainly not for young leafage of roses. I shall be very glad if I can be of any help in the matter.

TORRINGTON HOUSE, ST. ALBANS,
January 26, 1888.

Many thanks for your note received this morning. I shall hope to add some of it to my Turnip Caterpillars paper, which is not yet gone to press. Thank you for the offer of the specimens, but I do not quite see my way to showing live ones yet. My lecture [at the London Farmers' Club] is a terribly anxious prospect to myself, but I can but do my best, and I am endeavouring with the utmost care to form something that may be acceptable, but I am sure you will believe me that to address such a skilled audience is rather anxious work. I should much like to lay before the members of the Club some ideas for their consideration as

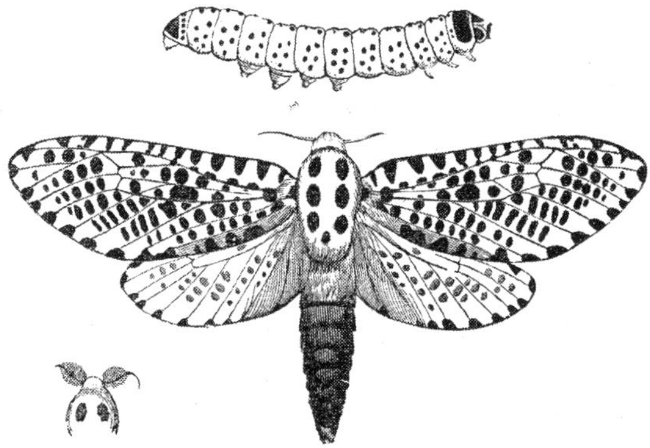

Female, head of male, and caterpillar.

FIG. 2.—WOOD LEOPARD MOTH, *ZEUZERA ÆSCULI*, LINN.

to how some reasonable amount of plain serviceable information might be got abroad. I do not believe in all this lecturing, examining and talking of classification. To my thinking it is beginning at the wrong end, and that the learners need first to make sure of their facts in the field and classify them when they have got them, if they do it at all.

February 17, 1890.

I have examined your caterpillars carefully, and I find that of the oak stem to correspond exactly with the larva of the Wood leopard moth, the *Zeuzera æsculi*. This is commonly found in (or at least it is usually sent me from) wood of fruit trees, but it attacks oak as well as forest trees of various kinds. Your specimen has also one of the characteristic habits of ejecting brown fluid from its mouth on disturbance. I think you have my "Manual," and there you would find a figure of the moth and larva. Your specimen is rather full coloured, but they vary greatly in this respect.

Your other caterpillar is a Lepidopterous larva, but I cannot name it with certainty. It is quite possible that it is the larva of the "Hornet Clearwing," the *Trochilium* (=*Sesia*) *bembeciforme*, but I have never seen a specimen, although the attack is said to be common, especially to

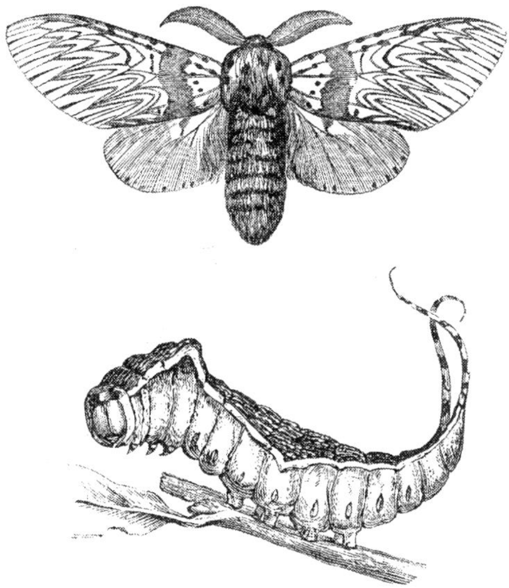

Male and caterpillar (life size).

FIG. 3.—PUSS MOTH, *DICRANURA VINULA*, LINN.

Salix caprea. The attack is stated to be mostly in the lower part of the stem. I think that you very likely have Loudon's "Arboretum" in your library, and if so you would find some good notes and fair figures of the hornet-like moth and its larva and pupa *in situ* in the wood at pp. 1481 and 1482, vol. iii. The larva is nearly dead now, so that the form is altered, but I do not see any reason against it being this kind; still I cannot say it is.

I have a very curious report of much damage attributed to Puss moth caterpillars at a locality in Lincolnshire, and am waiting with much interest for specimens to see what the cause can be. I rather expect it will be rabbits!

Yours very truly,

ELEANOR A. ORMEROD.

[The following notes by Mr. Robert Service[1] are explanatory of subjoined correspondence.

"THE 'HILL-GRUB' (the caterpillar of the Antler moth, *Charæas graminis*). Sheep-farmers are threatened with another plague. The 'hill-grub' has often done considerable damage to the upland grass-lands, notably in the years from 1830 to 1835. Just now complaints are rife from farms in many parts of the wide districts ravaged by the Voles[2] (in 1891–92–93). As usual the farmers look on these 'hill-grubs' as very sudden arrivals, but this is not the case, for last autumn the moths which these larvæ produce were in extraordinary swarms, and far in advance of their normal numbers. I remember noting at the end of last September when coming down from the neighbourhood of Loch Dungeon one evening in the twilight, how unusually abundant the Antler moths were flying. The evening was mild and very moist, and just as we got on to the level ground at the outside of a moss of perhaps six acres in extent, we found Antler moths flying in countless myriads in every direction. The time was 6.40, and there was still enough of the gloaming left to see the moths quite distinctly on every side, flying just below the level of the grass-seed heads.

"On August 23rd I happened to be going across the farm of Townhead, in Closeburn parish, Dumfriesshire, and about 10.10 a.m. the Antler moths appeared in myriads. Thousands upon thousands of them were flying in all directions, most of them just amongst and over the flowering heads of the spret, *Juncus articulatus*; but many were flying higher in the air, and some mounted up out of sight. It was a wonderful scene, and one that I would not have cared to miss. The effect was altogether different to that presented by the

[1] These observations are extracted from part of a series published under the geographical *nom de plume* of "Mabie Moss," this (sometime) moss district having been long under the observation of Mr. Service—not a young lady, as Miss Ormerod conjectured, but a well-known ornithologist who also takes a considerable interest in Economic Entomology (ED.).

[2] *Vide* Report of the Departmental Committee appointed by the Board of Agriculture to inquire into a plague of field voles in Scotland (Sir Herbert E. Maxwell, M.P., Chairman). Eyre and Spottiswoode, 1893.

evening flight I saw near Loch Dungeon in the previous autumn.

"A party of gentlemen fishing from near the Holm of Dalquhairn for some five or six miles down the Ken found all the trout they caught perfectly crammed with these 'hill-grub' caterpillars. Old shepherds will tell of times when they were so numerous that after sudden thunder-showers the sheep-drains have been completely dammed up with their bodies. The moth deposits its eggs, which produce larvæ that descend to and feed mostly about the roots of grasses during the autumn and early winter. After hybernation they commence in March and April to feed again with redoubled energy, and they turn to pupæ at the end of June and during July, producing the moths again in a few weeks (the perfect insect flies during August and September). Thus their cycle of existence in these various

FIG. 4.—ANTLER OR GRASS MOTH, *CHARÆAS GRAMINIS*, AND CATERPILLARS.

stages extends the whole year round. Their worst natural enemy is the common rook at the season when these birds betake themselves and their young broods to the hills, and I have reason to believe that many other birds devour them. The blackheaded gull, *Larus ridibundus*, and the common gull, *L. canus*, are very fond of the larvæ. Curlews take a good many, golden plovers and lapwings pick them up in numbers. Cuckoos also feed upon them, and I have found the stomachs of snow buntings, shot on the hills at midwinter, filled with these grubs" (R. S.).

Miss Ormerod says: "The caterpillars, when full grown, are about an inch or rather more long, with brown head, and the body of a deep bronze colour, exceedingly shiny on the back and on the upper part of the sides. The bronze colour is divided lengthwise by three pale lines, the back and side stripes meeting or almost meeting above the tail, and another narrower pale stripe or line runs lower down along each side."]

To Robert Service, Esq., Maxwelltown, Dumfries.

TORRINGTON HOUSE, ST. ALBANS,
August 1, 1894.

DEAR SIR,—It is many years since you gave me any of your good observations, but indeed I would gladly have profited by them, and it was only lately that I knew you were continuing them. Perhaps Mr. Bailey, the editor,[1] may have mentioned to you that I was so struck with the paper which he sent me, in which you mention *C. graminis*, that interpreting the *nom de plume* ("Mabie Moss") literally, I wrote to him expressing my admiration and asking if I might be put in communication with the writer; and now may I prefer the request to yourself that, if you please, you will kindly tell me anything you are inclined to favour me with about this recent outbreak of the *C. graminis*. Would it not be of great interest if we could make out something more about the parasites? There are, firstly, the threadworms—*Mermis*. Do you chance to have identified them? I have got no further than the specialist to whom I sent specimens, thinking they were most likely *Mermis albicans*—but this he was going to investigate. Then there is the bacterian infestation—the "flacherie,"[2] as they call it in silk-worms. This seems to me of great practical interest; and, thirdly, the larval parasitism of the *C. graminis* larvæ. I had so exceedingly few specimens that I could not work up the matter, but, whilst one cocoon sent to me appeared to be that of an Ichneumon, the only large larva which I found certainly in many respects resembled that of a *Tachina* fly. I should greatly like, if agreeable to yourself, to hear from you again on entomological matters. Besides the pleasure, it is a great advantage to me to have contributions of skilled and experienced information, and I would indeed most scrupulously acknowledge to whom I was indebted.

August 3, 1894.

I am much obliged to you for taking the trouble to send the morsels of *C. graminis* caterpillars. As you say, I am afraid we could hardly get results from them, but still with bacteria presence I do not know but dried bits may show something when moistened, so I am keeping them for the

[1] Of the "Dumfries Herald and Courier."
[2] Disease caused by *Micrococcus bombycis*.

present. That enormous appearance of the imagos must have been a wonderful sight; I should have liked to see it—and what (I wonder) will be the result?

Pretty surely I suppose there will be egg-laying and a consequent presence of larvæ? But if your convenience allowed you to inspect say two months hence, would it not be very interesting to ascertain—absolutely make sure—whether there is a presence of the "hill grubs" or whether the parasitism of their parents has been transmitted, to the weakening or destruction of their descendants? If we found no grubs, nor grubs with "flacherie" present, what a very interesting discovery this would be!

September 14, 1894.

I am writing a few lines at once on receipt of your letter, first to thank you for your geographical note, which helps me very much. [These attacks of "hill-grubs" were more or less general over the hill country of Kirkcudbrightshire and over the adjacent sheep-farms in Ayrshire, the Dumfriesshire hills, and the contiguous sheep-farm districts in Lanarkshire, Peebles, Selkirk, and Roxburgh. Seven counties were affected to my knowledge. R.S.] What a wide-spread outburst this has been! But I also write to beg you not to suppose for one minute that I see any reason to doubt what we have had laid down for such a length of time about date of hatching of larvæ of *C. graminis*. Mr. Wm. Buckler[1] "lumped" his observations of this and two other species, and it seems to me that what happened to caterpillars, which I gather he observed in captivity, in no way militates against correctness of other people's out-of-door observations.

With many thanks for all the information you give me.

November 20, 1894.

I am very much obliged to you for the very interesting note you have let me have about these dipterous parasites[2] of the *C. graminis*. How fortunate you have been to secure them, and in such good order too! As you have been kind enough to give me two of your specimens, I think I will presently send one of them to Mr. Meade, of Bradford. I am sure he would value it very much, and would doubtless identify it, which would be a help to me, for as you know I do not like to rest without verification on my own

[1] In *Larvæ of British Butterflies and Moths* (Ray Society).

[2] *Exorista lota*, "not an uncommon fly, and parasitic on several *Lepidoptera*."—Meade.

dipterous identifications. You would not mind about this part, as doubtless if you have not yourself identified, Mr. Percy H. Grimshaw, Museum of Science and Art, Edinburgh, would see to it (pp. 149, 185).

Do you ever come across the so-called "Turnip Mud-beetle," *Helophorus rugosus*, in your country? I had the beetle some years ago, as doing harm to turnip leafage, but we could not find the larva. Lately we found a larva doing a deal of mischief in the same neighbourhood by burrowing galleries in the top of turnips, and it struck me we might have what we wanted to complete the history. So I sent it to Canon Fowler, and he identified as beyond doubt *Helophorus* and being found where *H. r.* resorts, it is hardly open to doubt that we have got parent and child. Please excuse a short letter, for I am working as hard as I can manage.

Yours very truly,
ELEANOR A. ORMEROD.

[The parasitic and other enemies of the "hill-grub" are so effective in their attacks that in the year following a great increase in numbers a normal level of occurrence is invariably restored.]

CHAPTER XIV

LETTERS TO MR. WILLIAM BAILEY.

The Ox warble—Its destruction by the Aldersey Schoolboys—Annual gift of prize money—The Royal Party at St. Albans' Show.

IN addition to the entomological value of the next group of letters dealing chiefly with Ox warbles, Miss Ormerod's unselfish interest in promoting a wider knowledge of her subject is well shown in her words of appreciation and encouragement to Mr. Bailey in connection with his work (especially in relation to the success of correspondence with the Duke of Westminster), and the practical inducements, as well as sympathy, extended to his pupils.

To Wm. Bailey, Esq., Aldersey, Grammar School, Bunbury, Tarporley, Cheshire.

TORRINGTON HOUSE, ST. ALBANS,
November 24, 1887.

DEAR MR. BAILEY,—I am very much obliged to you indeed for kindly letting me see the documents which I now return, after most careful perusal, with many thanks. It is indeed satisfactory that the good work of our boys (destroying warbles), should have given such valuable help in this matter, which is so important to all who have to do with cattle, and consequently to the nation. The approval of His Grace the Duke of Westminster (so kindly given, too) will add great weight, and I am heartily glad also to see the Hon. Cecil Parker's confirmation from personal experiment and knowledge of the soundness of the plan and its success. I think if I can get time that I will write to him, to mention how strongly the many letters which I have received this year confirm the good effects of removal of the maggots (2 of fig. 5, and fig. 7), and likewise the prevention (in almost every case mentioned) of summer disturbance of the cattle.

I thought you would not object to my keeping a copy of your letter to his Grace.

The Committee of the "London Farmers' Club" which I daresay you know more about than I do, but which I believe to be the great Farmers' Club of England, has sent me an urgent request to read them a paper on Injurious Insects, at

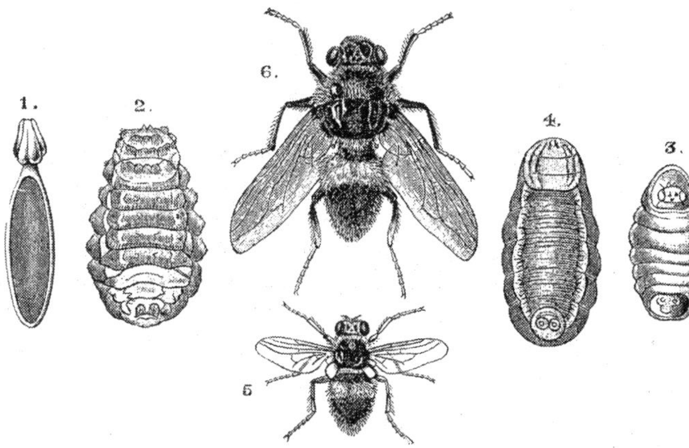

1, Egg; 2, maggot; 3 and 4, chrysalis-case; 5 and 6, fly. 3 and 5, natural size, after Bracy Clark; the other figures after Brauer, and all magnified.

FIG. 5.—OX WARBLE FLY, OR BOT FLY, *HYPODERMA BOVIS*, DE GEER.

their meeting place, the Salisbury Square Hotel, London, in next April. Professor Herbert Little, one of the Council of the Royal Agricultural Society, brought me the message, and at first I felt fairly frightened at the idea, and tried to "make excuse," for it is a somewhat anxious prospect (in the words of old John Knox) for a gentlewoman to look in the face of so many "bearded men and not be over much afraid," but I got such serious remonstrance, almost rebuke, from various quarters that I have consented to endeavour to prepare as good a paper as I can, and read it myself. Now if you permit me—I think that in the portion about warbles it would be very useful (and much more telling than any words of my own) to give your terse, clear and attractively worded account of what really has happened.

The following extract is the chief part of the letter by Mr. Bailey to the Duke of Westminster (October 28, 1887):—

MY LORD DUKE,—I was very thankful to see by last Saturday's Chester *Chronicle*, that at the Chester Dairy Show you drew the attention of our farmers to the enormous loss caused by the presence of ox warbles in our cattle. During the past three years, I have been directing the notice of my

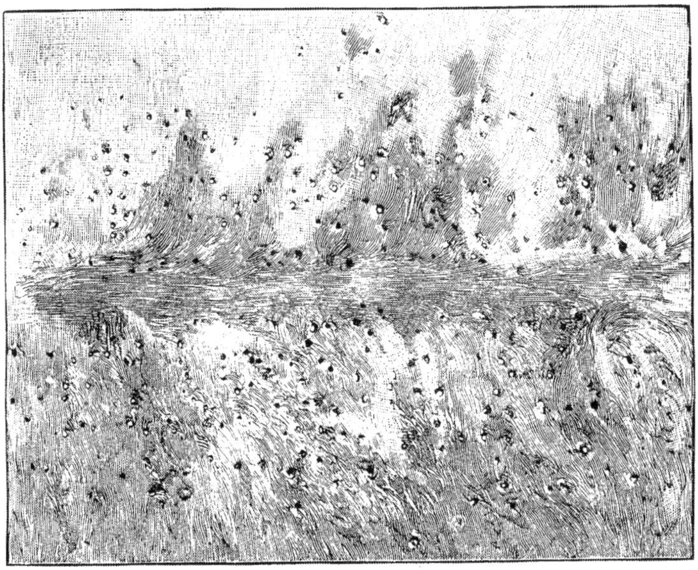

FIG. 6.—PIECE OF YEARLING SKIN WITH 402 WARBLE-HOLES.
(*Greatly reduced by photography.*)

pupils to the mischief done by these warbles, and, as we have now nearly stamped out this pest in Bunbury Parish, it has occurred to me that your Grace might be interested in learning the course which we have taken, and also in seeing how very easily our farmers might get rid of this enemy. The great majority of the boys in this school are either sons of farmers, or of farm labourers. After the boys had received from me a short lesson on the Warble fly, they were asked to examine their cattle at home, and to

FIG. 7.—PIECE OF UNDER SIDE OF WARBLED HIDE ; WARBLES ABOUT HALF SIZE.

From a Photo by Messrs. Byrne, Richmond, Surrey.

bring to school as many specimens as they could collect of the maggots of this fly. Hundreds were squeezed out and

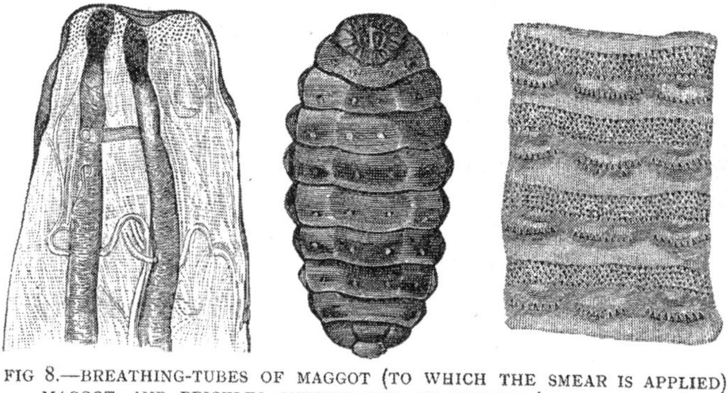

FIG 8.—BREATHING-TUBES OF MAGGOT (TO WHICH THE SMEAR IS APPLIED), MAGGOT, AND PRICKLES OUTSIDE SKIN OF MAGGOT (ALL MAGNIFIED).

brought in the course of a few days. One boy alone

destroyed 230 of these warble grubs in the spring of 1885 by the application of common cart grease and sulphur to the spiracle in the black tipped tail of the maggot or by squeezing out the maggots. [*Vide* Miss Ormerod's ninth Annual Report on Injurious Insects and Common Farm Pests, p. 92.] Last Easter I desired my pupils, during the week's holiday, to examine carefully the live stock at home for ox warble and to report to me. I enclose a copy of the first list which I received, and I am sure it will satisfy your Grace that this pest may easily be stamped out, if our farmers, their sons, or their labourers would apply the smear, or press out the maggots and destroy them. School boys can do this work, and feel a pleasure in the task. What has been accomplished by Bunbury boys can be equally well done by the boys of any other village school.[1]

[A leaflet which Miss Ormerod circulated widely says :— From £3,000,000 to £4,000,000 are lost annually through these pests. One-half the fat beasts killed in this country are afflicted with this grub. The farmer loses on his stock from poorer condition, and from death ; from less yield of milk, and damage to all, especially to fattening beasts, and cows from their tearing full gallop about the fields, besides loss to the butcher of from a halfpenny to a penny per pound on warbled hides. Look at the under side of the newly flayed hide of a warbled beast and see the grub cells (fig. 7). Maggots may be squeezed out, or easily killed by putting a dab of cart grease and sulphur, McDougall's Smear, or anything that will choke them in the opening of the warble, and the fly may be prevented from striking by dressing the beasts' backs in summer.]

May I add that during the past five years I have been drawing the attention of the boys to insects, which are injurious to food crops. They are quite familiar with such pests as the leather jacket, wireworm, turnip and mangold fly, caterpillars of the magpie moth, and the gooseberry and currant sawfly, &c., &c., for hundreds of living specimens have been brought to the school, bird's-nesting having to a very great extent been superseded by this new pursuit. The

[1] Recent record of Warbles extracted by the Aldersey Schoolboys and brought to the Headmaster :—
1895, 1,022 ; 1896, 2,596 ; 1897, 3,965 ; 1898, 1,706 ; 1899, 2,252 ; 1900, 1,851 ; 1901, 1,391 ; 1902, 1,066—Total, 15,849.

boys, having become well acquainted with the pests, were instructed as to the best methods of prevention and remedy. These boys will, in the course of a very few years, be the farmers and farm labourers of this district, and I am satisfied that even the little instruction which I am able to give them in what I may call "Practical Entomology" will then be found to be of considerable use to them.—W. BAILEY.[1]

Moth at rest, and with wings spread; caterpillar walking.

FIG. 9.—MAGPIE MOTH (CURRANT AND GOOSEBERRY), *ABRAXAS GROSSULARIATA*, LINN.

[1] Mr. Bailey writes in August, 1902:—"The Haberdashers' Company are the Governors of my school, and at our Midsummer distribution of prizes in June, 1882, Mr. Curtis, who was a member of the deputation who visited us in that year, suggested that it would be a good thing to give instruction to the boys on Injurious Insects. Failing to obtain a lecturer through South Kensington, at my suggestion, he called on Miss Ormerod. She suggested that I should take the subject, and added that she would give me all the assistance in her power. From that day up to the day of her death she took the kindest interest in our work. She presented to the school many books, beautiful diagrams, and a series of insect cases [prepared by Mosley of the Huddersfield Museum, after the cases arranged by Professor Westwood and Miss Ormerod for the S. and A. Museum at Bethnal Green], and was a liberal donor of prizes at Midsummer from 1885 to 1901 (both inclusive). Every Midsummer she kindly wrote a letter to be read on that occasion

November 24, 1887.[1]

DEAR MR. BAILEY,—The Farmers' Club meeting will be an exceptionally rare opportunity of pushing forward this, and some other important matters, as well as of laying before some of our leading agriculturists some important facts about a few of the pests of the corn crops of last season's notoriety. You will think my letter endless, but I want to congratulate you most heartily on your good success in the examinations (which must be a weary work to prepare for), and also on that of your assistant master and teacher, which is indeed encouraging, and to say how sorry we are to hear of your illness. I trust, if it please God, that you may have comfortable health again—it makes such a difference.

Since my sister and I came to St. Albans we are almost like different people. We have a beautiful house (pl. XIX.) with such thick walls that we do not feel the changes of temperature, and a lovely country view along the valley. We have also met with a most kindly reception, and, last but not least amongst blessings and comforts for which we are deeply grateful, is that educated earnest clergy form a decided element in the Society. But now I ought only to add thanks and very kind regards from us both.

December 11, 1887.

I must tell you the pleasure with which I heard your letter to the Duke of Westminster read at the "Seeds and Plants Diseases" Committee of the Royal Agricultural Society on Tuesday, and recommended for report to the Council, and I am glad to see it on the Society's report sheet sent me this morning, as being recommended for publication. I think this will do a great deal of good, and it cannot, I think, fail to be a great satisfaction to yourself that the excellent work done under your guidance and direction should thus be of such extended service throughout the land. I also figure to myself how pleased the good lads will be!

Will you accept the enclosed photo of my new and most comfortable home (plate XIX.); it gives a good idea of it, excepting in not quite showing the very rapid slope down from the terrace flower beds.

It would be a great and very true pleasure if when you

to the boys. I think I ought to add that the Haberdashers' Company were good enough to make a grant of £25 to start us with this new subject, and have since generously supported the carrying on of the work."

[1] Continuation of Miss Ormerod's letter to Mr. Bailey.

can spare time you would look in on us here for a couple of nights; I am sure that with our old Abbey and the many things of interest here, and some chat which you would let us have between whiles, the time would not lag. There are both pleasure and benefit in the work you allow me a part in. Pray believe me always, with kind regards and good wishes from us both.

Yours sincerely,
ELEANOR A. ORMEROD.

[On the warble question Miss Ormerod wrote on April 22, 1899, to Dr. Fletcher[1]:—

"Just now I am working hard on Warble affairs. The butchers (that is, leading men among them) very much wish that what is called 'licked' beef should be inquired into. I do not know whether you are troubled by this in Canada, but it is an alteration that takes place on the outside of the carcass of the animal beneath a badly warbled part of the hide. This part becomes soft and wet and blackish, and is popularly supposed to be soaked with moisture from the unlucky animal licking itself to soothe the irritation. Really it is the result of the chronic inflammation of the badly warbled hide. This causes much loss to butchers, and if I can get it well brought forward I think we shall through this rouse the farmers to better attention. The authorities at our Royal Veterinary College are most kindly helping me, and I hope before long to have enough sound information to be able to publish a paper on it."

To Mr. Medd[2] Miss Ormerod also wrote in Nov., 1900:—

"Do you chance to have noticed that the Warble fly of the United States, the *Hypoderma lineata*, is considered to be quite a distinct species to our *H. bovis?* I believe that investigation has proved that our *bovis* is very rarely found in the U.S.A., just as their *lineata* is very rarely, indeed, found here. Practically (that is, so far as injury to the hide is concerned), the trouble is similar, both in method of operation and in the frightful amount of damage caused; but it has been laid down by good U.S.A. authorities that in the case of their Warble fly, *lineata*, the attack is commenced by the quite embryo maggots making their way by the mouth to the gullet and there hanging on until it pleases them to make their way onward, by piercing through the coat of the œsophagus and onward through the tissues of

[1] See Chaps. xix.–xx. for letters to Dr. Fletcher. [2] See Chap. xxii.

the beast until they arrive after their long and curious journey beneath the ribs, whence they proceed to work beneath the hide like ours. The matter seems to me very curious, but I was not called on to enter into discussion, excepting giving my reasons why I felt wholly certain, and

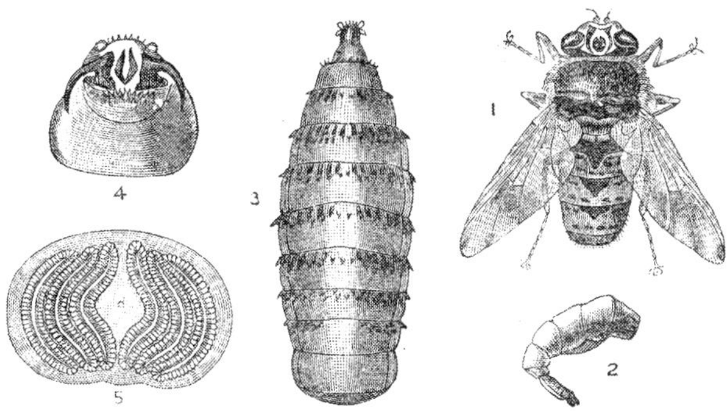

1, Male ; 2, curved extremity of abdomen of female ; 3, maggot ; 4, mouth hooks ; 5, spiracles at extremity of tail of maggot—all greatly magnified (after Brauer).

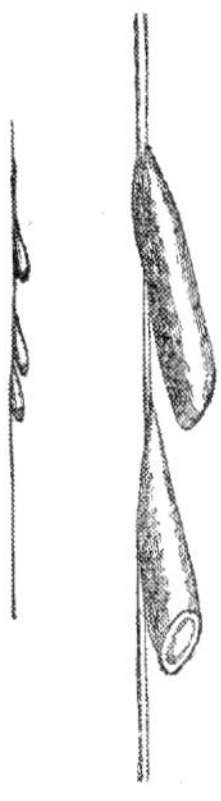

Eggs attached to hairs from a horse's fore-leg magnified and natural size. (After Bracy Clark.)

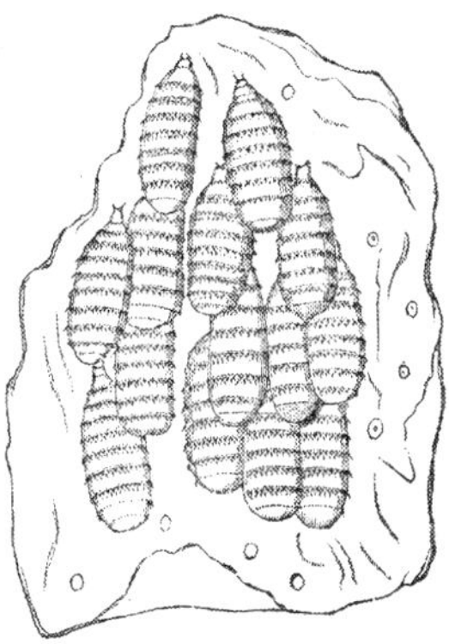

Maggots or horse bots attached to membrane of stomach. (After Bracy Clark.)

FIG. 10.—HORSE BOT FLY, OR HORSE BEE, *GASTROPHILUS EQUI*, FAB.

considered the evidence in our hands proved, that our *H. bovis* did not start on its travels in this way."

On May 14, 1900, she addressed another correspondent thus :—

"I have another formal application from the authorities

of S. Australia;—(this time from our friend Mr. Molineux) relative to Horse botfly—and very especially to make them sure regarding the precise differences between Bot, Warble, and Gad flies. I have explained that Gad flies, *Tabanidæ*, may be distinguished by being blood suckers, and by their maggots feeding in the ground, and that 'Bot' or 'Warble' are only two convertible names for *Œstridæ*, but that 'Bot' is usually most specially applied to internal feeding maggots, and Warble to those that live in the hide, notably in Warbles. But such difficulty continues to arise from haphazard use of the words, I have suggested that if possible the scientific name—(*Gastrophilus equi*) should be insisted on. An entomologist (?) had absolutely called this attack or kind of attack inside a horse that of 'Gad fly'! But as the attack has been well studied in the Department of Agriculture, Cape Town, I have suggested they should communicate with the Government entomologist, Mr. C. Lownsbury. For their practical needs, I have suggested clearing the Horse botfly, *G. equi*, eggs from the hair by dressing, and very especially that they should take care all droppings (in which the maggots pass from the horse, and where, or in the ground beneath, they go through their changes to the perfect state) should be so treated as to kill the maggots. It may possibly turn out that the *Gastrophilus* may be some other species than *equi*—I have not had specimens. When you are about to devote so much attention to Colonial Agriculture [in the "Garton" course of Colonial and Indian Lectures], I wished very much to tell you what I am about, lest I should, as this is sent me officially, go on other lines than you approve."]

June 9, 1891.[1]

DEAR MR. BAILEY,—I have now much pleasure in asking permission once again to place in your hands a cheque for £5 5s., to be used exactly as you may judge fit, in purchase of prizes for the encouragement of serviceable study of habits and means of prevention of ravages of injurious insects by your scholars. I have real pleasure in doing this because I believe the importance of those who are in any way connected with agriculture being serviceably acquainted with the causes of loss to crop or stock, and means whereby this may be lessened, cannot be over-estimated. I offer my hearty congratulations to yourself and your pupils on the satisfactory work achieved in my own department of agricultural entomology in one more year.

[1] Letters to Mr. Bailey continued.

I do not like to offer views of my own on these matters now that what is called Technical Instruction is receiving such widespread attention throughout the country. Still I should like, for the encouragement of any of your boys who may think themselves behind in the simply scientific race, to observe that instructions given (let them be conveyed in what terms the teacher will) must be founded to start with, on facts, trustworthily observed and trustworthily recorded; and the pupil who leaves your school with the knowledge of the appearance of the common crop pests, as the wireworm, the turnip flea beetle, the warble fly maggot for instance, and, as I am well aware is the case with many of your boys, adds to this a practical knowledge of how to lessen their powers of mischief, goes forth holding in his mind what will save him many a pound in the future, and be a benefit wherever he goes. It is a foundation on which as much as he pleases may be built, but the solidly learnt field knowledge will always be serviceable.

June 5, 1893.

I thank you very much for your kind letter. If I were nearer it would be a great pleasure to me to be present on your prize day, when I might have the gratification of making personal acquaintance with many of those whom I know by name as taking much interest in this important school as well as yourself, whom I should much like to meet; and also our "Aldersey boys," whom I have known and worked with, or they with me, for so many years.

It is a very great pleasure to me that they are continuing their attention, under your skilled help and guidance, to observation of farm pests, and their work stands first as a proof of what can be done in getting rid of one insect pest.

When careful search only produces twenty warble grubs, in a district[1] where a few years ago they were counted by hundreds, to my thinking we—that is, the boys, you and I—may fairly be proud of a thoroughly useful work. If I might venture on a kind of little moral reflection I should say that I should like the little prizes which I have so much pleasure in offering, to remind them sometimes of how much can be done, in many other things also, by even moderate attention given at the right time and under the

[1] This refers to Bunbury only, where we had nearly a "clean bill" in that year. The maggots brought were found in the adjoining parishes. I have in late years granted the boys a "roving commission." *On their bicycles* they visit farms which are many miles away from their homes. (W.B.).

guidance of sound knowledge. I trust they will continue their field work. With the increase of area under cultivation or occupied by stock so may their insect pests be expected to increase, and on sound knowledge of what really happens, and what at a paying rate can be brought to our aid, our hope rests of coping with the farmer's enemies. What I can do to help them by advice, or by reply to inquiries, will be gladly at their service. Whilst I congratulate those who have won my little tokens of goodwill, and beg to offer the same for the next prize day, I must say to all that in the information and benefit they have laid up in their working and observations they have each gained a prize far better than anything I can offer them.

May 29, 1894.

It is with most sincere pleasure that I hear from you once again this year of the good success of the Aldersey boys in their studies and of their steadiness in work. The methods by which serviceable instruction on this subject, namely, Agricultural Entomology, can be given is often a matter of difficulty and doubt, and I certainly think that the plan you mention to me is so good, and meets the points of combining practical knowledge with so much scientific information as is requisite, so well that I shall gladly draw the attention of those who apply to me for suggestions on these subjects to its serviceableness. You mention arranging the observations of the boys who take up the study of crop and fruit pests on a system which, though so simply worked, really forms an excellently complete course. You say that one week the boys bring samples of infestation injurious to fruit; in a second week attacks on garden vegetables; in another week on field crops; in another on timber; in another living examples of the subjects figured in the insect diagrams which my sister and I have had the pleasure of contributing to your school collections, and in yet another week you receive notes of serviceable means of prevention and remedies. This plan appears to me so sound and good that I hope I may be forgiven for intruding a few minutes on your time in greatly desiring to draw the attention of the influential visitors who will be present at your meeting to how excellently this plan meets many difficulties. A boy so taught knows his facts.

June 2, 1895.

Many thanks for your letter received yesterday morning, which is very interesting indeed to me, and which I hope to reply to very soon, but now I am replying to your note accompanying the caterpillars from the Peckforton Hills, though not so fully as I could wish, for disasters befell the letter, and it arrived by special messenger from the Post Office, with the announcement that the things had got loose, and were creeping all about ! Any way but little remained to judge by, so I report on what was visible. Most of the caterpillars were loopers (fig. 30), and the largest proportion of these, though differing so much in colour, appeared to me to be the *Cheimatobia brumata*. As you know there may be every variety of shade in these Winter moth caterpillars, from pale green down to smoky brown or almost black. Another kind of which I only find two specimens (small and very small, respectively), look as if when grown they would be the Mottled Umber moth, which is so injurious this year. There are just single specimens of a few other non-looper kinds, but at this present time all the kinds come under only one method of (feasible) treatment, and I am afraid this (even if feasible) would be much too costly on such a great scale. Washing with Paris-green or London-purple, or with kerosene emulsion, would be the right thing, or our British form of the emulsion, made by Messrs. Morris, Little and Son, Doncaster, and sold, I believe, at a very low price (consequent on the large demand for it), under the trade name of "antipest." This only needs diluting. But when we come to dealing with great areas like the Peckforton Woods, I believe that the only really practicable way of, in some degree, lessening the evil, and counteracting its effects, is throwing water from some large engine. If a fire engine and a supply of water were available this might do a great deal of good.

I was consulted by the late Sir Harry Verney about "an ancestral oak" at Clayden, which appeared nearly cleared of leafage, and I advised playing the house fire engine on it—and the plan succeeded. The moisture falling around the tree pushed on the second leafage and (conjecturally) saved the tree. But with woods it is most difficult to manage application. I am afraid I am only able to say what would be best, if it could be done.

For the future it is a grave consideration, and consultation is very desirable, as to what means could reasonably and safely be employed to destroy the caterpillar in the ground. They will probably be very soon leaving the trees, and burying themselves just below the surface, and will most likely reappear, in moth form, and ascend the trees, beginning in the early winter, and thus eggs will be laid to

It was a great pleasure to me to notice the appreciative interest that their Royal Highnesses now ~~to~~ our gracious King & Queen took in the habits of injurious insects. Her Majesty's discriminating ~~obs~~ observation made me permit myself to say that she should have been an Entomologist. And our King recognised at a glance the great water beetles the Dytiscus marginalis is a kind which he well knew as injurious to fish spawn.

start next year's attack. I do not know whether the ground growths would permit of anything like paring being done under the trees. The best way would be "sticky banding" in October. At the Toddington fruit grounds one year 120,000 trees were sticky banded, but still this is work on an enormous scale. These are the main points to work on, and I should be very much pleased to enter on any of them more in detail, but just now I am writing as soon as I can (before going to church), as with Sunday and Bank Holiday posts I am afraid this letter will not, at the earliest, reach you until Tuesday morning, so please excuse such hastily written lines.

April 6, 1896.

Now I am working on my Exhibit of Economic Entomology for the Bath and West of England Society Show at St. Albans. I think you will perhaps like to look at the enclosed set of labels for the cases.[1] There are only a few lines to be fixed outside each. In the catalogue there is a fuller account, with prevention and remedy. Is it not a triumph of condensation to get a little life history and prevention and remedy of Wireworm into about half a dozen lines ? But really there is enough if people would mind it. I try to give injured material wherever I can, and there are upwards of sixty infestations. Georgiana helps me with twenty diagrams—more beautiful than any of her previous ones—and the Council, who are very kind, have awarded us all the privileges of stewards and members of Council for the Show, so that we may have every convenience of transit there.

It gave me great pleasure to be appointed External Examiner in Agricultural Entomology at Edinburgh University—for besides enjoying such a great compliment it will help my work.

May 30, 1896.

N.B. *Confidential.* I want to tell you how kind and nice the Prince and Princess were at the Show. T.R.H. shook hands when they arrived, quite heartily, and when I had explained my own and my sister's exhibit I thought I was to retire, but I found I was to attend round the other exhibits in the building, so I walked on by the Princess—

[1] See Appendix C.

* * * * * *

SAMPLE OF THE SCRAP NOTES LEFT BY MISS ORMEROD (SEE PAGE OPPOSITE) RELATING TO THE GREAT WATER BEETLE RECOGNISED BY THE PRINCE OF WALES, NOW KING EDWARD VII., AT ST. ALBANS' SHOW.

just think, at the head of the Royal party, before the Prince and all of them! When we had gone round the Prince said, "Now, I think we must be going," and he shook hands again, and the Princess, who was a little ahead, turned back and shook hands also. I was told by one of the officials that the Prince expressed himself afterwards as much interested, and my informant had told the Prince that I was doing work in this country which was done in other countries by the State. H.R.H. was so interested about the warbles that he called up Lord Clarendon to look at the great photo of the warbled red deer's hide too, and we had quite a chat together.

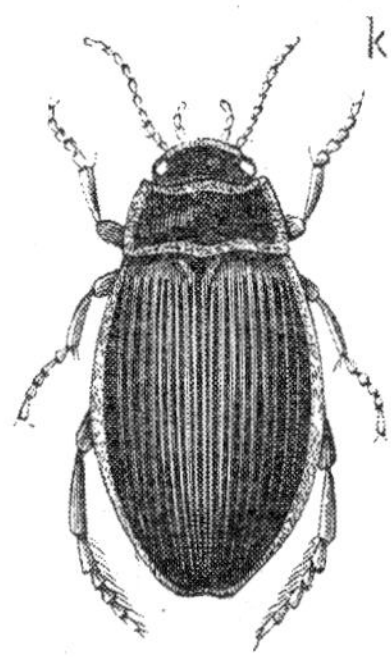

FIG. 11.—WATER BEETLE, *DYTISCUS MARGINALIS*, LINN.

June 15, 1899.

I had great pleasure in receiving your very kind letter, and I thought a great deal of you, and your flock, on the prize day. But now I am troubling you (the idea occurred too late to be of use at the time), to ask whether you would at all care to have (say) ten copies of my "Manual of Injurious Insects," to give just as you may think fit as an encouragement to the boys—or perhaps a present here or there to one who might be leaving school and taking up farming. I should like it very much. You have it yourself and (I think?) one for the school library, and Mr. D. E. Byrd must have his father's copy, but if you cared to have some copies it would really give me very great pleasure. Though fruit-insect prevention has made great advances in the last few years, this is not a special Cheshire interest, the agricultural observations are very correct still.

Mr. D. E. Byrd has kindly given me some very good

information about Cheese-fly maggot attack, just precisely what I was wishing for, and also something of the principle of prevention. Mr. Ward [Organising Secretary of the Cheshire County Council] was kind enough to procure me some good information from Miss Forster [of the Cheshire Dairy School], and I hope to form a good paper by and by. All I really want now in this matter are a few of the "hopping" maggots, which most likely will turn up soon. Curiously enough, just at the time, I had an application from a bacon-curing Co. and I think we have on both sides benefited.

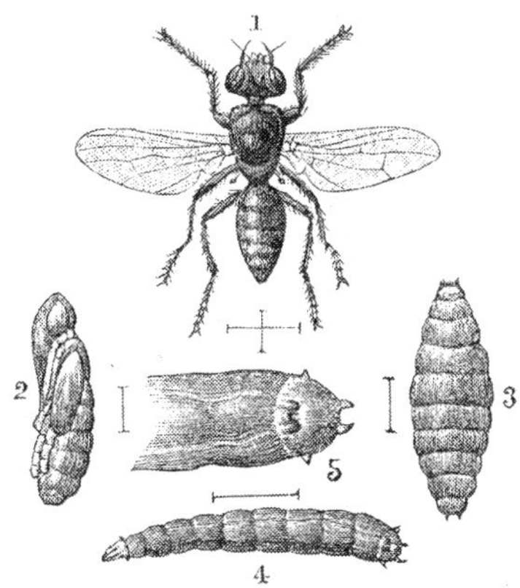

1, Fly; 2, pupa; 3, pupa-case; 4, maggot—all magnified, with lines showing natural length; 5, tail extremity, still more magnified, showing spiracles, tracheæ, and caudal tubercles.

FIG. 12.—CHEESE AND BACON FLY, *PIOPHILA CASEI*, LINN.

August 5, 1899.

I now, with many thanks for the clearness with which you have been good enough to note precisely the form of the presentation labels, enclose twelve, only altering by adding to the slips for the three boys, the prefix of "Mr." I am sure they will like it. I fancy I see them surreptitiously turning to the donatory slip, to enjoy their rise! Very many thanks to you indeed. I hope it may give the recipients pleasure, but I am very sure you give great pleasure to myself by allowing my little remembrance to these kind helpers.

I am sure you will be interested to know that the Meat

Traders Associations—at the Royal Lancashire Show—are distributing thousands of my Warble leaflets, with free leave to write up to London for more.

March 2, 1900.

Many thanks to you for your very kind letter. Indeed it is a trouble to me that I am not able to write oftener, but nobody knows better than yourself (who are so burdened with work for the good of others) how hard work can be, and if I quite overwork I am ill, so I am afraid to do all I wish.

Thank you for your kind congratulations. I take it as a very great honour for the University of Edinburgh to give me a Doctor of Laws Degree, &c., &c., &c. I am a little anxious about making such a very public appearance, but I dare say it will not be so alarming when it comes to the point. But I do not wish to go out of my own quiet lines, and I do not certainly wish to be called "Doctor." Would not the right thing be for me to just put LL.D. after my name where desirable?

TORRINGTON HOUSE, ST. ALBANS,
April 26, 1901.

MY DEAR MR. BAILEY,—I have postponed replying to your kind letter partly because I have had a long exhausting illness, and partly because I am sure that you will regret the subject of my letter, as I do myself. Still I think I ought to tell you that I am purposing quite to discontinue my regular entomological work. You would notice what I said about the Annual Reports, but the attention to insect inquiries and (almost worse) the requests for co-operation in philanthropic literary schemes had become a burthen so very injurious to me that I was warned both by my doctor and literary colleagues that without rest the consequences might be very serious. All last year my health was failing, and (though this is temporary) an attack of influenza early in March, followed by what are called "effects," has caused me great suffering.

But it is in reference to our long, kindly colleagueship that I am writing to you. Natural history is on a very different footing now from what it was in 1884, when with your good help our good lads started the investigations regarding Warble, which have proved to the whole world the possibility of checking this wasteful attack, and I may add they have carried the work on with their own steady, patient, long-continued energy. To this I must add my great appreciation of their useful work in real serviceable

Economic Entomology, and the kindliness and heartiness of their work.

But now yourself, your school and your scholars have a world-wide name, and as you will fully appreciate that to continue, however much I may wish it, publicly attached to any one philanthropic economic work throws me open still to whole hosts of applications, I am sure you will understand my wish to withdraw. You have I think my subscription for your next great June day, and after that I, with much regret, purpose to discontinue it. I look back on many years' kindly communication from you, but if you could have any idea of the labour which has been thrown on me from other quarters, I am sure you would think I am right. I earnestly and sincerely beg you to believe me with feelings of the highest esteem and friendship and every good wish,

Yours sincerely,

ELEANOR A. ORMEROD.

P.S.—Please to excuse handwriting, as I am on my sofa.

CHAPTER XV

LETTERS TO MR. D. D. GIBB

Great Tortoiseshell Butterfly—The Forest Fly—Numerous other fly-pests and fly-parasites—A few Moths.

THE subjoined letters to Mr. Gibb are unique in that they deal with a wider range of subjects than any of Miss Ormerod's letters to other British observers. She recognised and appreciated her correspondent's accuracy of observation, and gratefully acknowledged the assistance she received through the numerous specimens he so promptly collected for her when in need.

To D. D. Gibb, Esq., Assembly Manor Farm, Lymington.[1]

TORRINGTON HOUSE, ST. ALBANS,
June 26, 1894.

DEAR SIR,—I am very much obliged to you for kindly sparing time to let me have your careful observations received this morning, together with the specimens of the Great Tortoiseshell butterfly, *Vanessa polychloros*, infestation. I have been very carefully noting, measuring and counting, so as to secure details, and presently I think with your own observations these will form a very serviceably interesting paper. That patch of eggshells contained over three hundred eggs, as near as I could count by taking numbers in length and breadth. Your two caterpillars had been over hasty in their arrangements, and changed to chrysalis on the journey, and consequently made not a good business of it, but one of those you sent me previously, having better surroundings had done its work thoroughly well, and is a very beautiful specimen which I hope will develop. I

[1] Now "Kirkdale," Spencer Road, Bournemouth.

propose to have a good figure engraved of the butterfly, chrysalis and caterpillar.

All your other notes I have also read with much interest, especially those on turnip management, and your remarks about "warble," and in due time I shall be much obliged by being allowed to use these in my next Annual Report.

July 27, 1894.

I am very much pleased to hear that you have hatched two of the Large Tortoiseshell butterflies from your specimens. This is very interesting as completing your

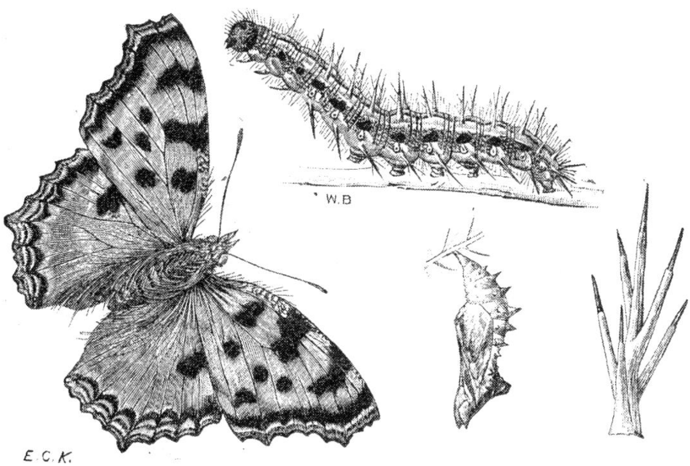

Caterpillar and chrysalis, natural size; branched spine from caterpillar, magnified.

FIG. 13.—GREAT TORTOISE-SHELL BUTTERFLY, *VANESSA POLYCHLOROS*, L.

previous observation, and I am particularly glad of this note of date of development for I am afraid that the only really good chrysalis which I secured from your larvæ does not seem likely to develop. However, it gave me an opportunity of seeing the beautiful colours and the six bright mother-of-pearl-like spots on the back. Many thanks for kindly offering me a specimen, but I should not like to take it—for it is of special interest with you to illustrate this rare attack, and also it is very difficult to ensure safety in transmission. Many thanks all the same, and also for your Hessian fly specimens received a short time ago, and for the further notes now. I am sorry not to have acknowledged them and the information in the letter accompanying them sooner, but I had a deal of work, and some temporary difficulty from breaking a blood-vessel in one eye. However I am thankful to say that is all right again.

I have no doubt you are right about the weather making a most important amount of difference in extent of injury both from Hessian fly and Diamond-back attack. If it had been hot I am afraid *Plutella cruciferarum* (Diamond-back moth) would have done a deal of mischief. The little Charlock weevil, *Ceutorhynchus contractus* (see my seventeenth, 1890, report), has been doing a great deal of mischief

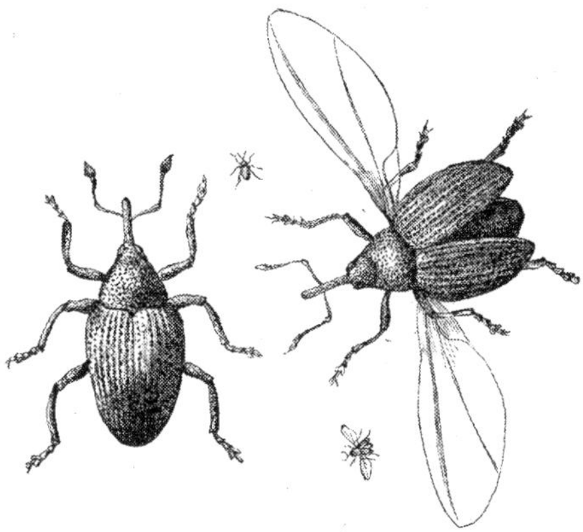

In usual position, and also with wings expanded—magnified; also natural size.

FIG. 14.—CHARLOCK WEEVIL, *CEUTORHYNCHUS CONTRACTUS.*

to young turnips at some places on the east side of the country.

July 30, 1894.

The *V. polychloros* specimen came to hand little, if at all, injured by its journey, and in beautiful order for figuring. I am very glad to have it, for besides proving the caterpillars to be of the "great tortoiseshell," I had the opportunity of seeing the row of long bristles or stout hairs about a third along the lower part of the front edge (the costa) of the fore-wings. This row of hairs is the structural difference between this "great tortoiseshell," and the "small tortoiseshell" (which is without them), but otherwise the two species are so much alike that there used to be doubts whether they were not merely varieties until this point was noticed by a Dutch entomologist, Mr. Snellen. I shall be glad to refer to this point, for it is important and was observed after our chief manuals of *Lepidoptera* were published.

On referring to your letter accompanying the Hessian fly puparia, "flax-seeds," in which you notice some of them being within the stalks, I remembered I had not precisely replied to this part, so I do it now. I think this position, though not characteristic, is not very uncommon, and is caused by a weakness of the stem. I have from time to

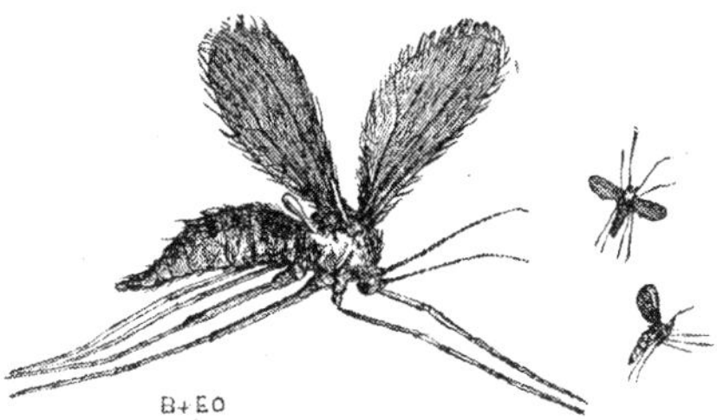

Natural size and magnified.

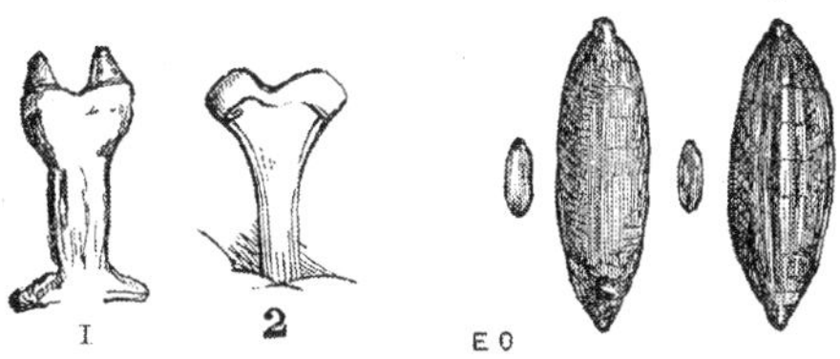

1, Anchor-process of larva of *Cecidomyia destructor*; 2, of *Cecidomyia tritici*—magnified; "flax-seeds," or puparia, in different stages of development, natural size and magnified.

FIG 15.—HESSIAN FLY, *CECIDOMYIA DESTRUCTOR.*

time found the stem cracked longitudinally and the "flax-seed" partly slipped into the cavity.

August 22, 1894.

I have to-day had a request from Dr. Ritzema Bos for some specimens of Hessian fly puparia *in situ* or otherwise. If you could do it without inconvenience, could you oblige me with some "flax-seeds" if you come on them at threshing time; and you will be good enough to let me have also a few pieces of barley or wheat stem just three or four inches long with the flax seed still adhering.

I hope you are having good harvest weather, but indeed this is the first really good bright summer's day we have had for a long time, and to my eye the wheat round here has a grey look instead of the bright colour.

August 28, 1894.

Your packet of infested straw came safely to hand this morning and I am very much obliged to you for kindly taking all this trouble. I have repacked the Hessian fly straws,

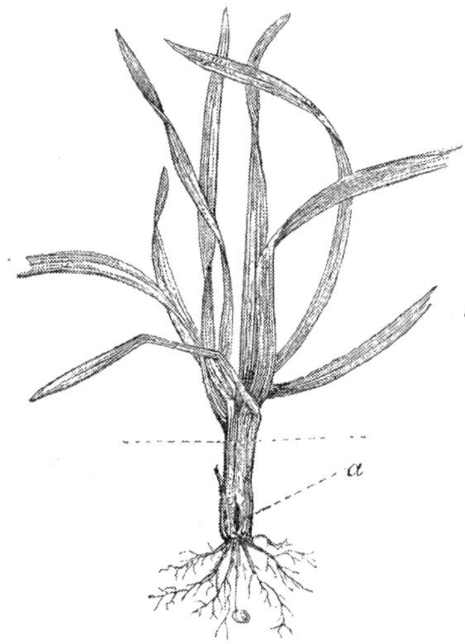

FIG. 16.—YOUNG WHEAT, WITH HESSIAN FLY MAGGOT AT "*a*." (After Prof. Webster.)

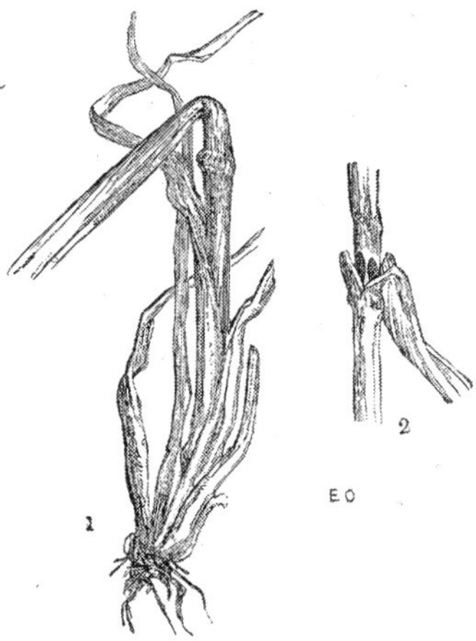

1, Straw bent over; 2, showing "flax-seeds."
HESSIAN FLY ATTACK ON BARLEY.

winding a thread over the place of deposit of the puparia on the barley straw for fear they should get from under the sheathing leaf and be lost. I am sure Dr. Ritzema Bos will be very grateful for the help, and also for its coming so promptly.

Thank you also for the *Chlorops* (Gout fly) specimens; they were particularly acceptable just now, for, if all is well, Professor Riley means to look in early next week before he returns to the U.S.A., and I think he would like to see them.

April 26, 1895.

If I am not troublesome I should be very greatly obliged if you would tell me anything as to the methods commonly used for keeping off attacks of the Forest fly, *Hippobosca equina*, which is such a special pest in the New Forest to horses not used to it. I mean the thick made fly of which I enclose a figure (18), natural size and magnified, which deposits an egg-like puparium or chrysalis case in the hair of the horses, from which case the fly presently comes out. I believe you will know exactly the infestation I refer

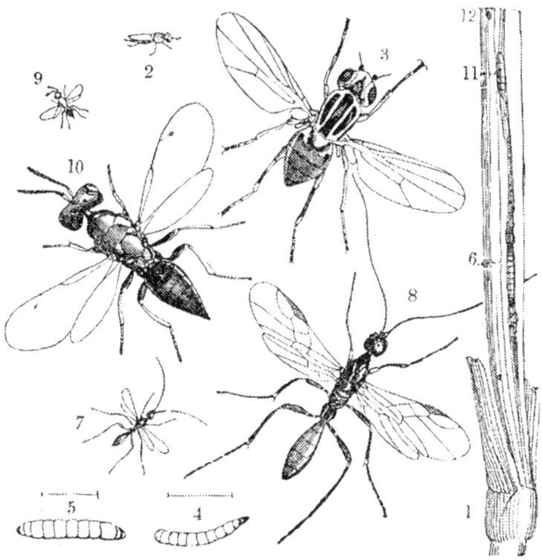

Nos. 1–6 and 11 and 12, Gout fly, grub, and pupa—natural size and magnified; with infested stem; 7, 8, 9 and 10, parasitic ichneumon flies, natural size and magnified.

FIG. 17.—GOUT FLY, RIBBON-FOOTED CORN FLY, *CHLOROPS TÆNIOPUS*, MEIGEN.[1]

to, and any information which you may be good enough to give me, as to how to prevent it coming at horses and settling on them, I know would be quite sound and reliable. I am receiving so much application for information about the habits, &c., &c., that I feel sure my best plan will be to issue a leaflet as soon as possible with figure included at the heading. I have, I think I may say, far more in the way of

[1] The attack is caused by the small black and yellow fly, figured above. She lays an egg on the barley sheath; the maggot from this attacks the ear, then eats a channel down one side of the stem to the first knot, and then turns to chrysalis state within the leaves.—(E. A. O.)

description and nature of the fly than can be needed, but it would help me very much indeed to have a recipe for any application which was really known to answer in keeping the attack off riding horses. I am sure you would allow me to add this to my leaflet, acknowledged to you. I make no doubt quantities of things, especially of the nature of soap or soft soap (not caustic) or lard, and a little paraffin or sulphur, would with careful attention keep the flies from congregating permanently, but the thing in hand is to prevent them coming at the horses and causing dismal downfalls! I have heard lately of a plan of rubbing horses with paraffin—very efficacious, I should expect, but not the thing to benefit the clothes of the riders!

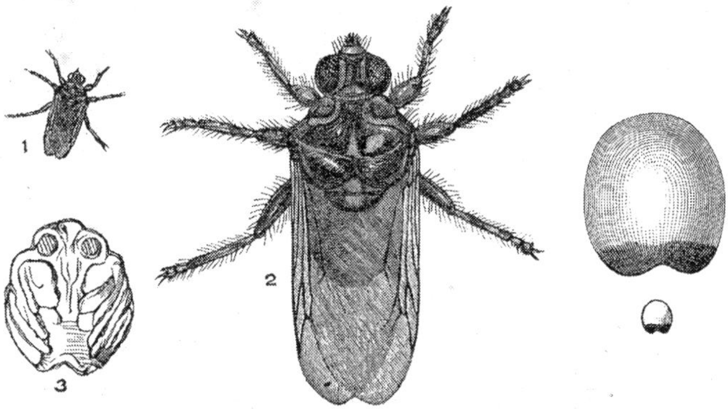

1 and 2, natural size and magnified from life; 3, pupa removed from puparium (after Réaumur); puparium, natural size and magnified, before complete coloration.

FIG. 18.—FOREST FLY, *HIPPOBOSCA EQUINA*.

Wednesday night, May 1, 1895.

I am exceedingly obliged to you for your most helpful letter and the live specimen, which I learnt a great deal from, before we re-captured it, and stopped its activity with some benzine. It slipped out of my fingers somehow, out of your careful packing, and kept flying at my light woollen shawl, varied by taking a promenade (which I was very conscious of) on the top of my head. It struck me as suggestive that it selected me (not my sister or our house-keeper) for this purpose, because I never use any kind of pomatum. I like my hair as smooth as can be, so the creature did not establish itself, but judging by feeling, it had much pleasure in its survey. I noticed the set of the wings, and perhaps I can get a figure.

When the flies are more plentiful, so that it would not give you too much trouble to secure some, I certainly should like two or three very much, but please do not let me intrude too much on your good nature and time. I will write again presently to say how I am getting on with

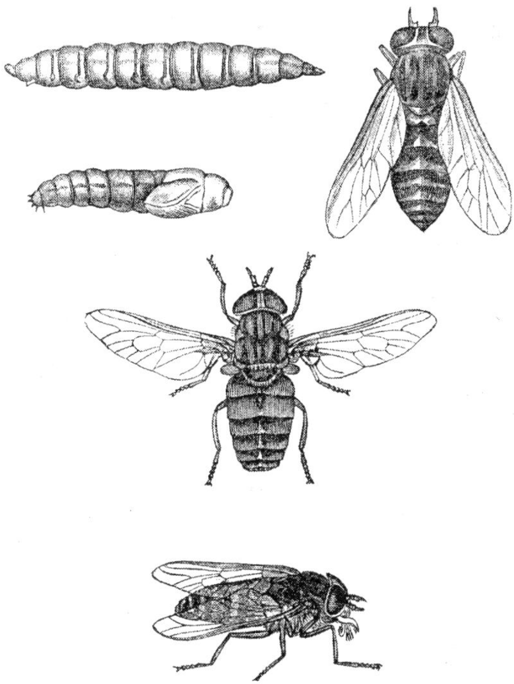

Fly, with wings expanded; also viewed sideways.

Larva and pupa, after De Geer.

FIG. 19.—GREAT OX GADFLY, *TABANUS BOVINUS*, LINN.

the leaflet, but I did not like to delay thanking you heartily longer than I could.

May 10, 1895.

I am very greatly obliged to you for all the information in your letter, and also for the four live and hearty flies. These have been very valuable to me, and I cannot help thinking I have discovered a point not previously observed in the structure of the feet which may prove of importance practically. However it may have been known, so I have written to-day to our great English authority, Mr. Meade, to ask him what he thinks about it and will write you again. I fancy that your specimen's being so fresh allowed me to make out the point. Still I may be wrong.

P.S.—I was told yesterday that a worse trouble in the forest than the Forest fly is the "Great Gadfly" the *Tabanus bovinus*. Do you think this is so? This fly is such a very large creature indeed, see figure (19) of it with wings laid at rest and expanded. I should have expected to hear of it before now.

May 20, 1895.

I received the first copies of my Forest Fly leaflet late on Saturday and now enclose you a few with great pleasure. Please tell me if more would be acceptable, as you know

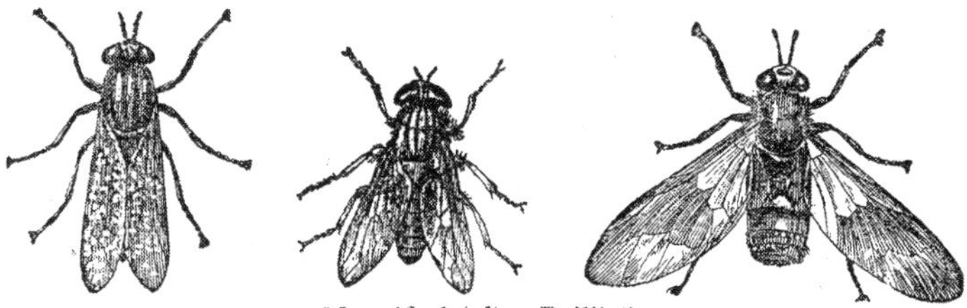

Magnified (after Railliet).

(*a*) CLEG, OR SMALL RAIN BREEZE FLY. (*b*) AUTUMNAL BREEZE FLY. (*c*) SMALL BLINDING BREEZE FLY.

FIG. 20.—BREEZE FLIES: (*a*) *HÆMATOPOTA PLUVIALIS.* (*b*) *TABANUS AUTUMNALIS.* (*c*) *CHRYSOPS CÆCUTIENS.*

how gladly I would send them, and you have helped me most importantly. I have only had a moderate impression struck in order that I might be able to alter or add as seemed desirable.

I thought a deal of what I could manage, as the flies came at me and I could watch them, but I did not see my way at all to making a more useful figure than that by Dr. Taschenberg, which tells little. Mine is after the figure by Professor Westwood drawn for the plates of "Insecta Britannica—Diptera," and these are regular standard reference plates.

July 1, 1895.

We have really captured some of the *Hippobosca equina* in North Wales. The account will be in next number of the "Veterinary Record." I have identified them with quite absolute certainty, but I suppose I must not forestall the "Veterinary Record," as it sent me the flies.

July 11 or 12, 1895.

I am very much obliged for your further consignment of the *Tabanidæ* (Horse gadflies), and especially for the liberal supply of the Great gadfly (fig. 19). What a very grand fellow he is, and how very painful the attack must be. I have to-day written to Mr. R. H. Meade about this great variety of Gadflies which you are letting me have, and offering to send him duplicates.

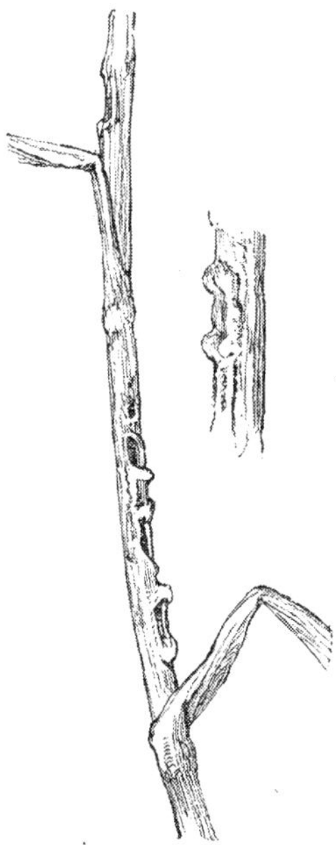

Red maggot attack on a stem of barley; and a saddle, magnified.

FIG. 21.—SADDLE FLY, ? *CECIDOMYIA* (*DIPLOSIS*) *EQUESTRIS*.

Many thanks also for first, and as yet only, note of presence of Hessian fly this season. About these curious markings on the side of the straw—are they not very like those of the maggots, "red maggots," of the *Diplosis equestris*, the *Cecidomyia* or Great midge, mentioned in my thirteenth Report, at p. 30? I think you have this report, and if you chanced to have leisure to compare some specimens with my sketch, you would see what you thought. The workings do not seem to me as regular, but yet there is a strong resemblance.

I am working up the Gadflies as well as time allows, and through courtesy of Mr. Janson have had a loan of a volume published in 1842 of a serial called "Isis" so as to be able to study the very special paper in it by Zeller, which is the authority on some of the important points, and which cannot now be bought by itself. I thought this was a kind help, for the whole book is very costly.

July 31, 1895.

I have a promise from Professor Mik, who is a special authority on flies, that when he returns to Vienna he will let me have such duplicates of the *Tabanidæ* as he has, which will be a great help. I have had an artist down from London who has made most beautiful drawings for engraving of the fly's foot (pls. XXIII. XXIV.), but I greatly want some dissections made of it, and I have only this morning heard where I could get this minute work done. Would you mind the trouble of once again letting me have two or three Forest flies? I should be very much obliged, for though I keep the specimens most carefully that you let me have, some quite fresh would answer much better for dissection.

It is very curious that until Mr. Goodall (a highly accomplished veterinary surgeon) noticed the long bristle attached to the *H. equina* foot, no one except that wonderful observer De Geer appears to have noticed it, or what is perhaps still more astonishing, repeated De Geer's observation and figure.

August 13, 1895.

I am much obliged by your letter of the 8th inst. with observations of the effect of temperature and weather on presence of Forest fly, and now again this morning, and very much, for the supply of Forest flies, which were alive I should say by the grumbling in the corn-stem, until I chloroformed them.

Your "black ants" appear to me to be *Formica fuliginosa*, of which it is stated in Frederick Smith's British Museum Catalogue of British Fossorial Hymenoptera [burrowing four-winged insects], p. 11, that "this species is at once recognised by its jet-black colour; its usual habitat is the vicinity of a decaying tree or old post." I only twice met with this kind in my father's woods, each time, curiously enough, one of my brothers who had a great fondness for

PLATE XXIII.

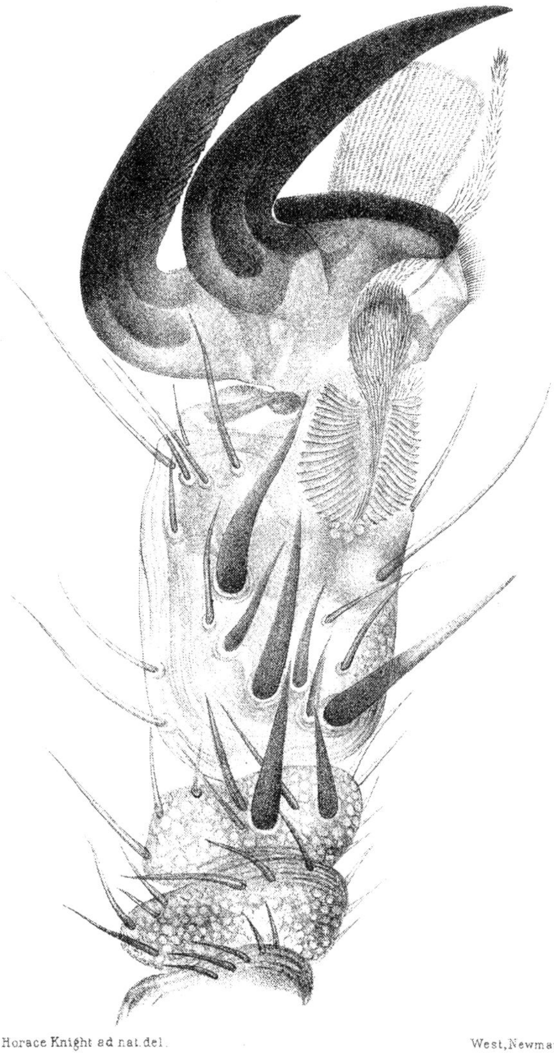

Horace Knight ad nat. del. West, Newman lith.

Foot of Forest Fly (Hippobosca equina, *Linn.*)
Side view greatly magnified.

To face p. 138.

PLATE XXIV.

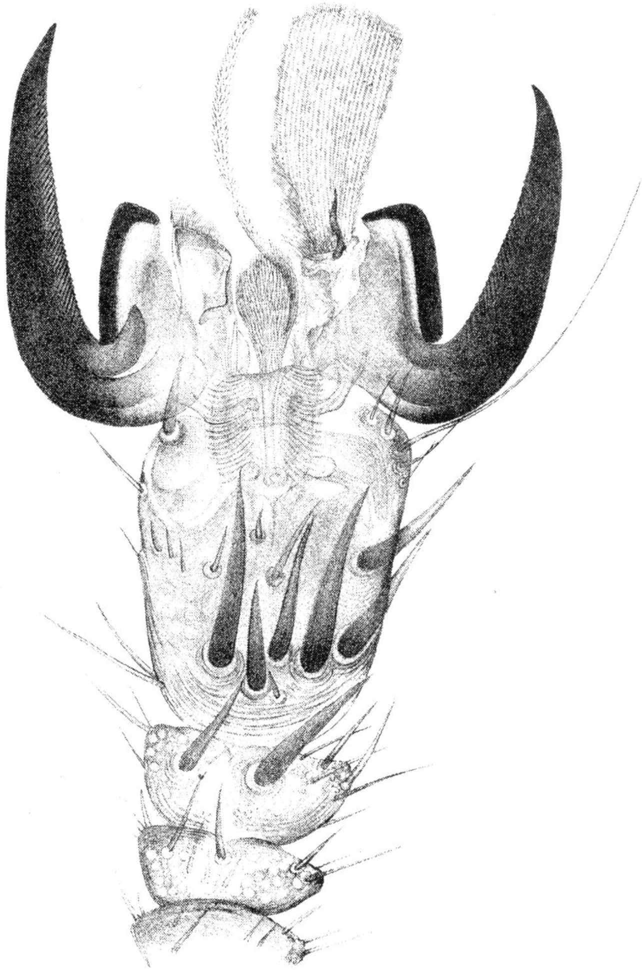

Horace Knight ad nat. del. West, Newman lith.

Foot of Forest Fly (Hippobosca equina, *Linn.*)

Seen from above greatly magnified.

To face p. 138.

ornithology saw the Hoopoe. As this rare bird is stated to have a fondness for this special kind of ant I conjectured its presence was caused by the *fuliginosa* being present. Their workings were wonderfully destructive in the felled stump which they chose for headquarters. I certainly think you need no advice from me on the head of dealing with them, but it just occurred to me that, if they come in a definite line still, and you could not run them up to their starting point, it might answer to put a couple of half-decayed stumps across their line of march. Might they not adopt the suggested new settlement?

I am getting on with the Forest fly and lately I have been studying the claws. I have only just discovered that along

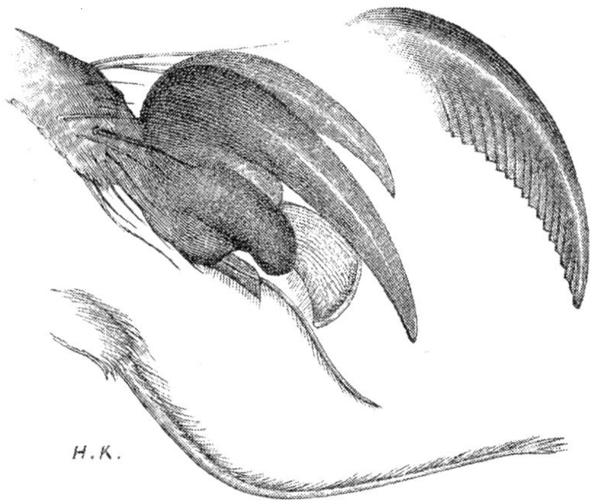

Much magnified.

FIG. 22.—FOOT OF FOREST FLY, *HIPPOBOSCA EQUINA*, SHOWING DOUBLE CLAWS, CENTRAL PROCESS, AND LONG PRICKLY BRISTLE; ALSO PORTION OF SIDE OF CLAW OF *HIPPOBOSCA MACULATA*, SHOWING PARALLEL GROOVES AND SAW-EDGE.

the lower part of the large-curved claw is a saw-toothed edge, and to this the slanting grooves which I had previously noticed run down one furrow to each notch so as to give an enormous power of holding and tearing. I think the thumb claw is also to some degree furnished both with saw- and file-like markings (fig. 22).

P.S. I can only see the saw and file mark with a good side light, when the claw is examined in natural state, not in balsam.

June 20, 1896.

I was very glad to have your note of first capture of *Hippobosca* (Forest fly) on May 6th. I wonder whether on your Red Deer (or Roe Deer, if you have them) you find the Deer Forest fly, the *Lipoptena cervi*. I am having a deal of communication about it as having been observed as a very noticeable infestation on Deer in one locality in the North of Scotland. I believe it is troublesome to people moving in the parts it frequents, but the odd thing about it is, that whilst the females are considered (or conjectured, for it is not quite certain) to be always wingless, yet the male flies are developed with wings and drop them, something like ants, on settling on a host animal. It would be very inter-

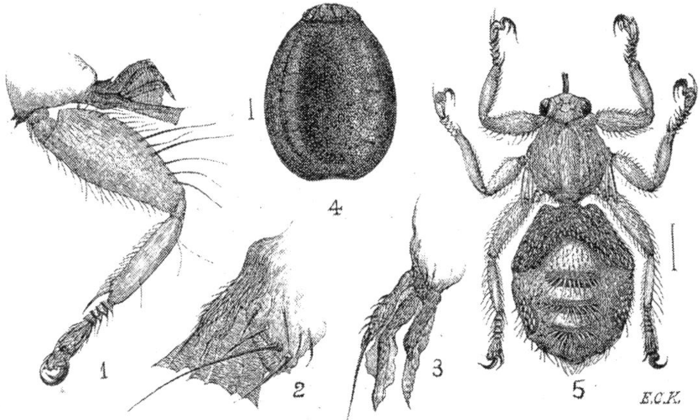

1, Leg and base of wing; 2, base of wing; 3, abortive wing; 5, female fly, with base of wings—all much magnified; 4, puparium, much magnified, and line showing natural length.

FIG. 23.—DEER FOREST FLY (FEMALE), *LIPOPTERA CERVI*, VON SIEBOLD AND LOEW.

esting if you found any of these; they come very near the so-called "Sheep tick" in their nature, only neither male nor female of the "Sheep Forest flies" is ever winged. It is also very curious that from some unaccountable confusion the generic name has gone wrong; it seems obvious it should be *Lipoptera*, "without wings," but—it is supposed by some error in printing—*Lipoptena*, which has no meaning connected with the fly, has got substituted. I think it would be well presently to try to get this put right.

August 29, 1895.

I am writing a few lines to mention that Mr. Meade has verified my identification of the New Forest *Tabanidæ* for me as being all correct, with one exception. He thinks the

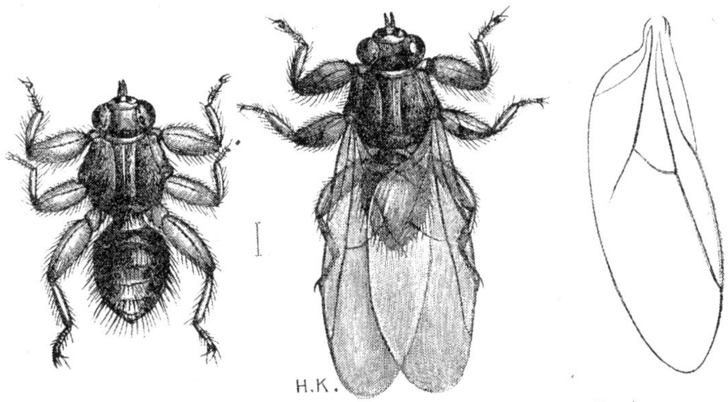

With wings thrown off; also still retaining wings; and wing—all much magnified. Line shows natural length.

FIG. 24.—DEER FOREST FLY (MALE), *LIPOPTENA CERVI*, VON SIEBOLD AND LOEW.

glaucopus is more like *cognatus*, but Brauer of Vienna says the latter is only probably a variety of the former, so this is no great matter. Mr. Meade is not only an eminently skilled dipterist himself, but he also possesses a collection of

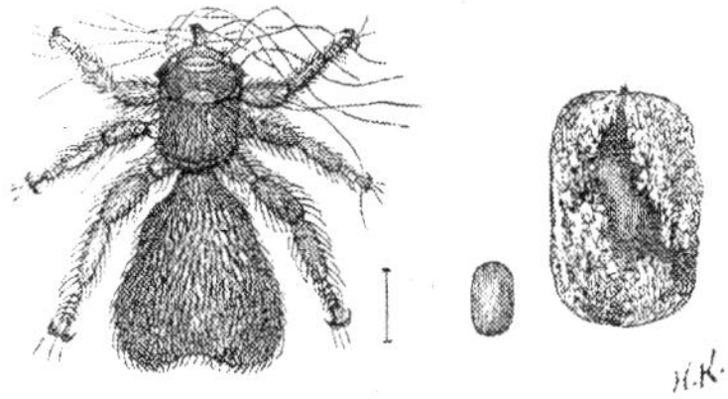

Fly, magnified, with line showing natural length; puparium, magnified (showing incrustation), also natural size.

FIG. 25.—SHEEP SPIDER FLY, "KED," OR "KADE," *MELOPHAGUS OVINUS*, LINN.

the *Tabanidæ* (our British kinds) named for him by Dr. Brauer, the great continental authority. So now we stand on a very firm footing (thanks to the trouble which you and Mr. Moens were good enough to take in supplying me with fresh specimens) as to the species of these bloodsucking pests which you have in the Forest. Would you tell Mr. Moens about this when you see him, with my compliments and thanks? I think you meet sometimes. I am longing to hear something of the military experiences.

October 8, 1895.

I am very much obliged to you for your letter received this morning, and (as you kindly allow me) I will just say what I should particularly like, but please believe me I should be very sorry to be really troublesome. First, about the Hessian fly straw. If you came on some that had been infested this would answer excellently. I have got some "flax-seeds" and I could slip some in. But really the "elbowed" straw (bent over) into an angle (fig. 16) is what I want to show. I have excellent Gout specimens. One thing I

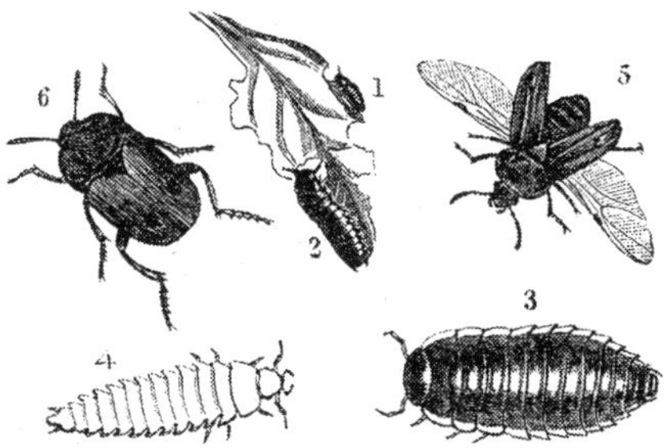

1 and 2, young and full-grown larvæ; 3 and 4, larvæ magnified; 5, female beetle flying; 6, male beetle, slightly magnified.

FIG. 26.—BEET CARRION BEETLE, *SILPHA OPACA*, LINN.

should particularly like is a little bit of Mangold leaf (say two or three inches square) showing Mangold maggot blister. I could dry this in blotting paper (like my pea- bean- and clover-leaf injuries from *Sitones*) and with a good supply of Mangold fly and pupæ which I have got, I think this would be very nice. I have good grubs of Carrion Beet beetle, which would be difficult to get, and I think plenty of the beetle (or at hand), but, for the mangold, if I could get them, I should very much like some of the Spotted or Black millepedes which were such pests earlier in the year. I am afraid though it is too late now. The only other thing which I am very much wishing for is a good specimen of apple twig, injured by American blight. A bit from six to nine inches long, which I could split down, would suit me very nicely.

I may mention that I am preparing an exhibit for the Bath and West of England Agricultural Society Show next May, but I am collecting beforehand to be sure. This afternoon I have arranged a nice case to show Bean and Pea seed and Leaf weevil injuries. [See Appendix C for list of cases and contents.]

October 22, 1895.

I am greatly obliged to you for the very acceptable parcel of specimens, which arrived in excellent order this morning. Indeed I feel very much indebted to you, for I know the trouble it takes to collect and pack in this careful way. The Hessian fly wheat was particularly acceptable as I had just two or three old straws, but this to freshen them up (with the insect and figures) makes a beautiful exhibit. The

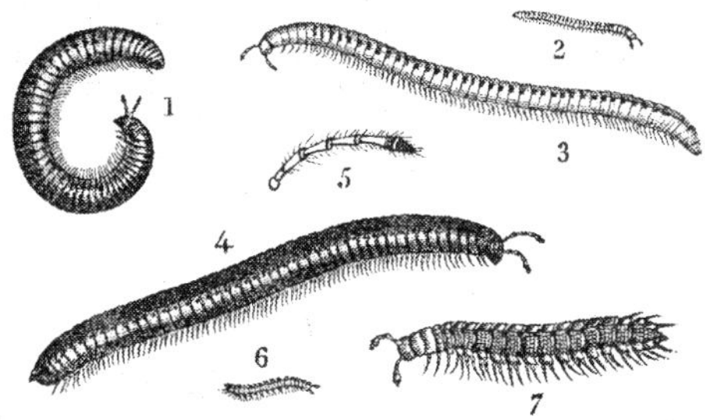

1, *Julus londinensis;* 3, *Julus guttatus* (*pulchellus*, Leach); 4, *Julus terrestris;* 5, horn; 7, *Polydesmus complanatus*—all magnified; and 2 and 6, natural size.

FIG 27.—CENTIPEDES AND A MILLEPEDE.

mangold leaves are also a great help; and nothing could be more characteristic than the American blight. I have not fully examined the contents of the bottles, but I see some nice *Julus guttatus* (Snake millepedes) and also a few of the long, thin, yellow, electrical centipedes, which I shall hope will keep their colour nicely in spirits. Indeed it is a very welcome contribution.

I have been ill with rather a bad quinsy, followed by something going wrong with my mouth and tongue, but I have nearly recovered now, and as I was directed to keep indoors, I have been getting on with the cases.

Besides the more customary crop and other attacks, I thought such things as liver-flukes (in spirit) and a good number of the little "water snails," *Limnœa truncatula*, (such tiny shells!), which is their host in the early stage, with figures of the intermediate conditions, would be of useful interest; also a couple of bottles with contents of sparrows' crops, showing the great amount of corn they eat, as well as a number of locusts in the condition in which they are importad in lucerne from Buenos Aires.

November 26, 1895.

This sort of brickdust-like deposit is, I think, eggs. I had a quantity of it sent me about six weeks ago by a fruit salesman and auctioneer who had got 10,000 apple trees

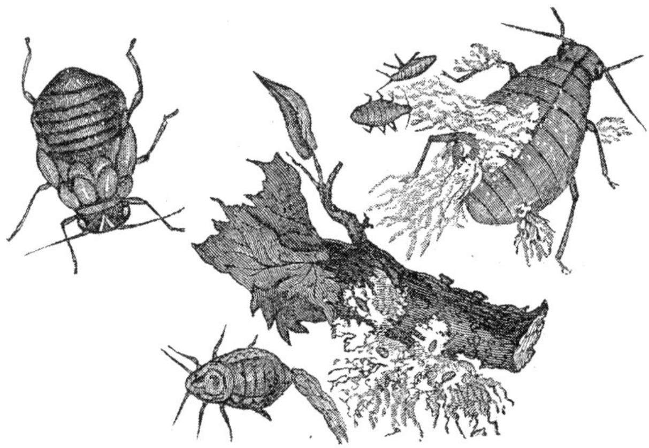

Infested apple spray, natural size; wingless viviparous female and young clothed with cottony fibres above; and small egg-bearing female beneath the spray; pupa with little cottony growth—all magnified.

FIG. 28.—AMERICAN BLIGHT, WOOLLY APHIS, *SCHIZONEURA LANIGERA*, HAUSM.

infested. It agrees in measurement and colour, &c., with the general description given by Mr. Frazer Crawford (of Adelaide) of the eggs of the Red spider, *Bryobia ? speciosa*, (fig. 52) found on apple in South Australia, but I do not think we can be quite certain of its nature until the contents hatch. About ten days ago I thought that I found fungi developing in the patches, so I sent a good supply to Professor M. C. Potter (Botanical Professor of Durham College of Science), for I was sure whatever he would say would be trustworthy. He wrote me that there was fungus amongst the red spheres. He did not believe that they were fungoid; but thought, like me, that they were eggs. Certainly you are right in considering them not American blight, although on one of the twigs you have sent me there is a swelled cankered piece that looks very much, to general observation, like that attack. I wish I could give you a plain straightforward answer, but the above is the best I can tell you at present. Mr. Nixon, whose name you will remember in my yearly reports connected with Red spider, says that he knows this "red deposit" well and does not think it does harm, but I should think it would be but prudent to have some soft soap mixture or antipest at hand, against hot sunshine in late winter days.

Many thanks for your good wishes, which I heartily reci-

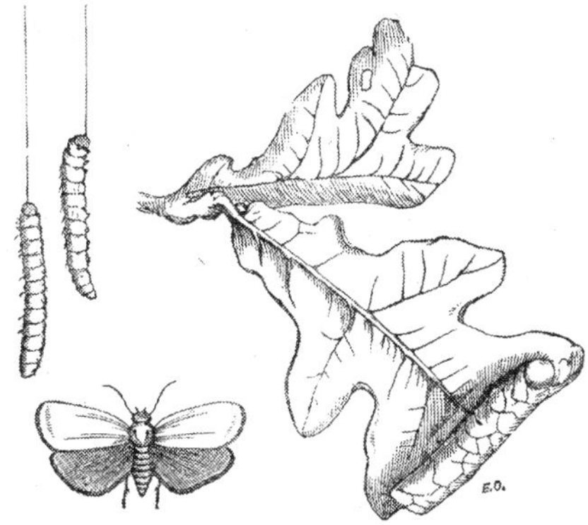

Moth; caterpillars hanging by their threads, slightly larger than life; rolled oak-leaf.

FIG. 29.—OAK LEAF-ROLLER MOTH, *TORTRIX VIRIDANA*.

procate, to you and to your young people. I cannot say I have been well. However, I am much better, but we are anxious, for my only remaining brother (who is nearly eighty) had a stroke of palsy last year, and on Sunday he had a second, but he is not suffering, which is a great comfort.

July 3, 1896.

I thank you very much for taking the trouble to send me this good supply of *Tabanidæ*, and still more especially for the Forest flies. I thought these were all dead, but whilst I was opening the bit of straw in which you pack them so cleverly, they began to tear out headlong—luckily I thought of catching the whole affair together in my closed hand, and then, pouring some chloroform in between my fingers, I got them all safe.

I am very much interested about this poor young woman's death from poisoning by a fly or insect attack.[1] I wish it had been possible to secure the pest, it would be so really useful to make out whether the evil was from the nature of the bite or sting, or whether from ill health or other cause the sufferer was unusually susceptible.

December 14, 1896.

I am troubling you with a few lines to ask whether you would kindly tell me if the caterpillars which did so very much harm to the oak leafage in your neighbourhood in May, were mostly "loopers"—or the dull, dirty green, or leaden-coloured larvæ of the *Tortrix viridana* (Oak leaf-roller): you just noted the very great amount of attack to me, in your letter of the 12th of May. I conjecture they would be loopers (? Winter or Mottled Umber moth),

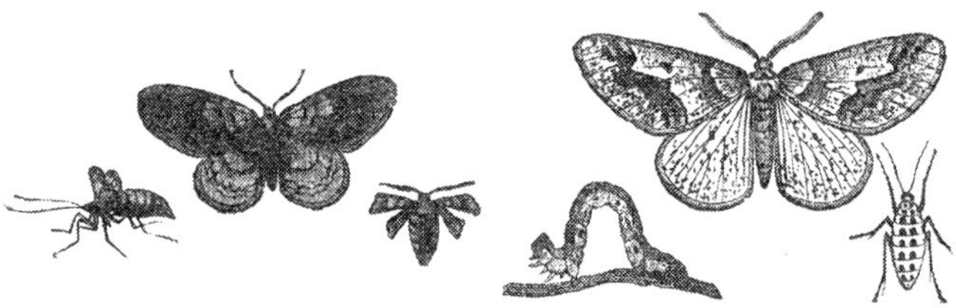

(*a*) Male; and wingless females. (*b*) Male; and wingless female; caterpillar.

FIG. 30.—LOOPER CATERPILLARS, (*a*) WINTER MOTH, *CHEIMATOBIA BRUMATA*, LINN.; (*b*) MOTTLED UMBER MOTH, *HYBERNIA DEFOLIARIA*, LINN.

for you note that "the moths appeared unusually early, and as soon as the bud began to open, the little caterpillars were upon them," and I think you would be referring to the early appearance last autumn of the Winter moth. But a note from you would be very valuable. I am wanting to make a really good paper on "Leafage Caterpillars"—people seem not to understand that though the remedies we know of can be used at a paying rate on orchard trees that we can get at, yet, for a mile of avenue "ancestral timber!" or for woods with their trees touching, and no passage for machines, the expense of treatment could not be met.

[1] The victim was a resident in the New Forest district, and the sting or bite was followed by severe local inflammation. Blood poisoning supervened and caused death. (ED.).

August 5, 1897.

I am greatly obliged to you for your very interesting and valuable observations, and for the accompanying specimens of corn attacks. What a collection to find in one field! I do not remember having had wheat attacked by *Chlorops* before, though it is subject to the attack, and it is years since I have had the Sawfly attack. In one stem the grub had spun itself a beautiful case just within the lowest part of the stem, and being kept steady in the transparent covering, it gave me an excellent opportunity of examining it.

I am very glad also of your definite observation of presence of Diamond-back moth. I should not much wonder if we saw more of it next year, for I have just had a very few specimens sent from widely distant localities.

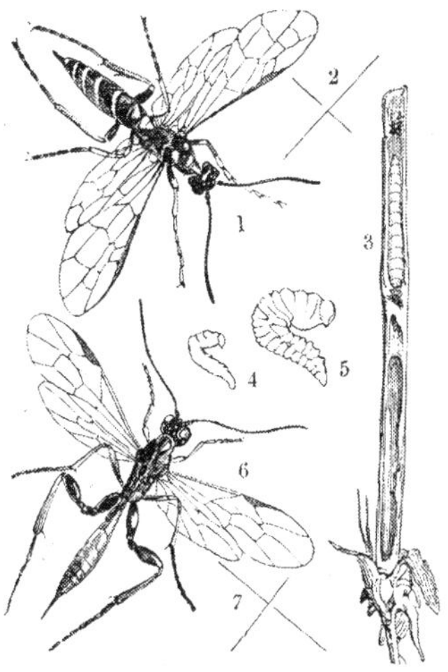

1, 2, Corn sawfly, magnified, and line showing natural length; 3, infested stem; 4, 5, maggot, natural size and magnified; 6, parasite fly, *Pachymerus calcitrator*, magnified, and 7, line showing natural size.

FIG. 31.—CORN SAWFLY, *CEPHUS PYGMÆUS*, CURTIS.

August 7, 1899.

I am very much obliged to you for your letter of the 3rd with notes of Hessian fly (fig. 15), and Corn sawfly presence. I have examined the specimens, and it seems to me that those of the Hessian fly attack close to the root are of the same nature as some I have had before. I think your notes would be interesting for my next Annual Report. I was very much pleased to notice some time back, that in an official U.S.A. report, attention was markedly drawn to the great importance of destroying puparia of Hessian fly as a means of keeping attacks in check. My name was given as having upheld the plan in England. I am truly glad that the States people have taken this improved view of preventive measures.

The weather has been quite distressingly hot here, with often a glare of sunshine on this exposed south-west slope that was very painful, and with the heat quantities of the Cabbage white butterflies came out. I got my gardener to syringe the brassicaceous plants with "antipest" as an experiment, and I certainly think that afterwards there was not nearly as large a proportion of the butterflies on the cabbage as in the adjacent flower garden.

Believe me,

Yours very truly,

ELEANOR A. ORMEROD.

D. D. Gibb, Esq., Barton, Marlborough.

CHAPTER XVI

LETTERS TO MR. GRIMSHAW, MR. WISE, AND MR. TEGETMEIER

The Red-bearded Bot fly—Deer and Ox Warble flies—Caddis flies—Black Currant mites—Crusade against the House Sparrow—Miss Ormerod's pamphlet and Mr. Tegetmeier's book on the Sparrow.

THE grouping of the letters to three correspondents, so differently interested in Entomology and other branches of Biology, was more a matter of dates than of any scientific relationship in the subject matter. (1) Mr. Grimshaw, the well-known authority on Scottish Diptera, was also the first investigator to show that the so-called "frosted" condition of heather was caused by a beetle larva; (2) Mr. Wise was one of Miss Ormerod's most interested correspondents in questions relating to fruit-growing and market-gardening; and (3) Mr. Tegetmeier was her colleague through the trying days of the Sparrow controversy, in which Miss Ormerod was subjected to bitter personal attacks by her opponents. He was always ready to lend assistance in relation to questions dealing with birds and the four-footed animals.

To Percy H. Grimshaw, Esq., F.E.S., &c., Museum of Science and Art, Edinburgh.

TORRINGTON HOUSE, ST. ALBANS,
August 14, 1895.

DEAR SIR,—I write at once to thank you very much for the copy of your paper on the *Cephenomyia rufibarbis* (Red-bearded botfly), in the "Annals of S. Nat. Hist." Will this be the attack figured (in its effect on the deer) in Dr. Brauer's spirited frontispiece to his "Œstridæ"? [1]

[In the last few days I have had sent a nice specimen of

[1] See also a paper on Deer botflies, in *Entom. Monthly Magazine*, 1898, by Mr. E. E. Austin, Brit. Museum.

the Throat Deer botfly, *C. rufibarbis*, which I alluded to in my nineteenth Report. It is a very handsome fly, more than half an inch long, and of very broad make (three-eighths across the abdomen), thickly clothed with very dark hair (but much either mixed with or tipped with orange), and on each side of the thorax a good-sized pale patch, and beneath the chin the red beard from which it takes its name. I scarcely think it would occur in the New Forest, but, if it did, it would be quite a rare prize.] [1]

Have you (if I may venture to ask) extended your researches to the *Hypoderma* (Warble fly), of our British deer? It would be usefully interesting, I think, if we could work this up. I am doing what I can, with help from some of the head-keepers, &c., and when deer-stalking is going on I am promised a warbled red-deer's hide for examination.

Rather larger than life; line showing natural length.

FIG. 32.—RED-BEARDED BOTFLY, *CEPHENOMYIA RUFIBARBIS*, MEIG., BRAUER, AND SCHINER.

,, 895.

I had much pleasure in receiving your letter this morning, and only wish I had a duplicate of the *Hypoderma bovis* (Ox warble fly, fig. 5), to spare—I would most gladly offer it, but now I have only one. I never had many, and with my best endeavours I cannot get people to rear them. I quite hope to have a hide of a red-deer presently, and I think one might make out the larva of the *H. diana* (Deer warble fly), at least, by reference to fig. 6, tab. viii.—what do you think?

May I ask you to do me the pleasure of accepting the enclosed copy of the "Œstridæ," lately come rather curiously to my hands. It was sent through a mistake instead of the separate impression of Dr. Brauer's "Tabanidæ," and as I knew how difficult it was to procure (especially with the plates), I kept it, feeling sure it would be useful to some friend. I have a copy which I have worked

[1] Extracted from a letter of Miss Ormerod to Mr. D. D. Gibb. (See Chap. XV.)

with for years, so I hope that you will not hesitate to give me the pleasure of making this copy as useful as I am sure it will be in your hands. I wish it were in better order. I see that beneath the frontispiece of this copy is a reference to p. 186 in the "Biologie von Cephenomyia, &c.," but I suppose my frontispiece is a "proof before letters," for there is no reference or description. The two are the same edition.

January 9, 1897.

My *rufibarbis* was sent to me by Mr. Dugald Campbell from Strathconan Forest, Muir of Ord, Ross-shire. I received it on June 8th, then quite fresh—and such a beauty! With its long thick coat it almost might be called furry, and the "glance" on the hairs was lovely. It was rather darker in some parts (that is, ran to rather more foxy red on the centre of the upper fore part of the abdomen), than is noted by some observers, so that it was very richly coloured, and its red beard was very handsome. I have had a figure taken of it, with great care, and if when you see it (for of course I hope you will accept a copy of my next Annual Report, on publication), you think you would like to borrow it any time for one of your papers, I should be only happy to lend it you.

Yours sincerely,
ELEANOR A. ORMEROD.

To Charles D. Wise, Esq., Estate Office, Toddington, Winchcombe, Gloucestershire.

TORRINGTON HOUSE, ST. ALBANS,
April 16, 1896.

DEAR MR. WISE,—If it would not give you too much trouble I should be very glad of some information about the case of Caddis worms attacking water-cresses. You will know these grubs quite well as the creatures that go about in shallow ponds or ditches with a case formed round them. Sometimes this is of very little shells, but at home the commonest kind was made of little morsels of rush or stick, with little leaves webbed up with it.

There is a very large trade in water-cresses from the little river here, but there are such quantities of trout in it, that probably these keep the Caddis worms in moderate limits, and I only now and then see their flies, the so-called "Water moths" in the summer. Mr. Richard Coe, Weston Farm, Guildford, has kindly sent me some excellent specimens of Caddis worms and cases, which I am very glad to have. The chief natural helpers against over-presence of Caddis worms appear to be fish of various kinds, but the increase of birds which naturally feed on fish—herons, &c.,—destroys the balance of nature, and Caddis worms increase.

[Miss Ormerod, quoting Mr. Coe in her Report for 1896, says (p. 156):—

"Whenever we find a bed of cresses attacked, we clear away all the plants, drain off the water, and leave the bed perfectly dry for two or three weeks in the autumn, previous to the winter planting. If afterwards we find traces of the

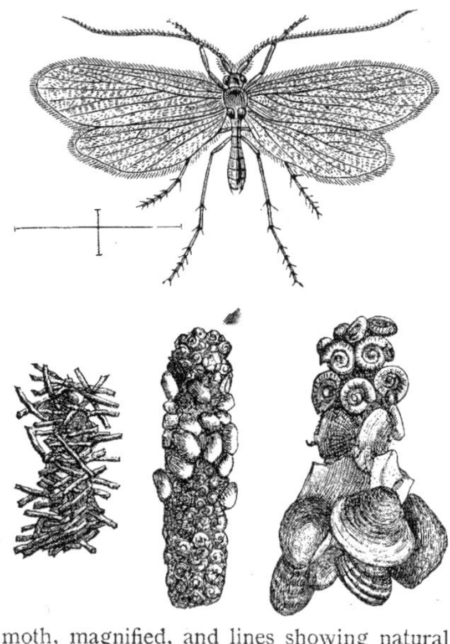

Water moth, magnified, and lines showing natural size (after Westwood); Caddis worm "cases" of *Limnephilus flavicornis*, magnified.

FIG. 33.—CADDIS WORMS, LARVÆ OF CADDIS FLY OR WATER MOTH, *MORMONIA NIGROMACULATA*.

worm, we wait until the plants are well established, then we increase the volume of water and swim the bed, and pass the backs of wooden rakes over the tops of the plants very thoroughly. This process brings the bulk of the worms to the surface, and they are let off down-stream with the surplus water."

To Dr. Fletcher she also wrote as follows:—"Did I

tell you about the Caddis worm attack on water-cresses? So much harm was being done that the unlucky grower was in much trouble, and on running the matter up it appeared that formerly there were numbers of trout in the water, but lately the landlord's wife had a fancy to encourage herons, and so came the curious sequence. The herons cleared off the insect-loving trout, so the vegetable-eating insects got ahead, and the watercress grower could not pay the rent of his half acre of cresses. I suggested that as the herons were encouraged by the lady, perhaps she, if applied to, might to some degree make good the damages!"]

March 5, 1897.

DEAR MR. WISE,—You asked my views about moles at Strawberry roots. I should say it would be quite worth while to spare them as you are doing, and see what comes of it. If they take the *Otiorhynchus* grub (of Orchard and Hop weevils) this would meet a difficulty which we hardly know how to fight at present, and if the moles took these grubs one might hope that they would take other underground kinds, which are kitchen garden pests, almost unconquerable by other remedial means. I should doubt, however, whether they would be of much service against Winter moth chrysalides (fig. 30). Very likely I am not right, but the mole seems to me to prefer more open ground and a larger scope of operations.

April 8, 1897.

So far as I know the only treatment for Black Currant Gall mite, *Phytoptus ribis* (fig. 65), which has been in a measure successful, is that reported by Mr. J. Biggs, of Laxton, East Yorkshire, in my seventeenth Annual Report, p. 93. There, if you will turn to it, you will see we have treatment to clear the pest from all localities, whether straying on the twigs or on the ground; or in the buds, this by breaking them off. Mr. Biggs observed, writing on the 20th of April, 1892: "You will, I am sure, be interested in knowing that I have, to a certain extent, prevented the *Phytoptus* utterly ruining my black currant trees. As you suggested in a letter of last March, we syringed the bushes twice with the solution of Paris-green, which I procured from Messrs. Blundell, and gave the soil all under the bushes a good coating of caustic lime; I also gave the bushes another dressing of the Paris-green. Just when the buds appeared this spring I had a boy gathering all the little knobs off the trees. The result has proved as satisfactory as I could expect, considering the condition of the trees last year, and I have every prospect of securing a good half crop. Our neighbour's trees in this village are utterly ruined, scarcely a leaf to be seen, and the trees completely covered with the affected knobs."

But with regard to the life history of the pest, I believe it breeds entirely in the infested buds, and I believe also breeds, *i.e.*, lays eggs, there at any time during the winter. I know that the nearly allied nut-*Phytoptus* does, for I have seen them. Outside the buds, so far as I know, the life is wholly spent in sheltering in crannies or straying about, on the stems, or on the ground. What we want, appears to me to be, to clear the mite by syringings from the stems when the buds (of which we have now the galled growth) are first beginning to form. But I do not see how we could do this, for we should ruin the fruit. My only hope for real prevention where black-currants are grown on this large scale, is in an alteration of the method of cultivation. As it stands now, the mites can convey themselves, or be carried by wind-borne leaves, or may creep from one bush to another on the ground, but if there could be a mixing of some field crop in strips with the black-currants, I believe it would do a deal preventively. If the ground between the rows were occupied by some crop that the *Phytopti* would not pass, it could not fail to lessen their presence. Even strips of strawberries or of gooseberries would be beneficial. I wonder whether kainite would be a good remedial application ? It might kill all the mites that are about, but it is quite plain to me that, as nothing that has been tried for so many years answers thoroughly, we are on the wrong lines and need a new plan. I wish you would, at your leisure, tell me what you think of mixing crops, and if you could let me have just a few little bits of galled twigs for figuring, I should be very much obliged. I wish I could help better about the matter, but so far the attack appears to have fairly baffled us all.

April 13, 1897.

I am very much obliged for these remarkably fine specimens of Currant galls, which reached me safely this morning. About the life history of the *Phytopti*, I do not think that anything more is recorded than what both you and I know. But as we know well that the mites are in the galls (such as you send me), it seems to me that what we have got to act upon is their condition (or locality, rather) in the time between their leaving these galls and when they are starting new attack in the embryo buds. I wish I could tell you more, but I do not see how to get at the point of locality, excepting by watching shoots with a hand magnifier. I really am quite at a loss as to what can be done.

April 19, 1897.

I wrote out to Vienna to Professor Dr. A. Nalepa, who is the great authority on the *Phytoptidæ*, and he is much interested in hearing about this great spread of attack, but is not able to give us better advice, as to practical remedies, than what we are already trying. (See also p. 248.)

He says very truly, that looking at the winter quarters of the mite pests being most especially in the buds, such measures as :—

(1) Breaking off and destroying the infested buds.[1] (2) Cutting off the infested shoots just above the ground, and so getting new shoots. (3) Only using uninfested pieces for propagation—could not, he thinks, fail to be of service, if carried out carefully. I quite agree with Dr. Nalepa so far as that, without these measures, infestation would be worse than it is. In a small amount of growth (such as bushes in a private garden), I can speak from my own personal experience of having sometimes satisfactorily checked the spread of these or similar causes of injury by employing dressings. But it is a very different matter where black-currant bushes are grown by acres together ; and I greatly doubt whether, even if consideration of cost were put aside, it would be within possibility to get this wood (or grove) of bushes, so examined and so expurgated of evil, as not to leave centres for spread.

It always strikes me as a very curious circumstance that (so far as I am aware) the black currant is not affected by this *Phytoptus* on the Continent, or at least in the large part of it in which the attacks are noted by Kaltenbach or Taschenberg. Do you think it can be that the black currant is there of a somewhat different kind which repels *Phytoptus* attack, just as some kinds of American vines are not as subject as others to *Phylloxera*? It occurs to me that it may be well worth while to import some hundreds of plants and plant them, of course on what is considered clean ground, and see what comes of it. I should like your views after you have well thought the matter over. I cannot expect the expense of an experiment

[1] This, or its equivalent, the immediate and diligent pinching of infested buds with finger and thumb, has proved the most practical remedy (Ed.).

of mine to be borne by any Company, but I should much like it trustworthily tried, and if you could give me some guidance as to where to apply on the Continent, and cost (a rough estimate), I might be able to get the plants, and with your permission send a good consignment to yourself.

April 27, 1897.

I have to-day heard from Dr. Ritzema Bos about the *Phytoptus ribis*, and he tells me that in Holland he knows many localities where this infestation is a scourge to fruit-growers, but it is always the black currant which is attacked. They do not have it there in the red currant, *Ribes rubrum*. He says that he is not acquainted with any better remedies than those mentioned in my letter, but that he considers it an excellent idea to seek for varieties or families of black-currants, *Ribes nigrum*, which may be "*Phytoptus* proof." He does not himself know positively whether there are districts in Holland not attacked by the *Phytoptus*, and whether in attacked districts there may be varieties that do not suffer. Therefore he is going to ask for information on this head from horticulturists and fruit-growers, and will write me again. I think it is very kind of him to take so much trouble to help us, and from his position I expect he will easily obtain whatever information is to be had, and I will be sure to let you know. It is very curious about the red currant being attacked in some parts of the Continent and not in others.

November 30, 1897.

I have this afternoon heard from Professor J. Jablonowski, Assistant at the State Entomological Station, Budapest, that he "sends now the promised black currants." I expect these will be supposed "mite-proof" plants, as he says that he hopes they will be serviceable for the proposed experiment—but he does not explain; only that they have been given to him by his friend, the Director of the Horticultural Institute, Desiderius Angyal (I do not know what prefix I should write). When the plants arrive I propose to divide them (if you please) between yourself and Mr. John Speir—it would be exceedingly interesting if there really should turn out to be a mite-proof black currant. But meanwhile Professor Jablonowski would very much like to have a specimen of the mite galls, for he has never seen them. If it would not be too much trouble, I should be very greatly obliged if you would be kind enough to let me have two or three bits of twigs with galls, if any are showing enough now to be noticeable, and I would send them on.

December 4, 1897.

Many thanks for the supply of galls, which I shall duly send to the Professor, and I earnestly hope that he will not infest Hungary with them! The consignment came to hand from him yesterday evening, but it is in the form of shoots as cuttings, so I now send you about half in a registered letter. If the pieces root properly I should think it would be best to plant them amongst the infested currants—as they are so few it would not be much trouble—and there is just a chance that they may be mite-proof. I do not myself (much as I regret it) think that there is any safety in washes and that sort of treatment, but as I write the idea comes into my mind whether, as with us, the *Ribes rubrum* (red currant) seems mite-proof—anything could be done by grafting black on red. Would they graft? or is my idea quite chimerical? The black currant shoots are var. "bang-up," which suggests England as their original country.

I do not know whether you have to do with importing apple fruit, but I see from Dr. Fletcher's (Canadian) Entomological Report that there is a newly observed fruit maggot in, I think (without special reference), the District of Columbia.

December 17, 1897.

I cannot be sure of your bulb attack without developing the fly, but I should conjecture that the mischief was most likely caused by the Narcissus fly. This is now known as the *Merodon narcissi*, Fab., but from the varieties in colour to which it is subject, I believe it has been known under all the following specific names: *ephippium, transversalis, nobilis, constans, ferrugineus, flavicans,* and *equestris.*

It is a fair-sized two-winged fly, and appears to be (in grub state) a severe plague to Narcissus and Daffodil growers in Holland, &c., especially in bulbs imported from the South of Europe.

In Verrall's list of British Diptera I only find one species of *Merodon* named and that is *equestris,* which on the principle mentioned on the preceding page, might be synonymous with all the other (?) species. The grubs feed in Narcissus and Daffodil bulbs and turn to chrysalides in the ground, but I do not find anywhere that there is any known remedial measure. It seems to me that the only way if a bed were much infested would be literally to trench it, and so turn down the chrysalides. You do not mention whether your bulbs are home grown. If they are imported, could not you suggest to your "consigner" that unless he sent you bulbs without maggots in them, you purposed applying elsewhere?

May 12, 1898.

Excepting one specimen your caterpillars are not yet nearly full grown! If you will turn to "Lappet moth"

Male and female; and caterpillar; also apple twig with leaves eaten away—all from life.

FIG. 34.—LAPPET MOTH, *GASTROPACHA QUERCIFOLIA*, LINN.

in my Annual Reports for 1893 and 1894, you will find "the brutes" figured—perhaps get a hint where they may have come from.

It was about this attack amongst others that I gave so

much annoyance to "Entomologists" by recommending that, notwithstanding their beauty and rarity, it would be highly desirable to make them yet more rare!

December 5, 1900.

Do you happen to have seen the Woburn Report containing, amongst a good deal of information, an account of results of experiments *re* Black currant mite? I would with pleasure lend you my copy, if you please; there is a little in it, as to their views about hydrocyanic acid—the very great difficulties of applying it to broadscale treatment—and a politely expressed hope that further experiment may lead to useful results. The experiment of moving cut down plants, even if steeped in methylated spirit and water, has not succeeded. Mine had a charming little crop of mite galls on those only moved to my clean ground, and even the steeped plants were not quite without them. In this case four of the twelve plants died, the others were sickly, and all of the two dozen sent me flowered profusely but did not produce one currant!

Yours very truly,
ELEANOR A. ORMEROD.

To W. B. Tegetmeier, Esq., F.Z.S., M.B.O.U. [1]

TORRINGTON HOUSE, St. ALBANS,
July 3, 1897.

DEAR MR. TEGETMEIER,—I am greatly obliged by what you tell me about your intentions as to publishing a book on "The House Sparrow," *Passer domesticus*. My idea is this—that for popular use (farmers and gardeners)—the evidence of what the food of the house sparrow really is, needs to be put plainly before them by means of records of trustworthy investigations of the contents of their crops. For this I have been taking the returns of Mr. Gurney, and some of Colonel Russell, who used to help me; an abstract of the U.S.A. Board of Agricultural Investigations, &c., &c.; also from my own Annual Reports, some lists, and observations of birds which are named as destroying insects—this to show that we do not wholly rely on *Passer domesticus!* With other material I propose to make a sort of 8 or 12 page "leaflet" or small pamphlet, and send it out gratuitously. I believe

[1] A great authority on the life-history of animals; author of a standard work on pheasants, and numerous works on poultry, pigeons, and horses, mules, and mule-breeding; on the staff of "The Field" for nearly half a century; an old Member of the "British Ornithologists' Union."

it would have an enormous circulation, and would not interfere with your much more valuable standard book. But I am exceedingly desirous to act completely in conjunction with you. To me it would be a very great advantage. I quite reckon on being violently attacked, but it did me no harm before to be threatened to be shot at, also hanged in effigy, and other little attentions. Still it was disagreeable!

FIG. C.—HOUSE SPARROW, *PASSER DOMESTICUS.*

[Miss Ormerod's case against the House Sparrow or avian rat is briefly given in the following summary, appended to the aforementioned leaflet, of which nearly 36,000 were printed and issued to applicants:—

"We find, in addition to what all concerned know too well already of the direct and obvious losses from sparrow marauding, that there is evidence of the injurious extent to which they drive off other birds, as the swallows and martins, which are much more helpful on account of their being wholly insectivorous; also that, so far from the sparrow's food consisting wholly of insects at any time of the year, even in the young sparrows only half has been found to be composed of insects; and of the food of the adults, it was found from examination that in a large proportion of instances no insects at all were present, and of these many were of kinds that are helpful to us or harmless. It is well on record that there are many kinds of birds which help us greatly by devouring insects, and that where sparrows have systematically been destroyed for a long course of years other birds have fared better for their absence. Attention should also be drawn to the enormous powers of increase of this bird, which under not only protection, but to some extent absolute fostering, raises its numbers so disproportionately as to destroy the natural balance.

"Here as yet we have no movement beyond our own attempts to preserve ourselves, so far as we legally may, from Sparrow devastations; but in the United States of America (of the evidence of which I have given a part) the Association of the American Ornithologists gave their collective recommendation that all existing laws protecting the sparrow should be repealed, and bounties offered for its destruction; and the law protecting the sparrow has been repealed in Massachusetts and Michigan. Dr. Hart Merriam, the Ornithologist of the U.S.A. Board of Agriculture, also officially recommended immediate repeal of all laws affording protection to the English sparrow, and enactment of laws making it penal to shelter or harbour it; and Professor C. V. Riley, Entomologist to the Department, similarly conveyed his views officially as to it being a *destructive bird, worthless as an insect killer.* In Canada, on October 6, 1888, at the Annual Meeting of the Entomological Society of Ontario, Mr. J. Fletcher, Entomologist of the Experimental Farms of the Department, strongly advocated the destruction of the sparrow; and in reply the Hon. C. W. Drury, Minister of Agriculture (who attended the meeting as head of the Agricultural Department of Ontario), stated 'that this destructive bird was no longer under the protection of the Act of Parliament respecting insectivorous birds, and that every one was at liberty to aid in reducing its numbers.' Reasoning on the same grounds as to procedure in this country, we believe that similar action is, without any reasonable cause for doubt, called for here. The amount of the national loss, by reason of ravaged crops and serviceable birds driven away, may be estimated, without fear of exaggeration, at from one to two millions a year. Much of their own protection lies in the hands of farmers themselves; and sparrow clubs, well worked, and always bearing in mind that it is only this one bird that is earnestly recommended to their attention, would probably lessen the load to a bearable amount; and we believe that subscriptions, whether local or from those who know the desirableness of aiding in the work of endeavouring to save the bread of the people from these feathered robbers, would be money wisely and worthily spent."

In his little book, "The House Sparrow," [1] Mr. Tegetmeier writes :—"There is no species with which *Passer domesticus* is likely to be confounded except the Tree sparrow, *P. montanus* (the only other species indigenous to this country) which is less numerous and which is readily distinguished by its smaller size, being only 5½ instead of 6 inches in length, and by its having black patches in the middle of the white feathers on each side on the neck, and two distinct bands of white across the wing in place of one."

FIG. D.—TREE SPARROW, *PASSER MONTANUS*

"The so-called Hedge sparrow or Dunnock, *Accentor modularis*, is wrongly named. It is a purely insect-eating bird, and neither in its structure, habits nor food is it closely related to the House sparrow. It does not occur in large numbers, and is highly beneficial as an insect destroyer."]

July 10, 1897.

DEAR MR. TEGETMEIER,—Your letter received this morning is a very great pleasure to me—in fact, a great relief to my mind, for I was truly sorry to feel I might be trespassing on far more authoritative work. I should like to shorten my work if I could, but when we meet, I hope you will set me right as to condensing and all other matters. If we could rout *P. domesticus* it would be a national benefit. Much looking forward to our meeting on Tuesday.

[1] *The House Sparrow*, published by Vinton & Co., at 1s., contains Miss Ormerod's original leaflet as an appendix.

August 4, 1897.

I think "House Sparrow" shapes up nicely altogether, and I have this morning received a letter from Dr. M. E. Oustalet, President of the "Comité Ornithologique permanent," at Paris, to say that he has not been able to find any indication of destruction of sparrows having taken place by order of Government in the districts that I inquired about.

August 16, 1897.

Application for our leaflet is very satisfactory. The Staffordshire County Council has taken up distribution, and the farmers and parish authorities are again encouraged to begin sparrow clubs. I have experienced tremendous denunciations of my own brutality from the Rev. J. E. Walker. I enclose the second, as he purposes to relieve his mind further in the "Animal's Friend." Please not to return it. I returned his book with my compliments and thanks for sight of the same, and requested that should he desire to make any further remarks relative to the leaflet that he would not address them to me, but to you as my colleague in the work.

August 21, 1897.

In very little more than a week a new impression was needed to keep up to demand—and we are making way well with this second 5,000. Many of the applications are from centres—and great satisfaction is often expressed at the information being made available. The Agent-General for New Zealand asked for a supply, and Mr. Morley, Lord Spencer's agent, is taking up the matter well; and as Lord Spencer appears to steadily set his face against sparrows, I hope that when he comes home we shall get some support there. A fair proportion of clergymen want copies for distribution to parishioners, or for sparrow clubs, which is satisfactory—and amongst all the great mass of applications there have not, I think, been more than five or six at all upholding *P. domesticus*, and these have been mostly quite trivial observations.

Mr. Morley was in a difficulty about how to keep the birds for counting, as in warm weather they got unpleasant. I suggested preserving their heads in salt and water—if I remember rightly this was how they managed the difficulty in South Australia. Altogether I think we are doing well—there are a good many inquiries as to the best methods of destroying the bird—but I always say that you will deal with this in your work. The good folks have not attacked me again personally by letter.

I should have liked to write just a short note to the "Field" to mention how well the matter has been taken up, but I did not feel sure whether you would wish me to do it? Would you think well of just mentioning the large demand yourself? On several days the applications ran to above a hundred letters. I am keeping the letters, for in some there is very practical observation as to the great injury done by sparrows—especially attacking corn on allotments.

August 22, 1897.

I am trying—if the thing be possible—to rout people out of the time-honoured old holes that they creep into—as the emigration of the sparrows—also the Maine and Auxerre story. These, I think, we have managed.

[The following is an extract from the "House Sparrow" pamphlet :—

"For many years mention has been made, by those who consider sparrow preservation desirable, of great disasters following on some not clearly detailed methods of extermination, or expulsion of the sparrow in the countries of Hungary and Baden, and also in the territory of Prussia; and, nearer our own time, in Maine, and near Auxerre in France. With regard to the three first named, a record will be found in our own 'Times' for August 21, 1861, p. 7.

"This gives a translation from the French paper, the 'Moniteur,' of a report on four petitions relative to preservation of small birds which had been presented to the French Corps Législatif. The report contains much information, but in respect to the emigrations of the sparrow because the bird was aware of the plots that were being laid against its safety, the statements cannot be said to carry any weight. The following extract is inserted, as it is important to agriculturists to have a correct copy of the baseless statements they are sometimes called on to believe. The passage is as follows :—

"'Now, if the facts mentioned in the petitions are exact, according to the opinion of many this bird ought to stand much higher than he is reputed. In fact, it is stated that a price having been set upon his head in Hungary and Baden, the intelligent *proscrit* left those countries; but it was soon discovered that he alone could manfully contend against the cockroaches and the thousand winged insects of the lowlands, and the very men who offered a price for his destruction offered a still higher price to introduce him again into the country.' . . . 'Frederick the Great had also declared war against the sparrows, which did not respect his favourite fruit the cherry. Naturally the sparrows could not pretend to resist the conqueror of Austria, and they emigrated; but in two years not only were there no more cherries, but scarcely any other sort of fruit—the caterpillars ate them all up; and the great victor on so many fields of battle was happy to sign peace at the cost of a few cherries with the reconciliated sparrows.'

"With regard to the destruction and consequent results stated to have occurred in Maine and near Auxerre, at present our very best endeavours have failed to find that the statement of this having occurred rests on any authoritative basis; and the only definite notice of the subject which we have found is, that in the neighbourhood of Auxerre there was an injudicious destruction of small birds generally, not only of *Passer domesticus*." See 'The House Sparrow at Home and Abroad,' by Thomas G. Gentry, p. 26, Philadelphia, 1878."]

August 22, 1897.

DEAR MR. TEGETMEIER,—But there is a third story—though I name this with more reverence than they always do—the New Testament allusions translated in our version, the "sparrow." I find in a copy of the "Ecclesiastical Slavonic" Scripture which I have here (the authorised edition of the Russian Greek Church) that the word is *bird;* in the ordinary modern Russian it is sparrow. Unfortunately I do not understand Greek—but this could easily be looked up in the Greek Testament. I am trying to find a scholar who knows what the respective words for bird and sparrow are in Aramaic, which I believe was the dialect of Palestine in the time of our Lord. Mr. Rassam, the explorer, can, I believe, talk a number of these Eastern dialects, but he always told me that he did not enter on them grammatically or technically.

September 3, 1897.

I see by a local paper that Miss Carrington's leaflet, "Spare the Sparrow," is out, and is procurable from the Hon. Sec. of the Humanitarian League, 53, Chancery Lane, London, W.C., price 1d. I have now written to the Hon. Sec., enclosing 8d., and requesting him to send six copies to myself, and two to yourself. This leaflet, I think, will be spirity. There are only a few lines quoted, but if the rest is so discourteous and inaccurate it will not be of much value.

Amongst applicants for my leaflet, the Duchess of Somerset and also Lady Alwyne Compton have asked for copies, which I am glad of. If it were "fashionable" not to protect sparrows this would go far with some people. I am longing to see the reply leaflet. I expect I am roundly abused, but I think it is rather strong to head something or other in the "Animal's Friend" for September "God Save the Sparrow." I expect we shall very likely have Maine and Auxerre, and Frederick the Great, and the cherries and cockroaches and the whole story resuscitated!

September 11, 1897.

The Secretary of the Yorkshire Union of Agricultural Associations asked for some leaflets, and with his consent I have sent him down 2,000 copies, which gives one for each member of the Agricultural Clubs or Chambers in the Yorkshire Union, and the matter is to be brought before the next quarterly meeting, with the view, the Secretary says, of seeing about asking the Board of Agriculture to remove *P. domesticus* from the list of protected birds. Mr. Crawford wrote me acknowledgment of receipt of the leaflets I sent by his desire to the Board of Agriculture, and said that next week, when the Secretary returns, they will be laid before the Board. I wonder what they will do? Daily applications are running from seventeen or eighteen to thirty—and some very good. To-day I have one from Smyrna and one from Stavanger, Norway.

September 19, 1897.

The applications are going on so well that I have had to order a fourth 5,000 of the leaflets to be printed as soon as can be managed, and of these over 2,000 are bespoken. A few days ago 3,000 were wanted for a Scotch centre, the Agent-General for New South Wales will send out 500, and other distributions are floating about; I think this is not bad.

October 16, 1897.

As you will see by the enclosed, I am now working on the twenty-first thousand. I have only about fifty copies left, and Mr. Newman has sent out some of the twenty-second thousand, so I think that we are doing well. One of the largest amounts asked for lately has been 1,000 for the Lancashire County Council, and also a little while ago Lady Aberdeen wrote for a small supply from the Government House, Canada.

October 27, 1897.

I hope you will be pleased to hear that I have brought

our sparrow work under the notice of Mr. [now Sir Ernest] Clarke, Secretary, Royal Agricultural Society—I hope in a way to advance our work. I sent him a couple of the twenty-second thousand, with a sort of report letter, giving some points. Mr. Clarke has replied very courteously that he is much obliged for my interesting letter, which he will lay before the Society's Zoological Committee. Also that, as he is occasionally asked for the leaflet, it might "save me (E. A. O.) unnecessary correspondence" if he were able to send copies to inquirers. I am delighted to follow up this suggestion—for practically it is the Royal Agricultural Society distributing for us, and thus giving their marked approval. I wonder what will come of the Zoological Committee's consideration. As the President of the Society has such an exceedingly bad opinion of the sparrow, I hope we may get some good colleagueship. I am perpetually asked how to destroy sparrows, but I refer the inquirers to you. I am longing to hear when your book will come out—surely it will have a good circulation. I am well advanced now in the twenty-second thousand, and the information is well spread, for we have a splendid notice—much more than a column—in the "Madras Mail," and I have had two applications from scientific U.S.A. centres.

I am still dispensing knowledge about the evil ways of *P. domesticus* so steadily that I have had to order a sixth impression.

The store of letters grew to such a size that a week or two ago I sent them (excepting about seventy which were to some degree private) in a great parcel to Mr. Janson, and I have arranged with him that this great mass, perhaps of 1,500 or 1,600 letters, should be sorted out into those that are merely applications for leaflets and those which contain any information.

The overwork and worry was too much for me, joined to my bad fall, and I was very far indeed from well for some time with gout and exhausting troubles, but I am better, and regaining strength.

September 14, 1898.

I most truly think it a great distinction that my name should be associated [on the title-page of "The House Sparrow"] with that of an Ornithologist of such world-wide reputation as yourself, and as it is your wish I very heartily agree. The only alteration I would suggest is that the word "Miss" should be removed. I do not like the word if it is not quite needed; and would it not be well to add a reference to my being an authorised agricultural worker? It may protect me from some "mendacities," and, a better reason, show that we are attentive to all three of the points (Ornithology, Entomology, and Agriculture) on which anti-passerine observation rests.

I like your frontispiece (figs. C and D, kindly lent by Mr. Tegetmeier) very much. It is very pretty as well as very useful. When your book appears I shall like to get some copies to send to some of my own friends, British and extra-British.

April 15, 1899.

It was a great pleasure to me to see "The House Sparrow" yesterday, followed this morning by your kind and cordial letter. I like your book exceedingly; it appears to me to be exactly what is needed. Chapter IV. [Diminishing the Sparrow Plague] meets the want which is greatly felt, and your voice being raised against poisoning will do good. I propose to send samples to the Agents-General of South Australia and New Zealand, where the "Avian Rats" are special pests; also to Mr. McKinnon, for the benefit of the Republic of Uruguay.

I think one or two would be well placed in the hands of the Department of Agriculture, U.S.A. I suppose that in an obviously much-needed matter like this it is hopeless to expect our Board of Agriculture to do anything. But I have, besides the above, several centres of work which I hope to make use of.

I do hope that your book will have the success that it deserves, and be of infinite benefit. I like it thoroughly—its pretty dress, the good figures and readable type on strong paper; it is a National gift, in your good and authoritative working up of the subject, and I feel myself honoured to be associated with you in the good work and the pummelling, which I dare say we shall get more of!

With my very kind regards and remembrances, believe me,

Yours very sincerely,

ELEANOR A. ORMEROD.

CHAPTER XVII

LETTERS TO MR. MARTIN, MR. GEORGE, MR. CONNOLD AND MESSRS. COLEMAN AND SONS

Elm-bark and Ash-bark beetles—Roman remains—Bladder plums—The Silver Y-moth.

A NUMBER of interesting and important fresh subjects are here concisely treated in letters addressed to various British inquirers. These are merely characteristic samples of a vast amount of correspondence for which space could not be found.

To the Rev. John Martin, Charley Hall, Loughborough.

TORRINGTON HOUSE, ST. ALBANS,
April 2, 1897.

DEAR SIR,—From your description of the elm-bark attack, I should certainly think that the maggots were those of the Elm-bark beetle, the *destructor*. If you do not feel certain after this hint as to the nature of the infestation, and will send me a little piece of bark, I will with pleasure examine it and report to you. This infestation does not injure the timber of the tree. The burrowings are mostly between the bark and the wood, though necessarily there are a number of borings through the bark, caused by the entrance and exit of the beetles. It would be desirable to fell the trees, and peel off the bark and burn it. The timber would be quite good (so far as this matter is concerned) but if the bark is left, the maggots will in due course develop to beetles and fly off to continue mischief elsewhere. Further I would suggest that you should direct your wood-superintendents to examine whether other elms show shot-like holes in their bark—the sign of the presence of the infestation. From your mention of the locality of the trees being rather damp,

I should conjecture that the trees were not in absolutely perfect health, and this is the state of things the beetle prefers for its attack. Injured boughs, or moderately recently-fallen boughs, or, above all, felled elm trunks in which there is still sap, but not flow enough to stifle the little maggots, are the very headquarters of infestation, and it is quite worth while to have such felled trunks peeled and the bark destroyed, or they will be the nurseries of great mis-

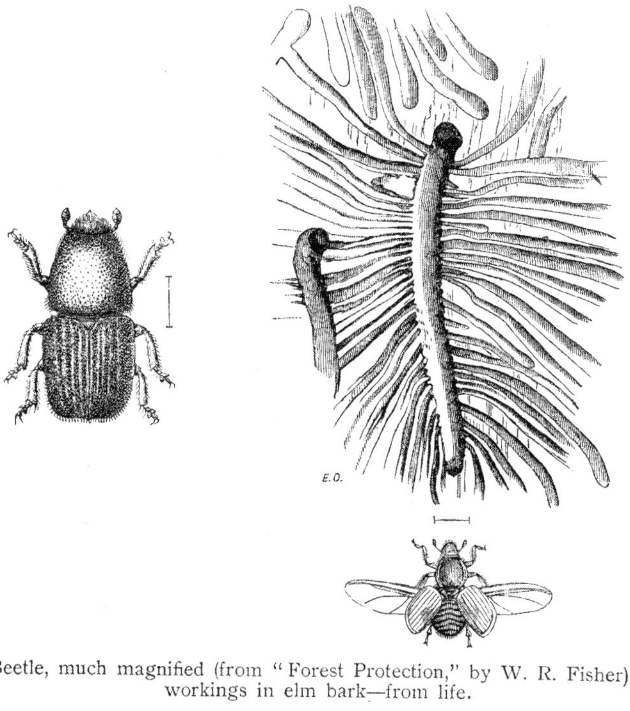

Beetle, much magnified (from "Forest Protection," by W. R. Fisher); workings in elm bark—from life.

FIG. 35.—ELM-BARK BEETLE, *SCOLYTUS DESTRUCTOR*, OLIV.

chief. If you will supply me with more detail I will with great pleasure give my very best attention.

April 5, 1897.

The little larvæ came safely yesterday and the specimens of bark this morning. Necessarily when the attack has been going on so long the burrows intersect each other so very much that they cease to show the typical patterning or tracks, but I do not see any reason at all to doubt that this is attack of the very great elm-pest, the Elm-bark beetle. With regard to its infestation of other trees besides elm, I have no knowledge of its ever attacking either oak or ash, but on careful search I find that one German writer records it as "sometimes" attacking the ash. I greatly doubt this having been observed in our country. Our ashes have, however, a bark beetle which tunnels much in the same manner between the bark and wood, and of which the presence may similarly be known by the shot-like holes in the bark. But you would distinguish the difference in pattern of gallery at a glance on raising the bark. As in the figure given, the mother-gallery is branched. This Ash-bark beetle, *Hylesinus fraxini*, does

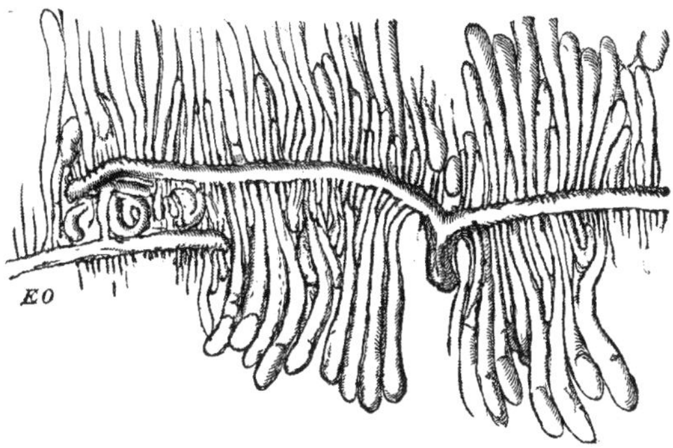

Workings, showing forked "mother gallery," with larval galleries from the sides.

FIG. 36.—TUNNELS OF THE ASH-BARK BEETLE, *HYLESINUS FRAXINI*, FAB.

not do very much harm, for it chiefly attacks felled trunks, or sometimes sickly or damaged trunks and boughs. It is not to be compared in its ravages with the *Scolytus*, well-named *destructor*. I am not aware of this ever attacking oak.

April 12, 1899.

You have certainly two kinds of bark attack present in the specimens which you send me, but without the beetles I am not able to say at all what species may have been doing the mischief. I can say quite certainly that I do not see any signs of the presence of the *Hylesinus fraxini* (Ash-bark beetle), but I have never, so far as I remember, seen the very long, narrow borings, hardly wider than a thread of silk, which are a good deal represented on the inner surface of one of your pieces of bark.

There are two or three grubs in fairly good condition which I have gently inserted into a burrow in the little bit of bark and have put carefully aside in the little box, and if these develop, we shall then know what we have to deal with. Perhaps you may be able to secure some beetles in a month or two; it would be of interest to make out the attack with certainty.

November 7, 1899.

I have very carefully examined your beetle and find that it is *Hylesinus crenatus*, sometimes known as the "Large Ash-bark beetle" to distinguish it from *Hylesinus fraxini*,

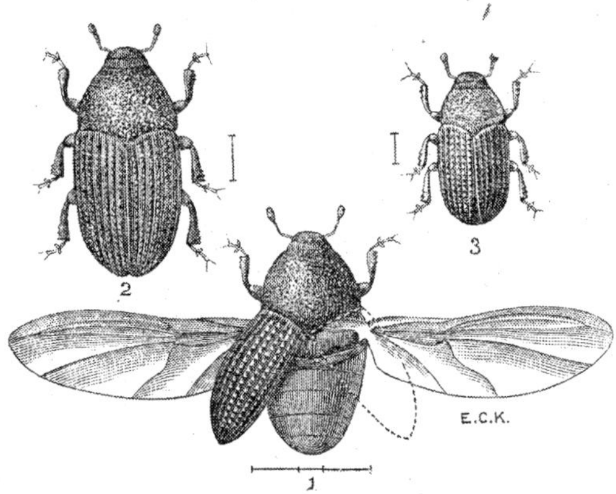

1, Beetle, with wings expanded, and one wing-case drawn only in outline, to show lower part of wing; 2, beetle as usually seen—magnified; 3, smaller and paler variety; also lines showing natural length.

FIG. 37.—GREATER ASH-BARK BEETLE, *HYLESINUS CRENATUS*, FAB.

the "Ash-bark" or the "Small Ash-bark beetle." The life history of each kind is stated to be the same, and I think, if I remember rightly, that some time ago, perhaps a year or so, in the course of our occasional correspondence, we have gone into the history of the *fraxini*, but if not I should have pleasure in either looking up the account in my Manual and sending the pages to you or condensing the points.

There appears to me to be this difference in method of larval proceedings: that whereas in the case of *fraxini* the parent galleries are formed somewhat in the shape of a T, with a short stem and long arms to the top, and the larval galleries placed at right angles to the others (fig. 36), so far as I understand this form is not followed by *crenatus* (fig. 38).

The beetle obviously pierces the bark, for the orifice is visible; and in or under the bark there are the mother-galleries, but I do not find the larval galleries feathering as it were from these, and the figure before me gives the idea of the body of larvæ having by their united attack cleared a flat space from which they have continued their solitary tunnels. Perhaps in cutting up your trees you may come

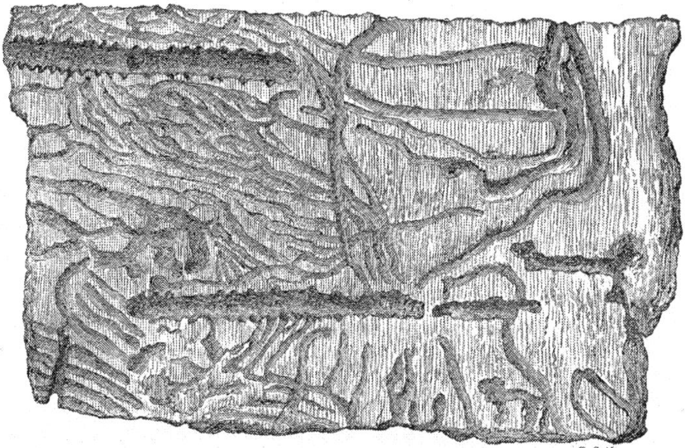

FIG. 38.—PIECE OF ASH BARK, SHOWING MOTHER GALLERIES OF *HYLESINUS CRENATUS* ON THE INNER SIDE.

on some of these markings. It is said that there are two generations in the year, of which the flight time of one is in April and of the other in October. This species frequents oak as well as ash, which is an important consideration, and I find it noted as frequenting old trees. These are the main points which I see about the history. I should think that if you find the trees which you have felled much infested, it would be a good thing to strip the bark off and burn it.

June 25, 1900.

I am very much obliged to you for all the great trouble which you have been good enough to take about the Ash-bark beetles, including your letter of the 23rd and the box of specimens received to-day. Some of the workings are quite certainly of *H. fraxini*. One bit catches the eye at a glance as showing quite typical galleries. In the long strip the workings are not so clearly distinguishable. According to descriptions or comparison with other specimens they appear to me of both kinds. But I really cannot think of giving you further trouble. We have all that is needed to make out a good, sound account, and I hope, if all be well, to do justice to the subject in my next Annual Report, and that you will be satisfied with my working up of the points of the infestation.

With renewed hearty thanks, yours very truly,

ELEANOR A. ORMEROD.

To A. W. George, Esq., Sedbury, Tidenham, Chepstow, Agent on Sedbury Estate.

TORRINGTON HOUSE, ST. ALBANS,
February 17, 1897.

DEAR SIR,—My work is chiefly on injurious insects, so I am afraid I am not qualified to give you the exact name of this curious collection of cement-like pupa-cases. Still I may say that your description most resembles those of the Mason bee, a kind of *Osmia* which constructs cells of a plaster formed of little morsels of stone, earth, &c., and then fills them with food and lays an egg on it, walls up the cell, and begins another. The grub in due course hatches and feeds, and goes through its changes to the perfect bee —and somehow or other manages to make its exit. These cells are sometimes made on walls, in parties of as many as a dozen (as shown in a figure before me), but as I said, I am not a "specialist" on *Hymenoptera* (Bees and Wasps), so I would not like to express a decided opinion. Your mention of the Roman coin found near the Severn cliffs is very interesting, for it was quite inexplicable to my father how it happened that, whilst coins are just the things often found in such great plenty amongst Roman remains in the pottery, bones, &c., of which there was such quantity in the site of the Summer Station of the Augustan Legion from Cærwent on the Sedbury cliffs, we absolutely did not *have* a single coin. Circumstances since we left have made me think that the word I have underlined may be more correct than that none were found. On one occasion it chanced I went when the ditch-diggers were at their dinners, and under a little shelter of turf (which naturally I

Ruins of Chepstow Castle, Monmouthshire.
(*p. 16.*)

inspected) I found a very nice little Samian cup. No more were reported as found; but after we left I heard of a box being in one of the lofts over the stables, addressed to myself, which when opened was found to contain more of these Samian cups, and also geological specimens from the cliffs. Of course I wrote down at once, but (perhaps equally of course) by that time the box had vanished. Your letter of this morning recalled all this to me, and made me think that very likely the domestic collector of curiosities who appropriated the Samian cups also made a little collection of the coins, whose total absence appeared so surprising. This is a very long story, but I thought it might be of some interest to you.

I suppose most of our old work-people are gone?

Might I venture to trouble you, in case you should be good enough some day to find time to write, kindly to let me know whether my father and mother's grave (vault) just below the high bank with the pathway on the top in Tidenham Churchyard (plate VII.) is in proper repair? If anything is requisite I think you would likely be so very good as to tell me, and to whom I should apply to do the work. Trusting you will forgive the intrusion on your time of such a long letter, I beg to remain, yours truly,

ELEANOR A. ORMEROD.

To Edward T. Connold, Esq., F.E.S., Hon. General Secretary, Hastings and St. Leonards Natural History Society.

TORRINGTON HOUSE, ST. ALBANS,
July 4, 1900.

DEAR SIR,—I think that perhaps before this reaches you, you will have heard from the Rev. E. N. Blomfield that these curiously formed damsons, of which you have forwarded me such excellent specimens, owe the galled growth to the attack of a parasite fungus. They are what you called popularly Bladder plums, or Pocket plums (fig. 39), and the cause of this extraordinary growth is the presence of the fungus *Exoascus pruni*. I do not myself work on Fungi, so I should not have considered myself qualified to give you trustworthy information, but I see in Professor Marshall Ward's good account of this attack, that, besides reproduction taking place by means of the spores carrying the disease from tree to tree, he mentions that the fungus can carry on its existence from year to year by means of its mycelium in the branches. Consequently much pruning back, as well as collecting and burning the "pockets," is needed to combat the attack to any serviceable extent. I am not troubling you with details, for you would find them so well entered on in Ward's useful little book, of which I gave the name yesterday to Mr. Blomfield, that I think you would prefer them in his wording. Hoping I may have assisted you a little in the matter.

December 19, 1900.

I am greatly obliged to you for the kind thought of sending me the photo of the Bladder plums. This shows the difference between the healthy and the diseased fruit so well that if I had not secured a figure of the diseased growth I think I should have asked your permission to copy part

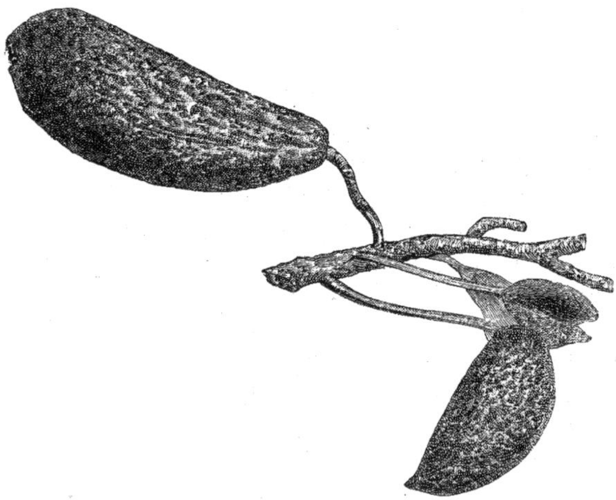

FIG. 39.—POCKET OR BLADDER PLUM INFLATED AND DISTORTED BY THE FUNGOID ATTACK OF *EXOASCUS PRUNI* (After Sorauer).

for my next Annual Report. This assuredly is not an insect attack. Still, as it may very often give rise to much perplexity, I thought that (with due explanation) there could be no objection to including your good contribution, and I hope that when in due time you receive your "contributor's copy" you will not disapprove.

About Dr. Nalepa's publications; I dare not offer to lend them, for all I have are copies presented successively during a long course of years, and if any mishap occurred, I should be in a difficult position. But if you have not yet applied to them, Messrs. W. Wesley & Son would be more likely to help you than anybody I am acquainted with. They would almost certainly be able to give you the titles of the successive publications and prices, and also procure for you such as are published. At one time I worked a great deal on vegetable galls, *Cynips* galls chiefly, but *Phytoptus* galls I have always found so very troublesome in several points of view that I have never worked on them more than I can help. Very truly yours,

ELEANOR A. ORMEROD.

To Messrs. W. J. Coleman & Sons, Fruit, Pea, and Potato Salesmen, Covent Garden Market.

TORRINGTON HOUSE, ST. ALBANS,
August 1, 1900.

DEAR SIRS,—I would very gladly help you about the moth-caterpillar attack on your potatoes, but I am afraid that without caterpillar or moth I cannot name it. There are very many infestations to potato of caterpillars, nearly allied to what you will, I think, very likely know well as the "Turnip grub." These are so numerous that it would be quite hopeless for me to endeavour to name merely from description and the chrysalides; and even with the caterpillar it would have been difficult (though I would with pleasure have tried), on account of some of these pests greatly resembling each other, and also some (identical grubs) altering their colours completely as they moult. I should have been glad to help you, but as these creatures are now turning to chrysalides the attack is presumably nearly over for the present.

P.S.—For general use in an attack of this kind the spray that you have been using, which is very nearly equivalent to the U.S.A. kerosene emulsion, is probably about as good as you could try; for I conjecture that you might not like to try "Paris-green"? Possibly this would not answer, and for various reasons—it being a ground crop as well as the tuber a food crop—it might not be desirable; still, I just name it.

August 4, 1900.

I am obliged by the fresh specimens of caterpillars received this morning from your agent, Mr. Carswell, and from these and the moths coming out to-day from the chrysalides previously sent me, I am able to say that the larvæ are those of the *Plusia gamma* moth, popularly known as the Silver Y-moth. I am not aware of these caterpillars having been recorded as injurious to potato leafage, excepting in the year 1892, when I had information of two attacks to this crop, in both instances from caterpillars migrating from clover. It is too late to-night to give you a detailed account, but I write now, as you will be interested to have the identification as soon as possible.

August 5, 1900.

Your potato attack is, as I mentioned last evening, caused by the caterpillar of the Silver Y-moth, so named from a small bright mark on the fore-wings, in shape like the English Y or the Greek *Gamma*. The moth is about half an inch in the spread of the fore-wings, which have a satiny lustre and are varied with rich coppery, as well as grey and brown, marks. The hinder wings are greyish, with a brown border. The caterpillars are fairly recognisable by being what are called "half-loopers." Having only two pairs of sucker feet beneath the body (besides the customary claw feet) they form a slight arch when they walk. The attack is occasionally very destructive and is one of those

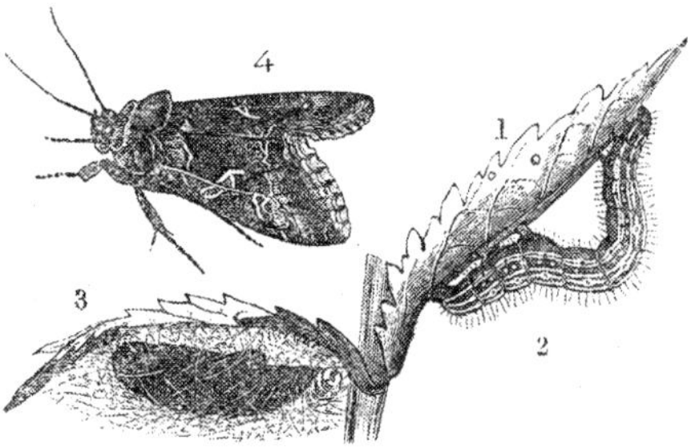

1, Eggs; 2, caterpillar; 3, chrysalis in cocoon; 4, moth.

FIG. 40.—GAMMA OR SILVER Y-MOTH, *PLUSIA GAMMA*, LINN.

which we have proof of having been blown to us, in moth condition, from the Continent; and, from some information which has come to my hands since I received your letter, I think it is not at all unlikely such may be the case now, with another kind of crop. The caterpillars feed on many plants, those of the cabbage and turnip kind especially; also on *Leguminosæ*, as peas and beans. Sugar beet they are destructively partial to. I should not at all think that the attack was likely to recur to potatoes, or that, as the infestation is now past its destructive stage, it was worth troubling yourselves about. If you should desire more about it than I can easily condense into a moderate letter space, you would find a careful account of the attack, with a good figure, in my sixteenth Annual Report on Injurious Insects. Hoping, however, that my few notes may be all you require, yours truly, ELEANOR A. ORMEROD.

CHAPTER XVIII

LETTERS TO PROFESSOR RILEY AND DR. HOWARD

Flour moth and Winter moth—Orchard growers' Committee—John Curtis—Entomology in Cape Colony—Handbooks and Reports—The General Index—The LL.D.

THE letters addressed to the two distinguished United States officials are unlike most of those we have passed. Miss Ormerod writes, as usual, in courteous and even in deferential terms to the two acknowledged chiefs among Entomological authorities in America. The considerable variety of subjects touched upon are dealt with in less simple language, and minor details give place to discussions on the higher polity of Economic Entomology. The letters contain internal evidence of the esteem in which her work was held by her correspondents.

To Professor Riley, Entomologist to the Agricultural Department, Washington, U.S.A.

TORRINGTON HOUSE, ST. ALBANS, ENGLAND.
March 6, 1889.

DEAR PROFESSOR RILEY,—We have got a flour caterpillar in England, newly arrived in the last two years, which is so very troublesome and injurious where it establishes itself that I should like to place a short account of it in your hands, hoping that at your leisure (I should rather say at your best convenience, for leisure you have none) you may kindly tell me whether you have it in the U.S.A., and, if so, whether you manage to keep it in check. The caterpillars were first observed in Europe in 1877 by Dr. Jul. Kuhn, of Halle, doing much mischief during the process of grinding some American wheat. The imagines from these larvæ were placed by Dr. Kuhn in the hands of Professor Zeller, who considered them to be *Ephestia* of a species previously undescribed, and they were named by him *kuhniella* (fig. 41) specifically after their observer. All this most likely you know well, but it is the appearance of this "pest" here which I am more particularly writing to you about. In 1887 the caterpillars did great harm in some large stores in London, and last year the attack established itself in a wheat-flour steam-mill in the North of England. The great harm caused is by reason of the caterpillars "felting" up the meal or flour by the quantity of web which they spin in it. They feed, of course, but this is not so injurious as working up the flour together, as thus they clog the mill apparatus to a very serious extent. I have much reduced their numbers by getting the manager of the steam-mill to turn on steam to scald them; and cleaning, whitewashing, and some use of paraffin have done good. The real cure would be to change the material ground. If we could use rye-

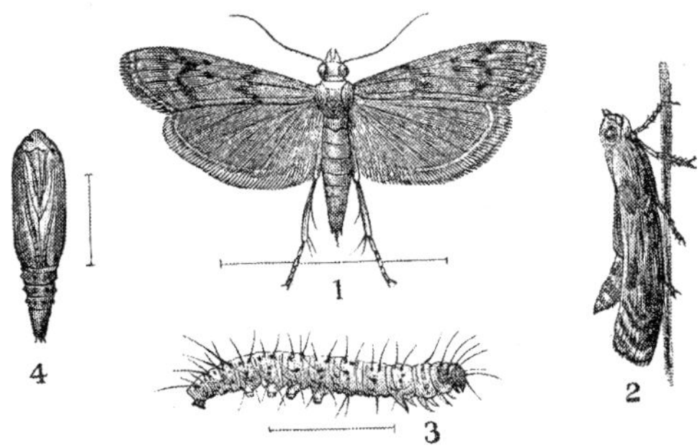

1, Moth, with wings expanded; 2, moth, at rest; 3, caterpillar; 4, chrysalis—all magnified; lines showing natural length.

FIG. 41.—MEDITERRANEAN FLOUR MOTH, *EPHESTIA KUHNIELLA*, ZELL.

meal for a few weeks we could clear out effectually this wheat-flour-feeding caterpillar. Unfortunately, however, the delicate apparatus of our recently arranged wheat "roller" mills does not allow of this. One point that would help us in preventive measures would be to know where the attack comes from. I am told it is a "scourge" amongst the flour (or rather the meal, as it prefers the more branny parts) in wheat from Russia and Hungary at the Mediterranean ports, so I am making inquiries; but Dr. Lindeman is not aware of this attack having been noticed in Russia. Under these circumstances I thought that I would write to you about it, and if you are acquainted with this moth and the larval working, and, still more, if you know how to destroy it, I should feel greatly favoured and obliged by any information that you may kindly give. I believe that unless it has very recently been placed on your American lists of *Lepidoptera* it is not noted as known there, and I am trying to persuade myself that it is not all selfishness which makes me trouble you thus, but that if by any possibility you may not chance to have heard of the serious nature of the work of these larvæ, you may care to have a few lines about them. The moth is about $\frac{3}{4}$ in. in spread of the fore-wings, which are of pale grey with darker transverse markings; the hinder wings remarkable for their whitish semi-transparency with a darker line from the point along a part of the fore edge. The larvæ, when full-grown, as far as I see, are about five-eighths of an inch long. You will not care to have full description, but they have surprising instinct for travelling, and amazing strength. One that I watched to test this power escaped from under a little smooth-edged cardboard frame which I had placed on a woollen cloth on a quite flat table and pressed down with a one pound weight.

I hope before long to forward my twelfth Report for your acceptance and that it may meet your approval.

June 22, 1889.

I have not until to-day been able to find time to study your interesting and instructive Report (which reached me a little while ago), and now after my best thanks I hasten to offer some observations about our use over here of the word paraffin—see p. 104 of your Report. So far as I know or can learn, the different oils sold under the name of paraffin, kerosene, or crystal oil, only differ from each other by reason of treatment to secure various degrees of purity or refinement. The common paraffin oil is the coarsest; kerosene I understand is a little more refined, and a trifle higher in price; and crystal oil—or (as it is sometimes described in the trade) "A1 Crystal Oil"—is limpid like water, and the purest of all. I do not know why, but kerosene is a name little used here. Paraffin is certainly not a correct term for the fluid form, but this fluid or oil is used so enormously compared to the solid paraffin that the appended word oil necessary for correct description is usually omitted as being understood. I quite feel it is a loose and inaccurate plan, but so the matter stands. In the same number of my Annual Report from which you quote—namely, that for 1884 published 1885—at pp. 66–67, is a recipe for a mixture of soft soap with "paraffin or any other mineral oil." It has been thoroughly tried over here, and found very useful. If you should think fit to experiment with it I should greatly like to know results.

A single report of appearance of Hessian fly (fig. 15) here has been sent me on June 13—with specimens accompanying—full grown but still in larval condition. These were on lower shoots of wheat of which the plant was then coming into ear at Revell's Hall near Hertford—the farm on which Hessian fly was first observed here.

September 23, 1889.

It was very kind of you to spare time to write to me before leaving England, and I well know how very much occupied you must have been, so must not be selfish enough to say how much I regretted not being able to have both the pleasure and the great benefit of a little conversation with you.

I beg to place in your hands the little brochure which I am now issuing on one of the consequences of warble presence, and might I ask Mr. L. O. Howard's acceptance of the other copy? You will see I have tried to condense the points of the subject into a space that workers would not be frightened at. It would be a great satisfaction to me if the inquiry met with your approval, and if you should judge fit to forward the cause of prevention in your country, your high authority would be a great help in strengthening my hands here. If you care to have a packet of the leaflets for distribution it would be only a pleasure to me to send some for your acceptance.

I have just seen with great pleasure that the Association of Economic Entomologists has been formed, and that they have elected the highest representative of the important work as their First President. This is a great satisfaction to me, and I hope ere long I may have the honour of being enrolled amongst its members.

You pay me a compliment in saying you would care to have an occasional contribution of mine in your valuable "Insect Life." If I had anything that I thought would be of sufficient interest to send, I would very gladly do so.

[Here a contribution on the "Shotborer Beetle" (Appendix D) followed, which was published by Professor Riley. See also page 199.]

April 10, 1890.

I must take up a little of your valuable time in offering

my best thanks for the exceedingly interesting transmission, received through your kindness this morning. Your own "Insect Life," 3 pts.; "The Root Knot disease"; and Mr. Koebele's "Australian Thrips" are all very valuable contributions to my library, and I greatly wish I were able to reciprocate more worthily. There is one point in reply to which, if you are quite willing, I should much like to be allowed to insert a few lines. It is to the paragraph headed "Traps for the Winter Moth Useless," p. 289, of March No. of "Insect Life." Mr. R. McLachlan is mentioned as having stated that traps which aim at destruction of the males of the *Cheimatobia brumata*, Winter moth (fig. 30) are useless, as enough will remain to fertilize the winged females. This I should have conjectured to be a well-known fact—but it is not this point which we are in any way working on, in any of the prevention details with which I am myself acquainted. Our difficulty, as you will see mentioned in my thirteenth Report, if you will kindly turn to p. 67, is the transportation of the females in the act of pairing by the winged males to the trees. This is a point much observed in this country, and I have to-day once again had my attention drawn to this difficulty in the matter of prevention, by a Somersetshire correspondent who in confirmation of his observation has preserved the pair in his collection. It is solely to meet this difficulty that we use tarred boards and lights in any preventive operations with which I am connected. I do not see the "Gardeners' Chronicle," and I am not in communication with Mr. McLachlan or I would have replied in my own country and given the necessary explanations, but, if you approve, I should much like to be allowed to insert the above observations, otherwise the various Superintendents and myself might appear to your readers (whose good opinion I should like to merit) as wonderfully ignorant of what I believe is a well-known fact.

We have now formed a kind of Society Conference with Experimental Committee of some of our best orchard growers in the West of England for the purpose of themselves experimenting, and reporting to the frequently recurring meetings—as to the effects of Paris-green, London-purple, &c. At last our people are roused to feel that "greasing" will not do everything.

I shall look with exceeding interest to the result of your *Hypoderma* or *Œstrus* (Warble and Botfly) experiments. I sincerely hope that you will be able to rear the imago.

I have been greatly disturbed (and am consequently not

writing you in as good form as I could wish) by a report being published in several of our London papers that I had been thrown from a carriage and met with serious injuries. This is altogether erroneous, but the many applications, and much writing and wiring to get the press to stop the report, has been indeed disturbing, and it has wasted me much time.

With kind regards and all good wishes from my sister and myself, pray believe me, yours very sincerely,

ELEANOR A. ORMEROD.

To Dr. L. O. Howard, Entomologist U.S. Department of Agriculture, Washington.

TORRINGTON HOUSE, ST. ALBANS,
July 26, 1894.

DEAR MR. HOWARD,—I do not myself know what arrangements the Royal Agricultural Society of England made with John Curtis.[1]

In the "Gardeners' Chronicle" for October 18, 1862, however, I find at p. 983, vol. iii., the following remarks in a short notice of the decease of John Curtis, which I transcribe in case they should be of interest. After mentioning that he had for many years been engaged in investigating the habits of insects injurious to farm and garden produce, the writer continues: "These he published in detached memoirs in the 'Gardeners' Chronicle' under the signature of 'Ruricola,' and in the 'Journal of the Royal Agricultural Society.' At a subsequent period they were collected into a single volume and published under the title of 'Farm Insects.' It was chiefly on account of the value of these articles that Mr. Curtis was awarded a pension from the Civil List which was augmented about three years since on account of the sad loss of sight which he experienced." The note is given as quoted from the "Athenæum," and in case you should not have references to Curtis having the pension he so well earned, I thought you might care for the extract.

Thank you for letting me know of Professor Riley's visit to England; I greatly desire to have a long talk with him. He may have comfort in having such a skilled successor. Special thanks also for your paper on the Army worm,

[1] The author of *Farm Insects* (to this day the most beautifully illustrated standard work in English on the subject) died at Islington on 6th October, 1862.

Lucania unipunctata.[1] It is such a good one, and the remedies so practicable. I hope to quote from this presently—duly acknowledged. You speak very truly as to information not being asked until the attack is so set up that much hope of victory over it is lost.

I should very much like to be allowed to offer my best regards, and respectful expression of my admiration of their good work, to the many kind friends who will be present at the Economic Entomology meeting in August, together with my hearty good wishes for the prosperity of the Association and its members. I owe much to the kindness of my U.S.A. colleagues and friends.

October 17, 1894.

I hasten to thank you for your letter received this afternoon, setting me right as to the origin of the bran-mash and Paris-green application for killing "cut-worms" (leather jackets). I should indeed be sorry not to give credit in the right quarter, and you may rest assured that the first time I have to mention the matter this shall be set right. I am sorry also on my account not to have known that this remedy was in use, and now you have pointed the way I shall be very glad to look the matter up. Through the kind liberality (public as well as private), with which I have always been treated by your country, I have a truly valuable library of your U.S.A. works, from which I often and gratefully profit.

I am looking forward very much to getting your paper on Economic Entomology, but at present I have only seen pleasant notices of it, and I am greatly desirous to read it *in extenso*. Attention to this subject is spreading very satisfactorily on the Continent. I am now in communication with Professor J. Jablonowski, of the Entomological staff of the Hungarian Government Department of Agriculture at Budapest. He is doing very careful and good work on *Thysanoptera* (Thrips). Also at Helsingfors (Finland) I hear from Dr. Enzio Reuter that they are contemplating arranging an Entomological Station, and I hope I may be in communication.

I am now beginning to pass my eighteenth Report through the press. One of the interesting appearances of the past season has been a widely spread outbreak of *Charæas graminis*, Antler moth (p. 104). This was more or less in

[1] The larva of a noctuid moth which now and then appears in great numbers in America, marching over the country and destroying young grain crops, grasses, &c.

seven contiguous counties in the South-west of Scotland, and though not remarkable in itself, yet, as there were one or two competent observers on the spot, some good notes were secured, especially as to presence of parasites, which I hope in due time you may find of some interest. There was much presence of a *Mermis* in one district. Out of a single larva I withdrew in three pieces about 18 inches of thread-worm. Also there was presence of "flacherie" and some *Tachina* larvæ. Dr. Ritzema Bos, of Wageningen, who is always most kind in colleagueship, helps me much about identification.

I hope to have a good deal to say about *Heterodera schachtii* (an eel-worm enemy of hop-roots). Different kinds of eel-worms seem each year to be showing themselves more, and I am greatly desiring to find whether the *schachtii* may not have come to the roots of oats here as well as in Holland. The Great Tortoiseshell butterfly, *Vanessa polychloros* (fig. 13), which is not common in this country, made a destructive appearance on elms and cherry leafage in one locality in Hants. And not far from Lymington was a destructive attack in one wheatfield of the caterpillars of a small moth, which ate out the heart of the young plant and was utterly ruinous. I cannot find the kind of attack on record (that is from a *Lepidopterous* butterfly or moth, larva), and we are all perplexed as to species. There seems little doubt that it is a *Miana*, and it appears to me most like *expolita*, but none of us contrived to rear it.

March 23, 1895.

I have been long in your debt for a letter, but sometimes it is very difficult to keep all work in hand, and I am sure you will forgive me. I had been endeavouring before your letter on Warble came to hand, and have since also been trying in some of what appeared the most likely quarters to gain information whether the form of attack which you mention in the U.S.A. was observable here, but as yet I have not been able to find that such is the case.

Many thanks to you for your presentation copy of your most interesting paper on "Rise and Progress of Economic Entomology," and your only too flattering mention of my own work (pp. 295–97). On the continent of Europe there is grand work going forward, and the colleagueship I am favoured with from many of the leading Continental Government Entomologists is most kind and gratifying to me.

September 23, 1895.

I think it is but a proper respect to you, as Entomologist of the Department of Agriculture of the U.S.A., to mention what I have been doing relative to the recent appointment of one of the U.S.A. staff of skilled Entomologists to the post of British Government Entomologist in Cape Colony. On the 17th inst. I heard from Mr. C. P. Lounsbury from Cape Town, with a letter of introduction enclosed from Dr. Fernald, which, he regretted, from pressure of time he had not been able to deliver. So did I, for I should very much like to have made his personal acquaintance, as well as that of Mrs. Lounsbury, of whom Dr. Fernald writes in such high terms.

I think it is a most happy thing for the Cape Colony to have secured the services of a good, trained Entomologist, but that he should bring with him in the person of his wife a lady so highly qualified to be a companion (an "*alter ego*") in his work was a good fortune past hope. I wrote at once to Mr. Lounsbury expressing the pleasure it would be to me to co-operate so far as lay in my power. And I have since written to the same effect to the Agent General for the Cape of Good Hope, especially drawing his attention to the fact (though of course I did not word it in this way) that really instead of one Entomologist they had thus secured the services also of an excellently trained assistant! Yesterday morning I received a reply, expressing his best thanks, and mentioning that he was then communicating the contents of my letter to the Hon. the Secretary of Agriculture at Cape Colony, who he felt sure "will be extremely glad to hear the high opinion you entertain of the newly appointed Entomologist, and he will also be grateful for your friendly offer of co-operation in the work of that office." I hope all this will meet with your approval. I am deeply indebted to the aid and encouragement I have received for years from the wonderful staff of workers of the U.S.A. and from its head—first Professor Riley, and now yourself—and if I can be of any service to a member of it by what I can do from here it would be a very great pleasure to me.

September 1, 1897.

I never before have ventured to submit one of my leaflets to you. I felt as if I should be taking a liberty. To-day, however, I have a request from the Boston Public Library for one of the leaflets on the House Sparrow, and I have therefore ventured to ask your acceptance of a few copies sent accompanying by book post. You will see that I have extracted largely from the excellent work of your own Board of Agriculture, but in a condensed work of this kind it is impossible to show the value and importance of the observations as I should greatly desire. At least I have acknowledged my obligation gratefully. I am sure I need not say that I should think it a pleasure and an honour if you cared to have some copies of the sparrow leaflet for distribution. The farmers here are delighted to have something reliable, and their reports confirm the severe losses which *P. domesticus* causes. But there is virulent opposition from a few people who rail at me in a most unpleasant manner.

Lately I had the great pleasure of a little visit from our

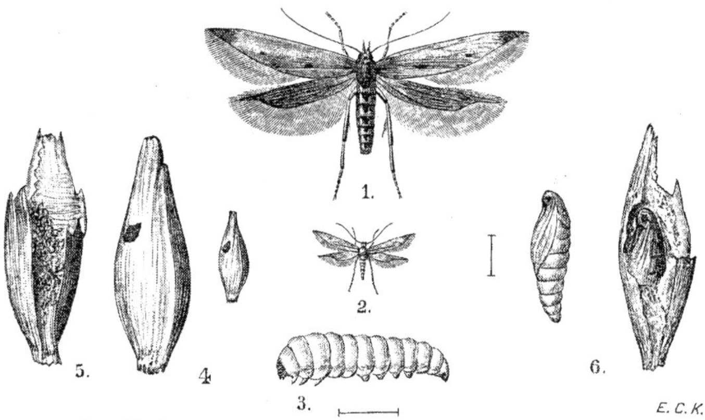

1 and 2, Moth, magnified and natural size; 3, caterpillar, magnified, and line showing natural length; 4, pierced grain, natural size and magnified; 5, grain with frass, magnified; 6, chrysalis in grain, and removed, magnified, and line showing natural length.

FIG. 42.—ANGOUMOIS MOTH, FLY WEEVIL (U.S.A), *SITOTROGA* (*GELECHIA*) *CEREALELLA*, OLIV.

good friend Dr. Fletcher, and we spent half an hour or so in cutting up some Plum-wood, infested by what I took to be the *Xyleborus saxeseni* (Shot-borer beetle) (fig. 46), given as a maker of flat cells, or burrows, by Eichhoff; but very likely you have heard about this from him already.

I have had some nice observations in the earlier part of the year of the workings of the Angoumois moth, *Sitotroga* (*Gelechia*) *cerealella*, which was imported in such quantity from North Africa in one or more cargoes of barley as to give some alarm.

The wings, such as they are, of the female *Lipoptena cervi* (fig. 24), have given me some good figures. There is demonstrably at times a mere abortive wing, but whether sometimes there has not been a developed wing which has been torn across so that only about an eighth of the wing remains, seems to me open to doubt. Also the Lesser earwig, *Labia minor*, has been locally a little troublesome. Altogether there have been a good many rather nice observations sent in, which I hope may presently be of some interest to you. Pray accept my sincere thanks for the enormous benefit I receive from the

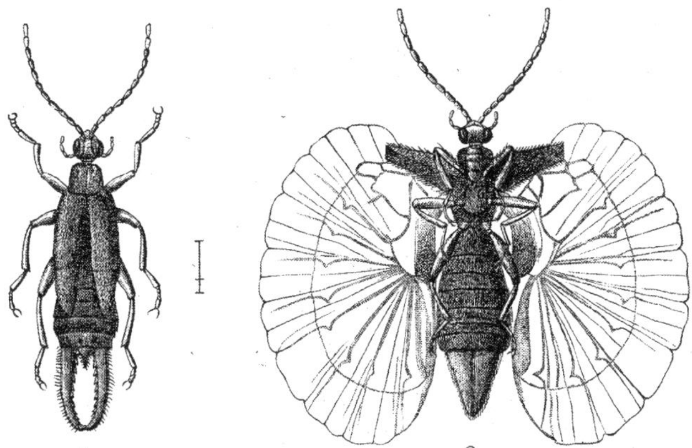

1, Male ; 2, female with wings expanded, much magnified ; line showing natural length of body and forceps.

FIG. 43.—LESSER EARWIG, *FORFICULA MINOR*, LINN., *LABIA MINOR*, LEACH.

valuable publications so kindly sent me, and believe me with most hearty good wishes, &c.

April 7, 1898.

Your letter of approval was a very great pleasure to me, and I greatly value your words of encouragement. Before this letter reaches you, you will perhaps have received a visit from Dr. Ritzema Bos, who gave me the pleasure of a visit on his way to the U.S.A. to investigate the amount of danger to be feared in Holland from this *A. perniciosus* (San José scale). From what I gather from the different publications with which I am most liberally supplied from your own headquarters and the experimental stations, I hope that we need not fear this veritable pest making a settlement here. I have an impression that a part of the commotion here is from a desire to exclude foreign fruit imports. I am working now on what I hope may make a "Handbook of Insect Attacks, injurious to Orchard and Bush fruits, with means of Prevention and Remedy." Fruit growing is extending very much with us, and so many little-known attacks have been reported to me in the last few years, that I thought a volume including these, with our old standing attacks brought up to date and very fully illustrated, would meet a need here. Also I was somewhat afraid that if I did not do it myself some one or other might be "good enough" to save me the trouble.

Our chief crop trouble during the spring and winter has been the presence of *Tylenchus devastatrix* (eel-worm), in clover. This still continues, but I hope that with good growing weather and sulphate of potash (as a manure dressing to encourage growth) we may fight it down.

March 24, 1899.

I am afraid that you will have been thinking me very negligent in not replying sooner to your kind letter, but I felt sure you would understand that if I could have sent any information in reply to your inquiry about the "Cigarette beetle" I should have hastened to submit it.

My Annual Report is late this year, for work on my Handbook, &c., &c., threw me late.

I have been following the urgent advice of our good and much regretted friend, Dr. Lintner, by having a "General Index" prepared to the series of twenty-two Annual Reports (chap. IX.). It is not a magnificently exhaustive compilation giving everything that can be desired, like that to your invaluable "Insect Life," but I think that both entomologically and practically it will be of service. When printed, I purpose to forward copies for your own acceptance, likewise to Professor Webster, to the State Entomologist, Albany, and a few other positions where I think they very likely have a set of my twenty-two annual issues, and therefore might care to have the Index. But if I were not intruding too much on your kind good nature, would you allow me to send a few, say a packet of ten or twenty, to yourself, which perhaps you would so greatly oblige me as to present to mutual friends whom you might see. I should think this a kind favour, for I might go rather astray in my sendings.

With my next number (all being well) I propose to commence a "Second Series"—altering my plan a little, so as to have a special section in which I could place any good short notes of information sent me, thus utilising what may come to hand, but without being encumbered by perpetual repetition, year after year, of life history and figures, of well known, or what should be well known, attacks.

June 26, 1899.

It is too good of you to give me the two copies of this valuable pamphlet, "Some Insects Injurious to Stored Grain," and I thank you very much. But I did not beg for more of your publications, and tried to get them *via* Messrs. Wesley, because you are so good to me, in constantly presenting information quite invaluable to me, that, as it is, I do not know how to reciprocate the kindness. We have nothing like your publications to fall back on here,

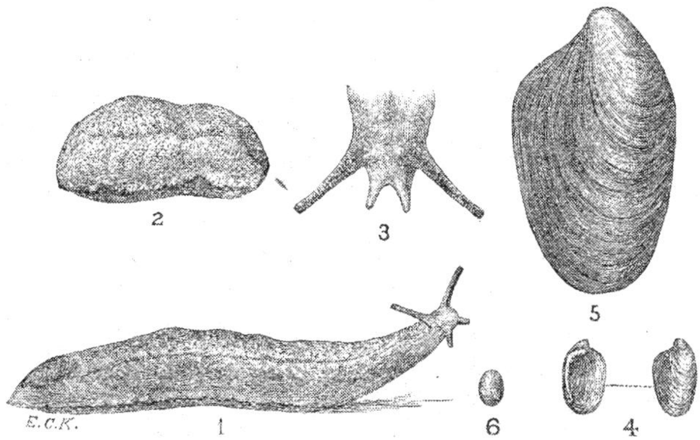

1, Snail-slug, in motion; 2, contracted; 3, head, with tentacles, magnified; 4, shell, upper and under side, slightly magnified; 5, shell, much magnified; 6, egg (4 and 6 from Plate v. of Jeffrey's *British Conchology*, vol. i.; the other figures from specimens taken at St. Albans).

FIG. 44.—SNAIL-SLUG, *TESTACELLA HALIOTIDEA*, DRAPARNAUD.

and when a very heavy case is brought to me I naturally benefit by your books.

I have lately been called in about a cargo of flour of 46,200 seven-stone bags, every bag (so far as examined) infested by *Calandra* (= *Sitophilus*) *granaria* (Granary weevil, fig. 68), and the Mediterranean Flour or Mill moth (fig. 41), and it was for the importers that I was trying to procure a copy, the other for my own lending. I am truly obliged to you.

My Index is not ready yet. I thought I could improve it,

and strained my eyes so badly that I caused delay without much good.

Now I am trying to work up *Piophila casei* (Cheese and Bacon fly, fig. 12) as a cheese pest. How curious it is that it should not trouble cured meats with us, as with you—nor cheese with you as with us.

The Shell-slug, *Testacella haliotidea* (fig. 44), seems to me to deserve a little notice, as (by its carnivorous habit) ridding us of various under- and above-ground troubles (slugs especially), and I have been gathering a few notes about the creature for some years. Another (I believe) unusual pre-

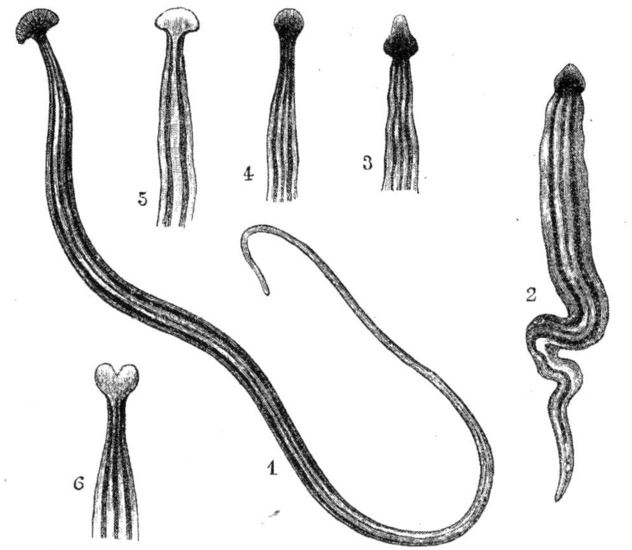

1, Worm extended; 2, contracted; 3, 4, and 5, different forms taken by the head—all life size (after figures by Prof. F. Jeffrey Bell); 6, bifid form of head, rather larger than life.

FIG. 45.—FLATWORM, LAND PLANARIAN, *BIPALIUM KEWENSE*.

sence lately sent me was a specimen of the Ground Planarian, *Bipalium kewense*, found eating plants "like a slug." I did not know the worm (so to call it) at all, but the name was given at S. Kensington. When it arrived it looked only like a very narrow slimy strip about three inches long—but I thought from its reported habitat possibly some slightly warm water would revive it, and immediately it roused up and swelled to a narrow cylindrical shape, and leaving the moss on which it lay made such fair speed (by adhesion of the lower surface) up the side of the bowl, bearing an unpleasant looking bilobed head before it, that I restored it to its box as soon as might be.

January 24, 1900.

I thank you most sincerely for this great trouble which you have been good enough to take for me. I feel very much gratified that you should place my Index in such distinguished hands, and I thank you very much also for your kind letter. Please allow me to add that if you should at any time care to accept copies of any works of mine which are in print, for yourself or friends, it would be a real pleasure to me to be allowed to send them.

I had a very pleasant letter from Mr. Lounsbury a few days ago. He is working with great interest on the "tick" [which conveys the disease known as red-water or Texas fever to cattle.]

March 21, 1900.

I do not know whether, according to etiquette, I am quite right in mentioning the following matter, but I think that to a kind friend like yourself I may mention the great gratification it was to me lately to hear from the University of Edinburgh that they were about to confer on me the Honorary LL.D. I feel this to be a great honour. It is not only the compliment to myself that gratifies me, but I greatly hope that one of our chief British Universities giving its approval to Economic Entomology will be a great strengthening to work in this country, which it has greatly needed.

April 30, 1900.

I was very much gratified by your kind congratulations (p. 295) on the great honour which the University of Edinburgh has conferred on me. They were all very kind when I went to receive the degree. I had the great pleasure one day of meeting His Excellency your Ambassador at the Vice-Chancellor's [Sir William Muir], and was charmed with the kind interest with which he conversed on Agricultural Entomology, and indeed all subjects which were brought forward. At the ceremony I was next to him, and now and then he kindly interchanged a few pleasant words. As I took my seat by him after receiving the degree he gently whispered, "I congratulate you; you did it splendidly," and I thought it very interesting that my first congratulation should be so kindly given me by the

Ambassador of the greatly advanced country to which I am so indebted for help in my work.

September 29, 1900.

It was a great pleasure to me (though it was only such a little visit) to make personal acquaintance with Dr. John Smith of New Jersey. Also Dr. W. Saunders (who came for the Paris Exhibition) and Dr. Mills kindly came to see me. These visits are very refreshing.

Meanwhile I have been learning a great deal from your "Notes on the Mosquitoes of the United States." It is a great gratification to me to possess this valuable work, and my medical adviser, Dr. Lipscomb, is only waiting until I can spare it, to borrow it for his own perusal. With kind regards and good wishes and grateful thanks for all your kind help and encouragement, pray believe me,

Yours very sincerely,

ELEANOR A. ORMEROD.

CHAPTER XIX

LETTERS TO DR. J. FLETCHER

General references to insect infestation—Progress of Economic Entomology—Success in using Paris-green in Britain—End of work done for the Board of Agriculture and Royal Agricultural Society of England.

THE series of selected letters to Dr. Fletcher in this and the succeeding chapter is the most comprehensive of the remnants of Miss Ormerod's correspondence with distant scientific authorities. Although only a portion of the original group of letters, it ranges over a period of fourteen years, and touches, sometimes only lightly, a great many of the leading objects of interest which had specially engaged her attention. Some phases of character come out here more conspicuously than in any other part of the volume. The mutual confidence in business matters which speedily established itself developed in this, as in most other instances, into intimate personal friendship.

To Dr. J. Fletcher, Dominion Entomologist, Ottawa, Canada.

DUNSTER LODGE, SPRING GROVE, ISLEWORTH, ENGLAND,
February 4, 1886.

DEAR MR. FLETCHER,—You ask about gas lime (as a top dressing for land). There is certainly need for caution in its use, but I do not think you would find a better short treatise on it than the little paper printed by the late Dr. [Augustus] Voelcker, of which I have had a copy taken for you (now enclosed with much pleasure), for I do not know where (or whether) it was published.[1] The kind old man sent me a copy when I wrote to him during his last illness,

[1] Printed by King, Sell, & Railton, Limited, 12, Gough Square, and 4, Bolt Court, E.C.

I not being aware how ill he was at the time. He had a great opinion of the lime, and I think it does immense good, but still, if too fresh or if too thickly applied, dire are the consequences. Even if the heaps are left standing a little while on the field, the chances are the spots will be poisoned. But I always use it in our garden. When we came here about twelve years ago it could be had as a gift, but when I wanted some a few weeks ago it cost about 7s. the cart load, and was only sold to me as a favour, there is such a run on it. One of the market gardeners said he could not do without it, and it is splendid for getting rid of the diseased growths in cabbage and turnip known as "Club root" or "Finger and Toe." But withal it does not do to trust the application to hands without heads. You will find reports (or rather notes in some of my different Reports) about quantities used.

I hope you will be able to come over, there are so many points it would be so pleasant to talk over, and Croydon is only a little way off by rail. It would give me great pleasure to make your sister's acquaintance.

July 19, 1886.

Lately I had good specimens of a Hippobosca, *H. Struthionis*, Janson, which is doing harm in South Africa to Ostriches at an up-country station. It appears to be a very curious instance of the migration of a parasite, as M. Lichtenstein (if I remember right, or M. Offer) thinks it may have been caught so to say by the Ostriches from the Quagga. It is very interesting as a quadruped pest on a bird.

March 15, 1887.

I was so very much gratified to receive your kind letter this morning, that I will reply as soon as I possibly can. Your Entomological Society of Ontario is the one of all others that I desire to belong to. I shall think it a real honour, one made still more welcome by the kind and courteous manner in which you notify I am likely to be permitted to have such a distinction [honorary membership]. Your society seems to me a pattern, a thorough example of what a Society should be, so truly scientific, and using its knowledge for the general benefit. I shall be proud to be allowed to add its title to my titles—prouder still to have the approbation and cordial friendship of its President, and its late President.

You have encouraged and gratified me very much by what you kindly say about my Hessian fly pamphlet; very few of our English Entomologists care for subjects of practical bearing, and it has grown me many a grey hair,[1] to endeavour to "keep the bridge." The "flax-seeds" are now being found near Errol in Scotland in the light grain or "shag," or "chog," as it is called, which is thrown down by a separate apparatus from the machine. Meantime I am trying to get a kind of cordon established for watch on the straw at such of our importing ports as I have influence near. We give the working men, through whose hands the straw daily passes, full instructions what they are to look for, where, and how, likewise a small gratuity, and a promise of a handsome bonus to the first who finds and produces specimens of infested imported straw. The working men can help enormously if they are kindly and properly dealt with, and I did not think sending an inspector would do much good. Hessian fly puparia would not have been "at home" on the day of his visit! Could you tell me whether straw is usually cut above the point of attachment of the puparia in Canada? This would make an enormous difference as to danger of infection.

Dr. Lindeman, Moscow, has given me a list of the Governments over which *C. destructor* has spread in Russia since its first appearance in 1879, and with his permission I am publishing it in my tenth Report (p. 104). Would you care to have a packet of copies sent over? Of course I shall send copies immediately on publication for your and Professor Saunders's kind acceptance, and to a few other of my Canadian friends; but if you will give me leave I should have real gratification in having a packet forwarded, and also begging acceptance of electros of any of my own figures which you thought might be acceptable to your Entomological Society.

TORRINGTON HOUSE, ST. ALBANS, ENGLAND,
April 22, 1889.

It was indeed a pleasure to me to see your handwriting again, and very soon after I received your Report which you have so kindly sent me. I have turned over the pages to see the general contents, and first of all I am exceedingly interested in your "Silver top" attack corresponding with our "white eared" wheat. They—these peculiar ears—appeared in Southern Russia, Dr. Lindeman tells me, two years ago, and he could not discover any insect traces any more than I could. It seems to me quite unaccountable, if it really is caused by Thrips, that they

[1] This was a purely metaphorical expression (ED.).

should not leave their cast clothing behind them! I wonder what you will think of my idea of ring vegetable disease? Dr. Lindeman writes me that he means to examine for *Anguillulidæ* (eel-worms).

I am particularly interested in your notes of *C. leguminicola* [American clover-seed midge], for I have long suspected we had the larvæ here, and to-day I succeeded in rearing my first imago, and have sent it off to Mr. Meade with Dr. Lintner and Professor Saunders's description and figures to see if he will agree with me. Will you kindly thank Professor Saunders from me for having the new edition of his excellent book on fruit pests sent to me. It is a pleasure to see it in this less expensive form, so many more people will buy it.

September 2, 1889.

You must indeed have had pleasure in your visit to Washington, but what a spectacle your study table must be on your return! Does not the collection, all calling "answer me first," quite make your heart sink? I cannot face it—it is such a terrible strain, so I stop nearly entirely at home like a limpet on a rock, and keep my work as well as I can in hand.

November 11, 1889.

Did I tell you that the *Xyleborus dispar*, Fab. (Shot-borer), has made what I hope may be only one of its strange intermittent appearances, in plum stems at the great Toddington fruit ground near Cheltenham? What a strangely destructive attack it is! I could not completely understand how it killed the young trees so wonderfully quickly until I dissected some stems, and found that, like your *X. pyri*, Peck, the creatures partly ringed the stem to begin with. And what a quantity in one stem! We need a descriptive English name, so I propose to call it the "Crowder," from the manner in which all the galleries are so crowded with the beetles, that there seems hardly room for another specimen.

December 6, 1889.

How very very curious is what you say about Professor Riley's now thinking *E. kuhniella* (Mill moth, fig. 41) may be a South Carolina insect. I shall await the letter you promise me with great interest. I suppose some records have been searched out, for in the spring he wrote me that he thought he could safely say that this species did not occur in the United States. Dr. Lintner also held the same view, and he is care itself. I am so glad you told me, for I had written quite a neat little paragraph for my Report on the remarkable circumstance of advance of one insect attack being so minutely recorded. How awkward it would have been! How good of you to spare me a male specimen. It is quite different your sparing me a specimen to my putting anything I have in your hands; I really hope you have not robbed your own valuable collection too much. I have been trying to compare them as well as I can manage under present circumstances, but I cannot of course do much without the microscope. The colour of mine is deeper, but this is not much. It was alive, but mature, when I took it.

I do believe all good work is done in concert, though we

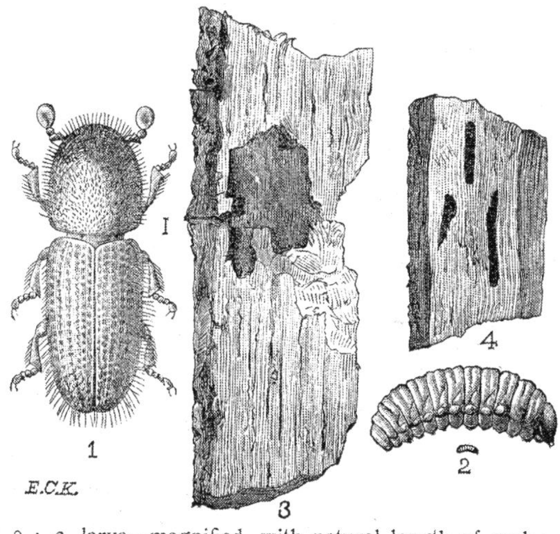

1, Beetle ♀; 2, larva—magnified, with natural length of each; 3 and 4, cell, natural size, showing broad and flat, and also narrow view.

FIG. 46.—SHOT-BORER BEETLES, *XYLEBORUS DISPAR*, FAB.

do not know how it may be fitting together yet. It is very often a great comfort to me to think so.

December 16, 1889.

I put off writing for a few days because I wanted to tell you more about the *Xyleborus dispar* (Shot-borer or Apple-bark beetle), which I am afraid is likely to be a very serious matter in other localities than where it first appeared, and it is doing much mischief: I do not quite like to raise the "danger flag" on my own sole responsibility, so I have sent out some of the new specimens to have my identification confirmed, and then I mean to write to you again and send a few more males. I found seven with hardly more than that number of females; also I found specimens of the white stuff that Schmidberger observed the larvæ fed on, and I have asked Professor Bernard Dyer to analyse it for me. He is a very kind as well as skilled helper. I cannot find the least sign of disease about the attacked trees: if the bark had been washed it could not be cleaner from Scale or moulds of any kind, but the havoc is dismal—what my correspondent calls "a slaughter" of trees.

We have now got the subject of Agricultural Entomology regularly announced as one of the subjects (voluntary) for examination of the Senior Candidates of our Royal Agricultural Society of England. I have been trying to get this arranged for some time, and I hope it will do good.

I have drawn up the questions as practically, *i.e.*, on as practical points as I could.

December 16, 1889.

Your letter was hardly started this morning when I received the confirmation from Mr. Oliver E. Janson of my identification of the fresh supply of Shot-borers from plum wood being quite correct, beyond doubt *X. dispar*. So I have great pleasure in enclosing two males and two females in a thin quill. They are packed in fine bark clippings, which they have shredded out themselves, so I hope they will travel safely. These are from plum stems, and in some cases they attack the branches. I have just now written a letter to the *Worcester Herald*, warning fruit growers to be on the alert, giving as much practical advice as I could compress into reasonable space, and especially recommending burning infested trees.

December 24, 1889.

I think that Agricultural Entomology is moving forward, but we are much hampered at present by various difficulties, which I fancy you would dispose of very rapidly on your side of the Atlantic. I suppose that in a sort of confidence I may mention that by private liberality of a Scottish advancer of science a lectureship of Agricultural Entomology is being endowed at Edinburgh University, but then comes the rather comical difficulty: Who ever is to take the position of lecturer? I am complimented by the expression of a wish from the authorities who have the election in hand that I should take it; but then Lady Professors are not admitted in Scotland. We know of "one man" fit for the purpose, Professor Allen Harker, of the Royal Agricultural College, Cirencester. He would do well, and as much desires the post as we wish to put him in it, but then the Principal of the Royal Agricultural College is very much set against his holding the post, as well as his Professorship at the college. It is a great puzzle. I have been doing my very best to help the Professor of Agriculture—a member of the appointing body—to find a suitable man, but what will come of it I do not know. This is not private amongst friends, but it is not yet before the public. Why, with you, I believe in a day you could fill the chair. I think I could do all that is wanted, but then, oh ! Shades of John Knox !

I am hoping each day to receive the copy of "Insect Life" Professor Riley kindly sends me, and to see what the Association of Official Entomology did at Washington.

[*Cablegram.*]

December 28, 1889.

Is not "Paris-green" the same as "Scheele's green," that is, arsenite of Copper, not arseniate ? With us arseniate of copper is a bluish powder ; please write.[1]

January 20, 1890.

I am exceedingly obliged to you for so kindly and promptly replying to my enquiry about the arseniate. I thank you most heartily, and Professor Saunders also, for so very kindly taking the trouble to make me sure how the matter stood.

I have been taking a great deal of pains to make my paper on the Paris-green as plain and sound as I can, but whether I can induce the growers to use it is yet to be seen. If any of your orchard operatives accustomed to application of it should chance to be in England, I believe that the best way to start affairs would be for his services to be engaged at Toddington, and from a proper method of spraying (and, without any doubt, its good effect), we should then, I quite believe, make progress. If you should know of any orchard workers being likely to come over, I should be very glad if you would give me a line, and then if none of my orchard applicants were disposed to engage him, I would myself ask for a lesson and a lecture, and he "should not lack his fee," as the old ballads say. Unless something is done to rouse the good folks they will go on smearing

[1] An arseniate is a salt of arsenic acid, while an arsenite is a salt of arsenious acid.

and smearing until their trees are one mass of grease, and swarming, nevertheless, with caterpillars of all kinds.

Now, I want to mention to you and to Professor Saunders that I have felt obliged to tell Mr. Whitehead, as gently and courteously as I could, that I must decline to continue the assistance which I have given since 1885 to the Entomological part of his work as Agriculture Adviser to the Board of Agriculture. I have recommended professional helpers who can aid him in the technical identifications, and if he needs more aid on general matters I have suggested that he should apply to Professor Harker, who has a great deal of strictly technical entomological knowledge, and of late years has given much attention to the agricultural application of it.

Even if the post of "Entomologist" should be offered to me, I should not think myself justified in accepting, for my great wish in my work is to be of immediate use, and if I had to wait for permission from boards and committees, &c., &c., before I came down on pests that want attention by return of post, I should not feel in the right place. Please forgive my telling you this story about myself, but though of course it is only meant for private friends, I thought I ought to let you know. My own work has steadily increased to such an extent that, with this sort of underground (unacknowledged) Government work in addition, I did not feel able to do full justice to it, and especially I wanted more time for experiment and correspondence.

February 13, 1890.

Many thanks for your kind congratulations on my better health. I am really better now. Work was bearing me down so very seriously I was obliged to make some degree of alteration. I regretted very much indeed not continuing any help I could give to Mr. Whitehead about his entomological Government work, but it was too severe a task, and it prevented my giving proper attention to my own, and likewise when the post of Agricultural Adviser was avowedly a paid one, I felt, and my friends felt, that if aid were needed it ought to be on a business footing and obtained from professional helpers.

March 24, 1890.

I thank you very heartily for the little box of *X. dispar* which you have kindly spared, for your own paper on the "Mediterranean Flour Moth" preceding the copy in the "Canadian Entomologist," and for all the information in your always truly acceptable letters. The little beetles came quite safely. I divided them duly, and I have no doubt both Mr. Janson and Canon Fowler will be very much pleased to possess them.

Our Worcestershire and Toddington people are really roused to see about these weary caterpillars. We have formed a "committee of experiment" with two or three very sensible and able men at the head, and I officiate as their entomologist, and benefit the stationer, at least! You should see the sheets of paper covered with sage advice!

At present I am trying to keep well before them that the very centre of all advance is to arrange our "washes" and our means of applying them, so that we may be able to destroy the hordes about May or June, when they are really and evidently doing harm. Your information is invaluable, not only in itself but because whatever may be advanced I can say Mr. Fletcher advised it, or more often, reported its success in Canada, and I feel secure. I really hope we shall make progress; the leading people are quite weary of this everlasting greasing, but I certainly do feel that our only excuse for asking you so many questions about it, is your own great knowledge of the subject, and great good nature; and, indeed, I am most truly grateful.

Professor William Fream, of Downton College of Agriculture, has just been appointed, by unanimous vote of Council of our Royal Agricultural Society, to be Associate Editor of their journal. This is such an excellent appointment it delights me. Professor Fream is an old friend of mine, so that besides the great benefit to the society of having such an able man in the post, I gain a skilled and heartily helpful colleague.

I hope that you will come over to England this summer, it would be such a benefit to me and such a pleasure both to my sister and myself. We hope you will stay here as long as you can make it convenient. This is a very good centre, and Rothamsted [the great English Agricultural Experiment Station] is only about four and a half miles off, and I am quite sure the staff would be delighted to show you everything.

July 7, 1890.

I believe that after our hard fight we have won the victory and Paris-green is now acknowledged, so far as the area of the work of our Committee has spread, as an indispensable insecticide in orchard-growing on a large scale. The caterpillars have been killed and the leafage not injured, and the Superintendents at Toddington are, up to date, quite satisfied and grateful. We are greatly indebted to you for your kind and able help, and what it has been to me I cannot say. It would fill a volume to record the progress of our work. It at first appeared as if the spirit of folly had got into the heads of the opposition; everything imaginable turned up one after another, and, as Entomologist to the Committee, I have hardly had a day's peace till now for weeks or months. We had one definite combination against us, and when all seemed quiet the beekeepers raised a commotion. This had to be answered publicly, but it seemed self-evident that if we did not spray when the trees were in flower we would not hurt the bees. One of our members made a commotion about his own health, and I had to point out to him that if he were not used to standing out in a March wind slopping with cold water (only I put it more politely) he was likely to feel uncomfortable.

If we meet, as I hope we may some day, I am sure you would be entertained with "The rise and progress of Paris-green." But really all the work and terrible anxiety have tried me very much, and I am going to have a little holiday with my sister for a couple of days at Oxford as a refreshment.

October 6, 1890.

You encourage me very much indeed by all you so kindly say, and I value your approval of my new book greatly, but I always feel, and I try to acknowledge, that the real usefulness of my work is derived from the kind co-operation I am allowed the benefit of. Just look at the Paris-green matter. I quite sheltered myself behind your name as an active referee. The good folks were hard of belief anyhow, but I really doubt if I could have driven the nail home without having you to fall back on. But for the pain that it could not fail to give, the history of our Evesham Committee's work, and what we had to meet, would be a most interesting chapter, and at last we had perfect success!

I think I told you of the wonderfully diseased strawberry plants, looking more like pieces of cauliflowers placed on the ground than their own graceful forms. Dr. Ritzema Bos has found that this is from the presence of a *Tylenchus* (eel-worm) (figs. 47 and 49), hitherto undescribed, and is going to bring out a preliminary notice in November, and as some portion of the observations (not the scientific parts) were mine, he will kindly let me use what I need for my Report. He is a very kind colleague.

November 18, 1890.

My sister is delighted to send you two copies of her Hessian fly maggot diagram, which she hopes you will kindly accept. This, as she says, is "her first public appearance," so she is rather anxious! But I have been doing my best to ensure her picture a good reception, and I revised it very carefully before it went out. I think you will like it. It should accompany this letter, but it comes so very near parcel post limitations of size that if it does not arrive please expect it shortly in a different travelling dress, by book post.

December 22, 1890.

For your collection you will, I think, like a regular letter of our good old Professor Westwood, but this is not in the least characteristic. He usually takes a postcard, and into it, by small writing, and adding in little bits where there is room, he gets in a surprising quantity of instructive matter. Mr. Meade's letter you would perhaps care for, as he is one of our leading Dipterists—he is very kind to me in identifying whenever I ask him; and the letter from Mr. Hormuzd Rassam is a contribution from my sister. He was, I suppose, our greatest British explorer in Assyria (after Sir Henry Layard) and was for a long time one of the prisoners of King Theodore in Abyssinia (to liberate whom this country went to war). I am not sure whether you saw him when you were at Spring Grove, but he was a near neighbour, and when he went on his Assyrian trips used to leave his very charming wife, and untoward little flock of Chaldee children, in what he was pleased to call "our care."

Many thanks to you for such gratifying notices of my Manual. They are only too kind, but it is very encouraging to have such approval, and very refreshing too, for sometimes I am nearly eaten up by anxiety.

I think the beneficial effect of Paris-green is quite established, and I hope that the use of it may spread widely next season; I fully believe that in it or in London-purple, lies the sole hope of keeping in check the crowds of miscellaneous kinds of moth caterpillars which appear with the leafage. In my fourteenth Report (that is, in the paper on orchard caterpillars which I am now preparing for it) I have tried to dwell with even tedious repetition on the points of the small quantity of the Paris-green to be used, and also the importance of the fluid being distributed as a mist or fine spray so as to coat the leaves, but on no account to be allowed to drip. Some of the good people seem to have an idea that they cannot have too much of a good thing, and results are dismal.

I am getting on as steadily as business allows with my new Manual. There are many new papers, and such subjects as Wireworm, Hop aphis, and others come out almost as new papers when the information which has been contributed piece-meal or in Special Reports, is sifted, and the information arranged in order. I am replacing figures that were not all that could be wished, with new ones. I am very anxious indeed to bring out what may be a really sound, up-to-date book, of our most important observations here. I think it will be about a quarter longer than my present edition, and "demy" instead of "crown" 8vo., so that it may be of comely form.

Economic Entomology is really doing better here. Our Highland and Agricultural Society of Scotland are looking about for an Entomologist, and this is a good step. [Dr. Stewart MacDougall was appointed to fill the office.]

December 23, 1890.

I have at once replied to your inquiry as shortly as I could manage, for I know how valuable space is, but indeed I shall be quite hurt and annoyed!—and your report will not give a right view!—unless you say that we applied to you, and that our work was in colleagueship. I really do not know whether I could have worked as was requisite, unless I could have had the advantage of being able to quote from your letters.

February 2, 1891.

Would you think me very greedy if I were to ask you for another copy of the "Proceedings of the Convention of Fruitgrowers," 1890. It would be a most acceptable help to the Evesham Fruit Experiment Committee. I should very much like them to read what you say about Paris-green, &c., but I am afraid if they had my copy it might not come home again. I have formed a short paper on "Paris-Green, its Uses and Method of Application for Prevention of Orchard Moth Caterpillars." I think it is all right, I have been very careful and plain, and I thought we must have some directions out before the season's work begins. We are finding wingless Winter moths and some other kinds going up the trees now, and this shows that there is no good trusting only to grease banding, for we should have really to grease from October to April to catch all the offenders! Our intermittent frosts let the creatures appear at intervals in a way which I suppose you are quite free from in Canada. Surely it should be recorded of me,

"SHE INTRODUCED PARIS-GREEN INTO ENGLAND"!

You should see the mass of correspondence since this time last year, from the first feeble efforts, through opposition and all sorts of things, up to success. The work is well begun, and though I may in fun mention myself, our Experimental Committee has worked wisely and grandly. Now they are going to publish the reports of all the members who have sent them in. That by Mr. Wise [1] is very good indeed, and I am to write a preface for them, so I can show the teachings, where they agree, and why they differ.

We have had a long spell of cold weather, bringing great suffering to the poor, and to my sister and myself the loss of a brother, who was "coldstruck" and carried off almost instantaneously by *angina pectoris*. I had a temporary share in troubles from a severe fall, my feet going from under me down a slope on hidden ice, and sending me down on the back of my head; but I think I am right again now.

There is a great want over here of some kind of lesson book for village schools telling something that would interest the boys—possibly, too, the girls. I do not know whether I could manage it, but I am thinking of trying to take some thirty or so of the very commonest attacks—including a very few to stock, which boys always care about—and seeing what I can do. I have a hope that through the boys we might get at the agricultural labourers and cowmen.

I like your address very much at the Economic Entomologists' meeting in reply to Professor Riley's grand and comprehensive address; but as yet I have not been able quite to make out the scope of the Society's arrangements for extra-American members. It must be a great pleasure to all members who can meet, to talk over serviceable points, and a great benefit conferred on the country, but I am puzzled about the external bearings. It does not seem to affect me say, for example, in my communication with such kind friends as yourself and Dr. Lintner. I would venture any way, I think, to ask at your convenience for advice or instruction, and where I can afford information I shall think myself honoured and happy to render it.

But I do not understand qualification. You have the names of Mr. C. and Mr. S. on your list. I do not know the gentlemen, so cannot tell what they may be doing, but our grand old chief, my entomological master, and friend

[1] See letters to Mr. Wise in chapter XVI.

almost of a lifetime, dear old Professor Westwood, is not there, and yet *ex-officio* as Hope Professor of Zoology he lectures on Entomology (to the best of my belief) regularly at Oxford. And what work Dr. Lindeman does! It would be a great help over here if we had some such Society. My work is so very solitary, but I do what I can.

Dr. Fream's lectures [Steven course in Edinburgh University] have been quite a success. This delights me. Professor Wallace has been exceedingly pleased with the sound manner in which he built up his Agricultural Entomology in the students' minds, and I think the course has given great satisfaction. He is a very sound worker, and I should greatly like him to be my collaborateur at the Royal Agricultural Society of England. I have not brought the subject forward yet, but if there were an Assistant Entomologist who might present my Reports instead of my personal attendance being necessary in all the business hurry of that great number of gentlemen, it would relieve me of a very distasteful part of my work.

March 23, 1891.

We have just got a full stream of applications for gratuitous distribution of "Paris-green" pamphlets, so we are very anxious to keep all in hand. I greatly hope that this will take hold. We broke through many objections last year, and now we can point to saved crops, and no disastrous massacre of gardeners—not even a sparrow defunct; also a lessened amount of Winter moth in autumn, and a glorious promise of flower bud on trees which have been reported on. Last year we did not know where to turn for a proper sprayer; now, on the day before yesterday there was to be a "contest of sprayers" at the Crystal Palace. I think this shows of itself how the matter on insecticide sprayings has come forward. I am fairly broadcasting the P.G. pamphlets. Many years ago when a railway bridge on a new method of constructic was made over the Wye (plate XXVI), near my old home, the natives were "afraid for their lives" to go over it, but the ingenious plan was struck, of running any one gratuitously over and back all day long—the trains of trucks were crammed, the people shouted for joy, and the victory was won; and now I am carrying out the same principle. Gentle and simple, wise and very unwise, are wanting "Paris-green" pamphlets, and I hope that by the sheets of advice, &c., that have to be sent accompanying, that the very silliest souls will not do harm; and meanwhile we are getting the subject popularised. You will think that I am *tête montée*

PLATE XXVI.

Railway Bridge on the Wye, near Chepstow.

To face p. 208.

about it, but it has been a long, severe labour, and I thoroughly believe that on the adoption of the arsenical insecticides depends the success of the English orchard growing in the future.

So far as I see, the "grubs" have not been the least the worse for the cold of the recent frost so long as they were in their self-made shelters below ground, but we carried devastation amongst hundreds of Cockchafer grubs, *Melolontha vulgaris*, by ploughing. The larvæ were too torpid to bury themselves, and the birds disposed of them very thoroughly.

Dr. Lindeman writes that he "had a district inspection set on foot" to find presence of *Tylenchus devastatrix* in

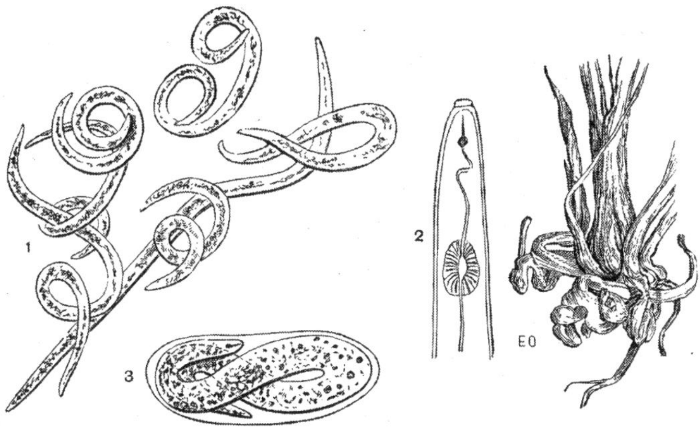

1, Adults; 2, anterior of female, showing mouth-spear; 3, embryo in egg—all greatly magnified, anterior portion 440 times (from figures by Dr. J. Ritzema Bos). One of the causes of clover-sickness.

"Tulip-rooted" oat plant.

* * * *

FIG. 47.—STEM EEL-WORMS, *TYLENCHUS DEVASTATRIX*.

Russia, but "always with negative results." This is very interesting.

June 26, 1891.

Did I tell you that my sister has been preparing a set of twenty-four diagrams—same size and in the same style as that of the Hessian fly? These are of our most destructive or most remarkable insect pests—and our Royal Agricultural Society has approved so highly of those which are printed that they have arranged for her to transfer to them the ownership of copyright of the set. This gratifies her very much. They pay her "out of pocket" expenses of printing and she presents the copyrights and her work. I think they form a very beautiful collection, and I believe the Society means to bring them out (together with my previous ones—p. 99) in little half-dozen sets. Thus, one set for village schools, one for fruit growers, one for forest use. I hope they will be very useful in this way for those who do not wish to purchase the whole.

We have certainly good proof this year that in our insular climate cold does not "kill the grubs." If it were possible it would even seem the Entomons were the better for it.

September 26, 1891.

A letter came from Adelaide to announce Mr. Frazer Crawford's decease. It was caused by chronic gout and heart disease. He had been as cheerful as usual, and when a friend left him about nine o'clock in the evening he set to work to prepare a scientific article, but not long after he went to bed. On the following morning, October 30th, the servant found the lamp still burning, but Mr. Crawford had quietly passed away as if in sleep with his book, a volume of Cryptogamic Botany, fallen from his hand. He was a perfectly indefatigable worker; even in the last month of his life, weighed down as he was by all the inconveniences and pains of hip disease besides those which took him from us, he prepared a long paper on vegetable and other plant pests for the "Garden and Field," in which he wrote, besides a review of my Manual. And a warning paper by him on the danger of importing *Phylloxera* appeared in the Report of the Bureau of Agriculture of South Australia accompanying the notice of his death. As a friend he was excessively valued by all who knew his kindness and his worth, and his loss is deeply regretted at Adelaide. To myself it is a very great cause of regret both as a true friend and an Entomological colleague.

February 6–8, 1892.

I have this afternoon sent the index to my fifteenth Report up to press, and am now enjoying myself by at least beginning a letter to you. I hope you will like the report. The paper on *Plutella cruciferarum* (Diamond-back moth) is quite enormously long, but I believe so far as evidence in my hands shows, that, taking all points of the attack together, it has been unexampled in this country before, and I was very desirous to present a trustworthy record, which would bear sifting at every corner as to what did happen, and readers could judge for themselves whether my conclusions are well founded. I think the moths were wind-borne. When the report reaches you I should very much like if you would read the "General Summary," pp. 157–164, first, or you may really wonder what could have induced me to give such a host of reports on the pest. I greatly doubt whether, without proper identification, we could trust to farmers distinguishing between Diamond-back moth caterpillars and those of Turnip sawfly, and there is no good at all in trusting to their reminiscences! No more than to moths being attracted to the dark side of a lighthouse (see p. 159 of my Report). I have taken great pains to be accurate.

In No. 1 of "Canadian Entomologist" for this year, which arrived on Saturday, the 6th, I read with much interest some of the observations on "Can insects survive freezing?" and I thought perhaps you might like to look at a

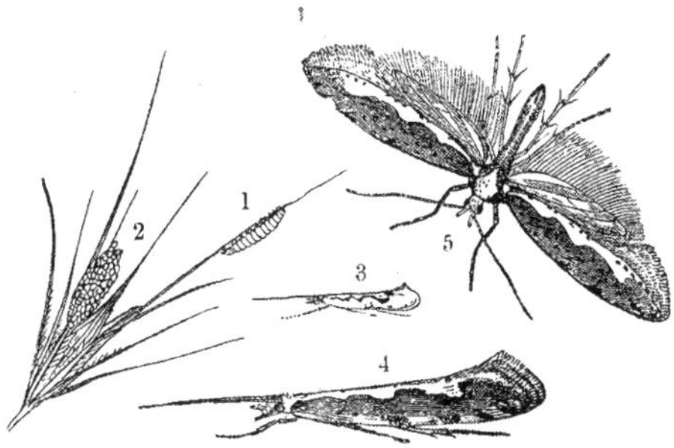

1, Caterpillar; 2, eggs; 3–5, diamond-back moth, natural size and magnified.

FIG. 48.—DIAMOND-BACK MOTH, *PLUTELLA CRUCIFERARUM* ZELL., *CEROSTOMA XYLOSTELLA*, CURTIS.

few slight observations which I read before our Entomological Society in 1879. At that time I was one of the regular daily observers of the Royal Meteorological Society, so I was able to be sure of readings of temperatures, but I could not get nearly as many examples as I wanted of the insects. Mr. Whipple's experiment, which I have added, was the best. I used to think it very interesting to see how some larvæ would crack across like little bits of stick, and their brethren when thawed would recover themselves. If you think the remarks are of any interest pray make any use that you please of them—it would delight me if they were of any use.

Have you chanced to hear from any quarter that the

Mediterranean flour moth (p. 179) has made its appearance in Moscow? It is now a few weeks since Dr. Lindeman wrote me that it had been found there in a chocolate or cocoa store brought by bags from London (England). Apparently the enemy was descended on with full power, and no delay, and he hoped it was stamped out. It puzzled me at first how *kuhniella* came to be in chocolate, &c., but it was suggested that these food-cake compositions were much adulterated with flour. The pest is steadily spreading here, and you will see in my Report that I have again reprinted a portion of your directions.

The weather has been so wet that very great breadths of wheat-land have remained unsown, so at present I have had little inquiry about the young plant pests, but with warmth and sunshine I expect they will come with a rush. I am just beginning a second edition of my little "Guide."

August 22, 1892.

After an operation on my knee the joint was right, but the long suffering had lowered my health exceedingly—and great pain pretty constantly in the troubled limb, with occasionally racking neuralgia, reduced me to such a state that I was gravely warned recovery was hopeless unless I lessened the enormous load of work. So as it was the engaged and routine work of my "office" which was so very harassing, I resigned my post at the Royal Agricultural Society as their Consulting Entomologist, and I have ever since been steadily progressing towards recovery. Sleep has returned, and the terrible pain of the neuralgia is gone, and I can work happily and comfortably.

I do not know how it happened, but the work (quite beyond what seemed my work) amplified on all hands—Continental and Colonial, and revision of papers, &c., &c.—until it would have required a good man of business and a staff to see to it all. So I cut the Gordian knot.

I hope not to make any difference at all in my Agricultural Entomological work for the country, especially as referee for the farmers and fruit-growers and the agricultural papers; also to continue my Annual Reports—and in all ways to work thoroughly. But this is very different to being obliged to attend *ex-officio* to people and things who or which appeared to me really often to take up time to little purpose, or even to prevent attention to really important investigation.

November 21, 1892.

One very great trouble last year was the fungoid attack to

cabbage and turnip roots, which we call here "Club" or "Anbury," or "Finger and Toe." I do not know whether you have it in Canada. You will recognise it perhaps best under the scientific name of the "Slime fungus" which causes it—*Plasmodiophora brassicæ* of Woronin. Our people confuse it so constantly with maggot root attacks that they send me a deal of inquiry about it, so I do not think there can be any harm (as I have really studied it for many years) in giving a paper on it in my next Report, and I have secured three excellent photos from life, which I hope will each give a good whole-page figure of the three chief forms respectively.

There are some nice new reports of infestation (so to

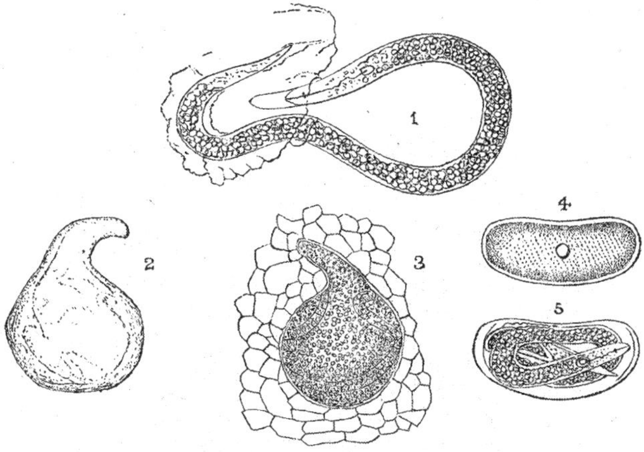

1, Larva; 2 and 3, females; 4 and 5, eggs in different stages of development—all enormously magnified (2 from sketch by E. A. O.; the other figures after Prof. Geo. Atkinson).

FIG. 49.—TOMATO ROOT-KNOT EEL-WORM, *HETERODERA* (*ANGUILLULA*) *RADICICOLA*, MÜLLER.

describe them), and I am working as steadily as I can, but I wish I could get on faster. I envy you your power of doing sound and good work so rapidly.

I have never thanked you for your excellent paper on the "Horn fly" (*Hæmatobia connicola*), which I read with very great interest and benefit, and lodged some of your liberal supply of copies where I thought they would be most useful—including getting attention drawn to the subject in the "Agricultural Gazette."

Dr. Bethune most kindly asked my sister and myself to

come over to stay at Port Hope for the Chicago Exhibition, but delightful as it would be to see all the friends who would be gathered to such a centre, neither sister nor self could manage the fatigue.

Our millionaire lady who is so known for her philanthropic work—Baroness Burdett-Coutts—wrote me that she had been elected President of the, or a Woman's Branch of the, Chicago Exhibition, and desired an account of the "Genesis of my organisation!" What could I say? There is not a woman but myself and my sister in it. I thought of Canning's famous "Knife Grinder" story, "God bless you, I have none to tell, sir." The Baroness wrote that she was obtaining information from the Bishops

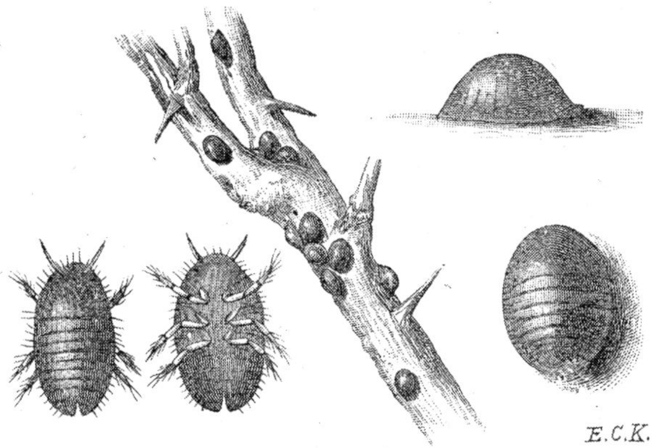

Female, showing side and upper surface; larval scales, with legs still visible—all magnified; infested gooseberry twig.

FIG. 50.—CURRANT AND GOOSEBERRY SCALE, *LECANIUM RIBIS*, FITCH.

and the heads of all the Churches, so I suppose her branch is *pur et simple* religious female organisations.

March 13–16, 1893.

You will see by a copy of the Report I have just issued that we have really got the *Heterodera radicicola* (Root-knot eel-worm). I should have liked to give the name of the sufferer, but he is our greatest English tomato grower, and it might have injured his business. He is trying many experiments, and at the end of April he is going to give me a report. It would be a pleasure indeed if we managed to make out any serviceable remedy.

At present I am trying to make a fair history and description of the Gooseberry scale, *Lecanium ribis*, Fitch, which has made such a headquarters here (I suppose set up when I was too ill to look after it) that I think I must almost have a chance of finding the desiderated male! But except the few lines by Dr. Signoret we do not seem to have a European description. Locusts came over in imported vegetables and fodder about a month ago, so that I secured three species, but no more are arriving now. Mine and the grower's chief investigation at present is as to finding measures to check the attack of the Mustard beetle, *Phædon betulæ*, and evil-doers of similar habits, and I am making a kind of link in operations with Messrs. Colman and Messrs. Keen, our two great rival mustard firms, and I greatly hope we shall make some advance.

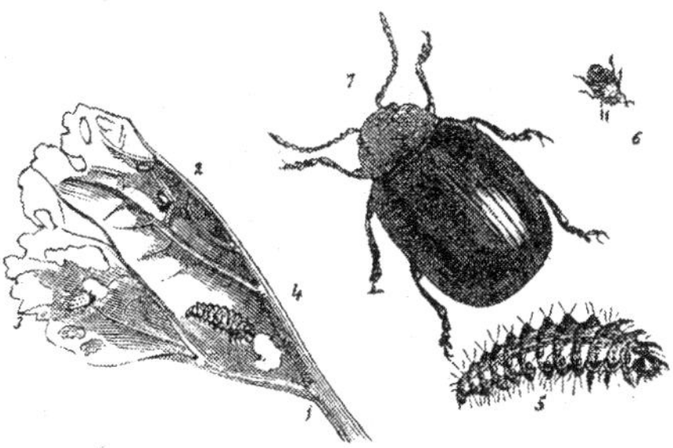

Beetle, natural size and magnified; maggot, magnified, and natural size on leaf.

FIG. 51.—MUSTARD BEETLE, *PHÆDON BETULÆ*, LINN.

One great worry is these (to my thinking) unqualified so-called lecturers sent out by the County Councils.

May 22, 1893.

I only knew as a fact a very little while ago that Professor Riley was standing for the post of "Hope Professor of Zoology" at Oxford, vacant by the death of our grand old friend Professor Westwood. Mr. Hachett-Jackson (Professor Westwood's assistant, I believe) wrote to me very urgently from Keble College, and I responded most heartily, mentioning everything I could think of that might assist Professor Riley's election. It would have been a benefit to myself past hoping for to have a really great Entomologist like Professor Riley in a definite post over here. The magician's rod would have beaten all kinds of underhand misrepresentations, scientific and practical, out of the field.

Anyway I fear that Professor Riley has hardly a chance, and indeed I wonder that he should contemplate changing his grand central position—central to the whole world—for such a very inferior post without genial colleagues around him.

By book post accompanying I send a copy of Mons. J. Danysz's paper on *Ephestia* (Flour moth), to your kind acceptance, in case you have not yet seen it; you will be interested to run it over and see his views of *Pyrethrum*. I very much doubt whether we could get our millers to try it, but it would be different with you.

CHAPTER XX

LETTERS TO DR. J. FLETCHER (*continued*) AND TO DR. BETHUNE

Foreign correspondents—Book by Dr. Napela—Efforts to endow Agricultural lectures at Oxford or Cambridge – Literary productions—Sympathetic communications.

THE letters addressed to Dr. Fletcher after his visit to Miss Ormerod and her sister Georgiana at St. Albans have here been grouped, as a matter of convenience, with letters to the Rev. Dr. C. J. S. Bethune, another Canadian Entomologist, who held a high place in Miss Ormerod's esteem, both as a man of science and as a sympathetic friend in whom to confide in times of sorrow.

To Dr. J. Fletcher, Dominion Entomologist, Ottawa, Canada.

TORRINGTON HOUSE, ST. ALBANS,
September 29–30, 1893.

DEAR DR. FLETCHER,—We were very glad to hear you had safely returned home. I wish we could have had a longer chat, but I will be thankful for the very great pleasure of chatting with you at all.

Just after you had left (or rather, I think, were leaving) England the Rothamsted Jubilee took place, which brought very many distinguished agriculturists to this part of the country, and you may imagine how much it was wished that you could have been present. I did not attend, but a few friends from long distances off looked in here on their way.

November 26 *and December* 1, 1893.

I have long been owing you a letter, and thanks, too, for your "Entomological Report," which I read at once when it reached me. You know the pleasure and the confidence I feel in all I learn from your writings. They and your kind co-operation have been an immense help to my work and me for many a year, which I have never ceased to appreciate most gratefully. I am working now on my next Annual Report. There has been a good deal of nice fresh matter sent in, and (so far as I could) I have tried not to go over old ground. I have a grand paper on Locusts (fig. 55), my specimens being identified at Madrid by Senor Don Igo Bolivar. Wasps were a terrible plague—and I have got some charming observations, so entertaining! but I have taken great care to have them on good authority—and M. Schoyen kindly sent me some notes by the Swedish State Entomologist of an enormous appearance at Tromsoe a few years ago. As this is so high up in the Arctic circle I thought the record would be of interest scientifically, and it is so spirited I have had many a good laugh over it (p. 239).

But what I hope you may be really pleased with is, that through the kind introduction of Dr. Friedrich Thomas, of Ohrdruf, whom you will know, I think, as one of our leading European Phytopathologists, I was put in communication with Dr. A. Nalepa (of Vienna), who for some years back has quite especially devoted himself to the study of *Phytoptidæ* (Blister galls). So that now we have in his successive publications first-rate specific descriptions, with measurements and everything requisite for certain identification of all the species which he has studied so far. Also in very many cases he gives good magnified figures, and he added to his many kindnesses to myself by sending me a plate with the details of the creatures marked with the technical names. In his treatises already published he has given excellent accounts of very many species as well as a good serviceable classification, and I rather think that the work which has been coming out in the Reports of the Imperial Scientific Society of Vienna is to be completed this spring.

This letter has been lying by me for a few days for an addition I wanted to make, and now I have to thank you very heartily for the great kindness which you have shown to poor Mr. T—— [a West of England farmer who had been unfortunate]. If he can manage to adapt himself to circumstances your timely and great assistance will have been the means of setting him up again. I doubted rather whether it was right of me to trouble you about him, still I thought I would venture, and indeed your help will have been the means of saving him from going quite down. I had no idea (no more apparently than Mr. T——) that his

Canadian prospects on his own and relations' standing were so hopeless. Do you think a little money would help? Say a couple of £5 notes or so, for possibly thick clothing is a matter needing supply. If you think it would be well, we would very gladly (if you would kindly give me his address) send out a little. One can get over scruples by calling it "a loan," and to be returned, if ever, at convenience, or not at all if more so, but I do not like to send without your leave.

December 5, 1893.

A hasty line to catch post, about Dr. Nalepa's books. I have just heard from Messrs. Wesley that they have ordered (as I asked them) a duplicate set of the four of Dr. N.'s pamphlets which I have, and sent you the names of yesterday. When these arrive I shall send them on to you, hoping you will kindly accept them, if for no other reason, to be a trifling reminder to you of how much I appreciate your always kind help to myself. The money value, as I mentioned to you, is small, but I am very desirous that you should have them as soon as possible, and ordering from here will save some delay.

Mr. Sinclair [the editor] wrote me thanks for your paper, and that he is having a figure of your fly copied for the "Live Stock Journal." This will attract attention surely.

December 21, 1893.

I wonder if you ever came across any observation of moths—*i.e.*, their larvæ—injuring silk in the raw material, as they habitually do woollen goods. I did not know that they did, but this morning I had an inquiry about it from Tiverton, and amongst the moths sent as offenders was a lovely white cocoon, which appeared as if it might have been made of the same material as the beautifully fine silk manufactured web or net sent with it, and outside this cocoon, now empty, were a number of little pellets of pale larval excrement, as if they were the results of feeding on very pale material. I hope to hear more of this. Would it not be a nice new observation?

March 13, 1894.

Very many thanks for the copy of your charming Report kindly sent to myself, and the six so liberally also presented, which I am placing carefully where they will be appreciated and useful. One I sent to our Lancashire and Cheshire Entomological Society, to the pleasure of the President. They are doing a good deal of nice work, and were going to have a special exhibition of *Silphidæ* (Beet carrion beetles), with observations (fig. 26). I like your Report very much; there is an immense amount of good, sound, straightforward information, both scientific and practical, in it, and it is quite an example of honest dealing with your body of observers. I have been very much interested in your Silpha notes, and I wonder whether we could get our farmers to try poisoning the cutworms, "surface caterpillars" as we call them here. I wonder whether I should not do well to follow your example and have short notes of anything interesting, even without giving a long story. These embody a great deal of useful information, but with us who are so behindhand in entomological information, I have been afraid that without a full account and a figure the readers would be all abroad. I was very much gratified to see the honourable place you give my name among your colleagues. Indeed this pleases me very much.

I was very much interested with what you told me of overplus of wasps having accompanied deficiency of rainfall in one portion of your part of the world. Our Press has been very kind to me, and I was particularly pleased with one remark, that (although retired from the Royal Agricultural Society) I had not ceased to be the "Consulting Entomologist of the Agriculturists of Great Britain."

Just now I am running a leaflet on *Bryobia prætiosa* (Gooseberry red spider), through the press, and this morning I had an order for 3,000 copies! Just think of that, and without the firm even seeing it!

April 9, 1894.

I am trying to bring kerosene, or mineral oil emulsion more forward as an insecticide. I have given a number of the best recipes in one of our leading agricultural journals—"The Farmer's Gazette," Dublin—with the information that for those who cannot manage permanent combination of the constituents, the so-called "antipest" makes a good substitute.

It appears that "formalin," as the trade name is called, is being brought out as a disinfectant. Mr. A. Zimmermann has been trying the effects as an insecticide on greenhouse plants, and he considered it so bad for the insects, and beneficial rather than hurtful to the plants, that he wanted my co-operation in getting it tried. Dr. Bernard Dyer told me he thought it would be well worth trial.

The point that occurred to me was could we use it against the Flour moth, *E. kuhniella?* At present we have got some flour well impregnated with emanation from some of the tablets, and Mr. Zimmermann was going to have a loaf baked of some of this flour, and consumed in his own large household, without letting them know there is anything peculiar about it! I am to know results; and I have said I should like a piece of the experimental loaf. I hope we shall not all be made very miserable indeed. If the flour rises properly, and the bread is fit to be eaten, then I am meditating getting an experiment made as to the destructive powers of the fumes by some of our folks here connected with milling, and also suggesting to Mons. J. Danysz, Director of the Laboratory of Parasitology, Bourse de Commerce, Paris, whether he might care to experiment in some of the French mills with which he had been in

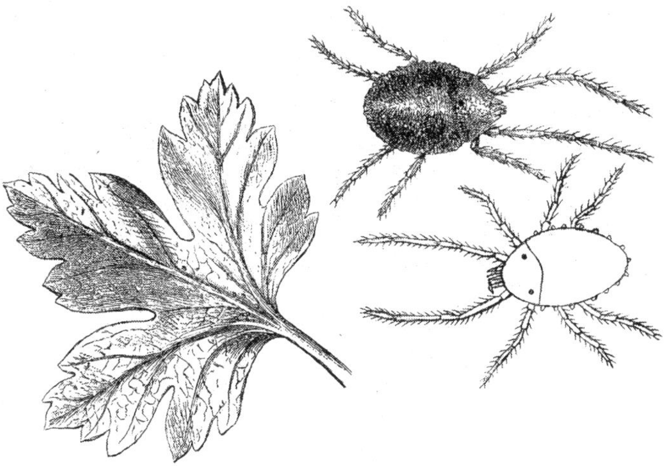

From life; Red spider (outline figure after Koch)—both magnified. Infested leaf, natural size.

FIG. 52.—GOOSEBERRY AND IVY RED SPIDER, *BRYOBIA PRÆTIOSA*, C. L. KOCH.

communication regarding destruction of *E. kuhniella*. The chemical is sold in tablets like large thick lozenges, and also as a fluid, and, I believe, in powder.

Enclosed is a little packet of seed of the pink hawkweed, which you thought pretty while here last summer, and a few seeds also of the white *Lathyrus* (vetchling). I hope they may remind you how welcome your visits here are.

June 20, 1894.

I was so sorry to learn from Professor Riley's circular that he really had resigned, and also from some observations in it to surmise that all had not been quite comfortable. Who will be his successor? Will it be Mr. L. O. Howard, I wonder? I expect that Professor Riley (unless he is really very ill) will work at his Entomology from morning till night or more.

The oak trees have been very severely injured by caterpillars in various places. Down near Lymington, Hants, one of my correspondents tells me the leafage is stripped so that the trees look as if it were the middle of the winter. Aphides also are very great pests this year, and we had a bad grass attack of them near Newcastle-on-Tyne. They were reported to be spreading rapidly from one large field (that is, large for us) of 15 to 20 acres, so I thought the best advice I could give was to mow the field—in the most literal sense, cut off the source of evil.

Is it not rather an interesting point to think of—that whether the weather be hot and dry, or cold and wet, there are some kinds of insect attack which appear to do equally well? The crops bear up better in special circumstances, but their unpleasant enemies seem to me just as comfortable.

I have got a very curious investigation on hand of the mischief of some beetles on the grassland of our South American Land Co. in the Argentine Territories. I will enclose or send you a little note I put in one of our agricultural papers. Is it not curious that the two Scarabæid beetles sent over with the Dynastids should so rarely come to hand here that there is only one specimen of each in our British Museum! I hope to work up the observations, or rather, to get a good deal of trustworthy observation to work upon, and to get some more specimens.

July 16, 1894.

I am now writing first of all to ask you kindly to accept a copy of the translation by Professor Ainsworth Davis of Dr. Ritzema Bos's "Agricultural Zoology." It seems to me a very useful book, but I think it is a mistake of Messrs. Chapman & Hall to have so arranged it that the price is 6s. This is almost a prohibitory price to many who could find 2s. 6d. or 3s. Also, if I had seen proof of title I think I would have asked for my name to appear in a much more secondary fashion. I should mention this copy is one of a few sent me for friends. I did not buy it or I would not have enlarged on the price! I have written, by request of Professor Davis, a short Introduction, and I was very glad to do it to show that I had no feeling of opposition, for much of it is on parallel lines with my Manual, and there might have been misunderstandings which I should have been very sorry for—for Dr. Ritzema Bos is always kind in helping me.

You will believe how intensely I was interested in all I could hear about Professor Riley's retirement. I was sorry for his indifferent health, but perhaps it was more the desire to be a free agent that led to his resignation. I think I could feel very much with him, but his was a magnificent post to resign.

October 28, 1895.

I was shocked and grieved to receive the news of our friend Professor Riley's fatal accident.[1] Dr. Bethune kindly sent me a paper with the full account, and as I did not know what any one might do in properly announcing it here, I wrote a short letter to the "Times" which they inserted at once. This was just what one might call a friendly notice;

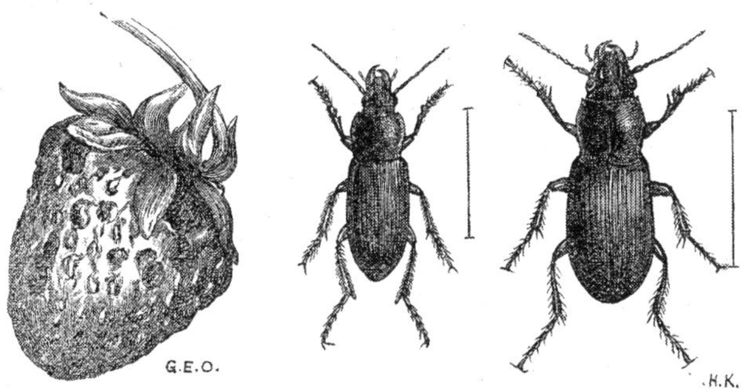

Magnified, and lines showing natural length; strawberry fruit gnawed by *Harpalus ruficornis.*

FIG. 53.—GROUND BEETLES—"BAT BEETLE," *HARPALUS RUFICORNIS*, FAB. (left), *PTEROSTICHUS VULGARIS*, LINN. (right).

an account of the accident and a few observations; the dry obituary notice (I mean the regular formal notice) had been inserted the previous day. I was very pleased to see yours in the "Canadian Entomologist." It was very sad, and I feel his loss much, for he was always, when we corresponded, kind and helpful.

Here, things are going on (or standing still) much as usual, but it has been a grand year for fresh observations. I have secured a long carefully watched observation of *Harpalus ruficornis* (Ground beetle) feeding on strawberry

[1] See Appendix E.

fruit. I watched and recorded until I got so weary of acting as their fruiterer that I thought seventeen days' observation was enough.

Amongst pine attackers I have had a lovely specimen of the *Astynomus ædilis* (Timberman beetle), sent me from the north of Scotland, the longest horned of the European "longhorns." It is wonderfully pretty to see the tiny beetle, not three-quarters of an inch long, comfortably bearing its delicate antennæ, nearly half a foot in expanse. Also I have got a good observation of the Pine Shoot moth's bad doings; the *Retinia buoliana*, the "Post-horn" attack as they call it in Germany, from the twisted shoots; and some other fresh work—but the great point of this year's observation is Horse and Cattle Diptera, Warble flies, Gad

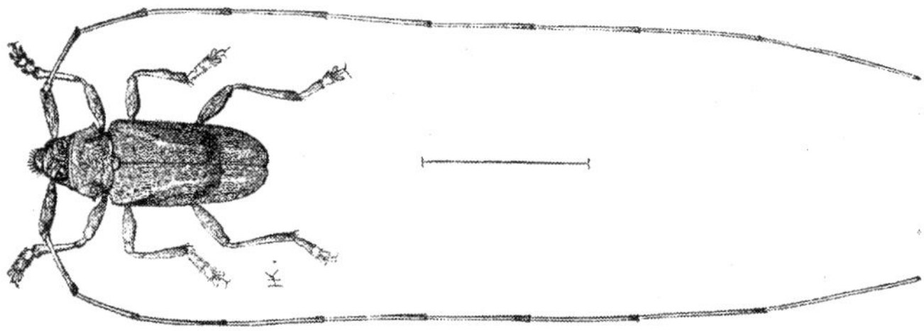

Slightly larger than life; line showing natural length.

FIG. 54.—TIMBERMAN BEETLE, *ASTYNOMUS ÆDILIS.*

flies, and Forest flies. Just now Forest flies are being sent me from India. The Indian species is very pretty. I have been working up the structure of the Hippoboscal foot, which is indeed wonderful (pls. XXIII., XXIV.). I do not understand the details, so I have had two great drawings made, and lithographed, for my next Annual Report, with the tiny foot magnified to a size of 6 inches by 5, showing every detail that appears to me observable, and I wonder what the parts will be considered to do. I think I have made out a good deal, but there is some apparatus that none of the few people I have consulted make out.

May 15, 1897.

You will have seen the state of enthusiasm this whole country is in about the celebration of the Queen's Jubilee. I trust that the exertion and excitement will not be quite too much for her, but it will be a great trial.

Another matter I feel more at home in—do you happen to have seen in some of our English papers that some of us are trying to get an Agricultural Lectureship established in the University of Oxford? It came about this way. It appears that the funds for support of the Sibthorpian Professorship of Rural Economy had fallen so low, that it was feared it would have to be given up. But the Clothworkers' Company came forward with the offer of £200 a year for five years on condition of Agriculture being made one of the subjects to be taken for degrees. I offered £100 on the same terms, and then it was offered by one or two people jointly, on the same terms, to clear off a debt which seemed growing like a snowball. The matter is now under consideration by the University authorities. They would gladly accept the money, I believe, for an Agricultural Lectureship on which attendance was voluntary, but the difficulty is accepting the matter as essential for a degree.

Instruction in agriculture (that is, chemistry, forestry, entomology, &c.) would do a great deal of good at such a centre of our "coming on" great landholders as Oxford, but the students will not attend the lectures unless the matter is compulsory. Prof. Warington is the Sibthorpian lecturer—a friend and neighbour (at least, he and his wife live very near by railway)—so we can talk over progress. He has his hands, I think, very full. In case after due consideration Oxford does not think it desirable to establish the Chair, I fancy it is very likely our offer may be then transferred to Cambridge; but this is at present uncertain.

[These efforts in the higher interests of science as applied to agriculture having failed, Miss Ormerod, in her *Last Will and Testament*, bequeathed, out of her ample means, a sum of £5,000 to the University Court of the University of Edinburgh, "upon trust for the benefit of that University."]

December 6, 1897.

I thank you very much for your two Entomological Reports lately received. I want to read your observations on "Hair-worms" carefully as soon as I can get time, for these creatures come, I think, as regularly as the summer.

You will perhaps have seen the turmoil that the Sparrow-lovers raised, and the floods of abuse they bestowed upon me. But it advertised the leaflet beautifully, and I could hardly print at first quickly enough to keep up to the demand. Our Royal Horticultural Society has asked leave to reprint the Sparrow leaflet in their Journal, which gratifies me much.

January 21, 1898.

I think you will be pleased to know that I am in

most pleasant co-operation with the Duke of Bedford's staff at the Woburn Experimental Fruit-ground as to endeavouring to find some way to lessen presence of *Phytoptus* (mite galls), on black-currants. We are going to try grafting on species which are not affected, for one thing; after I have been trying for I do not know how long to get growers to consider having their bushes in line, with other crops between, I hear to-day from Woburn that it appears as if those which had been grown that way were much the freest from attack.

February 16, 1898.

We are having an extraordinarily mild winter, and vegetation is said in some places to be one or two months over-forward. Of course insects are plying their trades heartily underground, but (so far) I do not see any difference in amount of above-ground appearances. If this is so generally, would it be too far-fetched an idea to think it was a still further confirmation of hibernation being constitutional, not an effect of weather? The underground workers that are sent me are larval "eaters" when not frozen torpid; also *Tylenchus devastatrix* (eel-worm) is, I believe, making wild work with clover, which is popularly attributed to *Sitones* (Pea weevil) larvæ. I found the little eel-worm (fig. 47) in quantities in abortive shoots of "stem-sick" clover sent me, and I am giving warning about it.

January 7, 1900.

I am very much gratified that you approve of the Index to my Annual Reports. You will believe that it was a weary work to make up our minds what arrangement would be desirable. The time and sight that I worse than wasted on it was incredible, for, I believe, I really complicated matters very much, and doctor, and business manager (Mr. T. P. Newman) spoke so seriously that I left off meddling, and I think Mr. Newstead did the work well.

I now very gladly forward a copy by book-post, and I should be only too pleased to send any copies that may be desired. My hope is that besides being just a paged reference list, it may stand for a sort of up-to-date "catalogue raisonné" of British Economic Insect attacks.

June 12, 1900.

I have owed you an answer to your kind letter so long that on receipt this evening of your very valuable pamphlet, which I am delighted to possess, I sit down at once to write.

I promise myself a great deal of information from your "Recent Additions," which is obviously of quite exceptional value. What you say of the number of injurious insects being greater, as well as the number of species, is very interesting. I am hoping to utilise the reports of forest insects which have been sent me up to date, in co-operation with Dr. R. Stewart MacDougall, the consulting Entomologist of the Highland and Agricultural Society of Scotland. I have much information scattered in my Annual Reports, but I have not strength to work it and attend at the same time (as I wish to do) to regular application, so we are thinking that, as a "Textbook of Forestry" is much needed for University use, we might work together; that is, Dr. MacDougall to take the heavy scientific part, as his engagements allow, and I to add what I can to the entomological notes which he has been collecting for years, and also give the figures. I should like this collaboration very much. Mr. Robert Wallace, the Professor of Agriculture in the Edinburgh University (an old friend of mine), is a very kind ally, and now I do not feel so very lonely in my work. By parcel post (posted with this letter) I am sending a photo of myself, taken in Doctor's robes, for your kind acceptance; I hope you will approve of the appearance of your old friend in her new dress! With very kind remembrances and good wishes, pray believe me, ever sincerely yours,

ELEANOR A. ORMEROD, LL.D.

To the Rev. Dr. C. J. S. Bethune, Editor of "The Canadian Entomologist."

TORRINGTON HOUSE, ST. ALBANS, ENGLAND,
April 1, 1895.

MY DEAR MR. BETHUNE,—My sister and myself were indeed grieved and shocked to see from the papers you kindly sent (received yesterday morning) what a disaster had happened.[1] What a mercy that all the boys were saved! The order and promptness speak volumes for the spirit of obedience and discipline—and we have been reading the whole history with the greatest sympathy and admiration. Poor boys — I feel so sorry for them — running out into the cold, to watch their pet collections and treasures burning!

I gather that for building purposes you are fairly insured, but will you let my sister and myself try to replace what we

[1] This reference is to the destruction by fire of the main building of Trinity College School, Port Hope, Canada, of which Mr. Bethune was Head Master for a period of 29 years ending 1899.

can of our own books and drawings? We are writing up to Messrs. Johnston to ask how best to forward my sister's and my five sets of Insect diagrams, which were published by our Royal Agricultural Society. When we learn, she is going to have them forwarded, and hopes you will kindly accept them as a little token of her great sympathy. By this post I am sending, in two book-post parcels, my Manual (2nd edit.), "Cobham Journals,"[1] and Annual Reports, vols. 13, 14, 15, 16, 18. These I have here, and I am going to write to my printers to forward some more to try and make up the set. Kindly accept these, and please excuse the "Cobham Journals" not being absolutely new. But it has long been out of print and I secured a presentation copy which was offered for sale and had it bound, and put a strip of paper to hide what might be on the title-page.

Mr. Fletcher is my chief Canadian correspondent, and it is a great delight when I get a letter from him.

You will not have time at present to think of entomological matters, but we were desirous to assure you as soon as possible of our great sympathy in your trouble. With my very kind regards to yourself and Mrs. Bethune, in which my sister begs to join me.

June 7, 1897.

I was very much pleased to see your handwriting again a short time ago—and a little while before exceedingly gratified with the long kind review. You, living among so many friends and colleagues in work, can hardly appreciate how very greatly indeed I value such kind encouragement.

Your beautiful letter was a great support and comfort to me in my loss last year,[2] and now my health is fairly established again. I had great trouble for many weeks, some months rather, from some very troublesome disturbance of sight, but I did as well as I could, and when circumstances allowed, I got one of our best London oculists to come and see what was amiss. To my great joy he told me that each of my eyes individually was in excellent order, but there was some such difference in their action that some special glasses were needed, and I find great comfort from them. He said he wondered how I had been able to work.

Just now Alfalfa (lucerne), infested with locusts is coming in from Buenos Aires, and one of my correspondents found his horses so ill after feeding on the infested lucerne, that I sent a copy of his notes to our "Live Stock Journal."

[1] Containing Miss Ormerod's Meteorological Observations.
[2] The death of her sister Georgiana.

One of the three animals was reported to appear to suffer from colic; another recovered when bran was substituted for the locust-infested hay. The third I should conjecture was very ill when I heard. But as I know nothing of veterinary matters, I thought it was but right to send the notes on, with a kind of apology. The locusts are of the South American migratory kind—*Schistocerca paranensis.* Pretty creatures—even all flattened out. My correspondent sent me about 120 of them.

July 20, 1898.

I am working now on what I hope to bring out in the autumn as a good thick volume, called, "Handbook

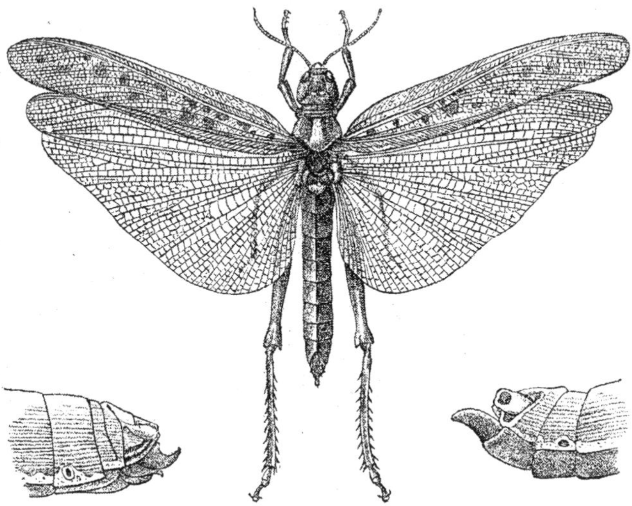

Locust with wings spread : tip of male abdomen to the right, and of female abdomen to the left. (After Conil, but reduced ⅛.)

FIG. 55.—SOUTH AMERICAN MIGRATORY LOCUST, *SCHISTOCERCA PARENENSIS* (*MALE*).

From Lawrence Bruner's Locust Investigation Commission Report, Buenos Aires.

of Insects Injurious to Orchard and Bush Fruits, with means of Prevention and Remedy," very fully illustrated. I am trying to include all the attacks of any real importance of which observations have been sent to me in the past twenty-one years, and though I give these from British observations to a great extent, I am trying to bring them all up to date. I hope you approve of the idea. Our fruit industry is increasing so much, that more information is needed for growers; but I do not feel sure I should have had courage to begin it, if some one had not written to me that he purposed bringing out a book on insect pests, and would like the use of my figures to illustrate it! It occurred to me that when he was about it he might like my letterpress also! So I have set to work and I have got to about p. 224.

There are more of the rarer attacks about than usual this year—*Atomaria linearis* at mangolds, for instance. This morning I heard from Messrs. Laxton, of Bedford, that they have gained a complete victory over that destructive pest, the Strawberry ground beetle, or beetles, I should say (in this instance cockchafers, fig. 58). They bought a multitude of pudding basins and sunk them in the strawberry beds, baited with sugar and water, and tempting solids, and the beetles were caught in hosts, sometimes by

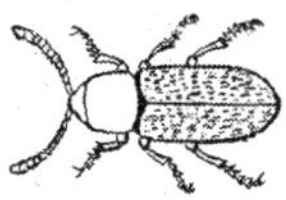

Magnified; natural length, one twenty-fourth of an inch. (After Taschenberg.)

FIG. 56.—PIGMY MANGOLD BEETLE, *ATOMARIA LINEARIS*, STEPHENS.

the half basin full. I think this is real good news for strawberry growers.

I wish I knew better how to manage my work. I do not think I should have any difficulty in keeping the real work in hand, but there is so much correspondence on subjects which, indeed, one can hardly call even allied, and yet I suppose one should return a reply, and that adds uselessly to the work. How well you must know this sort of thing!

I was grieved at the loss of our kind Dr. Lintner,[1] and I saw my good friend Mr. T. P. Newman about some not wholly inadequate notice being inserted in the "Entomologist." I could from my heart record his exceeding kindness to his weaker brethren.

July 28, 1899.

Your very kind letter to me of a few weeks back was a sincere grief to me in its information of your abiding sorrow under the heavy affliction with which it has pleased our

[1] State Entomologist of New York.

Father to visit you.[1] I scarcely know how to write to you, for it would be presumptuous in me to endeavour to enter to you on the only sources of consolation, which, in my own great loss, you placed so comfortably before me; but, believe me, I earnestly sympathise in your affliction, and earnestly hope that any arrangement you make may be to your comfort. I am much pleased to see in the paper of which you have kindly sent me a copy, that great care is being taken, that, so far as may be, you shall have a worthy successor in the office you have so honourably held for so many years [Head Master of Trinity College School, Port Hope].

I do not often hear from Canada, for Dr. Fletcher is

From Newman's "British Moths," p. 193.

FIG. 57.—"SPINACH MOTH," *CIDARIA DOTATA*, LINN.

so occupied and has to move about so much, that he has not time to give me the bits of entomological novelties he used to form most interesting letters with. I am trying this season to get my applicants to fill up their observations to some degree. Rather an undertaking this, you will believe! But I am getting a few new (or rather little brought forward) infestations.

The *Cidaria dotata*, sometimes called the "Spinach moth" is, I think, of interest at present.

I am sure that when you move to a new home you will kindly let me have your address, for I should be very sorry not to be allowed to still look forward to our occasional interchange of pleasant friendly communications, and with my very kind remembrances and most sincere good wishes, pray believe me, most sincerely yours,

ELEANOR A. ORMEROD.

[1] Mrs. Bethune was killed in a carriage accident in July, 1898.

CHAPTER XXI

LETTERS TO DRS. RITZEMA BOS, SCHÖYEN, REUTER AND NALEPA, MR. LOUNSBURY AND MR. FULLER

Eel-worms—Ladybirds—Wheat midges—Resignation from the Royal Agricultural Society—Wasps—Study of Norwegian and Swedish—Gall mites—Boot beetles—Experience of publishing.

REPRESENTATIVE letters to five foreign and colonial scientific entomologists have been gathered into this chapter, among other reasons to show the diversity of Miss Ormerod's work, carried on in close touch and in the most agreeable relations, with the highest wide-world authorities on various specialised branches of her subject.

To Professor J. Ritzema Bos, Amsterdam.

TORRINGTON HOUSE, ST. ALBANS, ENGLAND,
July 27, 1893.

DEAR DR. RITZEMA BOS,—I have not written to you for a long time, partly because I had nothing of sufficient importance to allow me to submit it to you, but also because both my sister and myself had rather severe illnesses.

Enclosed I beg to send you some pieces of potato, which I think it is just possible may be infested by (or at least have now) some slight presence of *Tylenchus devastatrix* (eel-worm, fig. 47). I received several tubers this morning from near Helensburgh, in Dumbartonshire, Scotland. Mr. Robert Howie, the sender, writes me that a large field recently dug up by him was very much damaged by being badly "scabbed" in the same way as the samples sent. But, when I came to examine the so-called "scabbed" parts after washing, the surface for the most part looked to me more as if it had been gnawed by some larvæ, than if it were a diseased state of coat. The skin of the potato is often left overhanging. I was going to suggest to Mr. Howie that he should search for *Agrotis* larvæ, or *Melolontha* (Cockchafer), grubs, but examining further at the end of one or two tubers, where the skin was still in its natural state, excepting small patches of what was as yet only a slight discoloured roughness, I found a few eel-worms. They were so few that they evaded me when using the higher power, but in one instance I thought I detected a bulb near the head end. I am afraid I may be taking up your time with what is of no importance; still I thought I should like to send you some pieces, and if the attack is one of any interest I would gladly forward more. The eel-worms I have seen are all anguilliform, the largest was about as long or longer than the largest *T. devastatrix* I have seen, the others were smaller. Mr. Rochford has been carrying on with great care and precision his experiments as to poisoning *Heterodera radicicola* (root-knott eel-worms, fig. 49). He has tried about forty

Larva, pupa, and antenna of male ♂ and female ♀.

FIG. 58.—COCKCHAFER, *MELOLONTHA VULGARIS*, FAB.

different applications—noting the amount given and the effect on the eel-worms and the plants. I certainly hope that a few will show successful results, but he is very careful, and is now going over his series of experiments a second time, that he may be quite certain before coming forward with statements of effects. As soon as I know anything of interest I shall be very glad to be allowed to tell you; Mr. Rochford has given me permission. I do not know as yet whether he will bring forward his results himself, or leave it to me to do. Pray believe me, with best thanks for all the kind assistance you give me.

September 7, 1893.

As I think that you have either returned home, or will soon be returning, I now (with your kind permission) send a few more of the "scabbed" potatoes, which it seemed possible might be infested by *Tylenchus devastatrix.* If it should be convenient to you at your best leisure to make any examination, and to let me know results, I am sure I need not say how acceptable your information would be, not only to myself, but to many interested in the cause of this external deformity. I send the potatoes in a little tin box by parcel post. Recently I have had rather an interesting observation of the little black, somewhat pubescent, "ladybird" beetle, *Scymnus minimus,* as a feeder on Red-spider, *Tetranychus telarius.* I have not been able to find any account of its life history, so I have had great pleasure in watching its progress from larval to imago state. It seems to me to be greedily carnivorous; after a few

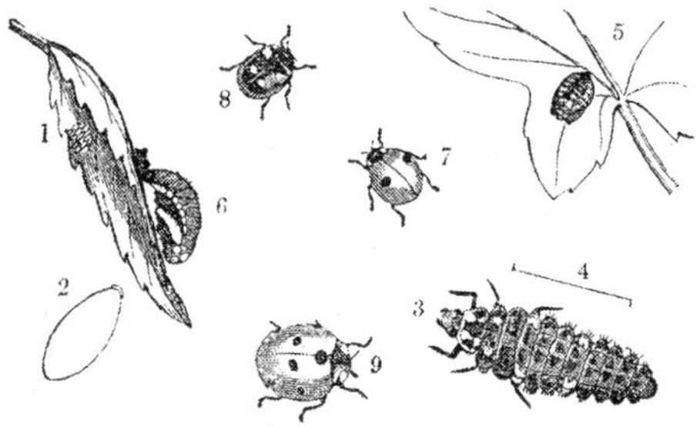

1, Cluster of eggs; 2, egg, magnified; 3, grub, magnified; 4, line showing natural length; 5 and 6, pupæ; 7 and 8, 2-spotted lady-bird, *Coccinella bipunctata,* L. (= *dispar*), and dark variety; 9, 7-spotted lady-bird, *C. septempunctata,* L., like in form but much larger than the black lady-bird.

FIG. 59.—LADY-BIRDS, *COCCINELLIDÆ.*

hours' want of food during their journey to me, the larvæ set to work to feed on what they could pick up on the back of a leaf infested by red spider, as eagerly as sheep on fresh grass; and as I found one day only a single larva remaining of three or four confined together, I suspect it was this survivor who had reduced his brethren to the small remains which were all I found. The final changes were rapid, for the above happened on August 28th, and shortly after it had pupated, and yesterday I found the little black ladybird in most active condition.

I have heard nothing further at present from Mr. Rochford about his *Heterodera* experiments. I think I must remind him soon that he kindly promised me a report.

May 14, 1894.

I have been quite sorry for a long time that I have had no specimens which would be of interest to you. I was afraid you might think I was not attending to these subjects, but now I have received a cucumber root quite beset with galls, of which I forward you a portion. It is from a nursery gardener at Rhyl, in Flintshire, North Wales, where they are much troubled by cucumber and tomato plants dying, some of both kinds having the "roots covered with galls but some have not." Messrs. Maxwell and Dalgliesh sent me some of the roots without galls, from plants that were nearly dead, but I could not discover the cause of the failure of these. On such inefficient examination as I make, I find in the soft pulpy centre of the larger galls some anguilliform nematodes, which I conjecture to be

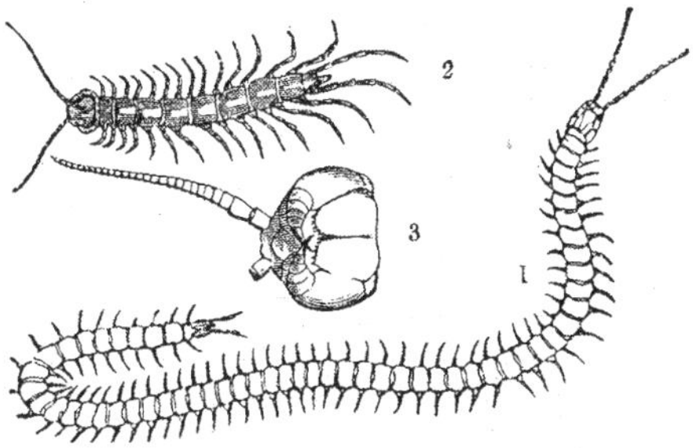

1, *Geophilus longicornis*; 2, *Lithobius forficatus*, "thirty-foot"; 3, head of *Lithobius forficatus*, magnified.

FIG. 60.—LONG-HORNED CENTIPEDES.

males, or larvæ, of the *H. radicicola*, but so far as I searched I did not find females; there were a fair number of eggs. On cutting the pieces of plant into fragments for packing I find the stem just about the ground-level much beset with diseased growth. I have not, however, delayed to try to examine this, for I might be only wasting specimens. Messrs. M. and D. have five houses fifty yards long each, so the infestation is a serious trouble to them. They tell me that they clear out all the soil each year, and bring fresh soil in. It "is rich alluvial soil." They have tried lime, soot, and nitrate of soda without effect, and I should certainly say that something requires alteration for the extermination even of an infestation much more easily dealt with; for they are troubled by millepedes (fig. 27), and also there are such great numbers of *Geophilus* (centipedes), that there must, I think, be something amiss whether these live chiefly on vegetable matter or on small animal vermin.

Some inquiry about *H. radicicola* has been sent to me from Glen St. Mary, Florida, U.S.A., but no new information.

On Saturday, Professor Ainsworth-Davis wrote to ask me to write a preface to his translation of your "Zoologie," and it will gratify me very much indeed to prepare such a one as I hope may please you. Your book will be a very valuable addition to our educational series, and I shall like very much to be permitted thus to appear in colleagueship.

October 3, 1894.

This matter of the ? *Tylenchus devastatrix* in the cortex seems to me most perplexingly curious. I cannot venture to form an opinion ; I have not the knowledge requisite, but looking at these *Tylenchi* being smaller than *T. devastatrix* is customarily known to be, and also their occurring in a locality where *devastatrix* is not known, the idea just floats in my mind whether they may be ♂ (males) or, alternatively, larval *Heterodera schachtii* ("Beet-root" eel-worm).

But perhaps I am almost wrong in taking up your time with a mere idea, as you work on definite proof, and though the shape of those I mentioned to you much resembled your larval *H. schachtii*, I had not sufficiently high powers to be sure of the species. I have been trying to make out whether there is ever a definitely formed opening for the exit of the contents of the ♀ (female) *schachtii*. In examining one specimen I found a circular orifice with what appeared to me a regularly formed edge—not a merely torn one. On putting this in glycerine under a thin cover-glass, and very lightly pressing it, there first came out a number of little eel-worms, without disturbing the condition of the orifice. I was, however, so desirous that my sister should see the interesting sight that I called her, and when I looked again perhaps in a couple of minutes, the regularity was gone ; the outer skin—the skin rather of the female—was cracking irregularly from the aperture and giving exit to a mixed collection of eggs and wormlets. I have tried to find another instance but without success. Very many thanks to you for also sparing time to explain to me the meaning of the word "schaümerde." [1] Now I quite understand and am very

[1] "Schaümerde," is a product of the fabrication of sugar, which contains the mineral parts, the salts, of the sugar beet. Therefore it is good for manuring this crop. (J. R. B.)

glad to know about it. Thank you also for your kind permission to use some of your figures of *schachtii*.

I should very much like to have some specimens of the hop-growth called "nettle-headed," but I have only received a very few leaves, in which I did not see anything amiss.

I received a specimen (though I suppose this is not rare) of the large *Coccinella ocellata* (Eyed lady-bird). What a pretty creature it is! I had never seen it before.

Also from a North British correspondent I received a number of what I do not think could be other than larvæ of one of the *Staphylinidæ*, which were doing mischief by feeding in turnips or their flower stems or leafstalks. They looked grey to the unassisted eye; magnified, they were whitish with grey patches along the back, and they much resembled the fig. by Professor Westwood (see p. 167 of vol. i. of his "Classification of Insects"), of which I give a

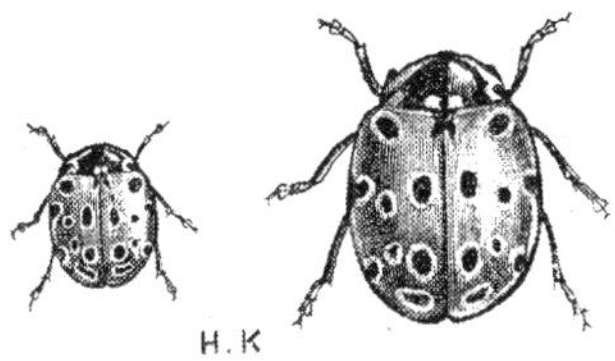

Natural size and magnified.

FIG. 61.—EYED LADY-BIRD, *COCCINELLA OCELLATA*.

rough tracing of the magnified larva and line showing natural size. Professor Westwood found numbers of these larvæ feeding on turnips, but, unfortunately, he does not give even the generic name. They are obviously very destructive, that is, those sent me.

I have been most carefully studying your observations on *schachtii* in oats with great pleasure and profit. With kind regards and ever with many thanks, believe me,

Yours very truly,

ELEANOR A. ORMEROD.

To Dr. W. M. Schöyen, State Entomologist, Christiania.

TORRINGTON HOUSE, ST. ALBANS, ENGLAND,
August 23, 1892.

DEAR SIR,—I have long been in your debt for grateful acknowledgment of your kind thought in sending me from time to time copies of your valuable pamphlets, and also of your portrait, which I have much pleasure in adding to my collection of portraits of the leading entomologists of the world. But I trust you will forgive my long silence because for a long time (that is, since last autumn) until about three weeks ago, I have been a great sufferer, and it has been with difficulty I have been able to keep up to work.

May I ask your kind acceptance of my fifteenth Report (accompanying by book post), and a little brochure I recently arranged by special request; also with them may I place a copy of my portrait, recently taken, in your hands? I value your pamphlets which you kindly send me, much; but, unfortunately, I have never been able to master your language—so when I have read the title, if it be a subject bearing specially on my own work, I get help from a linguist to enable me to benefit. Trusting that for the reasons given you will pardon my long silence.

October 25, 1893.

I thank you very much for being so good as to tell me of the appearance of the *Cecidomyia destructor* (Hessian fly, fig. 15) in Norway. This observation of the further spread of this troublesome barley pest is very interesting to me, and I am also greatly obliged to you for letting me have the characteristic specimens of *puparia*. There is no doubt that these are the chrysalis cases (the "flax-seeds," as we call them here) of the Hessian fly. I at once wrote to two friends to endeavour to procure the specimens you name, and it would have been a great pleasure to me to send them at once, but I much doubt whether I shall be able to procure any of the Wheat midge, *C. tritici;* I have not got any myself, nor have my two colleagues so far as they see.

About the Hessian fly, I have been more successful. I have secured some specimens well put up for the microscope. It is too late this evening to repack them properly, but I hope to send you three slides to-morrow in a registered letter, of which, with very great pleasure, I beg your kind acceptance. Should they not reach you in proper condition, you will oblige me by letting me know, that I may try to replace them. I should hope that the thoroughly well-advised treatment which you are endeavouring to get carried out in the infested district will be successful. I have great confidence in the efficacy of destroying the *puparia* in the screenings or siftings; and ploughing so as to turn down the "flax-seeds" also quite certainly answers well.

One special insect trouble during the past season in this country has been an unusual prevalence of wasps, *Vespidæ*, of various species. They caused much injury and loss by destroying fruit, and also were very troublesome by attacking horses ploughing, if their nests were turned up. I hear that they were also troublesome in Holland, and in the Hartz districts of Germany. Should you write to me, I should be very much interested to know whether they were also unusually plentiful in Norway.

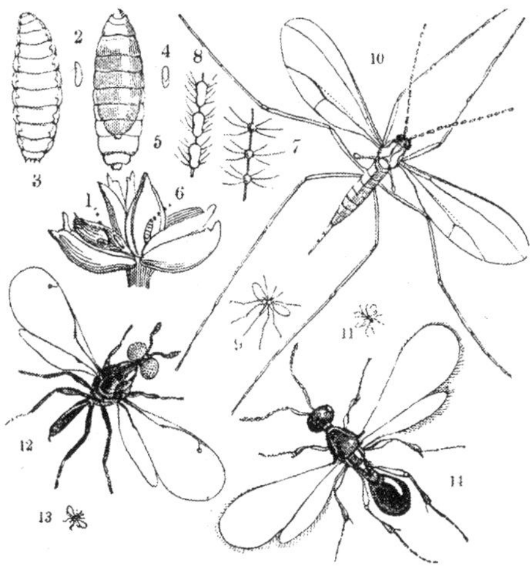

1, 6, infested floret; 2, 3, larvæ; 4, 5, cased larva or pupa, natural size and magnified; 7, 8, part of horns, magnified; 9, 10, wheat midge; and 11–14, ichneumon parasites, natural size and magnified.

FIG. 62.—WHEAT MIDGE, *CECIDOMYIA TRITICI.*

November 7, 1893.

I beg to offer you my best thanks for your very acceptable letter of the 31st of October. Indeed, I am greatly obliged to you for not only kindly giving me your own information as to amount of wasp presence observed in the past season, but also the translation into English of the account of their great appearance at Tromsö in 1883–4. This is exceedingly interesting, and also very entertaining. I have enjoyed reading this spirited account uncommonly, and I shall like very much to add it (of course duly acknowledged) to my paper on wasps in my next Annual Report.

[The translation appeared as follows :—

"In the years 1883–1884, there was an unusual prevalence

of them in the Arctic Norway, especially at Tromsö and other islands in the vicinity. Mr. J. S. Schneider, Conservator at Tromsö Museum, writes in the Swedish 'Entomologisk Tidskrift,' 1885, pp. 148, 149, about this matter as follows :— 'Who can tell all the tears which these wicked animals have squeezed from the poor children, or the swearings which the mowers have thrown out, the half-shut eyes, and the swollen hands and cheeks which have shown forth in the autumn months of these two years? Perhaps this may appear an exaggeration, but it comes, however, pretty near the truth. They built their nests everywhere, in the earth, in stone walls, behind the wainscottings of the houses, under garden benches, on the trees; it swarmed with wasps on all the flowers and bushes, the windows were filled with them, they crawled on the plates of the dining-tables, licked of the dishes with preserves, crawled under the clothings, and in the hair, and did not at all spare the ladies! When one was going in the woods, a humming warbling was heard, which is still sounding in my ears; wasps everywhere, it was almost a despair,' &c.

"I have not seen anywhere in the southern districts of our country the wasps so exceedingly numerous as they must have been in Tromsö in the said years. The species occurring here are: *Vespa crabro, media, saxonica,* and var. *norvegica, holsatica, vulgaris, germanica, rufa,* and *Pseudovespa austriaca.*" (W. M. S.).]

November 7, 1893 (*continued*).

Now I have much pleasure in begging your acceptance of a few pamphlets sent accompanying by book post—three on Hessian fly and one on Paris-green. Two of the Hessian fly pamphlets were condensed notes regarding its first appearance here, the other a report in full of the communications of my correspondents. I wished very much to send you a similar detailed report of the first year's observations of this *Cecidomyia destructor* (fig. 15) in Britain, but as yet I have not been able to find one remaining. Every year since the first appearance of this infestation amongst us, I have received some amount of information as to its greater or less presence, and I have given, so far as I could, my best attention to it. If it should happen that there is any point on which you would wish a reply to any inquiries, I would with pleasure do my best to answer fully, and would think myself honoured, as well as be very much pleased to be in communication with you on the above subject, or any other point of injurious insect presence.

[On the subject of wasps, Miss Ormerod wrote to Mr. Edward Connold on January 15, 1894:—

"I am very glad that you were able to procure my late brother's book on "Social Wasps" and that its perusal gave you pleasure. You ask me how the combs were removed from the nests. I do not know how my brother managed it, but I found the matter very easy,

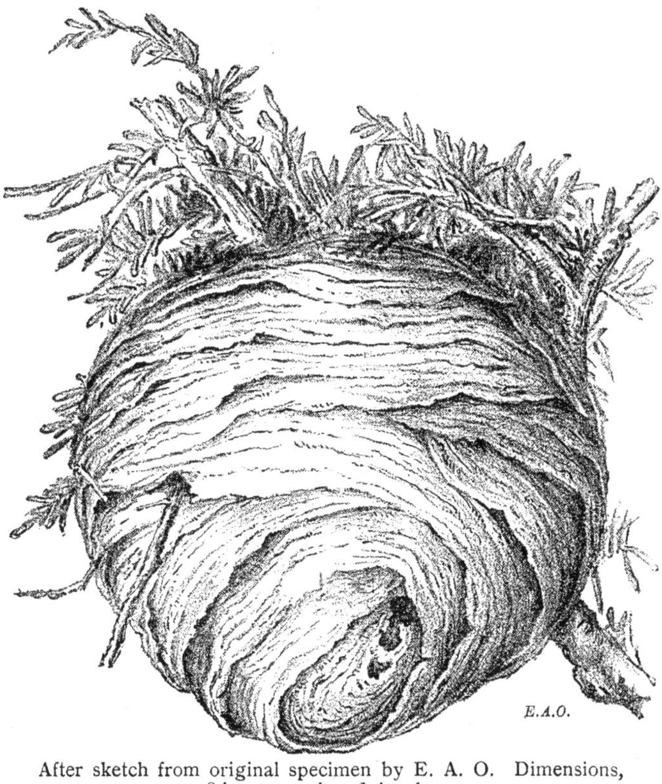

After sketch from original specimen by E. A. O. Dimensions, 8 in. across by 7½ in. deep.

FIG. 63.—NEST OF TREE WASP, *VESPA SYLVESTRIS.*

as long as the nests had been so recently taken from out-of-door localities, that the paper had not become too dry to be operated on. Indeed, the damp condition induced by the first stages of the very nasty state that combs with dead grubs get into, rather facilitated work than otherwise.

The first thing in working on a nest of any size was to get a pair of scissors, long in the blades, thin, and also very sharp. Then carefully make a clean vertical cut through the paper-case of the nest from the entrance below nearly to the top. Through this great gash I had no difficulty in removing the combs—so to say (although it is a disagreeable word) "eviscerating" the nest. I began with the smallest and lowest comb. Inserting my scissors horizontally I snipped through the little paper pillars by which it was connected with the comb above and withdrew it in a very convenient way, with fingers or forceps (or very likely by help of the scissors) through the opening. Continuing this process I do not remember that I ever failed to clear out the comb successfully. It did not always require to be entirely removed, if I recollect rightly. I think sometimes the upper comb did not require removal. When all was cleared out, I filled the empty paper case with cotton wool, and applying plenty of gum to this below the slit, I very gently pressed the paper back to its former position, and if the work had been dexterously done, the injury did not show much. If the paper had been broken of course the damage showed, and it was requisite to be careful that the gum or adhesive mixture used for keeping the cut edges in their places did not run about. Sometimes where circumstances permitted, I cut a little aside from the straight line in places so as to secure an uninjured piece of a layer to hide part of the slit. In this way very pretty specimens could be arranged, showing both nest and comb. I have been preparing a long paper on the wasp attack of last year for my next Annual Report. I have had very good contributions, and hope it may be liked.

"It will give me great pleasure to attend to any inquiry the Hon. Sec. of the Museum may care to send me as to starting a collection of pests to agriculture, and I think I might be able to help with suggestions where specimens are procurable.

"Many thanks for your suggestion as to membership, but I do not care to belong to more Societies than I can possibly help, so I hope you will forgive my not accepting your kind offer."]

March 10, 1898.

DEAR DR. SCHÖYEN,—In reply to your inquiry whether any measures are being taken in this country to prevent the introduction of the San José Scale, *Aspidiotus perniciosus*, I am not aware of any such measures being in contemplation. I have not heard of anything of the kind being proposed, nor have I seen any mention in our newspapers of preventive measures being contemplated in regard to imports. My own impression is that we are not likely to suffer from it. With our island climate (as a general thing, and as especially observed by Dr. C. V. Riley) the injurious insects of the Continent of America rarely establish themselves here, although ours adapt themselves to the American Continental circumstances, and this Scale appears to be remarkably susceptible to damp and cold. The Bulletin by Dr. John B. Smith, Entomologist of the New Jersey Experimental Station, published November 27, 1897, says, p. 6, "The Scale does best with us in dry, warm weather. It does not like dampness, nor shade, and will die out in a cold, moist locality. Large trees with dense foliage are therefore least troubled, and a dense mass of vegetation shading the ground completely will be infested only towards the tips of the twigs or branches nearer the surface, where sunlight and air are most abundant." I greatly hope, therefore, that even if this injurious attack should come, that it will not establish itself to a serious extent, as shade is a characteristic of many of our orchards.

Our chief trouble at present is an attack of eel-worms, *Tylenchus devastatrix*, on red clover, *Trifolium pratense*, causing what we call "Clover-stem sickness." I never knew the attack so widely prevalent before. But I hope that with the measures which I draw attention to in my recent Annual Report we may do some good.

March 11, 1898.

Relatively to the San José Scale, I find, from some information received this morning, that Mr. R. Newstead, Curator of the Grosvenor Museum, Chester, has lately attended by request at the Board of Agriculture, and stated that this infestation had not established itself in any way in this country. Also that he had not heard of, nor had he seen any instances of its presence, although he had made diligent search for it at Liverpool, &c. He thinks the matter is a "scare," and that the insect is not likely to establish itself here. In this opinion (the document before me states) he is supported by our Entomological Society. Mr. Newstead is, I believe, excellently qualified to form an opinion on the subject, as he is a practical Economic Entomologist, and he has also made the *Coccidæ* a subject of minute investigation. This I should say was more important than the views of a meeting of our Entomological Society, of whom few, if any (excepting Mr. Douglas), have, so far as I am aware, studied *Coccidæ* to an extent approaching Mr. Newstead's observations, and have no special bias towards applied Entomology.

The above will perhaps be of some interest to you as the nearest approach I am able to make to a reply to your inquiry, and I beg you to believe me.

Yours truly,
ELEANOR A. ORMEROD.

To Dr. Enzio Reuter, Helsingfors, Finland.

TORRINGTON HOUSE, ST. ALBANS, ENGLAND,
October 15, 1894.

SIR,—In acknowledging receipt of your obliging letter of the 8th of October, received here on the 12th, permit me to say that I think it not only a pleasure, but an honour, to be in communication with the leading Entomologists who, like yourself, are working for the good of their countries. I thank you much for your letter.

First, about the *Cecidomyia* (Wheat midge), larvæ (fig. 62) on the *Alopecurus pratensis*[1] (Foxtail grass), I cannot remember that any further observations were sent me about it, nor have I noticed anything in publications which come to my hands. My correspondents often send me specimens and details of some infestation which has caught their attention, but it is with the greatest difficulty in many instances that I can induce them to continue their observations for successive seasons, and the development of the imagines of the *Cecidomyiæ* from the early condition is much more trouble than they care to take.

By book post accompanying this letter I forward to your kind acceptance a copy of my seventeenth Report. In the pages of the Report I have placed copies of various leaflets. These, you will see at a glance, are not at all scientific, but intended quite for popular use by our farmers, therefore I have used the very simplest words I could.

You are good enough to offer to send me copies of some of your future reports in connection with Economic Entomology. If you can spare them I should value them very much. For although I am not able to understand more than a word here and there, yet with the help of the dictionary I can make out enough to see whether your information is applicable to the conditions here, and I can

[1] This species described by me later under the name *Oligotrophus alopecuri*, n. sp. (Zwei neue Cecidomyinen, Acta Soc. pro Fauna et Flora Fennica xi., No. 8, 1895, p. 3–9, Taf. i., Fig. 1–9) (E.R.).

get a good translation made for me. I can read German and French, but I am sorry not to be able to write with ease in either language.

November 21, 1894.

DEAR SIR,—I had much pleasure in receiving your kind letter yesterday, and also beg you to receive my very hearty thanks for your kind and valuable gift of so many of your writings received on the day before. But now I am going to ask you a further favour. At your leisure would you oblige me with the name of a dictionary which would help me to understand them? I do not understand Norwegian, but, with the help of the Dano-Norwegian dictionary of Mons. A. Larsen, I can manage to make out what I especially need from Dr. Schöyen's writings, which he is so good as to send me. But now I have been trying to translate your few lines on *Charæas graminis* (Antler moth) (chap. XIII.), and either from my own ignorance, which I much regret, or from not having the right dictionary, I have not been able to read them.

P.S.—It pleases me very much to hear from you that you approve of my reports, and it is kind of you to mention it.

December 11, 1894.

I thank you most heartily for sending me this useful dictionary. It is just what I was needing. With this help I can already make out short pieces of your reports and publications, which is a great pleasure and profit to me. It really was quite a vexation to see what I wanted so much to study and yet could hardly make out any connected meaning. I only just write now to say that both for your kind and helpful gift and your letter accompanying I thank you most heartily.

March 5, 1895.

I did not at once acknowledge your Report on Injurious Insects which you have sent me because I thought very likely you would send me a few lines about mine, and now I beg to acknowledge your note with many thanks. What a vast sum it is that you mention as the loss [about 5,000,000 Finn. Marks=ca. £200,000, in the years 1889–1891] caused by *Charæas graminis*, Antler moth (fig. 4)! I am so sorry that I am not able to read your reports, which, from the little bits I can pick out here and there, are, I see, so valuable and would help me so much. But please not to think that they are wasted on me, for I learn a great deal that helps me, and when there is something that I particularly wish to know I get the passages translated.

April 8, 1895.

I beg that you will never for one minute think of taking up your valuable time in writing to me at length about my reports. If you can at any time (as you have so nicely done in your letter received to-day) tell me that you think them serviceable, this is a most pleasant encouragement, for which I am grateful, but I know well what a tax it would be to write letters, so to say, merely for compliment. Pray believe me, I should indeed be sorry thus to trouble you. I value your writings that you are good enough to send me very much, and I got a serviceable Swedish grammar and studied it when I could get time, so I can make out a little now; at least so much that I can see where what I wish particularly to understand is, and get it properly translated. Accompanying I have much pleasure in sending two copies of my little brochure on Paris-green. I thought perhaps M., your brother professor, Odo M. Reuter, whose pamphlet on *C. graminis* I have studied with much benefit, might care to have one.

August 21, 1895.

Many thanks for kindly giving me a copy of your work on the "Zwei neue Cecidomyinen," which I am very glad to possess. Your minute description will be a most valuable assistance in identification. This year I have only had one report of presence of *C. destructor*, but there has been a great deal of insect presence, and sometimes of kinds not often observed here.

But the chief point of general interest, I think, has been what to do about the *Hippobosca equina* (Forest fly, fig. 18), relative to some of our military manœuvres in the New Forest, which is its especial English locality. I do not know whether you have the infestation so far north as your country? It is very troublesome at times here.

December 18, 1899.

I should be very glad to help you if I could by reference to publications on "Silver-top" or "White-eared" wheat, but I am not aware of anything having been written on it in this country excepting my own short and meagre notes in my twelfth Annual Report, for 1888 Specimens are sent me occasionally, but—as by the time that the top of the wheat (or grass) has faded so as to draw attention to the injury, the insect, if insect was there, has gone—I have never been able to identify the cause of the mischief with any approach to certainty. I conjecture the cause to be the presence of some species of thrips. The

American observations point to this, but these you probably are well acquainted with (and, indeed, it is not these you are inquiring about). In my notes I mention the peculiar manner in which the injured upper part of the stem can be withdrawn, the stem having been apparently severed about three or four inches above the uppermost knot. In the only instance I have seen in which the attack was still in progress (that is, the stem was not already parted, although it cracked asunder on being pulled), I found that at the point of fracture the straw tube had within an irregular swollen growth, what might be described as a granulated growth, filling up the tube; also the cross-section showed small open cells which had been cracked across in severing the stem. I had specimens of the attack also on barley, and at the time I was inclined, from the absence of all insect appearance, to ascribe it to some vegetable disease, but in the years that have elapsed since then it has appeared to me more likely to be attributable to thrips.

I am afraid that there is not anything worth your study in the page and a few lines of my remarks, but if you would care to see it, I would gladly direct a copy of my twelfth Annual Report to be sent for your acceptance. I would do so now, but I have not an unbound copy by me. Many thanks for your own publications which you have kindly sent me. I have read with great interest your remarks on the *Argyresthia conjugella*, Zell.[1] We have an apple attack here occasionally noticeable which agrees well with the characteristics of this infestation, but I have never been fortunate enough to identify the cause.

Yours very truly,

ELEANOR A. ORMEROD.

To Professor Dr. Alfred Nalepa, Gmunden, Vienna.

TORRINGTON HOUSE, ST. ALBANS, ENGLAND,
August 3, 1893.

MONSIEUR,—I am very greatly indebted to your kindness and courtesy in taking the trouble to give me all the very valuable and helpful information which you favoured me with in your letter of the 28th July. I also thank you much for your permission to make some extracts in my Annual Report from the information which you have placed in my

[1] The larvæ of this species infested badly the apple fruits in the whole of Finland in the summer of 1898. (Cfr. "Ent. Rec.," xi., No. 2, 1899, pp. 37–39, and "Can. Ent.," xxxi., 1899, pp. 12–14).—E. R.

hands. This is a very great favour, and you may rest assured that I will most fully acknowledge my debt to yourself. From the study of the pamphlet which you were good enough to send me I have already benefited largely. But I earnestly pray you, do not let me intrude on your kind liberality for any work that I might be able (if you were good enough to give me the name) to purchase. My London booksellers are accustomed to procuring Continental publications for me, and I am feeling myself so greatly indebted to you for valuable information that I am quite uneasy at not being able to reciprocate as I much wish. I have delayed writing in the hope of being able to procure some specimens, but as yet I have only the enclosed (Pear-leaf blister galls, ? of *Phytoptus pyri*) to send to you from trees in my own garden, and these I am afraid will be of little interest. Your valuable list of infestations has shown me that there are very many kinds of *Phytoptus* attack that I had no idea of the existence of, and I will indeed try to be of some service to you.

By book post accompanying I beg your kind acceptance of the current number of my Annual Report, in which are some remarks on a species of *Entedon* (or *Entedonidæ*, parasites of Dipterous leaf-miners especially) which we found in currant buds in watching for what we hoped might prove a parasite on the *Phytoptus*. I fear my report will be of little interest to you, but I just beg you to accept to show the kind of publication.

August 16, 1893.

I postponed replying to your kind letter of the 7th in the hope that I might have something of interest to send you, but I have only been able to procure the enclosed Prunus galls. They are from Toddington, Gloucestershire. I rather fear they will wither on the journey, but I forward them because the twigs have something amiss with them, which just possibly may be owing to *Phytoptus* presence. Thank you much for giving me the name of the *Phytoptus pyri*, which I have noted at p. 296 in your "Katalog," which you were good enough to send me, and which is of truly valuable assistance. My booksellers will, I hope, before long procure me five or six of your publications either in separate impressions or in the parts or volumes in which they were published, and then I shall hope to have the information that I am much wishing for, without troubling you personally. But should the special attack, which I desire to understand better, not be specifically described, then I should indeed be very thankful to avail myself of your kind permission to ask for further information, and a sketch would be a most valuable aid. I have too great a respect for the time and work of scientific men to intrude if I can possibly help it, and I am very grateful for the important help which you have already given me.

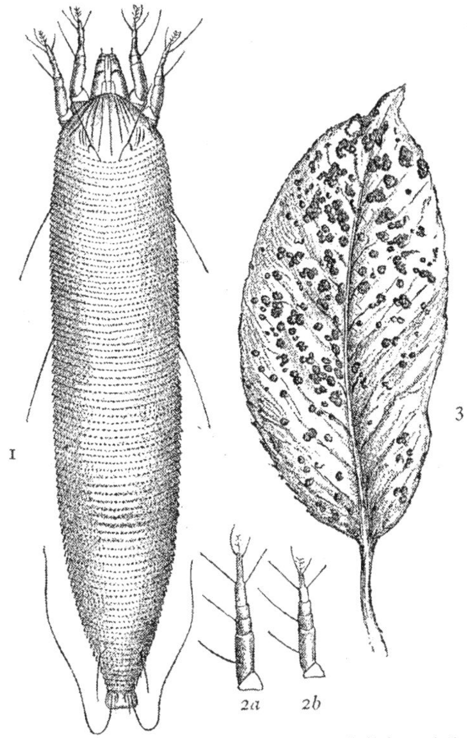

1, female (natural length circa 0·2 mm.); *2a*, left leg of the first pair of *Phytoptus tristriatus*, and *2b*, of *Phytoptus tristriatus* var. *carinea*, magnified 550 times—all after Dr. Nalepa. 3, infested pear leaf.

FIG. 64.—PEAR LEAF BLISTER MITE, *PHYTOPTUS PYRI*.

November 2, 1893.

I am greatly obliged for your kind letter received two days ago, and it is so very good of you to have taken the trouble of writing the names of the various portions of the *Phytoptus* on your plate accompanying so clearly for me that I hardly know how to express my thanks sufficiently.

This is indeed a most acceptable help, for there were some of the quite minutely technical terms that I had failed to make out the meaning of, and now you have most excellently got over my difficulties for me, and I thank you very much for the same. Since I wrote to you at Gmünden I have had great pleasure and benefit in procuring some of your valuable publications, so full of excellent descriptions and figures. One of these is the separate impression of your paper, read on January 24, 1889, with 9 plates, including p. 11, of which you have now sent me this valuably explained copy.

Another—the separate impression for February 13th—contains description, p. 11, and figure, plate iv., of *Phytoptus pyri*, and I have also a copy of your "Genera und Species der Familie Phytoptidæ," 1891. Now I think, thanks to study of your clear descriptions, I have a fair knowledge of the characteristics of a *Phytoptus*, and of the divisions of the Family Phytoptidæ. When I publish my next Annual Report I should very much wish to give my readers some better information than I have hitherto been able to do, and to point to them from what source I obtained it, and how they may obtain it for themselves. I think I have your kind permission to use one of your figures. I am therefore having a very careful copy executed of your *P. pyri* (plate iv., fig. 1), of the two claws (in your Genera and Species, plate ii., 9*a* and *b*), together with an attacked leaf from life (Fig. 64).

Your part would be a most soundly valuable aid to readers here, for really and truly I doubt if more than very few among us are aware (say) that the legs of the *Phytoptus* are made up of claw, tarsus, tibia, and so on, much less that the claw is of this peculiar shape. I confess to you I was ignorant of this myself. I should like to give a part of your description of the *P. pyri* to show what a description ought to be; also to allude to the species which you were so good as to name for me, and to your principle of classification (p. 317 of "Katalog"). Should any of this not be according to your pleasure, I beg of you kindly to tell me. I should indeed be ungrateful if, after all your kind help, I trespassed on your information against your wish. Should you allow it, you may depend on me to quote accurately, so that my quotations will send readers to your works, not enable them to use my report as a robbery of you; also I would fully and honestly acknowledge the source of my information, and be truly grateful. I wish I could send you specimens. Would you care to have some galls of the *Phytoptus ribis* from black currant in their (I think) very unusually advanced condition for this time of year ? If so, I think I could procure some from Kent.

It is with regret that I read in your letter that you are not in strong health. But if you could work less severely might not you hope to have benefit ? The excessively minute work

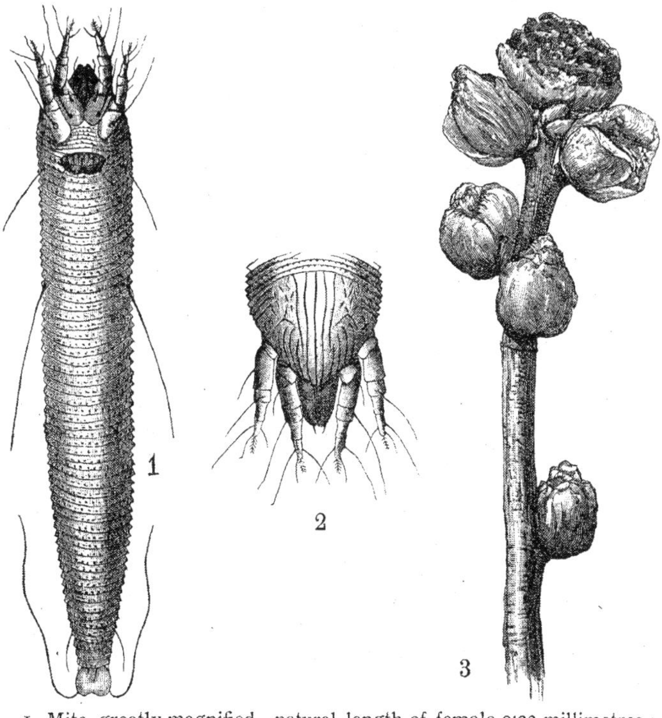

1, Mite, greatly magnified—natural length of female 0·23 millimetres ; 2, head and fore parts, still more magnified (by permission, after Dr. A. Nalepa) ; 3, mite-galls of unusually large size, with one withered and open.

FIG. 65.—CURRANT GALL MITE, *PHYTOPTUS RIBIS*, NALEPA.

of your elaborate investigations must be exceedingly wearing. In my own observations (which, indeed, are not to be compared with yours) I always find they tell very much on my health if I have at once to overwork my sight with the microscope and my mind in the record of my observations.

But I have not robust health, so that I can sympathise. With renewed thanks for the welcome contents of yours lately received.

March 12, 1894.

I am greatly obliged to you for your kind present of your "Beiträge zur Kenntniss der Phyllocoptiden," with its first-rate descriptions and magnificent figures. It is a very great advantage to me to be in possession of your noble work on these creatures, and I feel myself very much indebted for all the great help you have given me.

About the *Phytoptus ribis*. I delayed replying because I thought that if any thoroughly complete description of this *Phytoptus* had been published by Professor Westwood it would be sure to be known of by Mr. W. Hatchett Jackson, of Keble College, Oxford, who was Professor Westwood's chief assistant. But he tells me that "under the generic name of *Acarellus* I can find nothing but a brief paragraph without figure in the accounts of the meetings of the Entom. Soc." Mr. Jackson adds, "I remember the occasion very well, and making slides for him from specimens in our own garden. I shall search for those slides in the Hope Museum."—W. H. J.

After some search here I found the enclosed, and as I think you would desire to see the fullest account which I believe Professor Westwood published, I have detached the page. If he were still with us I know how he would have delighted in your splendid unravelling of what was then a mystery. At your best convenience, when you have quite certainly no further use for the page, perhaps you would kindly let me have it back.

In my own early observations of the habits of the Currant *Phytoptus* I noted it as *P. ribis*, Westwood, on the authority, or rather after the example, of Mr. Andrew Murray (see "Aptera," p. 355), for we had not in those days any more trustworthy and accepted guidance, but as to comparing these with such a work as yours, no one with the least atom of knowledge would think for a minute of such a thing.

Yours very truly,

ELEANOR A. ORMEROD.

To C. P. Lounsbury, Esq., Government Entomologist, Cape Town.

TORRINGTON HOUSE, ST. ALBANS,
September 17, 1895.

DEAR MR. LOUNSBURY,—It gave me great pleasure to

receive your letter this morning, in all excepting that I find I might possibly have seen yourself and Mrs. Lounsbury. I am really very sorry not to have done this, for there are many things so difficult to enter on in writing, which yet (as now you are on our British staff) I should like you to know, relative to entomological matters, and also, though I should have said this first, it would have been a pleasure to my sister and myself to become personally acquainted with you. How fortunate you are in having such a skilled colleague [his wife]; it must be a real comfort to you to have an entomological *alter ego*, and yet such a charming companion.

I do not know whether you have my little book on "South African Insects," so I beg your acceptance of a copy sent by this post.

You will have made acquaintance with your colleagues,

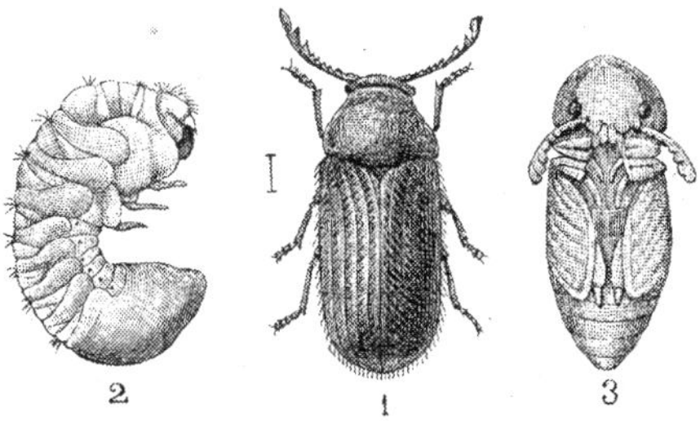

1, Beetle; 2, larva; 3, pupa, magnified (from Bulletin No. 4, New Series, U.S.A. Department of Agriculture, p. 124).

FIG. 66.—BREAD, PASTE OR BOOT BEETLE, DRUG STORE BEETLE (U.S.A.), *ANOBIUM PANICEUM* (=*SITODREPA PANICEA*) LINN.

and you will, I conjecture, find Mr. Bairstow useful if he be still attending to insect matters. He collected a great deal of information for me when I was compiling my little S.A. book. But now I am chiefly writing to indicate the pleasure it will give me to be in communication with you as occasion may occur, and with good wishes both for your success and comfort to yourself and Mrs. Lounsbury, &c.

November 4, 1895.

I had great pleasure in receiving your letter of the 12th of October, and first of all I will try to reply so far as I am able about the Boot beetle, *Anobium paniceum*. The English manufacturers did what is so very inconvenient—though one is not surprised at it—they begged that their names and localities might not be mentioned. But with regard to the use of a deterrent paste (or mixture in the paste), it was quite plain that they did not mean to do anything. They spoke of difficulties to the workers, &c., and as to using Paris-green!—really, there would have been a disturbance indeed, if I had ventured to suggest such a thing. The subject appeared to be making no headway, and my suggestions as to the all-importance of cleanliness in the workshop, so that the beetles might have no harbouring places, did not meet their views. So I strongly advised in order to make sure whether the infestation took possession in this country or at the Cape, that some boots should be

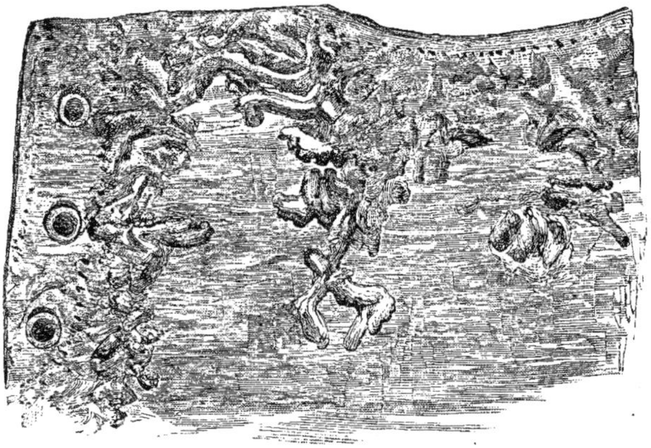

FIG. 67.—UPPER OF A BOOT INJURED BY MAGGOT OF PASTE BEETLE, *ANOBIUM PANICEUM.*

packed up and properly secured against all possibilities of external infestation, and sent to South Africa, and on arrival there, sent back to the exporters here unopened. Thus we should have learned on examination, if they were infested, that the mischief was started in this country. But not one word on the subject have I had from them since. Perhaps the result put the locality of the origin of evil being in this country beyond doubt. I have kept a quantity of the letters on the subject laid away, but now I think I cannot use them to better purpose than by forwarding them to you. Please do not return them. I have not re-read them, but it is impossible there can be anything confidential in them, excepting the names of the firms which the writers did not wish published, and it is just possible (in case you can spare time to run them through) that there may be points of interest.

What you say of inertness is just what is such a drag on the advance of work here. Instead of getting information, and acting on it, they (or many) propose to write to the Board of Agriculture or possibly to another quarter, and sometimes they follow advice, sometimes they do not.

Just now I had an application about *Strongylus filaria* (thread worms which produce husk or hoose) which is doing great damage in one district. They thought of writing to the Board of Agriculture. I suggested the excellent account in your Dr. Curtice's book on "Sheep Diseases," but it did not appear to have occurred to them to teach themselves.

June 24, 1896.

It was with great pleasure that I received your first Report about two days ago, and I must both very sincerely and heartily congratulate you on this good work. It seems to me quite an example of what a report should be. Clear wording that all can understand, and a short sound life history, with all requisite means of prevention of the specially detailed "pest" attacks, with a deal of excellent reading besides. Indeed, I congratulate you greatly on taking your place so firmly, and I consider the Colony is much to be congratulated also on securing your help. I am glad to see that the Government gives you good paper and printing. There is only one thing which I should much like to see added, and that is pictorial illustrations. Could not you have at least some figures? I believe they are available in the Government Stores. Sometime after the publication of my little book on the "Injurious Insects of South Africa," a request was made to me for a number of figures, which with much pleasure I presented. If you would like, besides those which could be looked up at the office of the "Agricultural Journal," electros of some of the figures which are my own, which I use in my own publications, I would gladly send you out, say a dozen or a dozen and a half, if the Agent General would (as I feel pretty sure he would) kindly allow me to send them out to you in the Government box. It would give me real pleasure if I could be of any help to you in your good work.

August 17, 1896.

I have this morning had great pleasure in receiving your letter, and I shall be very glad to send you electrotypes of the blocks of which you will let me have a list,—that is to say, of such as are quite my own. Those that I have from Messrs. Blackie and Son, Stanhope Street, Glasgow, I have only permission to use in my own publications. I think very likely, though, that, if you were inclined to purchase electrotypes from them, they would be quite willing to let you have them at the same price which they charge me, that is eighteenpence the square inch. About my own, I have no difficulties, as my wood figures and electrotypes are all in charge of my printers. There would be no charge for carriage, and I would charge you just the cost price of the electros. But there is one point, please, that I am sure you will forgive me insisting on as a condition of use of my electrotypes, namely, that they may be used in any publication of the Department of Agriculture of Cape Colony, or in any publication of your own, but nowhere else without my consent.

July 28, 1899.

I have, I am afraid, been owing you for a long time, more than one letter in reciprocation of your kind letters to me, but I have hoped you would forgive me, for you know how I am situated with a deal of application and no staff. I am wanting now to say that I hope you have not been vexed with me for having had a hand in robbing you of an efficient member of your staff (Mr. Fuller), which I am afraid must for the present be an inconvenience, but it surely will be an immense benefit to Natal, to have a trustworthy Entomologist.

I am trying to work up *Piophila casei* (Cheese and Bacon fly), which Miss Murtfeldt took up so well. I incline to think that it is more present than is supposed, only of course, "cured meat" dealers do not like to own to it. I have got a nice little family reared from bacon for observation under a glass, and some of their brothers and sisters loose about the room, which I see little or nothing of until the cheese is brought in twice a day, when they come, and so give me an opportunity of watching egg-laying.

August 9, 1899.

What a frightful thing this prospect of war is! I have not an idea what may be politically right, but it distresses me intensely to think of the sorrow, and so far as in me lay I have had a hand in getting poor Mr. Fuller right into the thick of the trouble.[1] You have assuredly been having

[1] Miss Ormerod had recommended Mr. Fuller for the appointment he secured in Natal.

trouble enough, with fire, water, and "sausages"! I am truly glad that your books and insects were not very much damaged. But I hope you will not peril your valuable health by turning yourself into a pasturage ground as you say, for these very detestable ticks. Much better try the convict! His nervous system will not be so delicate.[1]

July 5, 1900.

I learn with great pleasure that you and Mrs. Lounsbury are coming back through England, and I hope you will be able to give me the great pleasure of your looking in here. I should be so glad to see you, and you and I could have some delightful entomological talk. On Saturday next, I hope to see Dr. John B. Smith, State Entomologist of New Jersey.

What a business you must have in transporting your parasites from America to Cape Colony, but I hope you will have good success in obtaining the specimens you are needing. Yours sincerely,

ELEANOR A. ORMEROD.

To Claude Fuller, Esq., Entomologist Department of Agriculture, Pietermaritzburg, Natal.

TORRINGTON HOUSE, ST. ALBANS,
November 5, 1898.

DEAR MR. FULLER,—I would very gladly in reply to your request, offer you any suggestion in my power, but I scarcely know whether my ideas would be serviceable. Judging by my own experiences in purchase by farmers or fruit-growers of books which they certainly need and wish to have the information contained in, I should not expect any publisher to take any MS. of mine as a speculation. The good folks wish for the books, but they do not, at least only a very small proportion of them (I am speaking of agriculturists) wish to buy. My work is done at a great money loss, and my publishers do not take my books as a speculation, but act in fact as my agents. Could you not get your MS. published in a serial, with a stipulation, that you held copyright, and so your valuable information would be brought forward without cost to yourself.

There is another point. The differences in species, even in genera, are terribly difficult to be sure of amongst many of the Scale insects, and many of the Aphides, and unless

[1] This note refers to a fire in Mr. Lounsbury's department and to the investigation of red water fever in cattle produced by ticks.

fruit-growers have magnifiers and knowledge how to use them, I should not expect them to identify to any trustworthy purpose. If you brought out a strictly scientific work this of course would be very valuable as a book of reference, and Prevention and Remedies added would make it very useful indeed; but if you look forward to purchase by the public, I am afraid you will not find it happen.

Please excuse rather a hurried letter to catch the evening post, and believe me. Yours very truly,

ELEANOR A. ORMEROD.

CHAPTER XXII

LETTERS TO MR. JANSON AND MR. MEDD

Deer Forest fly—Flour moths—Weevils—Grouse and Cheese flies—Beetles—Agricultural Education Committee—The Water-baby Leaflet—Paper on Wasps.

MR. JANSON, addressed in the opening letters of this chapter, occupied the position of technical expert, to whom Miss Ormerod referred her generally accurate identifications of insects for confirmation. The cases of flour infestation referred to we have learned of in Chapter X., "Legal Experiences." The language employed is more technical than in any other part of her correspondence—the words of an expert addressing herself to another expert in the language of their common subject. Mr. Medd's name has been more associated with education than entomology, especially in relation to the comparatively new branch of "Nature Study."

To Mr. O. E. Janson, Technical Expert in Entomology, 44, Great Russell Street, W.C.

TORRINGTON HOUSE, ST. ALBAN'S,
February 13, 1897.

DEAR MR. JANSON,—I hope that in a very few days you will receive your copy of my twentieth Report, in which you helped me so especially about the Forest flies.

I am hoping you may be good enough to help me about the enclosed, or kindly put me in the right path, for I greatly hope that this may prove to be the long-needed observation about amount of wings of the ♀ (female) Deer Forest fly, the *Lipoptera cervi* (fig. 23). I received a day or two ago a good number, many still alive, or fresh on a little piece of Roe-deer's hide, which was infested with them even to being in clusters (from Strathconan forest, Ross-shire). On examining, I found on each side, at the hinder edge of the thorax, a little membranous kind of structure with a scalloped edge, and on very carefully raising it I found it was fixed to the thorax by a joint, and was, I think, quite certainly an abortive wing. I saw veins traversing the structure longitudinally, and though the scalloped and notched extremity was irregular in shape, it did not at all have the appearance (to my thinking at least) of being torn. Enclosed I send you half a dozen specimens, one of which has the structure very plain; the others I picked out at random, and what I am very much wishing you would help me about is whether these are females. They have the distinguishing dark brown colour (not the faint yellow colour of the male), and I should say they had the shape of the female, but I am not anatomist enough to be certain. If you cannot with complete convenience tell me yourself could you oblige by getting me a trustworthy opinion. I would most gladly give a most liberal consideration to any one you would get to investigate, for if these are females, we have here the long-wanted observation, and proof that they have abortive wings. I have plenty more specimens if you would care for some more; also I have two puparia.

February 23, 1897.

I am greatly obliged to you for helping me in this matter of the *L. cervi.* You will remember that you kindly helped me to a sight of a good number of German publications, from which I made large extracts, and, turning to these, I find notes of the male and of the female *L. cervi*, being found together in the hair of the deer all the winter through, and pairing there and the female depositing puparia. But the matter is much involved by the following statement regarding two varieties in the form of the males by Professor Stein, or Hartmann quoted by Stein: "The first are pale yellow, and the abdomen is slender and shrivels considerably after death; the latter are more yellow brown, their abdomen is wider and firmer, and the external organs of propagation clearly observable." There is a deal about abortive or shed wings, but the writers are under uncertainty. My belief is that our only hope towards clearing up the matter is our own observation, and if these creatures are really females, we have got the information that was being sought after. But do not let me tax your very great good nature too much. If you could give a specimen or two to Mr. Verrall and to

Mr. Austen I should like it, and you would hear what they say, and I would replace them to you. I have two puparia which I suppose are not likely to develop till towards the end of summer.

April 16, 1897.

I have been so fortunate as to find a puparium of a Deer Forest fly lately sent me in a consignment from Strathconan, and this gave me an opportunity of communicating with Professor Jos. Mik, Vienna, and he pronounces the specimens I sent accompanying to be females. He writes me (and I think it very kind of him to take the trouble) an exceedingly long letter, full of information and references, extending in a very small handwriting over five and a half large pages of note-paper, and, as he justly remarks, I have some difficulty in reading it!

I think of getting Mr. Pillischer to make some preparations of the *L. cervi* ♀ and their abortive wings so that we may have material for a good figure. Professor Mik is fearfully particular.

May 12, 1897.

Professor Mik identified my *L. cervi* as certainly well-developed females. I think he was a good deal pleased to have a mature puparium which I sent him and to dissect out an immature one. He says that he has himself ♀ of *L. cervi*, with abortive wings, so my work will not be a discovery as I hoped, still I think it will be of interest to illustrate.

May 24, 1897.

Your description of *L. minor* (lesser earwig) has helped me enormously, and I have translated as much as I think is likely to be needed of the technical part to help Mr. Knight to make a characteristic drawing (fig. 43).

I should like ♂ or ♀ and forceps of both, and I have material for this, but I should very much like a wing. I tried to unfold one or two and wasted my materials. Would your microscopist set one for me do you think? I should much like it; for I fancy (I have not been able to make sure) that there is a longer band of dark colour along the front edge than in our common earwig. But, any way, if I could have the wing set I should very much like to have a good figure of it.

October 5, 1897.

If you can spare time to help me in the present inquiry, I should be much obliged; it is quite a trade business matter. I am consulted by a London firm dealing in flour, as to infestation in their barrels, but as I gather it may be both from the Eastern and the Western world, and also may be infested by insect pests from whatever may be lying on the wharves, I want to be very sure of my identifications.

The presence of *Ephestia kuhniella* (Flour moth) was quite plain, so this I need not trouble you about. But about the "Weevils." I think those of which I enclose specimens in the bottle stoppered with cotton-wool, are the common *Calandra* (= *Sitophilus granarius*). I am quite sure *C. oryzæ* was present, but I do not think I have enclosed any. Messrs. Henderson write me to-day that they are quite sure their barrels took the infestation from oil-cakes which were swarming with *S. granarius*. To the best of my belief and

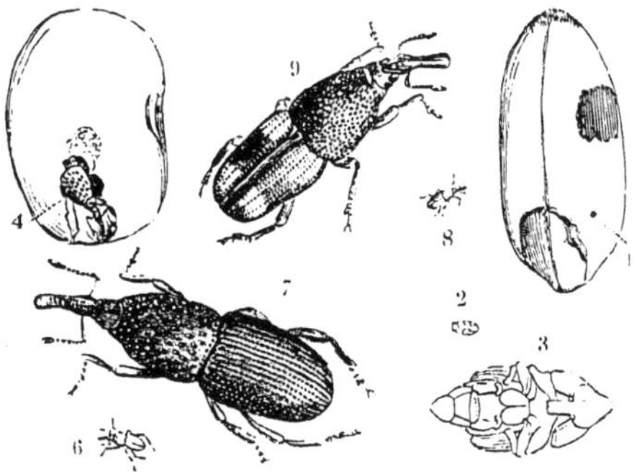

6, 7, Granary weevil; 2, 3, chrysalis, natural size, and magnified; 8, 9, rice weevil, natural size, and magnified; 1, 4, infested grains, also magnified.

FIG. 68.—GRANARY WEEVIL, *SITOPHILUS GRANARIUS*, AND RICE WEEVIL, *SITOPHILUS ORYZÆ*.

search, *Calandra* only lives on grain, so I fancy that its connection with the oil-cakes must be only as a shelter. I know *Calandra* will resort to remains of bread and milk or ripe apricots near a granary, but I supposed this was in search of moisture. But, nevertheless, as one weevil is so like another, it would be an important help if you would kindly verify my identification for me.

In the same little bottle are two small not-far-from-globose pubescent beetles, which I thought might be *Niptus hololeucus*, but when they came clean I saw they had not the beautiful bright yellow pubescence, nor were they so globose. I do not know them; you probably will at a glance, and your kind help would save me long search. Amongst the larvæ I found one answering to that of *Cucujus testaceus* (as given in Curtis) = *Lœmophlœus ferrugineus*—and in the flour there were numbers of the minute rusty little beetles of which I enclose some in a corked bottle. Will these be *Cucujus ferrugineus*? I do not think I have any types, and as this is such a decided business inquiry, I feel sure you will allow me to ask you to keep me right about it, at your convenience. The flour or barrels or something must have been (to my thinking) in a very neglected state.

October 11, 1897.

I am greatly obliged to you for your kind help about the flour coleoptera. I was puzzled about the *granarius*, as there was a slightly different look about it, from the specimens which I usually have, and I had no series for comparison. I have never had *Lœmophlœus* in this quantity before,—they run in all directions out of the flour. I cannot find another *Ptinus*, but the information you have given me is quite enough, I am sure, for my flour people. The really important attack that they have got is *E. kuhniella* (Flour moth) but as the flour is in barrels perhaps it will not trouble them

I have kept my *X. saxeseni* (Shot-borer beetles), in a good-sized glass-topped box, where the larvæ are still throwing out dust and the beetles come out and die, but I do not see any more, and I think that instead of giving you more trouble about them I had better get Mr. Knight to copy one of the U.S.A. imagos and add larvæ, pupæ, and strange "cleft" like cell from life. If the specimens you have are of interest to you pray oblige me by keeping them. I think I have material for a really interesting paper. Do you happen to know what has become of my very much valued correspondent, Dr. Karl Lindeman [the Russian Entomologist]? I have not heard from him for a year and a half, and I do not find his name in the U.S.A. Scientists' Guide. He was truly friendly and very punctilious in writing, but if he were dead I think I should have seen his obituary. I wonder whether he was so useful to the people that he has had to take a trip to Siberia!

October 26, 1897.

What work *Hylurgus piniperda* (Pine beetle),[1] continues to make in some of the great Pine woods in Scotland, consequent on the damage by high winds some years ago. I had

[1] With one possible exception the most destructive beetle of British forestry.

an application a little while ago from the forester on one of the great properties near Aberdeen, who reports great mischief on 1,000 acres. This afternoon I have a report of the woods at Craighlaw, Kirkcowan, Wigtonshire, being in most dismal condition.

I really wonder whether it will ever occur to our Board of Agriculture that there ought to be a Government Entomologist. It is only a short time since I had an application connected with the Austrian Embassy about a beetle attack that was eating the oats at Constantinople, but I suggested that Vienna was unsurpassed for its scientific men !

August 18, 1899.

I am thinking (though I have not mentioned the matter beyond just beginning at present) of (if I can find it) taking a comfortable villa and good garden at or in the outskirts of Brighton. I much wish to be nearer relations, for living so much alone is at times a very dreary kind of thing. Also there are many points in which Brighton would, I think, suit me better for my work, and possibly be more conveniently easy of access for entomological friends living on the South London lines. I know the place very well, and it has always suited my health excellently.

September 19, 1899.

I have a *Hippoboscid* this afternoon from Mr. Wheler, which was found on a lamb. He thinks it is a Grouse fly (or Spider fly, a near relative of the Forest fly). Surely oddly located ! But so far as I see I think it must be so. Shall I not send it you ? In any case it might be of interest, and I should very much like, at your convenience, to be made sure of what it is. If it be *Ornithomyia avicularia* (Grouse fly), I conjecture that it straggled into the nearest shelter when it developed. It is in beautiful order, but so lively that I have not been able to get a good look at the claws. [This identification was confirmed by Mr. Janson.]

September 22, 1899.

I am much obliged to you for all the points of interesting information in your letter. There is no hurry about figuring the Grouse fly, so that if Mr. Norman would kindly let me have the slide as soon as he thinks it would be safe to use it, I should feel very much obliged. I now enclose the specimen from a lamb. I quieted its very superabundant antics by slipping a little lump of cotton wool down the tube, about a third of the way, and it accepted the soft material moderately. It died afterwards, and I enclose it with some spirits in the tube. I should (if not inconvenient to you to ask), very much like this specimen also set by Mr. Norman, with the wings as they are at present—at rest, but showing the fore-nerves very nicely. I incline to think that if this be certainly *O. avicularia*, that it would suit better for figuring than the previous specimen as being in the same position as my *H. equina* and *L. cervi*, both ♂ and ♀ in previous Annual Reports. If you could oblige me with the two slides together I could make what personal observations I want; have which ever seems best figured, and afterwards, if one or both are of interest to you, I would very gladly beg your acceptance. I daresay you will be good enough to let

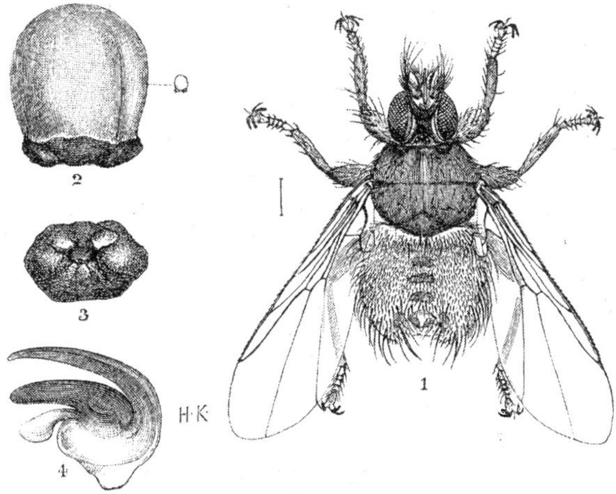

1, Grouse fly, magnified, with line showing natural length; 2, puparium, magnified and natural size; 3, end view, magnified; 4, claw, magnified.

FIG. 69.—GROUSE FLY, *ORNITHOMYIA AVICULARIA*, LINN.

me use your interesting short note about finding the specimen of *avicularia* alive in the box with the Horned owl.

I am working now on *Piophila casei*, Linn. (Cheese and Bacon fly, fig. 12), and hope to make a good paper, with some original observations of my own. Is it not a noteworthy circumstance that besides undoubtedly breeding in myriads in stores of cheese and bacon, that also they come in through the windows in such numbers that wire gauze, or equivalent, is a recognised protective measure? I think this points to there being some home of *P. casei* that wants looking up.

I did think Brighton might suit me better, but I found there was no suitable house, so I am staying here. I am very glad that you had a pleasant rest, and a beneficial one.

October 21, 1899.

Messrs. Forshaw and Hawkins, of Liverpool, have written me regarding beetle and maggot presence in flour and meal in two compartments of "Telesford," from New Orleans to Glasgow. They send me "a deal of" [1] report and two tubes with beetles, larvæ and flour. I believe these beetles (and larvæ) to be *Tribolium ferrugineum* (Rust-red flour beetle), and I enclose four beetles and six maggots. Will you be so very good as to let me know if I am right, and I enclose a telegraph form filled in, which would put me at ease for the present if you would be good enough to send it to me. The reason I am troubling you now is that the small

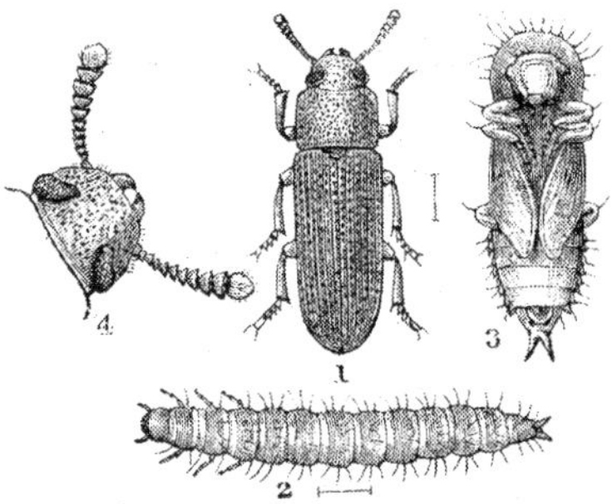

1, Beetle ; 2, larva ; 3, pupa—magnified, and with lines showing natural length ; 4, head with antennæ, much magnified.

FIG. 70.—RUST-RED FLOUR BEETLE, *TRIBOLIUM FERRUGINEUM*, FAB.

amount of flour in the little tubes has the characteristic (mentioned in Mr. Chittenden's paper in "Household Insects," &c., in a Bulletin of U.S.A.) of being greyish. See top of p. 113 as to "Flour Beetles."

This is quite different from the state of Messrs. Smyth and Co.'s flour, and if you are so good as to confirm my identification I might perhaps be allowed to use the information on our side on Tuesday, when Mr. Blyth comes down about depositions. The Glasgow case has every appearance of being on the road to a lawsuit, but now (after Friday's experience) I should not be so afraid of giving evidence, if you would make me sure.

[1] A favourite West Country expression of Miss Ormerod.

November 1, 1899.

I received the Grouse fly slide in perfect safety, beautifully put up; many thanks to you for procuring the same. If at your very best convenience you would settle my debt to Mr. Norman for his help, I should be greatly obliged. I am getting into your debt assuredly also, but whilst I am troubling you, thanks to these infested cargo people, I think I had better let this stand over. It is very weary work getting up information in this minute way, and as matter of choice I had rather be without a visit[ation] from six professional gentlemen and a shorthand writer all at once!

I have had a beautiful specimen of workings in willow of *Cryptorhynchus lapathi* beetle.

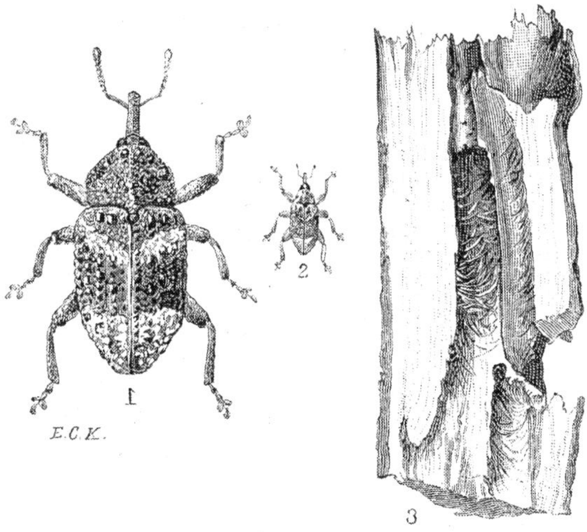

Beetle, natural size and magnified; willow stem, tunnelled by larvæ.

FIG. 71.—MOTTLED WILLOW WEEVIL, "ALDER-KILLER" (GERMAN), *CRYPTORHYNCHUS LAPATHI*, L.

December 29, 1899.

Many thanks for a sight of Mr. Fuller's letter (returned enclosed). I have enjoyed reading it very much; it is so interesting to have a real letter about the war, not made up "for press." I worked myself nearly stupid in running up the habits of the *Calandra* mentioned in "Insect Life," and there was some such roguery somewhere or other about the mate's report, which he stated afterwards was written under intimidation, that I felt a little uneasy about having anything to do with the matter.

January 12, 1900.

I have lately had an application about "White Ants" being destructive to young Cocoa trees in Ceylon. I do not know much about the great hill-building Termites as plant eaters, but I thought that probably exposing just the couple of inches or so subject to be gnawed, to the light might be useful.

September 16, 1900.

I am very much obliged to you for all the trouble you

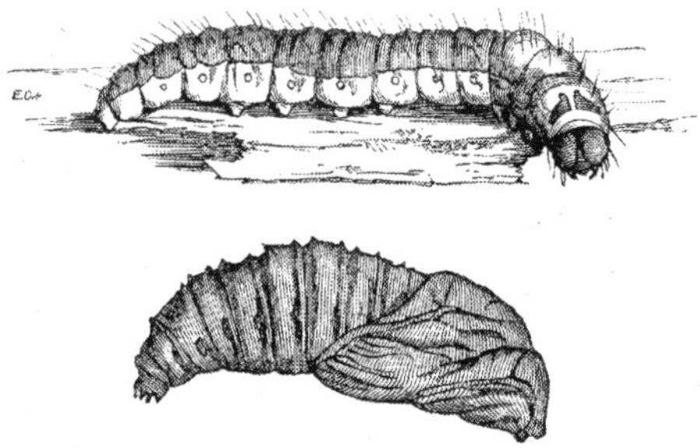

Caterpillar (not full grown) and chrysalis.

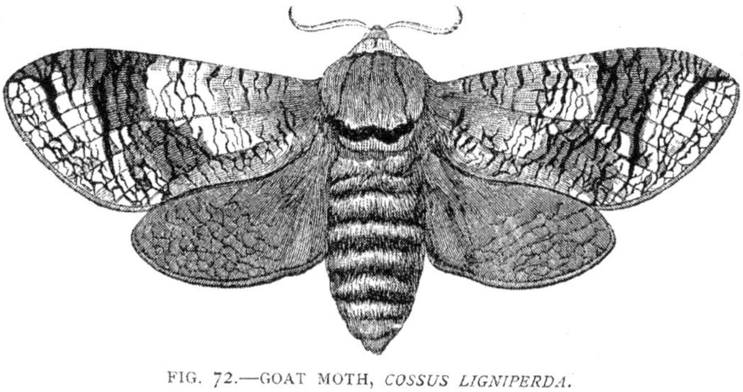

FIG. 72.—GOAT MOTH, *COSSUS LIGNIPERDA*.

have kindly taken in identifying the *Bruchi* for me, but on running the matter up there does not seem to be the least reason to suppose that these creatures had more to do with the barley than that they had strayed into it from beans, of which I find on special inquiry that the steamer carried also a consignment "in the same hold." I wrote to the importers (or rather my applicants wrote to them on my part) and I received a small consignment of the very identical beans from them (from Hull), and most of these I now enclose to you, as I thought you might care to see if anything of interest would develop. The specimens in the little bottle, including one or two hymenopterous parasites, are also from the beans.

In a little box with the beans is a fine specimen of the Goat moth, *Cossus ligniperda*, larva, which is very diligently spinning.[1] I have been much interested in watching the way it thickens its beginning of lacework web. I believe

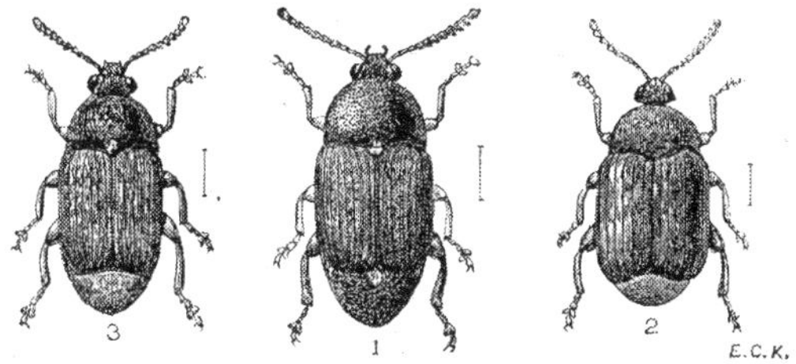

Bruchus brachialis. *Bruchus tristis.* *Bruchus rufipes.*

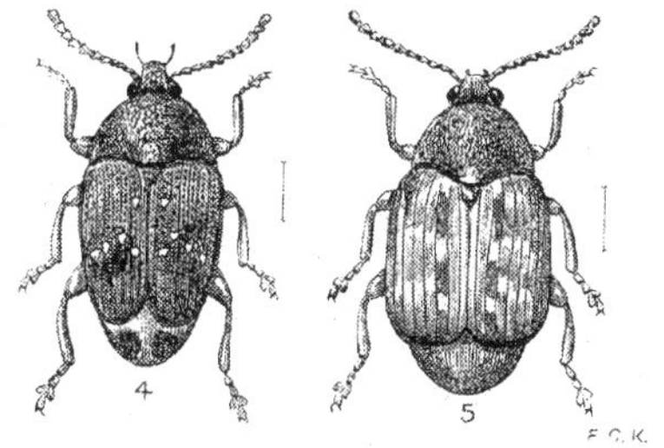

Bruchus pisorum = pisi. *Bruchus rufimanus.*
Magnified, with lines showing natural length.

FIG. 73.—PEA AND BEAN WEEVILS, *BRUCHI.*

(unless the top specimen has eaten it!) that there is another larva at the bottom.

September 23, 1900.

I am very much obliged to you for these nicely set *Bruchi*, and I do not think it would be at all out of place, although two of the species are not British, to give figures of the three kinds (*brachialis, rufipes,* and *tristis*) as found in a cargo including beans and wild peas from Smyrna, together with

[1] The caterpillars of the Goat moth feed in poplar, willow, elm, oak, lime, and beech, as well as in apple, pear, walnut, and other trees. (E. A. O.)

barley. (The consignees were very much puzzled about them.) I also found *rufimanus* in one of the beans which I was opening, a lovely specimen, so perfect in its marking. But now, if you please, I very much wish for a little further help. I cannot find any reference to *brachialis* or *tristis* in any book I possess, excepting just the names in Calwer's "Käferbuch."

I have been not a little disappointed about *Scolytus pruni*. I found nice larvæ in a piece of plum bark with this infestation, and had a good figure taken, but I kept on watching the small number of specimens to be fairly certain of species,

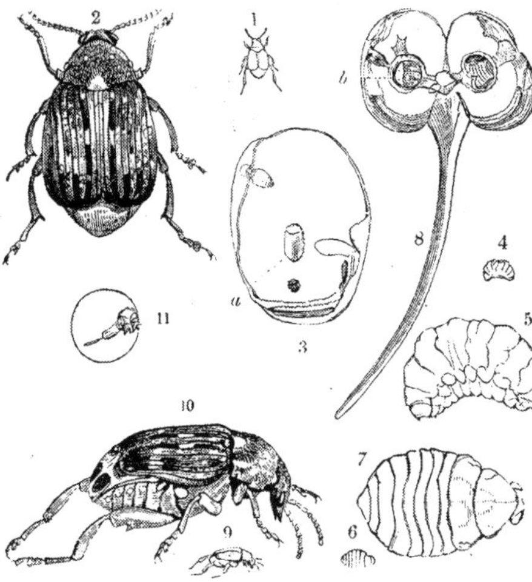

1 and 2, *Bruchus rufimanus*, natural size and magnified; 3, infested bean split open, showing cell; 4 and 5, larvæ, natural size and magnified; 6 and 7, pupæ, natural size and magnified; 8, bean, injured by beetle, vegetating; 9 and 10, *Bruchus pisi*, natural size and magnified; 11, injured pea.

FIG. 74.—BEAN BEETLES.

and to my vexation on development out came one as *rugulosus!*

With many thanks for your welcome and valuable help.

October 4, 1900.

I am very much obliged to you for lending me the two vols. of "Deutsche Ent. Zeit.," which will help me very much about those *Bruchidæ*—and more particularly with the specific distinctions which you have been good enough to give me. I will try not to keep the books over-long, and will return them carefully packed.

November 1, 1900.

Is it of interest to you (in case that you have not heard) to know of the decease, on the 13th of October, of Professor Josef Mik, of Vienna, after a short illness? I shall miss him, for he was a friendly colleague, and was good enough to send me a little collection of types of *Tabanidæ* which have been a great help.

I was rather perplexed how to name these three newly-imported species of *Bruchus*, but for want of a better I thought that sad-coloured bean-seed weevil, *B. tristis;* red-footed bean-seed weevil, *B. rufipes;* and red-horned bean-seed weevil, *B. ruficornis* [=*brachialis*] would do fairly.

Yours very truly.

ELEANOR A. ORMEROD.

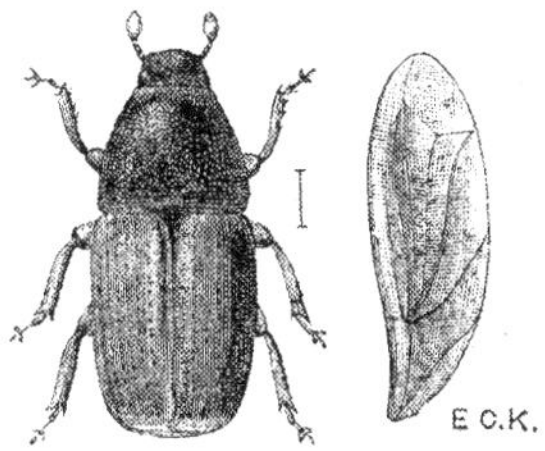

Beetle and wing, magnified; line showing natural length of beetle.

FIG. 75.—"SPLINT," OR SAP-WOOD BEETLE, *SCOLYTUS PRUNI*, RATZ.

To J. C. Medd, Esq., Stratton, Cirencester.

TORRINGTON HOUSE, ST. ALBANS,
March 12, 1900.

DEAR MR. MEDD,—I am much obliged by the packet of publications regarding the work of the "Agricultural Education Committee,"[1] and I note excellent names in your list of members, and some excellently true observations in your four-page leaflet, "Agricultural Instruction in the Elementary School." But it is with great difficulty that I am able to keep my own work in hand, and I have been quite unable to find time to study the other pamphlets which you have been good enough to send me, although, from their titles,

[1] The Agricultural Education Committee, 10, Queen Anne's Gate, Westminster, S.W., was formed in the autumn of 1899, with Sir W. Hart-Dyke, Bart., M.P., as Chairman, and the Rt. Hon. Henry Hobhouse, M.P., as Hon. Secretary. (J. C. M.)

I make no doubt that they contain both valuable information and suggestion.

Although I am sure that plain and interesting information on subjects of their daily surroundings would be gladly received by the boys, I do not in the least see my way to complying with your flattering suggestion of my pen being useful in the matter. You know how I am situated? There is a constant stream of applications sent me for advice regarding prevention of insect pests, which though chiefly about British troubles, involves much correspondence both with the Entomologists of our Colonies, the Continent and the U.S.A.—and to meet which I have no staff. I could not find time to write papers such as you desire; but if you wish I would send you copies of such leaflets as I have in which some of the ordinary crop pests are treated of very plainly; and from these I make no doubt that you could get passages arranged for your readers which the boys would like to read.

July 9, 1900.

It gratifies me very much that you should think my leaflets and "Manual" likely to be of use; and you have only to express the wish, for me to send another hundred of the "Manuals" as soon as they could be bound. I have been reading and much appreciating your observations in "Our Programme,"[1] of which you have kindly given me a copy, and it has occurred to me whether, now that I understand the scope of your work better, I might arrange a very simple paper on our commonest Live Stock attacks. I enclose a few pages as a sample of what is in my mind, just giving what could be taken in (and I think is needed) with addition of a little more life history, and the exceedingly simple methods of prevention. I have quantities of first-rate illustrations, but now I just submit the enclosed to you, hoping you will be kind enough to let me know at your convenience what you think of my idea.

July 14, 1900.

I am personally truly grateful for your letter of this morning, for I was very uneasy lest I should be, to put it shortly, giving sad offence. I certainly think the "Water-baby"[2] leaflet is a great mistake, but, as you judiciously remark, if it is to be issued we must make the best of it.

I will think over to the best of my power what appears

[1] One of the leaflets issued by the Agricultural Education Committee.

[2] Another leaflet of the series issued by the Agricultural Education Committee, but one which Miss Ormerod did not appreciate.

likely to be of use agriculturally on the subject of fly-attacks on farm-stock. Whilst I am preparing the papers themselves perhaps a good heading such as I may presently submit for approval will suggest itself. I should much like to have the primary heading "Agricultural Education Committee," for—with a footnote that the papers were prepared at the desire of the Agricultural Education Committee to give information—this would throw a shield over me, in writing on Cattle and Stock attacks. The ones selected do not infringe on what might be called "Veterinary"—things that involve discussion unbecoming in a lady writer, and those I propose to write on are what I have long had application about. There need be no difficulty about publishing if I do it in my usual way.

August 2, 1900.

After your visit, so pleasant as well as profitable to myself yesterday, I sat down as soon as I could to see what I could write about "Wasps," and I enclose the results. It is mostly an abstract of records of much personal observation of my own. If you like I would gladly lend electros of the figures.[1] If you care to accept the enclosed for any use to our Agricultural Education Committee that you may think it may be suited, I should be really pleased, only begging that it may not on any account whatever appear as part of the "Water-baby" series—that really I do not think I could bear.

August 8, 1900.

I thank you very heartily for your courteous reception of my letter about resignation. It is very good of you to write so kindly on the subject. I enclose you a copy of the letter which I have sent to the Secretary, which I have endeavoured to express with the friendliness which I feel. But, much as I regret leaving, I find that, independently of the considerations which I told to you, when I come to the real working my health does not allow it. If I am overpressed it brings on (without being unduly explicit) troubles both of health and sight, and I am very thankful that, beyond your exceedingly kind expressions, you do not press my remaining too hardly on me.

November 26, 1900.

Many thanks to you for Mr. Bathurst's paper on

[1] The paper on "Wasps" was lent by Mr. Medd to Mr. Chas. Roundell who incorporated it in his unique little volume, the *Rural Reader*, Horace Marshall & Co. (Ed.).

"Orchards;"[1] there is some excellent advice in it, particularly about sawing beneath the limb, trimming smooth, and not planting deep. But I think that as the piece of cloth to be tied round the tree is to "act as a trap," a little addition is needed (see my "Insects Injurious to Orchard and Bush Fruit," pp. 12, 13), viz., that the trap should be examined and the caterpillars cleared out every few days, or say every fortnight. If this be not done the sacking is very likely to make a nice little house for them. Please excuse my giving my views thus vigorously, and uncalled for. Yours very truly,

ELEANOR A. ORMEROD.

[1] Issued by the Agricultural Education Committee.

CHAPTER XXIII

LETTERS TO PROFESSOR ROBERT WALLACE BEFORE 1900

Washing Wheat—Text-book on Insects—Grease-banding Trees—Steven Lecturer on Agricultural Entomology—Australian agriculture—Examiner in Agricultural Entomology—Insect cases presented to the University—Death of Miss G. E. Ormerod.

THE four remaining chapters, consisting chiefly of letters addressed to the editor, are of a more general, less technical nature than those that go before. They deal more with University and personal matters, and with efforts being made to advance the cause of Economic Entomology than with the structural details and habits of insects.

To Professor Robert Wallace, University of Edinburgh.

TORRINGTON HOUSE, ST. ALBANS,
August 20, 1888.

DEAR PROFESSOR WALLACE,—I have delayed for a short time thanking you for your very kind present of your beautiful as well as valuable book on "Indian Agriculture,"[1] as I wished to make a little acquaintance with it before writing. Now I see what a great amount of serviceable information you have collected, and I am greatly obliged for such an addition to my library. I note what you wisely say about not substituting our implements hastily for native kinds better fitted to the land, but just now your explicit account of "wheat cleaning," beginning at p. 227, interests me exceedingly. I should be so glad if, when you have leisure, you would tell me a little more about this. You mention Messrs. Dell and Son, of London, as the firm that specially gave you information. I have been in communication about cleaning wheat with some of the Hull millers, one of the large corn brokers in Liverpool, and some other

[1] *India in 1887*. Published by Oliver and Boyd.

places, and had not heard of the washing, and this point, to me at least, seems a very important one. When I have gone carefully into the subject, and had the different kinds of screening sent in bags they do not seem to me to have been wetted. If they can wash at one mill they can at another, and we might have a chance of getting these pest-bearing extras neutralised as to evil qualities. I should greatly like to show you my set of screenings from Hull, labelled with their uses.

Do you happen to be aware of its being a regular business to supply weed seed, &c., &c., to deteriorate imports—that is of course exports of Russia, &c.? I had an interview with one of a firm who used to take orders for this at Samara! I believe these foul screenings most likely brought Hessian fly, and I rather think from a larva I saw in the spring *Meromyza* is come too.

It appears to me a deplorable thing that everything should be so absolutely arranged to import these nasty pests amongst us. If you will come I will show you my "pièces démonstratives." I have not a book like yours to reciprocate your kind thought, but will you give the enclosed "Manual of Injurious Insects" a place in your collection. With kind remembrances from my sister.

November 12, 1889.

About a text-book on Injurious Insects—it is not well to recommend one's own work, but I most earnestly wish that I knew of any better English book for plain work than my own "Manual." I formed it because there was no other book that met the everyday needs of Agricultural Entomology, excepting my own Annual Reports, and the Reports of the Department of Agriculture, which are formed in great part from my work and revised by myself. I do not know of any work on Agricultural Entomology which I can recommend.

If you want something very good about the lower creatures up to date I suppose you could not mend "Text Book of Zoology," by Dr. Claus, translated by Adam Sedgwick. This is a grand book, but I would not put it in my students' hands without a strong observation that I consider Darwinianism, &c., of this nature perfectly unproved and baseless. I certainly think that presently this view will follow "spontaneous generation."[1] But to go on, Curtis' "Farm Insects" is an excellent book up to date of publica-

[1] Miss Ormerod did not latterly oppose Darwinianism, but we are not aware that she ever accepted it. (ED.).

tion, but that is long ago now, and the second edition is an issue of the original sheets with a new preface—also £1 1s. is a great deal for students to give. If you want a book for your own study, "Die Praktische Insektenkunde," by Dr. Taschenberg is to my thinking unrivalled for practice and science—price circa £1 4s.

Now about your Australian larvæ. The longer and larger is a lepidopterous caterpillar; as far as I see nearly allied to our Turnip caterpillar, that is to say, of much the same nature as what we call Surface caterpillar here, and Cut-worms in America. This would probably turn to a good-sized moth. The larvæ in the two other bottles appear to me to be beetle grubs, of the *Lamellicornes*—you will notice the three pairs of well-developed legs, and the peculiar swollen form of the caudal extremity. I should suppose that like our Cockchafer (figs. 58) (or some other Chafer) maggots, that they fed at the roots of grass or other plants, but I should not like to commit myself to giving even a generic name to exotic pests in larval state. Would not a letter to Mr. Frazer Crawford, Adelaide, be the best way to gain information about prevention? And about figuring, if you sent specimens to Messrs. West, Newman & Co., 54, Hatton Garden, London, E.C., they would get them well figured—but still as the grubs and caterpillar have been so long in spirit the exact shape could not be conveyed.

I am delighted to hear that you are making progress about attention to insect pests in your University. When Professor Harker[1] was here lately, he told us something about these matters, and I cordially wished him the post of lecturer.

November 25, 1889.

I drew attention carefully in my first official report at the Royal Agricultural Society of England (when the Committee began again in November) to the need of caution [in connection with Codlin moth prevention] as to the adulteration that there might be in so-called cart-grease, and also to the success of the plan of before greasing putting paper round the trees. On the first glance it might seem doubtful whether papering was not one of the "study" applications which there are too many of, but it answers so well, that at the great Toddington Fruit Grounds the managers told me they were treating 120,000 trees in this way. The paper is what is used by grocers as "grease proof." It is passed in a broad band round the tree, and

[1] See note ante p. 79.

the overlapping ends fastened by paste and a band of bass mat or anything of that kind tied round to make sure of all being firm, and on this the "grease" is spread with a thin bit of wood—a sort of paper knife in fact. This kind of paper would, I should conjecture, be more certain to prevent the grease, &c., soaking into the tree than cloth. I have lately received copies of analyses of two or three kinds of cart grease which prove (in one case) to consist of grease and tar oils mixed with water and sulphate of lime. This did harm. Another consisted mainly of rosin oil, &c., mixed with a little carbonate of lime. This, I believe, answered quite well. I do not know how better to guard against mishaps than by starting the very earliest intelligence of important points round the newspapers as soon as ever I can; but you will believe me it is difficult to meet all sides. A Kentish correspondent wrote me that he was preparing his trees for dressing by cutting all the old bark off and then was going to tar on the fresh surface! If you would mention to your correspondent that my report of this month is in the "Agricultural Gazette" for November 18th, and that he would find some special cautions about grease banding at p. 501, column 1, I think he might be interested, but if he cares to write to me on the subject I would gladly reply, or I would with pleasure explain any point to you that you would care to have details of.

In the second edition of my Manual, which I am doing all I properly can to get time to start through press, I hope to give the very valuable practical teaching of the last two years about orchard insect pest prevention, and I hope to be able to add good results of a special (very cheap and very nasty) kind of fumigation we are going to try next spring.

P.S.—Do you see how the "I.L.N. Almanac has been helping itself to John Curtis' figures and mine—and then giving the credit to Mr. Jabez Hogg? I have had a little representation to make to the editor, and an erratum slip is to be added to all unissued copies.

January 21, 1890.

We expect Professor Harker here at the end of the week. Most likely he will come on here after his lecture at the Royal Veterinary College, at 4 p.m. on Friday next, and stay till Saturday, so we can bestow our best attention on affairs. I wish I saw a more hopeful state of things in (or for) the various matters [connected with entomological appointments].

Your letter came a few minutes after Professor Fream's arrival, and we said nothing about the lectures on Entomology in Edinburgh, but I told him how affairs were standing about the Board of Agriculture, and that I had recommended Professor Harker in case an entomologist was wanted. He was very pleasant. I have known him so long I always like a talk with him, and amongst other points we went over some special work about students' entomological examinations, and he left the impression on my mind that he would convey the requisite kind of information for your proposed lectures very satisfactorily to the hearers.

February 14, 1890.

Some time ago, before I knew that your University Entomological Lectureship [Steven course] was in a sort of way private, I mentioned something about it to Mr. James Fletcher (Dominion entomologist), and he is delighted with the hoped-for advance. He says how very much, if circumstances had allowed, he should have liked to give the course. You would, indeed, have had "a feather in your cap" if you could have secured him.

What a sad loss we all have in Professor Little.

April 18, 1890.

I return your two lists marked.[1] What you want is a set of cases with models and figures such as Mr. Mosley arranged for Kew. I told him he ought not to sell at as low a rate as he at first proposed, but I think that if strong card boxes were substituted for the nicely-finished mahogany ones, he could certainly let you have the cases at 7s. 6d. If you do not wish to open the cases (excepting for very special work), the board on which the exhibits are fixed might be fastened from below, and thus the cost of the beautiful work of one half sliding perfectly into the other half of the box saved.

July 21, 1890.

I was lately down for a few days at Oxford, and took the opportunity of asking Professor Westwood whether, if you arranged to have a course of entomological lectures, and asked him to deliver them, there was any chance of his granting such a favour? I thought it was too much to hope for, but I gained his permission that you might write to him on the subject, and I really think that if it were so

[1] Of Mosley's Insect cases with a view to suiting the Agriculture Department, Edinburgh University.

early that there was no fear of cold setting in, he would very likely undertake the set. Professor Westwood is, as Professor Riley well says, the "Prince of entomologists." I do not suppose any one living has such knowledge extending over all branches of entomology as he has. He is the Hope Professor of Zoology at Oxford, so constantly in practice of lecturing on his own special subject, and very fond of making things clear to young people. He has attended greatly to the economic aspect, and if you could secure him, his lectures as the commencement of the Agriculture Entomological course would give an *éclat* to the series that nothing else in the whole world would. To say he is Life President of the Entomological Society shows the respect he is held in on all hands. But you would have to be very careful of the good old man, for he never thinks of his 82 or 83 years, and he is not strong, though much more full of spirit than many a younger man. His address is: Professor J. O. Westwood, Walton Manor, Woodstock-road, Oxford. If you write to him he will think it over and tell you his views.

July 7, 1891.

It is very kind of you to give me the copy (received this morning) of your beautiful and so very useful book. ["Agriculture and Rural Economy of Australia and New Zealand."] I have been turning over a good many pages so as to have some idea of the contents before writing to thank you, and I cannot think how you could manage to collect all this very serviceable information there, or find time to condense it into this clear, readable form here. It is a very valuable addition to my library, and I value it much for its own worth, as well as your kind gift. How very honestly indeed you have acknowledged my little Cockchafer block; it is quite a pleasure to me to have it in your grand book.

I hope you have escaped the influenza, or had it favourably. It has been a serious visitation to us. My sister and I, and our housekeeper, Miss Hartwell, who acts as my amanuensis, were all seriously laid up in our beds at once! Such a time of misery, and inconvenience! I should like to write you about sundry matters of interest, but as very likely you are on the other side of the world, I had better postpone them.

Somewhat Private.

August 18, 1892.

I am very sorry to hear of your trouble in the loss of

your brother,[1] and with your grief, and also the effects of the long hard run of work, you must be greatly needing a rest.

I hope and greatly desire to continue all my work, Home, Colonial, and publishing; also to act as referee to our Agricultural Journals just as before, but it is much more comfortable working up important points, to having ever-lastingly to be going over a routine often keeping one from attending to what may be of importance. Who will they get to take my place [at the Royal]? It seems to me a great pity that there is not a properly paid and competent officer for the Board of Agriculture and R.A.S.E. I am safe in saying this, for I never intend to take office again, not for any amount of money that could be offered, neither do I mean to do the work of Government or Society under the polite name of "kindly co-operating!"

The only person I know who appears to me to be qualified to take the post at the Royal Agricultural Society is Dr. Fream, and I conjecture that his hands are much too full to allow it. Still I should be glad if it were so. Professor Harker has great knowledge of beetles, and indeed, I believe, of insect ways and customs generally, but I should scarcely think his tastes would lead him to this sort of work. However I have not the least idea what the R.A.S.E. proposes to do.

March 15, 1895.

As the time of your African trip is drawing near, I am just venturing to remind you, with what pleasure (if consistent with your own convenience) we would see you before you go. There appears to me to be a Gordian knot, and a few words (spoken not written) sometimes are invaluable on these occasions. I am pulling well with the European centres, but there are places where, much as I regret it, co-operation is not going on, and I think I might very likely get, as on a previous occasion, some most useful advice from yourself.

April 9, 1895.

I am very sorry and disappointed to say that I am ailing and so I do not know whether in your own hardly run time, you would care (or could at all spare the while) to run down for an hour or two on Thursday. The special trouble is that lately a very small bit of glass jerked up from something I was doing at my right eye. I thought it

[1] Quintin MacAdam Wallace, M.A., a Graduate (1st Class Honours) in Medicine and Surgery of Edinburgh University.

only hit the eye, but nearly a week after I found injury resulted from the bit having embedded itself in the upper part of the eyeball and formed a small abscess. Of course it had to be operated on and I hope put all right, but the very long, weary operation and the cocaine, &c., &c., have so tired everything concerned that I have not got over it all yet. So I thought I ought to tell you. What I want to say as distinguished from writing is more in detail.

March 19, 1896.

I make no doubt that I shall hear from our good friend Dr. Fream very shortly, or at least as soon as his much occupied time permits, but meanwhile I do not like to delay thanking you for kindly letting me know that the University Court had paid me the very gratifying compliment of appointing me co-examiner with Dr. Fream[1] in Agricultural Entomology. I think myself much honoured and much pleased also by their selection. If I might ask you to take the trouble, and it should be admissible, I should much like you to express to the University Court my grateful appreciation and assurance that I will endeavour to do whatever may be required in the office to the best of my ability.

March 27, 1896.

I am really very greatly obliged to you for the clear and full explanation you have spared time to give me, in your letter received this afternoon, of the arrangement of my co-examinership. It does please me very much to have even this little post, for I look on it as a mark of approval of your grand old University; also I am very glad that you approved of my letter to the Secretary.

I never knew the injurious insects so active as they have been this winter, in air, earth, and water—in the latter to the great damage of watercress (chap. XVI.). I had yesterday, some good specimens of great mischief from clover-stem sickness and for the first time found a nice way of collecting quantities of the *Anguillulidæ* (eel-worms) for observation. Generally they hide up in the rubbish, but I found that by teazing it out very finely in water on the slide and then carefully lifting it all away until the slide looked bare, that still such numbers of the eel-worms remained that they could be thoroughly examined.

[1] Dr. Fream had been, as a result of the recommendation of Miss Ormerod, appointed Steven Lecturer on Agricultural Entomology in Edinburgh University.

April 4, 1896.

I am now writing to you on a point on which I think that you—*ex officio*—are the first I should consult, and I should greatly like your opinion; and next (if, as I hope, you approve of my sister's and my own proposed presentation), that you will kindly tell me to whom to apply in requisite form. We have, by request of the Council of the Bath and West Society, been preparing an exhibit of Economic Entomology for their approaching Show here. My sister's part consists of twenty coloured diagrams, nineteen injurious insects and their works, and one finger and toe—these are very beautifully executed and fitted with loops all ready for hanging; size 26 ins. long by 21 wide. My part is seventeen cases—of which the enclosed slips, to be affixed on light slanting strips of wood at end or side of the cases, give just a general idea for observers without a catalogue (Appendix C.). I have tried, you will see, to give just a few illustrations of the main sorts of attack. Scientific names are used of course, but it is essentially an Agricultural Entomological exhibition made to help the plainest understanding, so I have not taken up space with mere scientific details, and I have spared neither trouble nor cost in procuring specimens, especially of the various *Œstridæ* (bot-flies). Also that there might be no possible doubt as to accuracy of nomenclature I got Mr. O. E. Janson to spend two or three hours in rigid investigation, and the only error in naming he found was in the name, or synonym, of a decayed wood-eating wireworm-beetle which I removed to make all sure. Fifteen of the cases are white pine, with what I call "detection" fittings outside. The glass is laid on the top but is kept in place by a handsome narrow brass band. Thus the inside of the case is at once accessible for any authorised purpose; but those not knowing the arrangements would cause such a clatter and disturbance that their misdoings would be very public. The cases are all as nearly as may be 12 ins. by 8 by 2½. Two of them completing the seventeen are "Live Boxes" of polished mahogany, same size, but of different make to prevent escape.

Now, I much want you to tell us whether you think that after exhibition here the collection, including my sister's diagrams, would be acceptable as a presentation to the museum of your Edinburgh University. It is not for me to speak of my own work, but I think it would be of use both in your work and Dr. Fream's, so I am writing to you first of all. If approved and we can arrange comfortably, I contemplate sending it (at my own cost) in charge of an expert who could repair damage. I shall wait your reply with great interest.

April 16, 1896.

Indeed, I thank you heartily for your kind letter of the 13th. It is a very great pleasure both to my sister and myself that you think our collection likely to be of use. I thought perhaps you had started on your long tour, so I wrote to Dr. Taylor, and yesterday we had a letter from him which pleased us exceedingly, with the kindly expressed acceptance of the University Court; and Sir W. Muir also was good enough to write, which we took to be very kind of him. I shall hope now, all being well, to collect, and (with permission) add as occasion allows. You would notice that some of the great attacks, *Tipula* (Daddy long-legs), leather-jacket *grubs*, for instance, and *Charæas graminis* (Antler moth), were not represented, for they were not about in the winter, but I shall hope to go on now. I should like you to see the cases, and we should much like a chat before you go; it is long since we met, and as the collection will not be free to go down till a little after the beginning of June, I suppose you will be far away then? I do not know the difference between the University Court and the Senatus. Very ridiculous you will think this; but I should like to understand about it.

May 30, 1896.

Many thanks for your letter received this afternoon, with address of Sir Robert Murdoch Smith [the curator]. From this I understand that the collection is to be placed in the "Museum of Science and Art," Chambers Street, as the property of the University Court of Edinburgh University? You will think me tedious, but I was under an impression that there was a "University Museum" *pur et simple.* I should not be easy at all in sending the exhibit down excepting in skilled hands. I had the great pleasure yesterday of showing them to the Prince and Princess (p. 123), and to-day I hear there is such a crowd that even our own people could only get a sight of two cases.

October 22, 1896.

I was very much pleased to see this morning that you had returned safe from your long journey to Australia, and I hope that besides the immense quantity of useful work which I make no doubt you have done, that you have come back in better health. You will have heard that my dear

Yours truly
Georgiana E. Ormerod

MISS GEORGIANA ELIZABETH ORMEROD.
Photo by Elliott & Fry.
(*pp. 16, 30, 37, 88, 90, 123.*)

To face p. 284.

sister has gone from me ; and for her I can be very happy, but I do miss her exceedingly.

But I am now writing to you about a little bit of business. When her failing health allowed, her great pleasure after you saw her was to execute some more diagrams, beautifully done, and I am sure there is no situation where she would have been more gratified for them to be placed than in Edinburgh University—and yesterday evening I had a truly kind letter from Sir Wm. Muir, telling me of the acceptance of my offer of them by the Senatus and University Court. But at present I am not able to lay my hand on her list of what was formerly sent. Would you mind the trouble of letting me have just the shortest possible notes of the subjects—a couple of words to each as Hessian fly, Wireworm, &c., would be quite enough—and then without fear of repetition I can present all the others to the University (excepting two or three which I should like to keep for her dear sake) ; and will you kindly further help me by letting me know at your convenience to whom I should address the package.

But though my dear sister did not work technically on my reports any more than I did on her beautiful drawings, I greatly miss her sympathy and colleagueship.

November 24, 1897.

I cannot say that I am well. The worry and hard extra work and my bad fall on the stone steps were not good for me, and I am painfully lame, and have got the gout, my doctor said a day or two ago, everywhere.

However, I am getting better, and hope to be much as usual soon. To-day I am looking up "Pine beetle." I think a trustworthy record of a thousand acres of Pine without (so far as seen) a tree not infested is a grand observation. This is a consequence of the 1893 and 1894 gales.

January 30, 1899.

I take it very kind indeed of you to write to tell me of the University arrangements about the Examinership.[1] I consider it a great honour to have held the office, and it has been a most thorough pleasure also thus to be associated in work with such a kind friend as yourself, as well as with Dr. Fream. But still, though not now one of the staff, I can work in colleagueship, and I have never forgotten the

[1] After a full term of three years, by ordinance, an examiner is not immediately eligible for re-appointment.

important help that you gave me some years ago. I shall look forward very much to a visit from you presently; besides the pleasure, it would help me, to have a good talk.

I am intending to make an alteration about my yearly reports. It seems to me that it would be the best course to bring the present series to a close with this number, giving with it a collective index of the whole series up to date. I should like the twenty-two years' work to stand complete, and not be liable to detraction, gradually, as to regret about Miss Ormerod not being this, that, and the other, which with advancing years is likely. I think, too, that I need a little consultation as to some slight alteration of plan. I do not like so much repetition as I see elsewhere. I have difficulty in avoiding it, and I am trying that my present Twenty-second Annual Report should be as fresh as I can make it. Kind regards from, yours sincerely,

ELEANOR A. ORMEROD.

CHAPTER XXIV

LETTERS TO PROFESSOR WALLACE ON THE LL.D. OF THE UNIVERSITY OF EDINBURGH

Announcement of the Honorary LL.D. to be conferred—Preliminary personal arrangements—Miss Ormerod's feelings of appreciation and of anxiety—Letters of congratulation.

THIS chapter is unlike any of the foregoing chapters of correspondence in its purely personal character. Interested readers will not fail to recognise in it the genuine feminine feeling of anxiety at the approach of a trying public ordeal to one so unaccustomed as Miss Ormerod to the pageantry of academic functions. Nor will they fail to appreciate the resolution with which she bore the physical strain put upon one whose strength had been well-nigh spent in the cause of science under a load of years and bodily infirmities.

To Miss E. A. Ormerod.

UNIVERSITY OF EDINBURGH,
February 24, 1900.

DEAR MISS ORMEROD,—I hasten to announce to you without a moment's delay that the Senatus of this University have only a minute ago agreed to do our University the distinguished honour of asking you to accept the honorary degree of LL.D. of the University. I may tell you without breaking any confidence that you are not only the first lady who has ever been asked to accept the degree, but it was in view of the necessity of recognising the great and distinguished labours which you have done for Science that regulations were made by which it became possible for us to confer the degree upon a lady. Any little share I had in this matter is more than rewarded by the great gratification which I feel in connection with this proposed act of the

Senatus, of which I believe you will most probably hear by the same post from the Principal. Should the announcement come a day later this will serve as a private intimation to yourself. It will be a still further triumph if you feel physically able to come to receive the degree in the presence of an assembly of about 3,000 people—the number who usually attend our graduations. If you are not able to come, of course the degree will be conferred all the same, but personally I would rejoice, if it can be without your running a serious risk, to see you among us and to get your name enrolled among the many distinguished men—all men but yourself—who have distinguished themselves in Science and Literature, and been pleased to accept our degree.—I am, dear Miss Ormerod, yours very sincerely,

ROBERT WALLACE.

Dr. Fream, "Steven" lecturer on Agricultural Entomology in Edinburgh University, wrote as follows :—

DOWNTON, *February* 26, 1900.

MY DEAR MISS ORMEROD,—As I have to catch a train I have only time to write you my very warmest congratulations on the LL.D. It was really settled a month ago, but had to be confirmed on Friday. Of course the secret "burnt" a little, but I was pledged to say nothing about it! It will appear in the University Intelligence shortly. The honour was never better won, and long may you enjoy it is the earnest wish of, in haste,—Yours very sincerely,

W. FREAM.

To Professor Robert Wallace, University, Edinburgh.

TORRINGTON HOUSE, ST. ALBANS,
February 25, 1900.

DEAR PROFESSOR WALLACE,—I feel wholly unable to express my respectful and sincere gratitude to the Senatus for such a high honour, and to yourself I am greatly indebted for your kind friendship and also letting me hear so soon. I value the honour exceedingly—the seal of approval of this highly scientific body. When the letter arrives which you tell me is coming I will endeavour to express myself to some degree adequately. To yourself just quietly I may say it is a pleasure, and such an unexampled honour that I am delighted. But still I feel that the great point of my work always is utilising the exceedingly kind help which is so cordially given me by my good, kind, scientific friends, and the practical observations to sift into shape that are given me as the foundation. If you were here I should like to say so much, but I do not know how to write more at present than that I am deeply grateful.

P.S.—I wish very much indeed to come, as you kindly suggest, but my very great and painful difficulty in walking movement from arthritis makes me fear that the risk would be too great, but anyway I am going to ask my doctor.

February 27, 1900.

Your exceedingly kind letter and the subject of it were such a surprise to me that in all the ideas suddenly arising I hardly know how to reply coherently. Now at least I can say I am deeply, respectfully grateful for such an honour to be granted me. I have written in reply to the formal notification from the Senatus what I hope may be a proper reply. I also mentioned that I trusted to be able to attend in person to receive this great honour. But now I hope you will be so good as to allow me to ask your help in arrangements. [Here followed a list of queries which are not of general interest.] Of course on such, to me, very great occasion I do not in the least mind expense.

The other matter is, Will you please tell me am I to wear Doctor of Laws' dress? and if so, will you kindly say to whom I should write to order it? When I come I am hoping you will instruct me in what to do, for unless you are good enough to help me with a little (or a great deal) of instruction I am afraid I am likely to be quite out of order.

Yours very sincerely,
ELEANOR A. ORMEROD.

UNIVERSITY, EDINBURGH,
March 1, 1900.

DEAR MISS ORMEROD,—I am delighted to see from your letter received this morning that you are going to be able to come to the graduation function, and that you have arranged to be well cared for on the way up. I shall take full responsibility for all necessary arrangements at this end. I should have done a lot to-day and reported progress to you, but unfortunately I have to go out of town to give a lecture on South Africa at Cauvin's Hospital, but I may tell you that I can easily secure the accommodation you mention for yourself, Miss Hartwell, and the doctor. You will wear a black cloak or graduation gown thrown over your ordinary dress very much like a Minister's robe. This is hired for a few shillings from a man who supplies them regularly to

Honorary Graduates, and I shall arrange all about that. A silk hood goes round the neck and hangs down the back. It is put on by the head Servitor after you have been officially capped by the Principal. It is part of the public function. You must not feel the least anxious about the event, as you will be surrounded by a host of people to whom your name is a household word, who know well the value which your work has been to this country, and who appreciate you accordingly. I shall be only too pleased to answer any question of detail you may write and help you in every way. Yours very sincerely, ROBERT WALLACE.

March 2, 1900.

DEAR PROFESSOR WALLACE,—I am very glad to know some part of what the form is on this great occasion. I hope that by following whatever directions you give me quite exactly that all will be right, *i.e.*, that I may do all I ought to do! But I cannot help being a little nervous; I feel the honour so very great indeed, and also the kindness I am receiving. Your account of the ceremony itself has made my mind much clearer. Walking upstairs is a great difficulty to me, but on flat ground, with my light ebony stick, I do not think my lameness is more than a very little observable. I am as near as possible 5 feet 6 inches. This is relative to the graduation gown. My head really is so full of this unprecedented distinction I am afraid I trouble you too much.

March 7, 1900.

I am very much obliged to you indeed for all the care that you have been so kindly taking for me, and for making everything so clear to me—amongst other points, your little note about convenience of cheques. I think you have arranged everything as nicely as possible for me. All matters for the journey I expect my doctor will look after nicely. But when you write again,—I suppose on the great occasion, as the cap is to be put on, that I appear without a bonnet? I have now read your letter over again that I may be quite sure that I thoroughly understand everything.

P.S.—There is yet one more inquiry I am venturing to trouble you with. My doctor [Dr. Eustace Lipscomb] is an M.B. (Cambridge); on such a special occasion, should he wear his hood?

March 3, 1900.

I shall be very much obliged if you would secure me rooms at the Balmoral Hotel, as you mention. Namely, a sitting-room and two bedrooms with doors opening one from the other, on the first floor to the front, for Miss Hartwell [Private Secretary] and myself, likewise a room for the doctor—from the evening (8 p.m.) on Wednesday the 11th until about nine on the following Sunday evening. I should like to be at the Balmoral; I have heard of it as such a good hotel. I can manage, though the operation is painful, to walk up just a few steps with the help of my stick (I have been trying five at my door), if somebody be by me in case I should slip, without, I think, attracting attention; and if I were too lame after the long journey to manage nicely, then I must be humble, and be thankful to be carried in a chair.

I feel greatly obliged to Sir Ludovic Grant for his kind intention of asking me to stay at his house. It would have been very pleasant, for thus, also, I should have doubtless seen many kind friends; but besides the great difficulty of the stairs, I am obliged to lie down a little each day, and I think after the long journey I had best keep quiet to fit me for the great day on Saturday.

But if the thing be possible without intruding on valuable time, might I not hope to see some of my kind friends at the hotel—yourself, of course, and I shall also be delighted to see Dr. MacDougall. Could you arrange some time? I should not myself see anything wrong in seeing friends on the afternoon of Good Friday, but pray do not let me do anything that might be thought not right. You and I will have a good deal to say at your best convenience.

P.S.—I was greatly gratified to learn that my letter to Sir L. Grant met with his approval. It was a matter of no small anxiety to me to try at least to express my appreciation rightly.

March 14, 1900.

I got a friend here to let me try on the square college cap "mortar board," and it fitted so nicely over my bow that I do not think I should be at all troubled by ideas of anything unusual being on my head; and I can take it off without trouble. Through your kind help I think all these arrangements are in perfect order, and I am looking forward much (preliminarily) to our meeting at Balmoral Hotel.

March 27, 1900.

I should have liked to beg a ticket besides the two which you kindly mention for my nephew, Arthur Ormerod, who has just taken his M.D., so I wired off to him at Oxford, but, to his great regret, he cannot come. I hope the weather will be better, but we have a good bright sunshine between the occasional light snow showers, and both Miss Hartwell and myself have good furred mantles, and with the snug small carriage all our own way, I think we shall do very well.

What a sight the hall will be! also your small flock of aspirant doctors; may be as anxious in their minds as some one I know of. But I am really not alarmed. I am sure you will keep me right. What time of day does the ceremony begin? And what happens after?—do we retire respectively like rabbits to our own burrows?

March 29, 1900.

The pamphlet on the McEwan Hall [the number of the "Student" describing the opening of the Hall] is a great boon to me, and what a noble building!

While in Edinburgh my idea is to have lunch at one o'clock, my usual time, and a sort of miscellaneous meal at 6.30, and rest in the evening after it, and I shall think it a great compliment and a very great pleasure if friends may do me the favour to look in after, say, about two o'clock. It will be much safer for me, under present circumstances of wanting to keep fresh and strong for the day, not to go out, so I should be on the spot. Sir Wm. Muir and his daughter, Mrs. Arbuthnot, kindly wrote that they meant to look in, but it would be only a pleasure to me to see any friends. Please to consider me as quite under your guidance for this, to me, so very great occasion, and wholly thankful so to be, excepting in the feeling of the great trouble that you are kindly taking. Yours very sincerely,

ELEANOR A. ORMEROD.

P.S.—Dr. E. L. thought it would be best for me to return by the Sunday night sleeping train, and the Midland manager has given permission for it to stop here on Monday morning.

Professor Wallace to Miss E. A. Ormerod.

UNIVERSITY OF EDINBURGH,
March 29, 1900.

DEAR MISS ORMEROD,—The box containing your most valuable contribution to the library arrived safely from Wesley & Son, and the ten volumes, [of her own works] all in excellent order, are standing on the Senate Hall table so that they may be seen. The Principal, Sir Wm. Muir, and the Secretary, Sir L. Grant, were the first, along with Professor Patrick and me, to inspect them in their present position, and all the others excepting myself were astounded at the magnitude of your work. I carried the books first into the library and had them entered in the catalogue before they went to the Senate Hall. They will have a shelf for themselves, so that they can be kept together as the "Ormerod Collection," or rather "presentation." I sent you a "Student" giving details of the Hall in which you will be capped. The capping is at 10 a.m., and after that, if you feel able, you will go on to St. Giles' Cathedral. I enclose one of the ordinary tickets to give you an idea as to how the general public are admitted.—(R. W.)

March 30, 1900.

DEAR PROFESSOR WALLACE,—What can I say? I am very much used to work just quietly in the hope of being of some service, but this kind commendation from those whose opinions I hold in such respect as those of the chiefs, whether the high officials or professors in your great University, is indeed a gratification, a comfort for troubles sometimes not light, and an encouragement which I gratefully and deeply appreciate.

I should like, of all things, if you will take charge of me, to attend the Commemoration Service after the capping. It will delight me to be there, and if I am tired I can rest after. [The graduation ceremonial was found to be quite enough for Miss Ormerod's strength, and no attempt was made to go to St. Giles' Cathedral to the service.] I usually breakfast at 8.15, so that I should be all ready at 10 o'clock. It seems to me that if the "low-hung carriage" which you have kindly secured use of for me were in attendance to convey us to the McEwan Hall, and when wanted at intervals onward, this would be exceedingly comfortable for me. But in everything of the arrangements I am hoping that all I have to do is to quite precisely obey as well as benefit by most thankfully all that you are good enough to arrange for me, and will instruct me about presently.

BALMORAL HOTEL, EDINBURGH,
April 12, 1900.

I earnestly hope that Dr. E. Lipscomb will find you better. It is a real grief to me that you should be going through such a painful illness [an influenza cold which developed at a most inopportune moment]. And, secondarily, not having all your kind advice and help and your companionship in all, does take away much of the pleasure of my honour.

We find the gown, hood, and trencher cap fit very nicely. This cap suits me much better than the soft velvet one, and I am sure that I should much prefer the black gown to the amazing splendours of scarlet faced with blue. I think on formal occasions, if desirable, I could get up my courage to wearing the quiet black gown, but I should be terrified about the brilliant garment. Dr. Lipscomb is going to tell you that, as matters have progressed, I do not feel as if it were at all necessary for me to have the convenience of a room in the Hall you kindly procured for me, and if it were permissible for me to "robe" here, and drive robed to the McEwan Hall, it would save me a world of anxiety. I might, I think, carry my cap in my hand until time for capping came. It is so exceptional a case that I do not see any impropriety in being bare-headed for a while. But I am truly anxious that I should appear before all the august body preliminarily under your wing, or, if there was risk for you, under the care of some other member of the University (if they will adopt me).

[The graduation ceremonial (p. 95) passed off without a hitch of any kind, and the students gave the first honorary woman graduate a magnificent reception.]

TORRINGTON HOUSE, ST. ALBANS,
April 17, 1900.

DEAR PROFESSOR WALLACE,—I really do not know how to begin my letter. There is so very much I want to say and to thank you most heartily for. But first I should exceedingly like to know that you are recovering, and were not seriously the worse for your kindness in really and truly coming from your bed to look after me. It would have taken greatly from my downright pleasure if you had not been there. I was much impressed by the ceremonial. I had not connected an idea of the perfect order, and in some respects solemnity, with the function of graduation. It is an impression never to be forgotten, any more than the exceeding kindness with which I was received. "Dr. Ormerod" also begs her best thanks for the most liberal supply of "Edinburgh Evening Dispatch" and "Scotsman" received this morning [containing accounts of the University function]. I am putting your letter, the very first with address of "Doctorate," carefully away amongst the special treasures of my Academic honour. I am trying to get, so to say, "into harness" again amongst the consignments of boxes waiting.

Now I hope you will not think me absolutely carried away by the feeling of the importance of the honour to myself, but amongst letters of congratulation I have one from Dr. L. O. Howard, the Entomologist of the U.S. Department of Agriculture, which pleases me very much. He says :—

Dating WASHINGTON, D.C., *April* 7, 1900.

"The receipt of your letter of 21st March and of your admirable twenty-third Annual Report reminds me that I have been remiss in fulfilling a strong intention to write you at my earliest convenience and congratulate you most warmly on the well-deserved honour which you are to receive from the University of Edinburgh. You are right; not only is it an honour to yourself, but it is an honour to Economic Entomology, the force of which cannot be over-estimated. I congratulate you very warmly. An LL.D. from Edinburgh has always seemed to me to be one of the highest honours which an Englishman (or woman now) could gain." L. O. HOWARD.

Dr. R. Stewart MacDougall wrote :—

SCOTTISH LIBERAL CLUB, EDINBURGH, *Saturday*.

A telegram received in the morning made it impossible for me to get to the McEwan Hall in time for my seat on the platform. Among the audience, however, I had an excellent opportunity of getting acquainted with "popular" opinion, and I only wished you could have heard all the kind things that were said about you. Somebody has said, "Beware when all men (and all women) speak well of you." Really I know no one so exposed to this temptation (if temptation it be) as yourself. The honouring of our various distinguished men naturally appeals most strongly to different groups, but there is in addition about this latest honour to yourself something which has touched the general imagination.

May you be long spared to wear the honour worthily.

I hope that on your return you will find yourself none the worse for your plucky journey north and all the attendant fatigue.

R. STEWART MACDOUGALL.

Dr. Ritzema Bos wrote :—

AMSTERDAM, *March* 16, 1900.

DEAR MISS ORMEROD,—I was very much enjoyed to read in your kind letter of 12th March that the Senatus of the Edinburgh University will confer on you the Honorary Degree of Doctor of Laws, as an acknowledgment of the great merits you have for the advancement of Economic Entomology. I am glad to hear that the important work you have done since so long years for Science and for Agriculture will be recompensed in this way. I hope that you may remain still for many years, what you have been already for so long time, the first Economic Entomologist of your country and one of the most famous Economic Entomologists of the world. My wife asks me to offer also her kind congratulations to you. December 19, 1899, it was twenty-five years since I received the Degree of Doctor of Natural Philosophy. On this day a deputation of representatives of our Dutch Agriculture and Horticulture came to me and offered me a statue of bronze—the genius of Science, with the subscription, "Ad lumen." It was presented to me in the name of many agriculturists and horticulturists in Holland and in Dutch India. The General Director of Agriculture came also to me, and told me that H.M. our Queen offered me the grade of Knight of the Dutch Lion (Ridder in de Orde von den Nederlandsche Leeuwen). It was a beautiful day for us indeed. With many kind regards, believe me, yours very truly,

RITZEMA BOS.

Lord Grimthorpe wrote :—

ST. ALBANS, *Ash Wednesday*, 1900.

DEAR MISS ORMEROD,—"I lose not a moment" (as the story is) in congratulating you, or myself, on the honour of our becoming a brother and sister in *Laws*, as one of my nieces points out in a newspaper. The Princess of Wales has only the inferior position of a sister in Music, and those in Medicine are quite common now. I am sorry that we, neither of us, dare venture to go out and pay our duty in person in this weather—as unique as your new position—and I was sorry to miss you the last time you came here. My dear wife, who has been worse than I am though more capable of recovery, is slowly doing so. She was in an alarming state for some time under the abominable influence of the general pest, influenza.

Though I write badly and with difficulty, I am better in general strength, but shall never be well. However, I am thankful to be no worse, and to have a nice series of benevolent relations of two generations here, and to be here instead of London or Bath. Tea generally goes on at 4½ now, and we shall hope not to be disappointed if you look in again, wearing your *red hood* when you have acquired it. With very kind regards and rejoicings from all our ladies

I am, yours ever,

GRIMTHORPE.

N.B.—I hope you are duly elated at the prospect of a Dean and Chapter here. I defied the late Archdeacon Grant who agitated for it, to tell us definitely any single practical bit of good it could do, and he declined to try.

Mr. L. O. Howard wrote again on :—

May 10, 1900.

MY DEAR MISS ORMEROD,—I am greatly pleased to receive your letter of April 30th with the newspaper clippings. I had read substantially the same account in American newspapers, but did not know, of course, of your pleasant meeting with Mr. Choate. He is a man who is highly esteemed on this side of the Atlantic, not only for his legal ability but for his tact and other good qualities. I do not know him personally, but he is a national character. His name is known from one end of the country to the other, and his clever sayings are repeated from Seattle to Key West, and from Portland to San Diego. In March I attended the annual banquet of the trustees of the Shaw Botanic Gardens in St. Louis, and responded to the toast of Henry Shaw. The man who sat at my right, a distinguished college president, told me many Choate stories, and succeeded in filling my mind so full of Mr. Choate that when I was called upon to speak I had almost forgotten what I had intended to say. We are all of us here delighted about your doctorate. Entomology and Economic Entomology have been steadily assuming a higher place in the minds of the people during the past twenty years, and this honour which has come to you is the culmination of our advance up to the present time. Wishing you many more years of work and happiness (work must mean happiness to you), believe me, my dear Miss Ormerod, sincerely yours,

L. O. HOWARD.

April 21, 1900.

DEAR PROFESSOR WALLACE,—It is a bright day when I see your handwriting outside the envelope, and I am truly glad your cold is better; it was no slight matter that wanted mending. My journey was not so successful as I hoped. The wind was very cold on St. Albans' platform and I got a chill, but I was up again yesterday, and hope to be just as usual in a day or two. I shall be so very glad to see you. Please fix your own time, and if you would tell me a little beforehand, I would try to get General and Mrs. Bigge to come to lunch. He I think knew Sir Wm. Muir in India, when he (General Bigge) was in military command. He would of all things enjoy a talk with you about horses.

One day (if you please that is) we would drive over to Batch Wood to tea, and Lord Grimthorpe will certainly come in and have a chat if he be well enough. In a parenthesis, would you care to drive over to Rothamsted? I know Sir Henry and Lady Gilbert and Mr. Warington.

I shall so like to be able to have a good quiet talk with you about various of my plans. I feel (may I be forgiven if I am too presumptuous) that now I have a real scientific home, and though I would not for the world intrude, I may I think ask my good colleague's advice. As you will be here so soon I think I had best not write to Sir W. Muir, as he kindly gave me leave to do, about my father's set of volumes of drawings. When you come you will guide my views as to whether they would be what might be liked for acceptance.

April 23, 1900.

I am doing just as you bid me, and after a little look at Mr. Garton's paper,[1] which I am sure must contain a deal of solidly valuable information, I have laid it aside to wait your helpful guidance. I have a letter just now from Dr. Fream saying he would like very much to come to meet you (as I begged him), but cannot manage it. I am looking forward exceedingly to much useful and pleasant talk. I generally go to church at St. Michael's (where Lord Bacon is buried) in the morning, but there is much good music at the Abbey close by, and you would do everything I hope just exactly as you like best. Yours very sincerely,

ELEANOR A. ORMEROD.

[1] "On the Production of New Breeds of Crop Plants by Multiple Cross-fertilisation."

CHAPTER XXV

LETTERS TO PROFESSOR WALLACE AFTER THE GRADUATION

London Farmers' Club Notice—Volumes of George Ormerod's drawings and a painting of Miss Ormerod presented to the University—Handbook of "Forest Insects"—"Recollections of Changing Times"—Papers on "Stock Flies."

THE letters in this chapter, written between the end of April and the middle of November, 1900, cover a period of extraordinary literary activity. Encouraged by the gratifying manner in which her academic distinction had been acknowledged by friends and public bodies, Miss Ormerod began with renewed vigour, and with something almost akin to prophetic instinct of what was to come in the not-far-distant future, to produce and to arrange for the production of, the literature that was needed to complete her life-work and to be a record of it. Another conspicuous feature of this chapter is the practical means she adopted to immediately show gratitude to the University for the perspicacity shown by conferring its degree, which was treasured by her above all things as the highest possible recognition of her scientific labours.

To Professor Robert Wallace, University Edinburgh.

April 29, 1900.

DEAR PROFESSOR WALLACE,—I have been reading parts of the "advance" proof of your paper [to be read before the London Farmers' Club in April, 1900], and it seems to me capital, and to meet the needs plainly and practically. I wish you much success. I can speak from personal knowledge as to want of dipping being excellent for increase of *Melophagus ovinus* [so called sheep tick] (fig. 25).

Mr. Druce [Secretary of the Club], writes me kindly that he intends to propose a vote of congratulation to me to-morrow on the honour conferred on me by the Edinburgh University, and this would be a great pleasure to me, for I feel it a very great honour indeed. From many good quarters I am receiving letters on this point, also on the benefit to agriculture which the approval of Edinburgh will give.

April 30, 1900.

I am arranging with Elliott and Fry, the photographers, 55, Baker Street, that they should send down a "representative" on Monday with proofs of photos, the bearer to be here by train arriving at about half-past ten a.m. But the truth is, that if you think I might ask acceptance, just as their first Hon. Lady LL.D., I should very much like to offer to the University one of Elliott and Fry's life-size chalk or oil portraits executed in their best way as a remembrance of the 14th of April. Do you think I might?

I am glad to know they spoke kindly of me at the Farmers' Club. I am sure I have some good friends there, and I thought it very kind of them to send me their vote of congratulation on my great honour.

[The London Farmers' Club, at its April meeting, 1900, passed with acclamation the following resolution:—"That the hearty congratulations of the Club are hereby offered to its Honorary Lady Member, Miss Eleanor A. Ormerod, upon the distinguished dignity of LL.D. recently conferred upon her *honoris causa* by the University of Edinburgh." A copy of the resolution was transmitted by the Secretary to the Senatus of the University of Edinburgh.]

May 11, 1900.

DEAR PROFESSOR WALLACE,—I had the books very carefully packed and sent off to-day, by luggage train, as they made rather a heavy consignment. [Volumes of her father's drawings, and copies of the "Manual of Injurious Insects" for free distribution.]

You will see I put a little note into the copies of the Manual, at "Red Spider," just in some degree to bring the matter of position of the spinning glands up to date; I do not know of any other point that needs correcting.

I enjoyed your visit exceedingly, and not only that, but you would hardly believe what a great amount of useful information you conveyed to me in the course of our conversations, as to many matters at Edinburgh. All these

PLATE XXVIII.

ORMEROD HOUSE, LANCASHIRE.
From an outline sketch by George Ormerod, 1808.

To face p. 300.

I have carefully noted, for though I do not really hold any post among you, yet I like to think myself now not wholly separate, and I should be entirely thankful should need occur at any time to avail myself of your permission to apply to you for advice. My friends greatly enjoyed all you said at lunch, and I shall hope you will come again presently.

I have written to Sir Wm. Muir about my father's books of sketches, but in real truth I feel such a fear of intruding on his high official position that I only just said what I thought was quite needed, but I entered a little more on the matter to Mrs. Arbuthnot.

ELEANOR A. ORMEROD.

The Librarian wrote :—

LIBRARY, UNIVERSITY OF EDINBURGH,
May 16, 1900.

DEAR MADAM,—I really do not know how to thank you for the honour you have done our University Library by making it the custodian *in perpetuitatem* of the delightful collection of sketches and water colours, the arrival of which has made the 15th of May a red-letter day for the Librarian at least. You will, I hope, be pleased to know that the priceless volumes have been placed in a room already rendered a sanctum by relics of such notable names as Shakespeare and Burns, Hus and Knox, Queen Mary of Scotland, King James VI., Queen Elizabeth, &c., not to mention Halliwell-Phillipps and David Laing, both of whom, I doubt not, Dr. George Ormerod would have recognised as his colleagues and peers. Professor Wallace has duly received his volumes. The drawings have been shown to Sir William Muir, who, I believe, is to thank you personally and who will lay them on the table at the next meeting of the University Court.

H. A. WEBSTER.

Sir William Muir wrote :—

UNIVERSITY OF EDINBURGH,
June 29, 1900.

DEAR MISS ORMEROD,—Your six volumes of drawings were yesterday shown to the University Court (as they already had been to the Senatus), and were well received and valued by them. And I was asked to communicate their obligations to you for them. They will be placed in the Library, and will be remembered as the gift of our First Lady Graduate, LL.D.

W. MUIR.

May 24, 1900.

DEAR PROFESSOR WALLACE,—Will you kindly accept the enclosed photograph. It does not seem to be quite me, but "me" does not quite know myself yet in cap and gown. At least it may remind you sometimes of most hearty gratitude for all your kind care which enabled me to come to personally receive the great honour symbolised.

Dr. MacDougall was good enough to send me some splendid specimens of bark infested by *Hylesinus crenatus* (Greater ash-bark beetle), which have enabled me to figure this attack. I should like very much indeed to form a "Handbook of Insects Injurious to Forest Trees," and I have a mass of material in my Annual Reports bringing the subject, I think, up to date, and a beautiful supply of figures, but there is such a run of application and correspondence that I do not see my way to doing it myself—and yet it seems a pity for the information to be lying comparatively idle.

May 29, 1900.

Now I must say that you wrote exactly what I was wishing about my proposed book, "Insects Injurious to Forest Trees."[1] In case Dr. MacDougall would not think me taking a liberty in suggesting the plan, I should very much indeed like to have the benefit of his skilled help in preparing the book, that is bringing it out in collaboration with him, and with our names on the title-page. Would you kindly take the trouble when you see him to lay the matter before him, for I scarcely like to come upon him suddenly without, so to say, a "sponsor." My idea is that the forest attacks would work out much like the papers in my "Handbook," of which of course I would gladly send a copy for his acceptance as well as material, *i.e.*, Annual Reports or sometimes, if more convenient, extracted papers and a copy of "General Index." I would undertake all expenses, *i.e.*, printing, publishing, furnishing figures, and the like. I think I have of my own nearly as many of good up-to-date illustrations as we should need to illustrate every attack, but where additions are needed I propose (as I am doing now from one of Dr. MacDougall's specimens) to have them figured from life by Mr. Knight.[2] I fancy the book would be about two-

[1] A suggestion that Dr. MacDougall should collaborate with Miss Ormerod in bringing out the book.

[2] Messrs. Knight, one or other, have been my artists for many years. I should like the printing to be, as usual, in the hands of Messrs. West, Newman & Co. Mr. T. P. Newman has superintended my printing for so many years. (E. A. O.)

thirds as long as my "Handbook of Orchard Fruits," but being intended at first for University services, possibly the plan would be different. This he, you, and possibly Colonel Bailey [lecturer on Forestry in Edinburgh University] might have a word to say about. I should like very much to hear from you on the subject, and perhaps from Dr. MacDougall.

June 5, 1900.

You will tell me presently when you can come, but would not Mr. John Garton [of Newton-le-Willows, Lancashire, the originator of the scientific system of producing new breeds of crop plants by multiple-crossing] come too? I should like it very much if it were agreeable to him, as there are so many points of interest we three could go over together. You could assure him that he can be as quiet as ever he likes, and rest in his own room, just as he pleases. Will you both come on Saturday for Sunday? When you come we can have a good talk about the "Forestry Insect Text Book." I am very glad to have it from you that Dr. MacDougall likes the idea of colleagueship. I have had a very nice letter from him with promise of one of details to follow, but when I found that he had been collecting notes for some years, I felt so very uneasy lest he should think me intruding on his projects (in fact very presumptuous) that I wrote him specially on this head. I shall be delighted to put every morsel of observations, and blocks, and all I can to help at his service, but it is to his skill that I look to form the book into what he knows, much better than I, will suit University needs.

The weather surely needs a little putting to rights. It caught me rather sharply, and I have had to spend some days in bed, but I am up again now, and getting some good observations.

P.S.—I have some such nice letters from Edinburgh about my photo. A very charming one from Sir Ludovic Grant, also from Professor Seth.[1] I mean to keep them as great treasures.

June 14, 1900.

I am in receipt of a long letter from Dr. MacDougall about the text-book of "Forest Insects," and it seems to me that his plan is excellent. For my good folks, who want the plainest facts fairly driven into their heads in the very plainest words, I think it would be too scientific in the

[1] Professor James Seth delivered the address to student graduates at the ceremonial at which Miss Ormerod received the LL.D.

possession of special entomological chapters, but I quite think in the present case these are needed, and my only fear is lest he should wish me to collaborate in these. All the rest I think I should be quite at home in, and I am going to write him about it, as I should very much like the joint work.

I am writing down bits (long or short as they come into my head) of "Recollections," on pages with appropriate headings in my letter book, which usually lies on the table most of the day, so is at hand; and most miscellaneous reminiscences go in which I feel sure I should not have courage to think of giving excepting on our plan. I rather think they might be interesting, and I mean to see in good time about the shorthand writer. The head reporter of our best local paper can take down well a report from my dictation. Do not you think that if we can get the "Recollections" (how would "Recollections of Changing Times" do for a title?) into shape that—instead of publishing as I usually do with any amount of trouble and little return for the expense—it would be a good plan to offer the MS. to some publisher, who might, I think, take it off my hands on terms to be agreed upon? But when next we meet I hope we shall go into all these matters comfortably, as you say, "after dinner."

P.S.—The French medal (plate XXII.) appeared to-day in a registered letter. I wonder whether Professor Ewart has got his? I have information of the worst attacks of eelworms in broad beans that I ever saw, after oats in the spring of 1898 and of 1899.

July 18, 1900.

I feel sure, wherever you are, that you are so much occupied that you have not a morsel of spare time, but if you could presently give me a little advice it would be of great value to me. I was urged to let my name be put on the Agricultural Education Committee, and agreed, and by way of something solid I suggested that I should form a set of papers on "Common Fly attacks to Farm Stock," and I set to work. But as I go on I really think that they are more fitted for regular agricultural work, and I should value a few words of guidance from you very much. The subjects I am thinking of taking as what I know personally are: Sheep—Nostril fly, with note of "Gad" as different, and "Spider" fly; Horse—Bot fly, Forest fly; Cattle—Warbles, Gad fly, and anything else that might occur.

Nostril fly and Horse Bot fly shape (as I think you

also would consider) nicely, brought up to date; and in *G. equi* (Horse Bot fly, fig. 10) I have really handled the only bit of the subject that was not pleasant, so that I do not think anybody could object. The two above-mentioned papers are about ready for press. But what I wish very much is that you would kindly let me know your view of it. Would it be better to print the subjects in my usual way, as leaflets, or make them into a little pamphlet? *G. equi* would fit nicely into a four-page leaflet. *Œ. ovis*, (Sheep Nostril fly), I think would be shorter; and the short papers which would go nicely along with their more important brethren in a pamphlet rather puzzle me how to deal with if in leaflets. I have excellent figures, and in an idea (possibly erroneous) of bringing the sequence out for the Agricultural Education Committee, I wrote a sort of little "fresh" preface on the creatures collectively. As I am sure

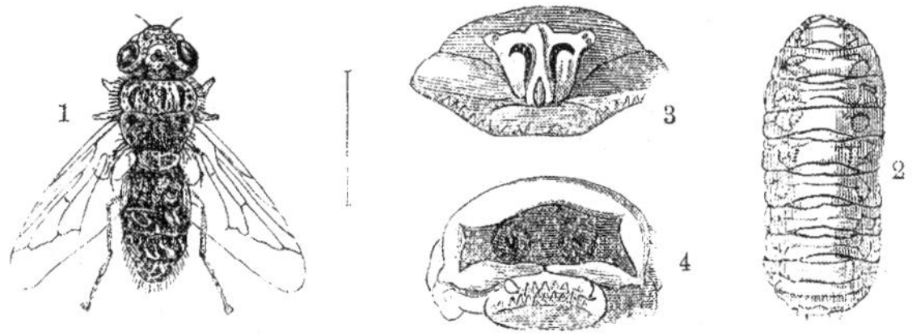

1, Fly, magnified, line showing natural length; 2, maggot; 3, mouth hooks of maggot; and 4, tail segment, showing spiracles, and lobes, acting as organs of progression—all magnified. (After Brauer.)

FIG. 76.—SHEEP'S NOSTRIL FLY, *ŒSTRUS OVIS*, LINN.

you will allow me the pleasure of thinking myself in some degree a colleague of yours (and if I drive well at work I should hope to have it ready for your winter session), I should be exceedingly obliged if you would tell me whether you think pamphlet or leaflet would be best. [The pamphlet form was ultimately adopted, and it was published as "Flies Injurious to Stock," &c., price sixpence.]

August 2, 1900.

I am very glad that Dr. Fream gave a good notice in the "Times," of your intended series of lectures on Colonial and Indian Agriculture—it will be a noble work, and I am glad you are enjoying the preparation.

"Reminiscences" are lying in a drawer, for there is such a quantity of work there is no spare time. When I have got the first sheet of "Flies Injurious to Stock," I should like to send one to you, please; not to trouble you, but just that you may see how it is getting on.

August 25, 1900.

Mr. Elliott tells me that "the oil painting" is to be quite ready on (or about) the fourteenth September, and I have ordered one of their best "rich" gilt frames in which it is to come down here. I hope much that I may somehow or other, be able either before completion or here, to secure the saving of anxiety to my mind by your seeing it. But I have not as yet written to submit my suggestion of acceptance to Dr. Taylor, for may be I had better see what I look like first.

Enclosed are two sheets of my progressing little pamphlet. Please do not trouble yourself by readin gthem, but, if at any time you care to glance over them, I hope you will like them. I had no idea till I set regularly to work what need there was of bringing the matters up-to-date. I think the brochure seems likely to run to about three and a half sheets, with Index. When you come you shall tell me, please, whether you will let me offer some for your class. I should very much like to—and you will tell me too, about Manuals.[1]

September 4, 1900.

It was a great pleasure to me to receive both your letters, but I was afraid of intruding too much on your time, so I put off thanking you for them till I received the enclosed proof this morning. It is a real comfort to me that you can approve of my little pamphlet, for I have been very anxious over it, and I hope you will think sheet "D" right. I am delighted to be allowed to send it to you.

At page 33 you will see I have utilised the colouring of the eyes of the *Tabanidæ* (Gad flies), specially for identification. I do not think this point is much brought forward, and I found it very useful. Many thanks for your two pamphlets and suggestion *re* dips. I have been studying your S.S.,[2] and mean to try to get a little bit into my paper as an addendum. Also I want to study your "Nature Knowledge" [opening lecture to a class of teachers.] I don't seem to understand this subject yet, and your address, I feel sure, will help me very much.

[1] One hundred copies of Miss Ormerod's *Manual of Injurious Insects*, were distributed gratuitously to persons specially selected by us as likely to be interested in the subject matter and capable of spreading a knowledge of it (ED.).

[2] Lecture at the London Farmers' Club on Sheep Scab.

Yesterday I had a long letter from Mr. E. P. Stebbing, Chittagong, Bengal, accompanying a large pamphlet on "Injurious Insects of Indian Forests," published by the Indian Government. He wrote that he was taking up the subject of Injurious Insects (agricultural as well as forest), and that the Indian Government having "put him on special duties for two years to tackle the question," he wanted me to advise him on a number of points. I am sure I do not feel competent. However, I wrote him as well as I could, and had to look up the shorthand writer we have talked about, and get him to put it in typewritten form—so I helped myself, at least. When I get the copies I propose just to put one in an envelope for you to see what I have been suggesting. But I only send it because you are so very importantly engaged in Indian, &c., work. I should like you to be able to look at it, if you like, but only if you like. Pray put it in the rubbish basket if it is the least trouble.

September 25, 1900.

Here is "Prevention and Remedies," and the other odds and ends for "Stock Flies."

"The picture" has come, and I think that as Mr. Elliott said, it is really a "great success." I hardly know how to comment on my own appearance, but if you should be writing to Dr. MacDougall he would tell you about it. I almost think I shall be glad when it goes on, it is such a curious feeling to have my own eyes looking at me so steadily. I suppose when we get into the next month I may write in form to Dr. Taylor, to inquire if I may be permitted to ask acceptance.

I very much enjoyed Dr. MacDougall's visit. We talked Entomology most pleasantly, and I think arranged very satisfactorily all necessary preliminaries for our proposed Forest Insect book. The little visits which have been given me this summer have helped me very much, as well as being a great enjoyment—though none so much as yours—and it is a fact, as you mention, that if the ladies come too, it perplexes the talk very much! I want to learn all I can in the time.

September 27, 1900

I was very much surprised yesterday to receive about six dozen large Plant bugs,[1] with a communication from the Chinese Minister Plenipotentiary (in London), over his own

[1] *Tessarotoma papillosa*, Dravy. (O. E. J.)

signature, begging for information as to how to prevent their ravages in the lee-chee orchards in China. It seems very odd (in the present state of affairs especially) that the Chinese Government should consult me.[1] However, the treatment wanted was plain, so I hope I did not do wrong in replying as he wished.

October 16, 1900.

Lord Grimthorpe is very much interested about your Indian Famine lecture, and he would very much like to have a copy.[2] I think he will do what he can to study it, likewise expect me to give him so much commentary as I can; not much this, I am afraid.

I assure you your little visit was a great pleasure to me. These excellent talks freshen me up delightfully for dry work. I shall look forward to some more in due time.

October 21, 1900.

I do not know how to thank you for this kind gift.[3] I know how to value such a literary treasure, and to me it is of exceeding interest also; but as your gift to me I treasure it much, and gratefully thank you for your kind thought. The twelve copies of "Indian Famine" preceded it an hour or two yesterday afternoon, and I am reading it carefully and slowly (that I may thoroughly appreciate it), and with great admiration; indeed, I think such a clear condensation of the mass of information to be dealt with is splendid. I have sent copies to Lord Grimthorpe, the Bishop of St. Albans, &c.

With my very kind regards and grateful thanks for all the help you give me, which is a great deal more than probably you have any idea of.

October 26, 1900.

I am delighted to read both the letters you send, but what an especial pleasure it must be to you to have the nice courteous message of acceptance sent by our good Queen. [In acknowledgment of a copy of the address on "Famine

[1] We were at the time actually at war with China, although nominally the united Powers of Europe were fighting the Boxers.

[2] A digest of the Indian Famine Commission Reports down to October, 1898, read as the Inaugural Address on the opening of the course of "Garton Lectures" on Colonial and Indian Agriculture. Published by Oliver and Boyd, Edinburgh.

[3] A copy of *Quasi Cursores*, portraits of the high officials and professors of the University of Edinburgh and its Tercentenary Festival. Drawn and etched by William Hole, A.R.S.A. David Douglas, Edinburgh, 1884.

in India."] I congratulate you exceedingly. How much you must treasure it! Thank you very much for letting me see it, and also that from the Chancellor [of the University, the Right Hon. A. J. Balfour].

My people have been much pleased to receive the copies you kindly let me give them, and Dr. Lipscomb has asked me to thank you for him. But I do not know that any one has been more interested than Mr. T. P. Newman. He, as one of the "Friends," has been working in their society to help, and I find they collected £27,000. [The Friends' Foreign Mission Association collected this sum to use in relief of the famine of 1900].

October 29, 1900.

I have, with much pleasure, written to Messrs. West, Newman & Co., to send you (to University, Edinburgh) one hundred copies of each of the two pamphlets. Please write when some more (or Manuals) would be at all acceptable.

I am placing your Famine pamphlet carefully, so I have some still on hand, but I will not fail to ask you if more could go out well, *viâ* my presentation. I have been studying it to the best of my power. I am not able to condense such a mass of information fully, but this is what I think I have learnt. These famines originate meteorologically, the crops consequently failing for want of moisture. The only places (three districts if I remember rightly) exempt from them, are so, consequent on climatic circumstances or irrigation. The chief preventive measure, being irrigation, is not always easy of application, as, for instance, the possibility of a canal raising the height of the water-table too much. I follow to some degree the difficulty of bringing relief arrangements to bear on special bodies of men, as the weavers, for instance. It is also very interesting to read of the method of dealing with the "Wild Tribes," their power of finding wild food, and of bringing in wild forest products adapted for sale. Some information as to details of kinds of food and preparation, also of the sums of money represented by Indian names, must surely remain adherent to one's mind, but one special thing is the splendidly arranged work of our Government, which is a comfort to think of. I inflict the above on you, that you may see I have really been trying to benefit by your grand work, and I do congratulate you on the result of your heavy labour.

November 8, 1900.

I should be very thankful if you would tell me where

Professor Jablonowski might safely apply for sulphate of copper at "an acceptable price"! I could, I suppose, look him up some sort of an address, but I should not feel sure it was trustworthy, and he is such a centre of work, also an old correspondent, I should much like to help. I should be very much obliged if you could conveniently tell me, or him—he is director of the Government Entomological Station, Budapest—where he could get a price list and a supply.

I have been ailing with some sort of slight feverish and gout attack, but nothing serious, and I am up again.

To-day Mr. Newstead is come to see what the experimental black currants are doing [in the garden]. I gather that even soaking the cut-down plants, roots and all, in methylated spirit has not proved a wholly certain means of prevention of Gall mite (fig. 65). If so, I incline to think that I had best make an end of my black currant hospital, there is no use in simply bringing in infestation.

November 9, 1900.

I shall be delighted to see you at next week's end, Saturday to Monday, 17th to 19th, as you mention. Many thanks to you for helping me to an answer to the Budapest professor about the sulphate of copper. I fancy "the picture" would arrive this morning at the University. I hope it will give satisfaction, and I make no doubt that it will have great honour done to it in the hanging. Perhaps some day I may see it!

"Reminiscences" had not been getting on, on paper, but when your letter arrived I took up a pen and wrote like a very whirlwind some points that were in my mind regarding the beginning of my insect studies. I wonder what you will think of them. I hope to have some progress to show you. I am having twenty feet accommodation for books put up in my dining-room. I think this will look well and be very convenient.

Yours very sincerely,
ELEANOR A. ORMEROD.

The Rev. Professor Taylor, Secretary of the University Court, wrote:—

November 10, 1900.

DEAR MISS ORMEROD,—The portrait has arrived uninjured. It is an excellent likeness, and with gown, hood and cap, vividly recalls what is in reality an event of historical importance as well as a most interesting graduation ceremonial. I propose to have it placed so that it may be on view, so to speak, to the members of the University Court on Monday at their meeting of that day, and to the members of the Senatus Academicus when they next meet. Thereafter it will no doubt find a permanent place on our walls.

I would venture to tender anew the thanks and best wishes of the University Court, and with the assurance of my profound esteem, beg to remain, dear Miss Ormerod,

Sincerely yours,

M. C. TAYLOR.

November 14, 1900.

DEAR PROFESSOR WALLACE,—This is very kind of you; it is a great pleasure to me to know that I am allowed to hold such an honourable place, and I thank you very much for all the trouble that you have been taking. I really do not know how to express what I feel about all the kindness shown me, but you, knowing how I have been situated till the University of Edinburgh showed me such honour and kindness, will believe the heartfelt comfort and encouragement it is to me to have their authoritative approval and support. But this is private to you. "The Chancellor' and Secretary might think I was *tête montée* if I wrote in such a fashion. I have had some nice letters, two from Dr. Taylor and a charming little letter last evening, delightfully worded, from Sir Wm. Muir. I am going to look at the picture of Lord Inglis again in your beautiful book ("Quasi Cursores"), that I may see whom I am allowed to sit next to in this very distinguished company, but I am writing to catch the post now, so I only thank you also for the papers which I have not yet had time to give my head to. With most kind regards and hearty thanks.

November 15, 1900.

I feel I gave a very insufficient acknowledgment (writing in a hurry last night) for all the kind care and, I feel sure, no small trouble you have been taking about putting my "representation" nicely on view. I have refreshed my memory of Lord Inglis, and indeed I feel I have a right to be proud that my portrait is allowed to be placed by such a grand representation of such a distinguished man. I am glad the "Court" liked the picture in itself (I urged all concerned to good execution), and indeed it is a pleasure to me to think that the memory of endeavours at least to work of E. A. O. will be so markedly protected by the University.

Yours very sincerely,

ELEANOR A. ORMEROD.

P.S.—My new arrangement of books is so convenient, it helps me almost as much as an assistant! (E. A. O.)

Eleanor Anne Ormerod, LL.D., F.R. Met. Soc.
First Woman Hon. Graduate of the University of Edinburgh, 1900.

From the oil painting (Academic costume) in the University Courtroom.
(p. 306.)

CHAPTER XXVI

LETTERS TO PROFESSOR WALLACE *(concluded)*

The "Reminiscences" and the last Annual Report—Warnings of serious illness—Proposed pension—Gradual loss of strength—Death.

THIS closing chapter records the peaceful close of the wonderful career of a remarkable gentlewoman who devoted her life to work in the successful effort to benefit her fellow men. The pages are replete with human nature and human sympathy, and full of unselfish interest in the interests of others whom she numbered among her sympathetic friends and trusted confidants. The "Reminiscences" on which she did but desultory, yet interested, work, during the intervals of temporary respite from the burden of disease and increasing physical exhaustion, were as she feelingly expressed it "a perfect blessing." Her letters belonging to this period are a noble record of fortitude and resignation during a trying struggle for health and life, and the close is touchingly pathetic.

To Professor Robert Wallace, University, Edinburgh.

November 19, 1900, Monday evening.

DEAR PROFESSOR WALLACE,—I return Sir W. Macgregor's letter[1] with many thanks for letting me see it, for it is very gratifying. It is a great pleasure to me to see how those who understand appreciate your work. I am very glad you are able to tell me that you enjoy your visits to me, but next time I hope that our going to church may be of a less airy sort. I hope that you did not get serious harm ?[2]

[1] From the Governor of Lagos arranging a personal interview.

[2] This reference was made to a cold draught experienced in church.

I feel much pleasure (not to say relief) at results of our "Reminiscence" work, and at all those papers being safely lodged in your hands.

P.S.—I am working steadily on the twenty-fourth Report, but if a bit [of "Reminiscences"] comes into my head (the "awen," as the Welsh say), I mean to put down the ideas.

December 5, 1900.

Here comes such a long story [here cut short] about the "Reminiscences." I hope it will not be quite too tedious, but really I think we are thriving.

A messenger has just been down from London, and carried off material for ten illustrations.

The materials for letterpress are appearing fairly out of holes and corners also, the chief prize a book of Memoranda for 1891, by my sister Georgiana, giving numbers of dates of my letters, &c.

I was glad to see the "Creameries"[1] in the "Times," and glad to see also that it was properly placed at the top of the column. I thought you wrote very firmly and well.

P.S.—I have not sent [copies of the Manual] (though you kindly said I might) to the Clubs. I have not the courage; so many of the members might not care for Economic Entomology.

December 15, 1900.

I think I am being very good! in seldom letting the "Reminiscences" meddle really with work, but rest time (wet afternoons) helps. One thing more, I remembered I had a part given me by my mother of my father's "queue" (Anglice, "pigtail") cut off in the year of their marriage, 1808, and I think this might come in nicely.

December 21, 1900.

I quite forgot to thank you for your Indian Examination questions,[2] which was wrong of me, for I like very much to have all the information they point to, though I am afraid there are scarcely two I could answer.

January 18, 1901.

My account of myself is—I am fairly well all but rheumatism; only, last Saturday the disaster happened of a blood-vessel breaking in my left eye. These affairs seem

[1] A letter written to defend the position of the Board of Agriculture for Ireland against an unwarranted attack of a Cork correspondent of the London "Times" (ED.)

[2] The first examination paper set in connection with the "Garton" course of lectures (ED.).

seldom of consequence, but this time my doctor told me (after two or three days) that he did not remember excepting from external circumstances that he ever knew such a great breakage. So I was an absolute spectacle for some time, but the sight is not at all injured, and the organ recovering well, and I may write as much as I like. I now enclose six more illustrations—I think in their way they are all nice.

January 27, 1901.

As you kindly say that even more than a good report of "Reminiscences" you would like to hear I am better, I am truly thankful to say that I am quite as usual again, and my eye recovered. There has been some sort of illness about but I had it very lightly. I hope the very bad day for His Majesty's Proclamation brought no serious harm to yourself. An Edinburgh "inquirer" informed me that he thought numbers of the spectators would catch their deaths of cold. I was truly pleased to see that the King duly promised to support "The Church of Scotland," a matter I have more at heart than on my tongue here! You will value Her Majesty's approval of your "Indian Famine" lecture more than ever now. I certainly should have liked myself to have a tiny bit even of approval.

"Reminiscences."—This is just for your best leisure (and pleasure) to advise me on, but I very much need a good "paper talk" with you to start me on a reasonable plan. I quite believe that in a fortnight or sooner I may begin regularly.

But now—publisher! Messrs. A—— B—— wrote me that the book would be so sound it would be sure to command public approval and they would like to publish. Mr. Newman wrote he thought I had best go to the top of the tree, and suggested John Murray. I answered that in real truth the very idea of applying to such a leading man made me quite uneasy—and yesterday he replied that as he understood you were aiding me in the work, that my best course would be to ask you whether when the time comes you would act on my part with a publisher. I am sure he is right—I am as ignorant as a reasonable person can be of how to "approach" a publisher, but, if I am not asking too much, it would indeed be a relief to my mind if you think fit to give me this help.

If it is possible I certainly should much like to print with Messrs. West, Newman & Co. Is it possible to have a part of the book printed before beginning negotiations just to show what it is like?

February 4, 1901.

I feel sure you will be pleased to hear that this morning I sent Messrs. West, Newman & Co. all that I believe is needed for my present Annual Report, excepting for completion of Index; and I have really begun "Reminiscences." Will not my best way be to take any subjects that I think I have enough material for, and work them up just as I think they might go to press? Thus you would see how you like the writing and suggest improvements, and there would be something, if you please, to show a publisher. Turning to your letter—I think that if at your very best leisure you would kindly let me have the parcel of MS. which you were good enough to take for safe custody it would help me now.

How dreary the past week has been with our national sorrow and all the anxieties. I hope we may be more cheerful now.

February 8, 1901.

Your beautifully secured parcel has arrived safely, and I have locked it up carefully in my safe, with a very legible inscription that the contents are the property of Prof. Wallace, University of Edinburgh. There is nothing like making sure, in case of as people say "anything happening"! I should like to think that this mass of documents which I have been accumulating should pass to your hands.

I hope the work for your lecture[1] on the twelfth prox. is getting on quite to your liking. It is always a great pleasure to me to hear your plans are prospering.

February 14, 1901.

It has been very much on my conscience that I did not say a word in my hasty letter about your beautiful and valuable present.[2] How very pretty it must be, and a very great pleasure to yourself as a kindly acknowledgment.

About the "Reminiscences"—what you suggest about typewriting is just what I should like, but I did not care to trust MS. here. Before parleying with the typewriters, I should like very much indeed to read to you all the papers that I can get ready before the ninth. I feel a little anxious about the new style of writing.

February 21, 1901.

I have made up a good bit on "birth, childhood, and

[1] A paper on "Agriculture in South Africa," read before the Royal Colonial Institute on 12th of March, 1901.

[2] A silver tea service of Indian work presented in recognition of a public service.

parentage" (chap. I.) not forgetting with "an action of humility"! Edward I., and Eleanor of Castille. At present I have "Series of Annual Reports" (chap. IX.) on hand, —very pleasant work.

But now I want you, please (and very much indeed), to be kindly thinking of some advice about my entomological work that I am sure you could help me greatly with when we meet. The burthen has become so very great that it seriously affects my health. I am in bed now with another of these attacks; the constant pressure of work to suit other people's time and convenience, and maybe a tremendous worry, brings on painful and exhausting illness. I hope to be up again to-day, but the doctor is very anxious I should —may I call it?—"Take in sail." My wish is that the present Annual Report should be the last of the series with an addendum slip of explanation inserted. There is not the important information needed or forwarded that there was twenty years ago, and working hard for months over so much repetition is dreadful drudgery. I heard lately from Dr. Fream, and he very strongly advises me to drop it. If your opinion—which I thoroughly trust —is the same, I should have no doubt. The difficult thing is to moderate the applications, but I think I see my way to that very nicely by having plenty of the addendum slip printed and sending a copy to an unreasonable applicant. I do not want to give up Entomology entirely.

How nice it must have been to have a good turn at curling!

February 24, 1901.

In answer to your very kind letter I must tell you I am much better. It was quite my fault that I got so out of sorts; I ought to have asked my doctor weeks ago what was amiss, and then the difficulty of how I, "all of my own head," was to get that "old man of the sea"—the Annual Reports—off my shoulders, came on me like a brain shock. However, now I hope things are getting quite nicely into order again. Meanwhile I am trying to arrange what can hardly fail to be a rather explosive announcement. When I came to set to work it did not seem to me that an addendum slip would do. It would have been on such different lines to the statements in the Preface that folks would have wondered what could have happened! So I mean to have a Cancel, and hope all will be nice.

One word which I forgot—I quite hope to pass on quietly as much Economic Entomology as I possibly can to Dr. MacDougall.

March 1, 1901.

This is very kind of you, and if you are very much shocked at my explicitness please consider yourself an extra nephew, M.D. for the occasion, and put this in the fire.

I have had a kidney attack. I believe something "gouty" (?) has been wrong for weeks, but I had not asked the doctor until such pain set in that there were no two ways about it, I had to go to bed; and he put me on a "course" (of alkalis, I believe) to get out the enemy. Of course this was very weakening, but I was soon up—and really absolutely, I believe that if it were not for a nasty barking cough—very tiresome by day, and more so by night—I should be much as usual. I should be grievously disappointed if you did not come for any reason connected with me. Speaking very selfishly, and besides all the good the pleasure of one of your visits does me, I do not feel as if I could settle comfortably until I have the benefit of your sound and skilled advice about how to re-arrange my entomological work.

"Reminiscences" are in enough trim to show you something of even now.[1]

March 2, 1901.

I am so sorry regarding what I am writing that I hardly know how to put it, but I find to-day I am so much pulled down that I am obliged to tell you. It would be a sad disappointment to me if I did not see you, but my nights are so bad from this cough that I cannot depend on not having to ring to call Miss Hartwell to attend to me, and this makes a great commotion. I believe, as I wrote you yesterday, that the illness (as well as the pain) has gone, but it is the cough which has been keeping me pulled down, more than I knew.

March 4, 1901.

Indeed, you are quite too kind and good to me, and now I want to say that my doctor says he does not see any reason why I should not be able to enjoy your visit on Sunday next without any difficulty or risk whatsoever. If it was convenient to you, would the train suit that would bring you to St. Albans about a quarter before 11 from St.

[1] On this date a note of instructions was left to Miss Ormerod's trustees to deliver to us the "Reminiscences" papers, &c. The end of the note is as follows:—

"And I request Professor Wallace, being a friend in whom I feel complete confidence, to accept the above, and use or not use them for the purpose precisely as in his good discretion he may think fit."

Pancras, and could you stop till the (I think) 8.30 train? I am truly sorry not to be looking forward this week to a whole week-end, but I am still obliged to get up and go to bed at unusual hours; but, indeed, I am very much better—the pain went, but one of the bad sort of cold or cough attacks followed and I could not sleep properly for three nights nor rest lying down. Now I can rest and sleep again.

March 7, 1901.

Please do not think that a good talk tires me or is any strain. It is the want of conversation that I find so wearing, and there is so very much that it will be quite a delight and a rest for me to be allowed to go over with you.

I am writing this to-day so that you may know that (so far as anything in this world is certain) there is no possible reason why I should not look forward to the pleasure of our meeting next Sunday. I am not able to give you my doctor's verdict for the good reason that he did not think I needed looking up yesterday.

March 12, 1901.

You do not know how good and kind I think it of you to let me rest on you for advice in this way, and it brings a great brightness when you come and I can hope you are making yourself at home. I am glad you like Mr. Newman. I always feel that he is a quite true and well-judging friend, very kindly, but at the same time so grave that I do not at all times feel free to express all I am thinking about! I fancy that you "not being a lady" he would feel freer to express what was uppermost.

Thank you for all you say about Mr. John Murray, and very especially indeed for your good advice. I do really mean, and am trying to act on it, but cannot you imagine the difficulty in not working as hard as body and mind will allow?

However, I have made a thorough beginning; amongst various points, returning to Mr. Newman a great bundle of proofs sent to be looked through, just think, unlooked at. I also disposed of a regular onslaught with special letters from Lady Warwick and Miss Edith Bradley, &c. I am minding what you said [about curtailing work] very nicely.

I am thankful to say I am feeling better every day, and I am looking forward very much to being a better kind of hostess if you will kindly spare me a week-end by and by.

7 p.m.—You are, I conjecture, just beginning your lecture [on "Agriculture in South Africa"]. I hope it will be thoroughly pleasant and satisfactory and that you will have

a comfortable journey home. Please accept the enclosed [the twenty-fourth and last Report]. I have only received a parcel late to-day, but I want to send you a copy "from the writer."

March 18, 1901.

I am very glad your colonial lecture was successful. It is no good my not telling you, for some way or other you would have an idea, but I have not been thriving. Of course there was a flood of letters about discontinuing the Annual Reports, and, however kind (and some were very kind indeed) yet not being in full working order, they were rather too much, and I got feverish "rigors" (though not bad) with temperature 100°, and the doctor on Saturday ordered me straight off to bed. Here I am still, but as far as I know, now only as a matter of precaution. I would not have said anything about it, but I was sure you would have an idea.

Now about something much nicer. I wrote to Miss Ashworth (28, Victoria Street, London) and had a most pleasant and businesslike reply. She told me that publishers preferred quarto size and typed a few lines to show the size of type and style they like best; and I sent up the "Chartist Outbreak" (chap. VII.) and asked her to type it for me accordingly, and to let me have one copy and two carbon copies. Thus there would be one for you, one for me, and the third would be useful for the publisher. I should be very much obliged if you would kindly tell me how to offer a copy of my twenty-fourth Report to the University Library. Would it be sufficient just to send a copy c/o The Librarian. I do not want to give more trouble than I can help about such a little thing.

P.S.—I assure you I mean to attend to your kind advice of not making what might be a great pleasure into a toil.

March 20, 1901.

Here comes the first instalment of "Reminiscences" and I hope to forward more to you in due course. The history of "Rise and Progress of Annual Reports" is in Miss Ashworth's hands. Indeed, I am very thankful to you for helping me about the typewriting. I had no idea of the helpful difference it makes even to me. Please, I earnestly beg of you, do not think that your delightful and helpful visit, only too short, had anything to do with my having to call in the doctor again. I am sure he does not. But I am sure, too, you will understand how very trying indeed, though mostly very kind, the outbreak of newspaper and private comment on what they call "my retirement" was. So to get my cough really cured, and drive constitutional coincidences out of the field I went to bed with the best possible effects (really). I think the doctor will let me get up to-morrow, but he wants me to keep safe from snow chills.

March 24, 1901.

Here is another bit [of autobiography] begging your reading when you are inclined, and now "Birth, Parentage, &c.," is gone up to London. I should so very much like (if not too much trouble) if you would make some sort of mark on the margin of your copy, wherever you think some alteration is needed, and then when I have the pleasure of seeing you here we could go comfortably into it.

Now (as the fates permit) I am working on "The Severn and the Wye" (chap. V.), and I think it will be interesting, there is such a variety of fresh observation, "Fish, fishers, and fisheries," some specialities in zoology and semi-marine botany, and something of a good many sorts of things.

I am much mended and doctor says I may tell you I am getting on all right, but the long illness has pulled me down very much so that I am only allowed at present to be up in my own room—such a little thing brings the cough back and we have snow showers still—but as soon as ever I can get about again I have no reason to doubt I should be much as usual.

March 29, 1901.

I seem very unlucky this winter, but on Tuesday, when I hoped I was pretty well again, a chill so bad and so strangely sudden seized me, that breathing got hurried, I could not speak with comfort; and an acute pain set in in my right side. Doctor set to work and did not mention that congestion of the lungs was present, but taking affairs at once did great good, and the enemy was routed; still, I am a good deal pulled down, and do not mean risking another chill at present. I had greatly hoped this time not to tell you any long stories about my health, but it is no good pretending, so please you must let your friendly sympathy in my troubles be my excuse.

I wonder what you will think of the enclosed ["copy"]. I incline to think the subjects are rather nice, but that as we get on bits of this may fit into future papers, or of future papers here? It seems to me best to write whatever I can as well as I can manage, and sift by and by. "Am not I 'umble" (as Uriah Heap says) about Edward I.? (page 13).

April 1, 1901.

I know I shall always have your kind sympathy in these unpleasant visitations, and I wish they did not come to intrude so often. But this time I really and truly do hope, unless some luckless draught gets hold of me, that I shall pick up quickly, and not have such dreary stories to tell you.

Dr. Lipscomb says that it is just having let my health run down that is the reason, and I mean to be very careful. I am up in my room part of the day comfortably, and hope to get downstairs to-morrow.

I greatly look forward to a good talk by and by over many matters, and I was very sorry that Dr. MacDougall could not come this week, but further on I hope we shall have a chat. You will doubtless (or very likely) have seen flourishes in the papers about a testimonial! to my unworthy self—but to my horror yesterday I had a letter from Mr. —— stating that he was trying to procure a pension for me; and the Member for H—— and (I understood Lord ——) would most likely use their influence.

Just think what could possess him—what a to-do there would have been. But I wrote earnestly representing how misappropriate such a grant would be to a person so well off as myself, and it being such a troublesome matter, I got Dr. L. to read my letter. I hope I may have quite stopped his operations (and politely), but assuredly I should feel inexpressibly lowered if I accepted a "pension."

I have been collecting for "Reminiscences" very fairly well, but I have been afraid to prepare whole papers lest they should not be bright.

April 2, 1901.

I must write a line to give, I believe, a soundly good report of myself in reply to your letter, which arrived 4.50; it is very good of you to write so kindly. I have been down to-day for about six hours, and I do hope now to steadily regain my strength.

You will let me have your address, will you not? And I shall hope to write something more worth reading.

Mr. —— has on my urgent representation stopped his applications as to a pension.

P.S.—The typewriting seems to me beautiful, and I hope soon to have more work ready.

April 8, 1901.

You will know from your own experience the deluges of publications which come—what can I do with them? They might be measured by feet, if not by yards. Some valuable, some ——!

Would not it be my best way to keep them all until you will, as I hope, come some day—and you could see if there are any that you would like. Besides what are of no very obvious use, there are quantities of amazingly learned entomological treatises which, in case they do not float in the way of our good friend Dr. MacDougall, he might at least like to place on his shelves. You will tell me, will you not, some time what you advise? Meanwhile, with all possible good wishes and kind regards, &c.

April 19, 1901.

I should like to give you a better account of myself, but for weeks back I could not think why I got on so slowly, with "relapses," and it is only just lately that I have extracted out of my good doctor that the illness I had was that horrid influenza, and I am going through the weeks and weeks of "after effects"! I am not allowed to go down, but sit up a few hours in my room, and am certainly better, but I am told I must not expect to be well for a long time. One of my doctor nephews looked in yesterday, and he told me that a characteristic of some of the influenzas which have been about is that they do not seem much at the time, but they leave those detestable effects on the system.

You will believe how very pleasant (as I get stronger) I find looking up bits for "Reminiscences." Miss Hartwell brings me books, and I can "rummage" and copy. Now I enclose you some pages, of which I think some part is right, but I did not feel as if I could put the whole paper right until I had it typewritten.

I should very much like too if you would give a thought to my "Scriptural Commentary" (page 21). I do not see how the description I object to can be right. I hope you will think the paper is hopeful. I am not up yet, therefore please excuse this stupid scrawl, and with my very kind regards and best wishes, &c.

May 2, 1901.

How I long for the day to come when I may tell you that I am well, and am going on as usual. But this disgusting, tenacious remains of influenza seems to be always coming back. I had got on to coming down on Friday last a little after 9 a.m., and was full of hope and absolutely striving to recover, but yesterday something went wrong, so I am on a treatment of milk and seltzer-water and bed, but I felt I must write you, and hope soon to send you a much better letter.

"Reminiscences" are a perfect blessing, and I enclose two portraits of my father received yesterday to show the illustrations are getting on. Is not the one of him as a little laddie of about five years old, charming? (pl. XXX.)

May 15, 1901.

Many thanks for the additional copy of your lecture, "Agriculture in South Africa." It is so interesting, I am sure I can find a home where it will be welcome. I was glad to find you were out in the country, and I hope the bracing air will enable you to work on this load of papers without killing yourself.

For myself, I really am afraid that, excepting hope, I have a very indifferent account to give you. I was always getting better off and on! But the result was, that I got weaker and weaker, until on Saturday Dr. Lipscomb wired for Sir Dyce Duckworth. He was away, but my nephew, Dr. J. Arderne Ormerod, who is taking Sir D. D.'s practice at present, came down, and I think the change of treatment that they arranged is really doing good. The trouble was that, though there did not seem any reason why, what they call the "after effects" of influenza should not move off (the sort of gastric catarrh and its detestable allies), yet they didn't, and my medical tormentors made up their minds that it might be from "Liver." The plan has been altered as to treatment, and at my urgent request I am allowed to take one glass of port a day, and I do think it is doing me a great deal of good. But excuse more now, for sitting up at my writing-table tires me.

May 22, 1901.

I am very sorry to tell you in reply to your kind letter that I am very ailing. I seem to get fairly well of the influenza, and go down and sit for a few hours in the dining-room in the easy chair by the fire. Then, as sure as can be, in a very few days I get a "recurrence" of illness and have to go to bed for days. I think I am now going through about the fifteenth. Dr. Lipscomb says he does not know the reason, but it is very like the recurrence of Indian fever. I know that there may be scentless or other sewer gas, and from what Mr. R—— F—— told me some time ago of the recurrence of a very parallel attack to the Duchess of C—— from gas under her invalid sofa, I mean to have the matter properly seen to. I know there may be reason close to my door.

P.S.—Since the above was written Dr. Lipscomb has

Miss Ormerod's Father, about five years old.
From a Miniature of 1790.
(p. 323.)

Miss Ormerod in childhood.
From a Silhouette, date 1835.

been called and thinks the present attack was caused by a chill; and with staying in bed a few days Miss Ormerod hopes to be better.—A. HARTWELL.

May 28, 1901.

I am afraid I have seemed very negligent, but my varying illness made it very difficult to tell you, and now I do not want to go away without telling you my deep gratitude for all the great, helpful, affectionate kindness you have showed me. And about the "Reminiscences," which I hoped would be our pleasant joint work, I have a large collection of material which I give to you for your own property to use as you please—with the requisite paper [dated 1st March] with it. I believe myself the end may come any time now, but I go in happy hope, and that it may please God to bless you is the prayer of your affectionate friend.

June 4, 1901.

I pencil a few lines to say what a delight your visit yesterday was to me. I longed very much to see you again, and also I was wanting to give you the various documents about the "Reminiscences." To-day Miss Hartwell has been rummaging out for me what I think must be nearly all the material I have more, including the "Edinburgh book" [relating to the LL.D.], which please accept from me as a keepsake. It was left you in my will, so will not there be a hunt? And now I should much like to write more, but I feel too weak, and with every good wish.

P.S.—Please notice I give you all the contents of the box sent to-day—as well as the documents we looked out yesterday.

June 8, 1901.

I was delighted with your letter—that you had a nice talk with Mr. Newman—and besides such an interview with Mr. Murray. This is a great pleasure. I am miserably weak, but I am trying to do as the doctors tell me, and lie here waiting for—what I am sure will be for the best.

My very kindest regards. Yours most sincerely,

ELEANOR A. ORMEROD.

[The *Times* of Saturday, July 20, 1901, published an admirable record of her life and work in the sympathetic obituary notice, from which we have made the following brief extract: "We regret to announce the death of the accomplished entomologist, Miss Eleanor A. Ormerod, which took place at her residence, Torrington House, St. Albans, after a severe illness. She had been gradually sinking for the last six weeks from malignant disease of the liver. Her loss is not to this country alone, but to the whole civilised world, though the farmers of the United Kingdom will feel in a special degree that a trusted friend has been taken from them. Many people will feel that such a magnificent record of unselfish work as she has left behind ought to have received some official recognition of a national character. Nevertheless, almost the last honour bestowed upon her, that of the honorary degree of Doctor of Laws in the University of Edinburgh, was peculiarly grateful to her," &c., &c.

Having regard to the special interest which Miss Ormerod took in the progress of Economic Entomology in Canada and the United States, and the high appreciation in which she was held by the enlightened exponents of the subject on the other side of the Atlantic, we conclude with an extract from the September number of the "Canadian Entomologist" for 1901 :—

"Entomology in England has suffered a great loss through the death of this talented and estimable lady, who died at her residence, Torrington House, St. Albans, on Friday, July 19th. Practical entomologists throughout the world are moved with profound regret that a career so remarkable and so useful should be brought to a close, but one could hardly hope that the aged lady would long be able to sustain the burden of increasing infirmities and the trials of a painful and protracted illness. Miss Ormerod was one of the most remarkable women of the latter half of the nineteenth century, and did more than any one else in the British Isles to further the interests of farmers, fruit-growers, and gardeners, by making known to them methods for controlling and subduing their multiform insect pests. Her labours were unwearied and unselfish; she received no remuneration for her services, but cheerfully expended her private means in carrying out her investigations and publishing their results. We know not now by whom in England this work can be continued; it is not likely that any one can follow in the unique path laid out by Miss Ormerod; we may therefore cherish the hope that the Government of the day will hold out a helping hand and establish an entomological bureau for the lasting benefit of the great agricultural interests of the country."]

APPENDICES

Appendix A (p. 37).

Salmon Fishery.—Both locally, and thence to the country at large, the bay beneath the Beachley and the Sedbury Cliffs was very important, as being one centre of the Severn Salmon Fisheries. The following notes by Mr. Frank Buckland,[1] Government Inspector of Salmon Fishing for England and Wales, are interesting: "The visitor will observe in the lower estuary stretching for a considerable distance into the water from the muddy banks, rude piers made entirely of wicker work, which look like large eel-baskets; these are called 'ranks' of 'putchers.' Each putcher is about 5 ft. 6 in. long, and 21 inches across the mouth. A framework is made by driving stakes into the mud, and the putchers are then fastened together in rows one above the other, often to the height of 10 feet or more; these great walls of baskets look not unlike, as my friend the late John Keast Lord remarked, 'a gigantic wine rack filled with bottles, encased in wicker work.' As the salmon come along with the tide in the thick muddy Severn water, they run their noses into the open mouths of the putchers, and speedily get jammed up at the narrow end; the poor things cannot turn, and the more they struggle to get out, the firmer they become wedged in; as the tide recedes they are left high and dry. I have often observed that wasps wait about till the tide goes down, and then take first cut at the salmon. A great many first-class Severn salmon are caught in these putchers and sent to the London market."

[1] See *Log Book of a Fisherman*, &c., by Frank Buckland, M.A., pp 366, 367.

With regard to another form of baskets used for catching flat fish, &c., at p. 368, he says :—

"Besides the putchers another kind of basket is used which is called putts ; . . . . the wicker-work is much closer in this instance than in the other. The putt in its most special form consists of three parts, the large part or mouth, called the 'putt' ; the middle called the 'butt' ; and the small end or bag, called the 'firwell.' . . . The diameter of the opening is about 5 feet, and the length from 12 to 13 feet ; they are used to catch flat fish, &c." The illustration (fig. A, page 36), given by Mr. Buckland shows the putt, with the small end or "firwell" removed.

The above technical description of the arrangement, measurement, &c., of the "putts" and "putchers," corresponds in most points with the details of the long rows (three or four in number) running out into the river beneath the Sedbury cliffs (plate x.).

APPENDIX B (p. 67).

The following notice appeared in the "Times" of March 11, 1901 :—

"*Miss Ormerod's Retirement from Entomological Work.*"

"Widespread regret will be felt, both at home and abroad, at the announcement which we are able to make, that Miss Eleanor A. Ormerod, after many years of unremitting toil, has decided to discontinue the Annual Reports on injurious insects and common farm pests, which she has prepared for a period now extending to close upon a quarter of a century. When in the year 1877 she issued the first of these annual records, and thus placed at the disposal of the public the fruits of her intimate acquaintance with many departments of natural history, very little systematic work had been done in the direction of saving crops and live stock from the ravages of insect and other pests. In this respect the position of the farmer and the stock-keeper to-day, as compared with what it was in the middle of the seventies, is vastly improved. It is true that the farmer may still lose his turnip and swede crops through the ravages of the active little beetle, which is perversely termed the 'fly'; that fruit-growers may bewail the loss of their apples and plums owing to the abundant presence of the winter moth; and that stock-keepers may view with dismay the damage both direct and consequential that their cattle incur through the activity of the warble-fly. But these and similar losses are entirely preventable, provided that there be no careless indifference, and that time and trouble be devoted to the object it is sought to attain. It is to Miss Ormerod's persevering efforts that this change is due; it is to her persistent enquiry year after year into the causes of mischief and into the means of removing them that the subject of agricultural entomology, which so long had languished in this country, gradually forced its way to the front, until it has become recognised that some serviceable knowledge of it is indispensable to the mental equipment, and cannot be omitted from the technical training of the aspiring agriculturist. Readily and gratuitously she has answered day after day all inquirers, whilst for twenty-four consecutive years her pen and pencil have been devoted to the preparation of the annual reports, every one of which she has generously published at a nominal price, which year after year involved a substantial loss. 'But the work was hard,' she now tells us—and the simplicity of her words renders them eloquent—'for many years for about five or six months all the time I could give to the subject was devoted to arranging the contributions of the season for the Annual Report of the year.' In spite of indifferent health, at times accompanied by much physical suffering, Miss Ormerod has carried on her self-imposed task, and the result is that she has revolutionised the subject of agricultural entomology, as it was understood in this country twenty-five years ago. Not only at home, not only throughout the British Empire, but in all progressive countries Miss Ormerod's name takes first rank amongst the Economic Entomologists of the day, and correspondence reaches her from beneath almost every flag that flies. And, now that the time has come when this talented lady feels it expedient to no longer work at the high pressure which has so long been maintained, all who have benefited by her disinterested labour—and they are very many—will join in the hope that she may long live to enjoy the comparative leisure to which she is looking forward."

APPENDIX C (p. 143).

Contents of Insect Cases Shown at the Bath and West of England Show at St. Albans (May, 1896), now the Property of the University of Edinburgh, kept along with Miss Georgiana Ormerod's Diagrams in the Museum of Science and Art, Edinburgh.

CASE I.—WEEVIL ATTACKS TO PEAS, BEANS, AND CLOVER SEED, AND LEAFAGE. 1. Infestations of Pea-seed. 2. Infestations of Bean-seed. 3. Clover-seed "Pear-shaped" Weevils. 4. Leaf-eating Weevils, and gnawed Leaves.

CASE II.—ATTACKS TO CORN STEMS. 1. "Gout Fly" attack to young Barley, also to ear and stalk. 2. Hessian Fly attack, showing Wheat-stems elbowed at point of feeding of Maggot.

CASE III.—INFESTATIONS OF STORED CORN AND MEAL. 1. Granary Weevils in Wheat. 2. Granary Moth in Wheat. 3. Meal and Flour Beetle in Meal. 4. Mite in Granary Rubbish.

CASE IV.—STORED CORN. Common Granary Weevil in Barley.

CASE V.—INFESTATION OF WHEAT MILLS AND STORES. Mediterranean Mill Moth, and Flour felted together by its Caterpillars. (A very bad Mill Pest).

CASE VI.—WASTE MATERIAL CLEANED OUT OF IMPORTED CORN. 1 and 2. "Rubble." 3. "Hencorn." 4. Broken Bits, used for bedding Pigs. 5 and 6. Uses not given; supposed to be used for Adulteration.

CASE VII.—INFESTATIONS IN IMPORTED OR STORED FODDER; ALSO SPARROW'S FOOD. 1. Locusts in Lucerne from Buenos Aires. 2. Hay-stack Moth from Clover or Sainfoin Stacks. Food from Sparrow's Crop containing Corn.

CASE VIII.—FIELD CROP AND GRASS-ROOT INFESTATIONS. 1. "Click Beetles" and their Grubs, known as "Wireworms." 2. Turnip "Flea" Beetles and Mustard Beetles. 3. Chafers and their Grubs.

CASE IX.—FIELD CROPS, ROOT, AND LEAF INFESTATIONS. 1. Cabbage and Turnip Moths, and their "Surface" Root-feeding Caterpillars, also Cabbage, and Pea-leaf Caterpillars. 2. "Mangold-leaf Fly" Maggot attack. 3. Death's-head Moth Potato-leaf Infestation.

CASE X.—APPLE INFESTATIONS. 1. American Blight. 2. Codlin Moth. 3. Winter Moths, and their "Looper" Caterpillars, also Cabbage and Pea-leaf Caterpillars. 4. Goat Moth, of which the Caterpillars feed in Wood. 5. Lappet Moth, and its leaf-eating Caterpillars.

CASE XI.—PINE INFESTATIONS. 1. Pine-sheets distorted by Tortrix Moth Caterpillar attack. 2. "Timberman" Beetle, with longest horns of any European kind. 3. Pine-beetle infestation in bark and shoots.

CASE XII.—ELM AND ASH-BARK INFESTATIONS. 1. Attacks of "Common" Elm-bark Beetle, and of "Lesser" Elm-bark Beetle. 2. Attacks of "Ash-bark" Beetle.

CASE XIII.—INSECT INJURIES TO WOOD AND LEATHER. 1. Sirex Tunnellings in live Silver Fir. 2. "Death-watch" Beetle's Borings in Oak and Beech Timber. 3. Injuries of Maggots of another kind of Death-watch Beetle to manufactured leather.

CASE XIV.—INFESTATIONS PARTLY BRED IN PONDS AND DITCHES. 1. Water Beetles injurious, in Beetle or Grub state, but chiefly in both, to young Fish in Ponds. 2. Liver-fluke of Sheep, and "Pond Snails," in which it lives in its early condition.

CASE XV.—FLY ATTACKS, INJURIOUS TO CATTLE, HORSES AND SHEEP. 1. Forest Fly; also Sheep Spider Fly (popularly known as "Sheep Tick.") 2. Bot Flies, Common Horse Bot Fly, and Sheep-nostril Bot Fly. 3. Gad or Breeze Flies.

CASE XVI.—OX AND DEER WARBLE. 1. Ox Warble Fly and Deer Warble Fly, in different stages, with Maggots in spirit. 2. Piece of young Red-deer's Skin, showing swellings caused by Warble Maggots in the under-side.

CASE XVII.—INJURIES TO CATTLE HIDE, FROM OX WARBLE. 1. Pieces of Hide, showing swellings with Maggots within, from the under-side; also perforations in the outside, leading down to the Maggot-cell; also sections of Hide, showing Channel down through the Hide, and Maggot-cell cut through. 2. Pieces of Tanned Warbled Leather.

APPENDIX D (p. 182).

Injury by Xyleborus dispar in England.

Professor Riley, in "Insect Life" (the U.S.A. Official Entomological Journal), says:—"Miss E. A. Ormerod wrote us on September 23, 1889, as follows: '. . . The beetle which is considered one of the rarest of the British Coleoptera, *Xyleborus dispar*, Fab. (formerly known as "Bostrichus" or "Apate," Fig. 46) has appeared in such great numbers in plum-wood in the fruit grounds at Toddington, near Cheltenham, as to be doing very serious injury. I found, on anatomising the injured small branches, that one of the galleries which the horde of beetles (packed as closely as they can be) forms or enlarges, passes about two-thirds round in the wood, more or less deeply beneath the bark, whilst another of the tunnels, likewise occupied with its closely packed procession of beetles, was in possession of about two inches of pith, so that the rapid destruction of the tree was fully accounted for. The attack appears, as far as I can see, to disappear usually very rapidly, but I am advising owners to make sure. This disappearance, I conjecture, may arise from the excessive rarity of the small male of this species. Amongst about sixty ♀ (female specimens) which I extracted from the tunnels I only found one ♂ (male).'"

Appendix E (p. 223).

Professor Charles Valentine Riley was killed by a fall from his bicycle in the streets of Washington. He was riding, as usual, to his office in the morning, accompanied by his young son. It was down-hill, and he was evidently going rather fast, when his wheel struck a stone carelessly left in the roadway after repairs. He was thrown violently, and died from the effects of the fall a few hours afterwards.[1]

'Biologist, artist, editor, and public official, the story of his struggles and successes, tinged as it is with romance, is one full of interest. Beginning life in America as a poor lad on an Illinois farm, he rose by his own exertions to distinction. His nature was a many-sided one, and his success in life was due to sheer will-power, unusual executive force, critical judgment, untiring industry, skill with pencil and pen, and a laudable ambition, united with an intense love of nature and of science for its own sake. This rare combination of varied qualities, of which he made the most, rendered him during the thirty years of his active life widely known as a public official, as a scientific investigator, while of economic entomologists he was *facile princeps*.

'He was born at Chelsea, London, September 18, 1843. His boyhood was spent at Walton-on-Thames, where he made the acquaintance of the late W. C. Hewitson, author of many works on butterflies, which undoubtedly developed his love for insects. At the age of eleven he went to school for three years at Dieppe, afterwards studying at Bonn-on-the-Rhine. At both schools he carried off the first prizes for drawing, making finished sketches of butterflies, thus showing his early bent for natural history. It is said that a restless disposition led him to abandon the old country, and at the age of seventeen he had emigrated to Illinois, and settled on a farm about fifty miles from Chicago. When about twenty-one he removed to Chicago, where he became a reporter and editor of the entomological department of the "Prairie Farmer."

'Near the close of the war, in 1864, he enlisted as a private in the 134th Illinois regiment, serving for six months, when he returned to his editorial office.

'He also enjoyed for several years the close friendship of B. D. Walsh, one of our most thorough and philosophic entomologists, with whom he edited the "American Entomologist." His industry and versatility, as well as his zeal as an entomolo-

[1] The substance of the foregoing statement was supplied by Dr. Bethune. The following (condensed) obituary notice by Professor A. S. Packard, of Brown University, and referred to by Miss Ormerod, appeared in "Science," and subsequently in the "Canadian Entomologist."

gist, made him widely known and popular, and gave him such prestige that it resulted in his appointment in 1868 as State Entomologist of Missouri. From that time until 1877, when he left St. Louis to live in Washington, he issued a series of nine annual reports on injurious insects, which showed remarkable powers of observation both of structure and habits, great skill in drawing, and especially ingenious and thoroughly practical devices and means of destroying the pests. It goes without saying that this prestige existed to the end of his life, his practical applications of remedies and inventions of apparatus giving him a world-wide reputation. In token of his suggestion of reviving the vines injured by the Phylloxera by the importation of the American stock, he received a gold medal from the French Government, and he afterwards received the Cross of the Légion d'Honneur in connection with the exhibit of the U. S. Department of Agriculture at the Paris Exposition of 1880.

'The widespread ravages of the Rocky Mountain locust from 1873 to 1877 had occasioned such immense loss in several States and Territories that national aid was invoked to avert the evil. The late Dr. F. V. Hayden, then in charge of the U. S. Geographical and Geological Survey of the Territories, sent Dr. P. R. Uhler to Colorado in the summer of 1875. Mr. Walsh had made important suggestions as to the birthplace and migrations of the insect. Meanwhile Riley had since 1874 made very detailed studies on the migration and breeding habits and means of destruction of this locust. Dr. Cyrus Thomas had also been attached to Hayden's Survey, and published a monograph on the locust family, *Acrididæ*. As the result of this combined work Congress created the United States Entomological Commission, attaching to it Dr. Hayden's Survey, and the Secretary of the Interior appointed Charles V. Riley, A. S. Packard, and Cyrus Thomas members of the Commission. Dr. Riley was appointed chief, and it was mainly owing to his executive ability, business sagacity, experience in official life, together with his scientific knowledge and practical inventive turn of mind in devising remedies, or selecting those invented by others, that the work of the Commission was so popular and successful during the five years of its existence. In 1878, while the Report of the Commission was being printed, Riley accepted the position of Entomologist to the U. S. Department of Agriculture, but owing to the lack of harmony in the Department, he resigned, Professor J. H. Comstock being appointed. Congress meanwhile transferred the cotton-worm investigation [on which Riley had been engaged] to the Entomological Commission. Dr. Riley was reappointed to the position of U. S. Entomologist in June, 1881. Mr. L. O. Howard said of the administration of this office: "The present efficient organisation of the Division of Entomology was his own original conception, and he is responsible for its plan down to the smallest detail. It is unquestionably the foremost organisation of its kind at present in existence." Again he writes: "Professor Riley's work in the organisation of the Division of Entomology has unquestionably advanced the entire Department of which it is a part, for it is generally conceded that this Division has led in most matters where efficiency, discipline, and system were needed."

'His Division published the first bulletin, and in "Insect Life" began the system of periodical bulletins, which has since been adopted for the other Divisions of the Agricultural Department. In an address, says Howard, before the National Agricultural Congress, delivered in 1879, in which he outlined the ideal Department of Agriculture, Professor Riley foreshadowed many important reforms which have since become accomplished facts, and suggested the important legislation, since brought about, of the establishment of State Experiment Stations under the general government.

'His practical, inventive genius was exhibited in his various means of exterminating locusts, in the use of kerosene oil emulsified with milk or soap, and in his invention and perfection of the "cyclone" or "eddy-chamber" or Riley systems of nozzles, which, in one form or another, are now in general use in the spraying of insecticide or fungicide liquids.

'Although the idea of introducing foreign insect parasites or carnivorous enemies of our imported pests had been suggested by others, Riley, with the resources of his division at hand, accomplished more than any one else in making it a success. He it was who succeeded in introducing the Australian ladybird to fight the fluted scale.

'Riley's scientific writings will always stand, and show as honest work. He was not "a species man" or systematist as such; on the contrary, his most important work was on the transformations and habits of insects, such as those of the lepidoptera, locusts and their parasites, his Missouri reports being packed with facts new to science. His studies on the systematic relations of Platypsyllus as determined by the larva evince his patience, accuracy, and keenness in observation and his philosophic breadth.

'His best anatomical and morphological work is displayed in his study on the mode of pupation of butterflies, the research being a difficult one, and especially related to the origin of the cremaster, and of the vestigial structures, sexual and others, of the end of the pupa. Whatever he did in entomology was original. He was also much interested in Aëronautics, and took much delight in attending séances of spiritualists and exposing their frauds, in one case, at least, where another biologist of world-wide fame, then visiting in Washington, was completely deluded.

'Riley was from the first a pronounced evolutionist. His philosophic breadth and his thoughtful nature and grasp of the higher truths of biology are well brought out in his address on "The Causes of Variation in Organic Forms," as Vice-President, before the biological section of the American Association for the Advancement of Science in 1888. He was a moderate Darwinian, and leaned, like other American naturalists, rather to Neo-Lamarckism. He says: "I have always had a feeling, and it grows on me with increasing experience, that the weak features of Darwinism and, hence, of natural selection, are his insistence (1) on the necessity of slight modification; (2) on the length of time required for the accumulation of modifications, and (3) on the absolute utility of the modified structure." Riley, from his extended experience as a biologist, was led to ascribe much influence to the agency of external conditions, remarking, in his address: "Indeed, no one can well study organic life, especially in its lower manifestations, without being impressed with the great power of the environment." He thus contrasts Darwinism and Lamarckism: "Darwinism assumes essential ignorance of the causes of variation and is based on the inherent tendency thereto in the offspring. Lamarckism, on the contrary, recognizes in use and disuse, desire and the physical environment, immediate causes of variation affecting the individual and transmitted to the offspring, in which it may be intensified again both by inheritance and further individual modification."'

'"Evolution shows that man is governed by the same laws as other animals." "Evolution reveals a past which disarms doubt and leaves the future open with promise—unceasing purpose—progress from lower to higher. It promises higher and higher intellectual and ethical attainment, both for the individual and the race. It shows the power of God in what is universal, not in the specific; in the laws of nature, not in departure from them."'

INDEX

23

O

P

LONDON: WEST, NEWMAN AND CO., HATTON GARDEN.

WORKS BY THE EDITOR OF THIS VOLUME.

2121037R00231

Printed in Great Britain
by Amazon.co.uk, Ltd.,
Marston Gate.